The Studio System

Rutgers Depth of Field Series

Charles Affron, Mirella Affron, Robert Lyons, Series Editors

Janet Staiger, ed., The Studio System

Linda Williams, ed., Viewing Positions: Ways of Seeing Film

Edited and with an introduction by
Janet Staiger

The
Studio
System

Rutgers
University
Press

New Brunswick
New Jersey

Library of Congress Cataloging-in-Publication Data

The Studio system / Janet Staiger, ed.
    p.   cm.—(Depth of Field series)
    Includes bibliographical references and index.
    ISBN 0-8135-2130-0 (cloth)—ISBN 0-8135-2131-9 (pbk.)
    1. Motion pictures—California—Los Angeles—History. 2. Motion picture industry
—California—Los Angeles—History. 3. Motion picture studios—California—Los
Angeles. I. Staiger, Janet. II. Series.
PN1993.5.U65S77   1994
791.43′0979494—dc20   94-14489
                                                                                                                        CIP

British Cataloging-in-Publication information available

To David Bordwell
Great scholar, teacher, mentor, and, best of all, friend

Contents

The Studio System

Introduction

Hollywood filmmaking has always been guided by numerous conventions and ideologies about the product it is producing and the production processes that will achieve a success. Who (or what) is responsible for what shows up on the screen? A list of credits for any movie suggests that tens to hundreds of people are involved in making the film. What those people think is required for entertainment or artistry or good box office is perhaps as complicated as assigning credit. Here are some representative remarks by its creators about what makes a good movie or a good working relation among the creators:

> It is obvious that the *appearance* of a *picture* is far more essential than that of any other product manufactured by man, although appearance will never *make* a picture if the story lacks in interest or is faulty in direction.
>
> It is then one of the duties of the cinematographer always to keep present in his mind that his work, to have a real commercial value, must be in accordance with the story, enhance the story telling qualities of the production and not distract from them as happens unfortunately much too often.
>
> J. A. Dubray, *The American Cinematographer*, 1922[1]

> I don't mean this in a baldly literal sense, . . . but suppose I ask Victor Milner to photograph a scene in an absolutely realistic way. That may mean that he must underplay technical perfection. He must do many things in what, to a trained picturemaker, will be a crude way.
>
> Of course he will try to do it to please me as a fellow-worker. But with each succeeding "take," he will unconsciously polish it up a little. Always in the back of his mind will be a little worry about what Charlie

Lang—and the Vic Milners and Charlie Langs in every other studio—will say at seeing him do a scene so crudely.

Ernst Lubitsch, *The American Cinematographer*, 1938[2]

The choice of stories for [Americans and Europeans] must inevitably be basically different. One prefers meringue; the other, stark, red meat. And the choice of stories must with equal inevitability dictate the style of camerawork to be used in bringing them to the screen.

Victor Milner's reply to Lubitsch,
The American Cinematographer, 1938[3]

Yes, well, the *auteur* theory led to such nonsense. The entire premise was based on ignorance, lack of information. If John Ford was the supreme creator of *How Green Was My Valley*, then who was Darryl Zanuck, me, Richard Llewellyn who wrote the novel, or William Wyler, the director who prepared the script for production with me?

Pinky is now called a film by Elia Kazan. But Kazan came in at the very last minute when John Ford had to drop out. Kazan was assigned on a Saturday and started shooting on Monday. And he didn't change one word that was in the script approved by Zanuck.

To give sole authorship to a non-writer director is just absurd.

Philip Dunne, *Screenwriter: Words Become Pictures*, 1987[4]

As a director you come in and this very strange waltz begins [with the studio]; the director wants as much time [to shoot] as possible. And so begins the endless confrontation between management and creativity. They want it great, but they want it cheap.

John Carpenter, *Gaffers, Grips, and Best Boys*, 1987[5]

One guiding thread among these remarks is that conflict exists—among norms and among roles in the work process. In terms of product conventions, standards of appropriate or effective storytelling may not synchronize with notions of beauty or the value of spectacle. Beliefs about colleagues' views of what counts as, say, appropriate lighting practices or suitable camera movements may operate to transform subtly a worker's activities.

Likewise, production processes for such an imaginative art as moviemaking request not only individuality and creativity from each worker but also cooperation from the multiple people needed to produce the film. Personal goals must at times be sacrificed to group efforts. Finally, a third conflict exists: production needs (often in terms of cost requirements) may demand an alteration of the product standards held by the craftspeople. So beyond conflicts within product conventions and production practices also exist conflicts between the norms of a good movie and the practical restrictions on achieving that outcome.

The aforesaid series of conflicts is what this collection of essays attempts to illuminate. The collection does not pretend to resolve the conflicts, but it does offer examples of how such tensions have been embedded and then played out in the creative processes of producing culturally significant narratives within the conditions of high finance. Movies might have been made inexpensively (and they have been and are still being made for very little money). However, movies that end up costing a lot of money seem to be the ones that attract the interest and pleasure of massive numbers of people. Although people may have varied attitudes about the assessment that capital is what drives the creative process, studying that phenomenon becomes exceptionally important given films' cultural impact.

The essays in this collection are grouped under the term *the studio system*. I want to distinguish the domain of this book from works often labeled similarly. All the essays will be focusing on a social investigation of Hollywood, not an economic one. By this, I mean that they have been chosen to present problems concerning the way workers interrelate to the work process and to their individual functions, roles, and beliefs, and not problems concerning the industry or the firms as the object of study. Even though the economic structure of the film industry (including its performance and conduct) affects the day-to-day lives of workers, other books are good surveys of both the history and operations of "the industry."[6]

Instead, what I want to present is a detailed sense, through a series of case studies, of what it is like to work in Hollywood amid the complexities of conflicting demands, such as the norms of what constitutes good product, how production teams should operate, and when a worker either should accede to the group's conventions or should deviate from them. Moreover, I want to expose the reader to the variety of forces entering into the mix that produces the films from that production source.

In an earlier work, *The Classical Hollywood Cinema: Film Style and Mode of Production to 1960* (coauthored with David Bordwell and Kristin Thompson), I stressed that older descriptions of Hollywood as a mass-assembly, completely oppressive operation were ones that did not quite understand three major contravening factors inherent in the process by which movies are manufactured. First of all, even were one to follow a strictly critical (Marxist) analysis of moviemaking, Marx makes an important distinction between a manufacturing and a machine-tool (or modern) industry. More specifically, in manufacturing, a product can be made in a serial form. In serial manufacturing, a commodity is produced by a group of workers in connected phases of development. Although labor is divided and a hierarchy of workers develops, Marx argues that some cooperation among the workers is possible. This is not so in the case of the machine-tool industry, for which the labor structure is appropriately described as mass assembly. In the Hollywood mode of production, workers interrelate in a routine process with many conversations among the various segments of the sequence. As I concluded earlier, such structural organization, necessitated by the type of product being produced, permitted "some collective activity and cooperation between craft workers."[7]

For many members of a firm, that collectivity and respect for opinion were insufficient, but for those in the middle-level and upper-level ranks, much evidence exists that these more privileged workers were relatively pleased with the social processes of working on movies. They were not happy with other aspects of the experience, not the least of which were the few rewards it provided in terms of public recognition and sometimes money—hence, for example, screenwriter Philip Dunne's complaints about the auteur theory's apparently neglecting the roles of almost everyone else in the work process. Although director D. W. Griffith once supposedly said about products of his early moviemaking days, "There's another sausage,"[8] I would argue either that Griffith was exaggerating or that at least by the time the movie industry was actually producing reasonably sophisticated narratives (from about 1915 on), such a remark was unjustified. The type of product itself and its extreme complexity required collective interchange among the workers involved.

A second contravening factor to the film industry's being simply a mass-assembly, oppressive experience is also structural. Built into capitalism is an economic tension that inhibits the cookie-cutter approach to making films. Although it is important that much of the work be routine (this is cost-effective), capitalism markets its products in ways that work against pure repetition of the product. This is especially true for certain items such as those in the luxury field of expenditures. Hollywood (in addition to most other types of industries) has discovered that product differentiation is valuable in re-creating demand. Thus, it is completely within the capitalist system to cultivate innovation in products, particularly if the novelty can be advertised. The value placed on change encourages the industry to seek creative ideas and differences. The degree to which the business can actually tolerate unconventionality, and of what kind, is worthy of study, but it is a mistaken notion to describe Hollywood management and Hollywood firms as resistant to novelty. Rather, Hollywood industry feeds off such behavior by its employees. Thus, creativity—by the individual or within a group process—is a valued and promoted activity within the workplace, not something inhibited by management.

What may be less valued are particular types of nonconventional changes. A good example of this is the joke in Robert Altman's film *The Player*, in which two writers pitch a story that will have no stars and no happy ending. They land the deal, but the final movie features Julia Roberts, Bruce Willis, and a last-minute rescue for the happy couple. By that point in *The Player*, however, the writers have been socialized to the system: they are ecstatic about the new version's appeal. The humor of this sequence of events derives from a baring of the fact that in Hollywood some rules are inviolate, and discovering which norms are sacrosanct and which are not is a prerequisite for both the academician and the worker who wants to be a "player."

It is also valuable to consider the structural conditions that may either facilitate or hinder more unusual deviations from the norms. In studying innovations in the television industry, Joseph Turow concludes that unconventional ones are more likely when competition is aggressive, technology is changing, demands by distributors are in flux, and government policies are altering.[9] Paul DiMaggio and Paul M. Hirsch call such industry "expectations about what a market, middleman, or federal and state agency *might* do" "imaginary feedback loops."[10] Such emphasis on the imaginary is critical, for the term aptly recognizes the projected nature of management's calculations. Thus, both the internal ideologies of a good product and industrial conditions generate the environment for the degree of latitude offered to workers that they may experiment within their individual areas of expertise. Again, controlled creativity is not against the system but part of it. Moreover, anticipation of the values (or dangers) of change constitutes part of management's daily routine.

The third contravening factor to Hollywood's being a pure assembly line is once again structural. This factor, however, is not tied to economic conditions, as were the previous two. Rather, its source is cultural. What counts as so-called good storytelling in the United States (and in much of Europe and elsewhere) has a history that precedes and exceeds that of the movie business. Some people have argued that narrative is essential to human ecology. Narrative is indeed a way to master incoming information so that we may operate within and among the physical and social conditions of our reality. That said, however, narratives can take an incredible variety of forms, with a vast array of practices involving causal sources (e.g., God, fate, nature, social behavior, personal character psychology, or psychopathology); ideologies of verisimilitude and beauty; aesthetics about story coherence, repetition, fidelity, or continuation; and procedures for telling the story (i.e., narrational choices and preferences). Those narrative and narrational options have not been equally prized among the workers in Hollywood, in part because the options do not seem equally successful in drawing large numbers of people to movie theaters.

On the other hand, it is conceivable to argue that what has become successful is not due to any popular, unmediated demand by audiences. Rather, audiences may tend to enjoy the familiar, especially if narratives are pleasurable in part as a way to master an overwhelming array of stimuli. What Hollywood may do is offer the security of ritual, of routine, with even the deviations being well within the bounds of the conventional. Thus the chicken-and-egg issue—the audience versus Hollywood—is worth serious study, for it sets historical terms for future policy making. The present collection of essays will not particularly address finding the origin of the source for why the films that Hollywood makes are (moderately) popular. It will, however, watch the film workers grapple with attempts to repeat or improve upon the narrative successes of the past and present.

The aforementioned three factors—the complexity of the product, the need for both standardization and differentiation in the manufacturing process, and the desire to create narratives satisfactory to consumers—have produced the conflictual tensions that operate whenever anyone tries to make a movie. Thus, several major questions circulate throughout the essays included in this book. They are as follows.

1. What are the norms and rules for the formulas and *for the innovations?* One should expect these to change historically. Only one of the essays addresses this specifically (Bordwell, "Deep-Focus Cinematography"), but it would be possible to research this question more widely through close attention to workers' comments (available through historical documents) and the films themselves. And while attention is being paid to this, the norms and rules should not be limited to considerations about good storytelling (the product) but should embrace the norms of the production processes as well. As Clinton R. Sanders indicates, industry conventions also involve such areas as the materials to be used, the types of interactions permitted by personnel, and the procedures for evaluation.[11] To anyone who has watched a film being made it is obvious that a whole set of rules about personnel interaction are operative, such as who may talk with whom, when, and about what. Although we know fairly well why labor divided as it did and when,[12] a study of the sociology of the work process has not yet been attempted. Nor has a discussion of the ways in which violations are perceived and dealt with by the operating unit and then the effects those ways have on the creative process.

2. *What are the tensions between product conventions and production conventions?* This seems to require much more rigorous analysis as well as description along a historical axis. Some attention has been directed toward specifying product norms on the large scale (i.e., the Hollywood system as a whole and then individual genres).[13] However, little work has been done on the relation between those product conventions and the work processes that produce them. The essays in this collection are the best examples that I know of to deal with these relations at the micro level. However, a future project might be to sort out which product conventions were likely to affect the work processes at various points. For example, the study by Wayne E. Baker and Robert R. Faulkner of the impact of the blockbuster on which work roles have more clout (and why) is a useful essay to start considering whether anything similar to this was occurring during the 1930s and 1940s in Hollywood or at least whether equivalencies of any sort were operating. Were some product conventions capable (and in what ways) of altering behaviors? What kinds of behaviors? Which work practices were exceptionally resistant to change? Examining this from studio to studio might also be a possibly illuminating venture. Although most of the firms followed certain generalized practices (making movement from company to company easy), each studio had its particularities. A study of the ways in which this tension played itself out at each firm, under different management structures and heads, would constitute a valuable contribution to our understanding of the making of movies. An important start on such a project is the work of Thomas Schatz in *The Genius of the System.*[14]

Moreover, it is possible to consider product conventions as also liberating (not just as constraining). When operating within a formula, writers (or viewers) can place their creative (or interpretive) energies elsewhere, enjoying other parts of a cinematic experience. When attention does not need to be directed toward unraveling a plot or figuring out a character's motives, then watching lighting, spectacle, or performance is made easier. The freedom from some product conventions (through particular genres) might alter production routines as workers focus more on other features of a film. For example, attention has been directed to the Freed Unit at MGM as a particularly integrated set of workers. However, because the unit was making musicals—a genre in which plot is of lesser significance than in many other genres—we might consider how the unit's work routines altered because the members were required by the genre and its product conventions to attend to issues of rhythm, formal repetition, movement, and rhyme.

3. *What happens when part of the system changes?* In a seminal essay on the production of culture, Howard S. Becker writes, "A system of conventions gets embodied in equipment, materials, training, available facilities and sites, systems of notation and the like, all of which must be changed if any one segment is."[15] Many people, including the workers themselves, have described filmmaking as an equation. Change *X* and everything alters, including the solution. Given that change is a requirement in the business, the transformations at particular moments are worth investigation. Some of those transformations have been made in equipment and materials—such as changes in film stock—and some in the movement to color, sound, and the wide screen ratio. Although some work has been accomplished on these changes from an aesthetic point of view and although a bit has been done on the implications those changes had for the work organization and the workers, this is still a very underexplored area.

4. *How have work routines and tensions among the various conventions affected individual workers?* Some explorations of labor have been made. It is hardly surprising that within the history of this area of research, it is in fact the workers who have been the focus of more study than the other questions posed earlier. And this is appropriate. Intelligent analysis of labor described the Hollywood system from the 1920s onward while labor was attempting to organize collectively so as to secure better working conditions and a greater share of the profits. The study by Hortense Powdermaker, *Hollywood: The Dream Factory*, published in 1950, is still a powerful description of the day-to-day sociology of the film business.[16] The firms making up Hollywood, as in many other businesses, have exploited their workers. The complaints leveled at certain parts of the experience are certainly justified. One of the most

significant questions is, Who had (and has) the power to make what kinds of decisions and when? This is of paramount concern in fostering an understanding of the tacit rules of an institution.

However, to recognize the validity of the criticisms leveled against the system of Hollywood is not to accede to the mistaken inference that every part of the experience was horrible. As I indicated previously, especially for middle-level and upper-level workers, the pleasure of collaborating on aesthetically powerful and culturally significant narratives had personal and social rewards. We might also want to investigate more specifically the subcultural organizations operating both informally and formally among various groups of workers and contributing to their self-esteem and negotiation within the studio system.

I am sure the attentive reader, stimulated by this set of essays, will think of other research questions, and it is for that reason that I have put the collection together. I would like to point out as well that the essays represent a mixture of theories and methods, and this is intentional. I do not personally believe that every question can be adequately handled by one master theory. However, I am also not so naïve as to presume that theories are ideologically neutral. What I do offer to the reader is the possibility of considering how different theories and methods approach the topic of the social institution of Hollywood so that both the advantages and disadvantages of the theories and methods can be weighed. The gamut within this collection runs from functionalist to conflict sociologies, from quantitative to qualitative methods.

As I indicated earlier, I have chosen a set of case studies to provide very specific examples of the general tensions I have laid out as existing within the overall institution of making movies in Hollywood from the time when films became complex enough to require a moderately well-organized production system. I date this as occurring by the mid-teens of this century. Beyond that, I have grouped the writings under several more specific headings to draw out certain problems (although I think all of these issues could be found in each example).

The first essay, by Edward Buscombe, is a seminal work that advances the problem of the sociology of Hollywood to the foreground of concern in film studies. Published in 1975, it was one of the earliest attempts to query how workers' beliefs might be related to the films they produced. As Buscombe ironically reminds us in the opening of the essay, that question is raised because trying to separate art from industry is not only impossible, but it misses the point. Films are neither "autonomous, self-sufficient entities" nor simple "reflections of society." We know that somehow the real workers have some relation to what appears on the screen. Buscombe gives a very good review of the work that led to his reformulation of the problem. He also attempts to study one specific studio (Columbia) in terms of who worked there and the films made there between 1926 and 1941.

The next four essays are specific studies of individuals function- ing in roles usually considered to have the most potential for power in the filmmaking situation. Richard B. Jewell and Paul Kerr study directors Howard Hawks and Joseph H. Lewis, respectively; Thomas Schatz looks at star Bette Davis; and David Bordwell writes about the career of cinematographer Gregg Toland. (Writers and producers would constitute the other two of the top five players.) Each of these essays shows how situated these workers are within the conventions and latitudes for innovation that exist in Hollywood. Bordwell is particularly explicit in setting out (1) how Toland tried to promote his own career through the practice—unusual for cinematographers in the 1930s—of developing his own style and (2) how Toland's coworkers responded to and modified his unconventional innovations in deep-focus camerawork. Jewell sets out to take on directly the mythology that directors who supposedly over- came the system were romantic heroes. He astutely describes the predic- aments faced by the producer of *Bringing Up Baby* that permitted Hawks to recognize how the production routine constraining the firm was to his advantage. Hawks manipulated the system to be sure, but he could have done so only if the system itself had its own internal operating rules available for use by a savvy director.

Kerr's study of Lewis is also a criticism of auteur theories that neglect to consider the institutional situation of the worker. Moreover, Kerr argues that the subgenre in which Lewis worked (the B film noir) may have been as influential in raising Lewis's name to the level of auteur as were any specific acts of creativity on the director's part. Schatz investigates one principal resource of a studio—the star, who when she or he achieves public recognition also gains some potential semblance of power in the creative process. That power is not assured an individual, however. Rather the ability to make choices about one's career has to be secured. Schatz details how Davis did so at one of the studios most interested in economical production. Thus, Schatz's essay is valuable in laying out the particular operations of Warner's as well as how contract players functioned within those processes. Moreover, Schatz describes well the constraints that studio bosses respected when dealing with directors who were able to elicit great performances from their stars. Thus, a checks-and-balances system regarding authority and expertise operated—in this case in Davis's interests.

Individuals operating within roles in the industry are of concern in any analysis of causality within an institutional framework. I have suggested that conventions and ideologies are also exceptionally important. The next three essays are examples of product conventions that affect the work processes. Robert C. Allen's study of the Fox studio's attempt to create an "art" movie to better the company's reputation is just such an example. Working from period notions of high-quality filmmaking (and prestige personnel), William Fox specifically permitted the production team to have its own way, because he hoped to use *Sunrise* as an announcement that his firm intended to compete with other major firms for the first-run market. When publicity threatened to imply that the movie would be *too* innovative (i.e., exotic or freakish), Fox tried to control the image of the film, noting that it was based on a well-known story. He was not particularly successful in his manipulation of the movie's publicity, but the story of his attempt to use innovation (in the form of art cinema) is a good instance of how product differentiation and creativity may be utilized by a capitalist firm for its own benefit.

The other two essays in the group deal with the product convention of fidelity. In the first case, Jeffrey Sconce analyzes how a production unit tried to negotiate just what counted as the true story of *Jane Eyre*. Market research indicated that the narrative of "Jane Eyre" had accumulated a set of social and cultural encrustations sometimes unjustified by the original novelistic source. Whereas production conventions suggested that writers ought to be faithful to certain aspects of an original source (because that is what made it popular in the first place), now the conflict between the popular image of a narrative and its original source meant responding to that difference. How David O. Selznick's firm dealt with this in its research and writing practices is the subject of Sconce's essay.

The second fidelity case is also a case of a "social" narrative, this time the story of Tarzan. Derral Cheatwood's discussion of the process and progress of the Tarzan movies from studio to studio is an excellent attempt to query the degree to which specific studios make a difference when a narrative moves around. Cheatwood especially tries to determine when conventions (for this narrative at least) seem inviolate and when they can be altered. In the case of the Tarzan story, Cheatwood argues that it is the producing agent (the studio) that seems to be the significant variable in formula changes.

The third grouping of essays deals with issues involving workers who are not in positions within the labor hierarchy that permit much control or power over their work situation. Martin F. Norden's essay on the initial possibilities for women in the film industry (until about 1920) is an important reminder that those early openings soon closed off to women and became rather restricted domains in the 1930s and afterward. Even today, official data from the industry suggest little progress for women. James Lastra's essay articulates the conflict between different professional aesthetics and conventions when sound engineers met studio technicians. Sound engineers defined realism differently from those in Hollywood, coming as they did from the area of "science." What their practices would achieve, however, was quite at odds with problems in making movies that were edited and for which comprehension of dialogue mattered more than so-called fidelity. Lastra describes how sound engineers accommodated their original norms to the new needs of filmmaking.

One of the burgeoning areas of research about Hollywood has been the history of labor's attempt to organize collectively so as to improve working conditions and financial rewards. I have chosen Denise Hartsough's study of the collusion between management and a corrupt labor union (the International Alliance of Theatrical Stage Employees during the late 1930s) because it illustrates how multiple factors operated to give management the edge over workers. Those factors included not only jurisdictional conflicts among organizing labor groups but also government regulation. As Hartsough concludes, "motion picture executives were . . . 'smart' shoppers who selected the 'bargain' in labor that best fit their current needs."

Hollywood, like most industries, has occasionally experienced unusual determinants of its day-to-day operations. A fourth group of essays considers such situations. Notorious for its influence on the product and production conventions was the existence of the self-regulatory systems over subject matter operating from at least 1909. Richard Maltby's discussion of the period from about 1930 to 1934 is an outstanding analysis of how Hollywood firms as a grouped institution dealt with social problems displaying themselves through sexuality and violence. Maltby's thesis is that product conventions already well established within Hollywood's ideology of narrative and narration were plunged into crisis when the Depression raised questions about capitalism's ability to expand continually. Maltby thus connects the appearance of a specific genre with increased sensitivities about how consumption was portrayed and about how the self-regulatory system would respond to those images. Thus, he describes how production norms were altered by the production process involved with regulation of film content.

In another instance of self-regulation, Clayton R. Koppes and Gregory D. Black provide a fine synopsis of how the film industry responded to government's needs during World War II. Their history of the Office of War Information suggests how easily Hollywood could adapt its product conventions to specific demands about subject matter—if it chose to do so—although Koppes and Black's story also indicates how much the government learned about making movies that would sell to audiences. As the authors point out, entertainment became safer than significant themes for both Hollywood and the Office of War Information.

A final example of external influences on the normal processes of Hollywood filmmaking is the arrival of demographic analyses of audiences. By the middle of World War II, professional pollsters such as the Gallup organization had informed Hollywood that a massive portion of the latter's audience were teens and young adults. As the professionals continued to survey who came to the movies and why, some filmmakers chose to target those most likely to attend their films. The "teenpic" of the late 1950s was one result, and Thomas Doherty describes its formation as a genre that seemed to offer a sense of security that was otherwise being lost as audiences shifted their everyday moving-image viewing to television. How one individual, Sam Katzman, recognized the need for a somewhat unconventional innovation at that time is the subject of Doherty's study.

As I suggested previously, many possible research questions arise from the issues at stake in these essays. The stimulus for further inquiry that they provide is the value of this collection for scholars. For students of Hollywood, and especially for young filmmakers, the book has been organized to illuminate the contradictions operating in the film industry. But the discovery that cinematographers and directors differed among themselves, and still produced important films, is worth pursuing. Important as well is the recognition that movies are the consequence of many individuals' labors. Finally, examination of the reasons for the various ways that conventions about how to make a good film narrative affected what appeared on the screen prevents us from considering movies as magic. A dream factory Hollywood may be, but the dreams are made by people.

Janet Staiger

NOTES

1. J. A. Dubray, "Art vs. Commercialism," *American Cinematographer* 1 February 1922, 4, 6.

2. William Stull, "Camera Work Fails True Mission When It Sinks Realism for Beauty," *American Cinematographer* February 1938, 59–60.

3. Victor Milner, "Victor Milner Makes Replay to Ernst Lubitsch as to Realism," *American Cinematographer* March 1938, 94.

4. Philip Dunne in Lee Steven, *Screenwriter: Words Become Pictures* (Pittstown, N.J.: Main Street Press, 1987), p. 110.

5. John Carpenter in Eric Taub, *Gaffers, Grips, and Best Boys* (New York: St. Martin's Press, 1987), p. 70.

6. See in particular the following recent surveys: Tino Balio, ed., *The American Film Industry,* rev. ed. (Madison: University of Wisconsin Press, 1985); Douglas Gomery, *The Hollywood Studio System* (New York: St. Martin's Press, 1986); John Izod, *Hollywood and the Box Office, 1985–1986* (New York: Columbia University Press, 1988); and Douglas Gomery, *Shared Pleasures: A History of Movie Presentation in the United States* (Madison: University of Wisconsin Press, 1992). These books have good references to more detailed studies.

7. David Bordwell, Janet Staiger, and Kristin Thompson, *The Classical Hollywood Cinema: Film Style and Mode of Production to 1960* (London: Routledge & Kegan Paul, 1985), p. 92.

8. "Advice to Hollywood," *Motion Picture Herald* 167:8 (24 May 1947), 61.

9. Joseph Turow, "Unconventional Programs on Commercial Television: An Organizational Perspective." In *Mass Communicators in Context,* ed. D. Charles Whitney and James Ettema (Beverly Hills, Calif.: Sage, 1982), pp. 107–29.

10. Paul DiMaggio and Paul M. Hirsch, "Production Organizations in the Arts," *American Behavioral Scientist* 19:6 (July/August 1976), 742.

11. Clinton R. Sanders, "Structural and Interactional Features of Popular Culture: An Introduction to the Production of Culture Perspective," *Journal of Popular Culture* 16:2 (Fall 1982), 82.

12. See my chapters in *The Classical Hollywood Cinema.*

13. See Bordwell and Thompson's chapters on the product conventions for the whole system in *The Classical Hollywood Cinema;* numerous books are available on the specific genres.

14. Thomas Schatz, *The Genius of the System: Hollywood Filmmaking in the Studio Era* (New York: Pantheon, 1988).

15. Howard S. Becker, "Art as Collective Action," *American Sociological Review* 39:6 (December 1974), 772.

16. Hortense Powdermaker, *Hollywood: The Dream Factory* (New York: Little, Brown, 1950).

Historical Research and
the Studio System

Edward Buscombe

Notes on Columbia Pictures Corporation 1926–41

I

The film industry, the cinema. How are these terms related in film criticism? *The film industry* describes an economic system, a way (or ways) of organising the structure of production, distribution, and consumption. Historically such organisation has, in Britain and America, conformed to the usual pattern of capitalist activity; film can be seen as an industry like any other. It has passed from the primitive stage of small-scale entrepreneurial activity to the formation of large-scale monopolies, securing their position by vertical integration, spreading from production into distribution and exhibition. Since the war the industry has, like other forms of business, developed towards diversification and the formation of multinational corporations. In other respects too film has developed like other industries. Production in particular has been based on a division of labour, of a fairly extreme kind. From early days the industry has employed the techniques of mass advertising, and it has required the injection of huge sums of capital, resulting in turn in the passing of control of the industry from its original owners and from the primary producers.

In film criticism, then, the term *film industry* implies a way of looking at film which minimises its differences from other forms of economic activity; a way which is of course predominantly that of those

From *Screen* 16:3 (Autumn 1975), 65–82. Reprinted with permission of the author and *Screen*.

who actually own the industry. Its characteristic descriptions are sufficiently indicative of a perspective: *the trade, marketing, exploitation, a package, product.*

The cinema suggests something else. While the term might, notionally, encompass the industry, the pull is surely in a different direction. *The cinema* implies film as art. As Raymond Williams has shown with convincing detail in *Culture and Society,* the opposition between art and industry has a long history in our culture. The division between the two is experienced everywhere as deep, but nowhere deeper than in film. On the one hand, we are given to understand, is the industry, churning out product for financial gain. On the other are artists, creating enduring works of personal expression or comment on life and society. Such an opposition has taken different forms at different times. Sometimes it has been geographical. In America there was Hollywood, the industrial system par excellence. In Europe (usually excluding Britain, apart from its documentaries) there were artists: Renoir, Dreyer, Bergman, Antonioni, etc. Later the auteur theory, as applied to American cinema, changed the emphasis. Though Hollywood was still an industry, through diligent critical work some artists could be winnowed from the chaff, artists who against the odds managed by luck, cunning, or sheer genius to overcome the system, the industry. The auteur theory, whatever its "theory" may have been, did not in practice abolish the distinction between art and industry; it merely shifted the line of demarcation.

One might suppose that a little common sense would tell us that such a distinction is nonsense, that all film is both industry *and* art, in some sense. Even the lowest, most despised products (choose your own examples) are made with some kind of art. Do they not share the same language as the acknowledged masterpieces: do they not tell a story, try to affect the spectators' emotions? They may do it more or less effectively, but isn't this a difference of degree, not of kind? Conversely, in the making of the most spiritual and sublime films grubby bank notes change hands. The film stock on which the masterpiece is recorded may come from the same batch used to shoot the potboiler on the adjoining stage.

Yet proof that the mutual exclusion of art and industry operates at a level too deep to be affected by mere common sense can be found not only in the dominant critical attitudes but in the organisation of social institutions. To give an example close to home: the British Film Institute (BFI) was set up, as its Memorandum of Association states, "to encourage the development of the art of the film." At the same time it is stated that the BFI is permitted neither "to control nor attempt to interfere with purely trade matters." Art not only can but must be divorced from industry. And the split is preserved even in the structure of government. Whereas the BFI is administered by the Department of Education and Science, the film industry comes under the Department of Trade and Industry. Thus the opposition art/industry has to be seen not merely as a mistake in film criticism which can be easily rectified by a more careful look at the facts but as the result of a whole practice of thinking, talking, writing, and disseminating inscribed in institutions like the BFI, those parts of the education system that handle film, plus also exhibition/viewing practice—the art-house circuit and its audience(s)—the immaterial thought both reflecting and being part of this apparatus; in short, as part of an ideology.

The main concern here, however, is not with the origins of such an opposition but with its consequence for film criticism. This may be baldly stated: there has been scarcely any serious attempt to think the relationship between art and industry with regard to films produced in what have historically been for us the two most important film-making countries, namely, Great Britain and the United States. Criticism has been devoted not to relating them but to separating them out, and in practice this has meant that critics have concentrated on the beauties and mysteries of art and left the industry, presumably a tougher plant, to take care of itself. Study of the industry might require knowledge of, say, economics or of how films are actually made, knowledge which critics have not been expected to acquire. The main effort of criticism, therefore, has gone into the study of film texts viewed as autonomous, self-sufficient entities or, occasionally, as reflections of society, but certainly not as reflections of the industry which produced them, unless they are being dismissed as rubbish. Even recent work deriving from structuralism and concerned to open up the text, to deconstruct it, has tended to take the film as given and has ignored questions of how the organisation of a film text might relate to the organisation of an industry or to specific working practices.

It is in respect of Hollywood, the largest field of activity in both film-making and criticism, that the lack of a history of the industry is most glaring. Of course there is a certain amount of information around. Statistics have occasionally been assembled (a number of government and trade reports on Hollywood in the 1930s are listed in the notes of Leo C. Rosten's *Hollywood: The Movie Colony, The Movie Makers*, a book which has some useful material on this period). There are one or two books, again on the 1930s, which assemble some facts about the economics of the industry (for example, F. D. Klingender and Stuart Legg, *The Money behind the Screen*, and Mae D. Huettig, *Economic Control of the Motion Picture Industry*). But of course they don't attempt to make any connections between the economics and the actual films produced. There is also the ragbag of publicity releases, inaccurate box-office returns, and general gossip which makes up the trade press (*Film Daily, Motion Picture Herald, Variety, Hollywood Reporter*, etc.). To this may be added a host of biographies (or ghosted autobiographies) of prominent industry figures, of which *Hollywood Rajah*, by Bosley Crowther (on Louis B. Mayer), and *King Cohn*, by Bob Thomas (on Harry Cohn) are representative examples. Little that is useful can be gleaned from such works, which mostly string together collections of anecdotes about the "great men." On such questions as the financial structures within which they were obliged to operate or the actual working methods of their studios they are for the most part silent. Of studio histories, properly speaking, there are none, with the possible exception of Richard Schickel's book *The Disney Version*, which is hampered by Schickel's failure to get any cooperation from the Disney studio itself—a fact, of course, that is not without its significance, since it indicates the difficulties of this kind of work.

Indeed, the neglect of industry history is not only a consequence of critical attitudes and priorities which have abandoned the field to those whose interest does not go beyond personalities. It is also the result of very real practical problems. The fact is that the history of the American film industry is extremely difficult to write, because many of the basic materials that would be needed are simply not available. The statistics are incomplete and unreliable. The trade press presents only the acceptable face of the business, even when one can get access to it (the BFI Library, virtually the only collection of such periodicals in Britain, has no run of *Variety*, though there are plans to acquire one). The biographies, and studio histories, where they exist at all (for example, Bosley Crowther's *Lion's Share*, on MGM), are based largely on reminiscences. Concrete documented evidence in the form, say, of studio memoranda, accounts, and other records, is almost totally lacking. If such records still exist they are mostly locked away in studio vaults. And the history of technological development in Hollywood has still to be written. Lastly, the films themselves; such prints as have been preserved are often impossible to see. The situation is little different from that which exists in relation to the history of the Elizabethan stage, with this exception, that infinitely less method and application have gone into researching it.

The result is that when Hollywood has been written about, its industrial dimension has been ignored. Much of the writing has been based on an idea of history as one damned thing after another. Even such a prestigious work as Lewis Jacobs's *Rise of the American Film* scarcely rises above this, most sections being simply annotated film lists. The only principle to compete has been auteurism, which leaves film history at the stage which history proper reached in the nineteenth century when Carlyle defined it as the lives of great men. Deliberate attempts to get away from auteurism, such as Colin McArthur's *Underworld USA* (on the crime film) and Jim Kitses's *Horizons West* (on the western) are ultimately broken-backed books. Genres may be related to aspects of American history, but in the end it is the auteurs who dominate the account.

Some recent, more promising directions have been pursued. Patrick Ogle's work on deep-focus (*Screen*, v. 13, n. 1) and that of John Ellis and Charles Barr on Ealing Studios (*Screen*, v. 15, nn. 1–2, v. 16, n. 1) have from different perspectives tried to make connections between films and the nature of the industry which produced them. *The Velvet Light Trap* has brought to light valuable material on the studio system, though the use that has been made of it has often been disappointing. But the gaps in our knowledge are still enormous.

II

One consequence of the existence of such gaps has been that attempts to relate Hollywood films to the society which produced them have simply by-passed the industry altogether. The result has been a series of short circuits. Hollywood films are seen as merely reflecting society. On the one hand is society, seen as a collection of facts, attitudes, psychological patterns, or whatever. On the other are the films, where one sees such facts, attitudes, etc., mirrored. Though it may be conceded that the mirror sometimes distorts, insofar as there is a theory behind such a view it is a naively realist one, and indeed how could it be otherwise? If there is no conception of Hollywood as an industry with its own history, specific practices, economic relationships, and technological and other material constraints, if film is seen as something that somehow mysteriously appears and having appeared is simply there, fixed and given, then how is one to understand the nature of any mediation? To confine ourselves again to the period of the 1930s, a book such as Andrew Bergman's *We're in the Money* devotes a mere four pages to "A Note on the Movie Industry and the Depression," which ends thus: "The preliminaries completed, we proceed to the black and white footage itself." And in the black-and-white footage the social comment can simply be read off as if the films were so many sociologists' reports. Here is an admittedly rather extreme example: "Tod Browning's 1932 MGM film, *Freaks*, had a cast made up of pinheads, human torsos, midgets, and dwarfs, like nothing ever in the movies. And what more stunted a year than 1932 for such a film?" (p. 168).

One might expect that more specifically Marxist attempts to relate Hollywood to American society would display a little more rigour and subtlety. Bourgeois cultural theories, with their assumptions about the values of artistic freedom and personal expression, are obviously ill equipped to deal with a medium so conditioned by money, technology, and organisational structures. Books such as Bergman's, which dispense with most of that theory (though never completely, for some auteurs, such as Capra and Vidor, make an appearance), seem to have no theory at all to replace it. Marxism, on the other hand, proposes a sophisticated understanding of the relations between society, a system of production, and the actual product. Yet such Marxist models as have been put forward for understanding Hollywood have suffered from a crudity which has had the effect of deadening further thought. The crudest model of all is that encapsulated in Godard's phrase *Nixon-Paramount.* The model implied in such a phrase has had obvious attractions for the political avant-garde and indeed contains some truth. But the truth contained in such vulgar Marxism is so vague and general as to have scarcely any use at all. Ideological products such as films are seen as directly caused by the nature of the economic base of society. A capitalist system produces capitalist films, and that is all there is to it. Alternatively—but the slight sophistication is scarcely a modification—the products of Hollywood are bourgeois and capitalist because the particular industry which produces them is capitalist. And the more specific the model becomes, the more its crudity is exposed. Thus in the first section of the *Cahiers du Cinéma* text on *Young Mr. Lincoln* (translated in *Screen*, v. 13, n. 3), we are told that since Hollywood is involved with big business, its ideology is not just a generally capitalist one. It supports the more reactionary wing of the political spectrum, represented by the Republican Party.

The *Cahiers* text is only one example of a desire to show not only that Hollywood is a part of bourgeois ideology in general but that some Hollywood films are intended to carry a specific and reactionary message which has a direct reference to a particular political situation. Another example of such over-politicisation comes in a recent issue of *Jump Cut*, n. 4, Nov.-Dec. 1974, which contains an interpretation of *King Kong* as an anti-Roosevelt tract. The article conveniently states its premises in a footnote:

> This article is built round two suppositions. First, that all huge business corporations (such as RKO) are conservative Republican unless demonstrated otherwise, and that their products (like *King Kong*) will reinforce their interests instead of betraying them. Second, that the auteur theory in its standard application is not a germane approach when dealing with a political film, especially under the tight studio control of the 1930's. A political film would only be allowed release if its philosophy was in line with that of the studio which made it. Therefore, RKO studio will be regarded as the true "auteur" of *King Kong*, despite the innumerable personal touches of its artistic crew.

Although the phrase *unless demonstrated otherwise* indicates that the author, Gerald Peary, is aware of the dangers of oversimple generalisations, his assumptions still seem open to two major objections. First, is it not possible that even in Hollywood (not noted perhaps for its political sophistication) there were in the 1930s people who could see that the survival of capitalism (and hence of their huge corporations) was not necessarily synonymous with the victory of the Republican Party, especially a Republican Party so discredited as the one which had been led to electoral disaster and intellectual bankruptcy by Herbert Hoover? Second, what exactly *are* the interests of such corporations? In the long term, obviously, the survival of a system which allowed them to make profits. But in the short term surely it was those profits themselves. Is it to be assumed that studio executives saw the possibility of profits in attacking a leader who had so recently demonstrated his popularity at the polls (especially among the cinema going section of the public)? Or should we assume that the political commitment of the studio executives overcame their dedication to profits?

It seems unlikely, but our ignorance about Hollywood generally and about the particular organisation of RKO is such that we cannot answer these questions. Precisely for this reason we ought to beware of assuming any answers. Even if we do assume, with the authors in *Cahiers* and *Jump Cut*, that a studio is owned by big business and that one of its products promotes the political and hence economic interests of the company (I say apparently because the actual interpretation of the films seems open to question), it does not necessarily follow that the political meaning is the direct result of who owns the studio. Post hoc is not *propter hoc.*

The lack of any detailed knowledge of industry history, then, suggests caution on the question of the political orientation of Holly-wood in the 1930s. First, is it true that the film industry was controlled by big business? And is this the same as the Republican Party (there was business influence among the Democrats too)? Second, if it is true, can one assume a direct effect on the ideology of Hollywood films? Even the term *ideology* seems to pose a problem here. It is one thing to argue that, using the term in its classical Marxist sense (or as refined by Althusser) to mean a general worldview or structure of thought situated primarily below the conscious level, Hollywood films are ideological expressions of bourgeois society. It is quite another to argue that they support a specific set of political attitudes. Bourgeois society is more than simply the Republican Party. And in any case Marxist theory claims only that ideological products are determined in the last instance by the economic relations existing at the base of society. The arguments about *Young Mr. Lincoln* and *King Kong* appear to assume that facts about who controls the film industry can provide a sufficient explanation of a film's ideology, ignoring the dimension of the institutional structures which may inter-vene between the economic base and the final product. Without a knowledge of these structures one cannot say that these films are *not* propaganda; but if they were intended as such, as the *Cahiers* and *Jump Cut* articles imply, it is a strange sort of propaganda, which requires an ingenious interpretation thirty or forty years later to make its point. Surely it would have to be demonstrated that such a reading was available to an audience at the time.

III

These problems were thrown into relief by a viewing some time ago of *American Madness*, directed for Columbia in 1932 by Frank Capra. The story of the film concerns Dickson, the manager of a small-town bank (played by Walter Huston). The directors of the bank are financiers of the old school (pre-Keynesians), dedicated to tight money policies, which they pursue ruthlessly and selfishly. Dickson, however, has a different view of what the function of a bank should be. He believes that money should be put to work to create jobs and opportunities. His policy is to lend to small businessmen, trusting in his own assessment of their good intentions rather than in the security they can offer. His beliefs are put to the test when a run on the bank occurs; the run is stopped and his faith in his clients vindicated when the little people he has helped rally round to deposit money and so restore confidence in the bank.

The programme note which accompanied the screening of the film at the National Film Theatre suggested that the character of Dickson might have been based on A. H. Giannini, a California banker who was influential in Columbia's affairs in the 1930s. Such a suggestion raises one immediate difficulty, in that it seems to assume that the apparent, or manifest, meaning of the film is the only one, and ignores the possibility that the latent meaning may be quite different. The film might be about other things besides banking. It excludes, that is, the possibility of analysing the film along the lines of the *Young Mr. Lincoln* text, which finds that despite the film's apparent project of supporting the Republican cause in the 1940 presidential election, the "real" meaning of the film undermines this. (The problem of such readings, despite their obvious attractions, is that it is never explained how in practice the subversive meaning of the film becomes available to the people to whom it might be some use, i.e., the working class.) Nevertheless, the suggestion seemed worth following up because of the possibility that it might throw some light on the question of Hollywood's relation to politics in the 1930s and on the nature of the production system generally. And this might in turn tell us something about Capra's films.

Robert Mundy, in a review of Capra's autobiography in the American *Cinema* (v. 7, n. 1, Fall 1971, p. 56), speculates on how it was that Capra was able to make films which so closely embodied his personal ideas. He suggests two reasons: firstly, that Capra was working for a small studio where freedom was greater, and secondly, that Capra's vision "was unusually consonant with the vision of America which Hollywood purveyed with such commercial success in the 1930s. Ideologically his films were rarely at odds with the image of life which the studios believed the public wanted to see." Mundy avoids the facile assumptions that Capra was "in touch" with America and that his films arise out of some special relationship to the people and the mood of the time. Instead, he suggests that his work is an expression of the point of view of his *studio*. He concludes, however, that we need to know more: "A persuasive history of Columbia in the 1930s [is] needed before an informed critical account of Capra's work can be written." Quite. The problem is to know where to start, given the problems of such research outlined above. Mr. Giannini seemed to offer a way in.

He is referred to in a number of books about Hollywood, but as far as I know never more than in passing, as a prominent Californian banker who was involved in movie financing. In several of the references there is a curious uncertainty about his initials. Sometimes he is called A. P. Giannini, sometimes A. H. Thus Philip French in his "informal" history of the Hollywood tycoons, *The Movie Moguls,* mentions him on page 25: "In fact the first banker to take the cinema seriously was the Californian A. P. Giannini, the son of an Italian immigrant, whose Bank of Italy (later renamed the Bank of America) has played an important part in movie finance since before the first world war." On page 79 we read: "A H Giannini, the influential movie financier whose Bank of Italy had a special claim on Hollywood consciences of whatever religious denomination."

The mystery of A. H. or A. P. was only cleared up when I looked up Giannini in the *National Cyclopædia of American Biography*. It appears that there were two of them. (Obviously I am not the first person since Mr. Giannini pére to be aware of this fact, but it seems as though Philip French was not when he wrote his book. Of such confusions is film history made.) It's worth giving some details of their careers, since they are relevant to Capra's film. A. H. and A. P. (or to give them their full names, Attilio Henry and Amadeo Peter) were brothers. Both their parents were natives of Italy; their father had been a hotel keeper but had come to California to try farming. Amadeo was born in 1870 and his brother four years later. The older brother had gone to work at the age of twelve in his stepfather's firm of wholesale commission agents in San Francisco, and while still in his twenties he formed the Columbus Savings and Loan Society. In 1904 he founded the Bank of Italy. Giannini's bank was at the time of a novel kind. Branches were set up in small towns across the country to attract the savings of the man in the street, and Giannini even started savings schemes in schools. His bank specialised in making loans to small businesses with minimal collateral and introduced the practice of lending money for house purchase repayable in monthly instalments. He appears to have been a man of some determination and imagination; during the great San Francisco earthquake and fire of 1906, Giannini was the first to reopen his bank, setting up his desk on the waterfront while the fire still raged. By 1930 he had built up his banking interests to the point where the holding company, the Transamerica Corporation, was the largest of its kind in the world, with assets of $1,000 million. Giannini's unorthodox methods did not endear him to more conservative financiers on Wall Street; particularly deplorable was his policy of encouraging wide public ownership of his corporation and of assisting his employees to become stockholders through profit-sharing schemes.

His brother Attilio (sometimes called Dr. Giannini, though he abandoned medicine when made vice-president of his brother's Bank of Italy) was involved in various movie companies between the world wars. In 1920 he lent Chaplin half a million dollars to make *The Kid*. In 1936 he became president and chairman of the Board of United Artists, and though he resigned from this position in 1938 he retained an influential position in the film industry by virtue of his place on the voting trust which controlled Universal Pictures. He was also involved with several so-called independent production companies such as Selznick International Pictures and Lesser-Lubitsch. It's worth pointing out that none of these organisations possessed large chains of movie theatres. It was the tangible assets of real estate which tempted the Wall Street banks into movie finance in the 1920s. Giannini does at least seem to have been more interested in making pictures.

Giannini's main importance for present purposes in his role in Columbia. The company was originally formed in 1920 as CBC, the letters standing for the names of the three men who set it up: Harry Cohn, Joe Brandt, and Harry's brother Jack. All of them had previously worked for Carl Laemmle at Universal. Attilio Giannini lent them $100,000 to get started. In 1924 the company changed its name to Columbia Pictures Corporation (possibly an echo of the Columbus Savings and Loan Society?). Giannini continued to be closely involved. Although in 1929 the studio decided to establish stock on the New York exchange, 96 per cent of the voting stock was concentrated in the hands of a voting trust. In 1932 Joe Brandt was bought out by Harry Cohn (after Jack Cohn had attempted to enlist Giannini's support in a coup against his brother), and thereafter the voting trust which controlled the company consisted of the two Cohns and Giannini. Unlike most studios at this time Columbia had no debts to the New York investment banks and instead was run as a family business.

Giannini's position was therefore a powerful one. Unfortunately one has no actual knowledge of how he used it. All that can be done is to suggest what his influence might have been given the kind of background from which he and his brother came. The Gianninis were quite separate from the New York banking establishment. Not only was theirs a different kind of business (deposit as opposed to investment banking), involving them with different kinds of clients; they were Catholics (unlike the Rockefellers and Morgans), they were second-generation immigrants, they came from the other side of the country, and their social attitudes were, as far as one can tell, less patrician. A. P.'s entry in the *National Cyclopædia* says that he "has ever been known as a friend of the poor and struggling" and if ever a banker could be so described it seems likely that he was. Not surprisingly, therefore, he supported the Banking Act introduced by Roosevelt in 1935 because, he said, he preferred a measure of government control to domination of the banks by the Wall Street establishment. In 1936 he actively supported Roosevelt's campaign for a second term, at a time when Wall Street considered FDR as no better than a Communist. It seems reasonable to assume that his brother shared his liberal views.

The Gianninis might, then, be seen as a kind of contradiction in terms: populist bankers. The populists of the nineteenth century had regarded bankers as the physical embodiment of all that was evil, and believed that the agricultural problems of the Mid-West were largely caused by a conspiracy of monopolists on Wall Street keeping interest rates up and farm prices down. (Amadeo Giannini was, we are told, greatly interested in agricultural progress.) The little man, the populists contended, stood no chance against those who commanded such resources and used them for selfish purposes. But the Gianninis believed in deliberately aiding such small businessmen and farmers who got no help from Wall Street. In this respect they are in line with the policies of the New Deal, which attempted to get big business under some kind of government control while at the same time trying to raise farm prices and help small firms and individuals by encouraging banks to make loans, by refinancing mortgages, and so on.

This too is Dickson's policy in *American Madness* and it seems plausible that the character is indeed based on Dr. Giannini. The question then is, What do we make of it? A simple and tempting theory might be constructed: Capra's film doesn't so much capture what "people" were thinking at the time as represent the thinking of a New Dealer on the voting trust controlling Columbia. Such a theory certainly has its attractions. Firstly, it provides a corrective to the crude assumption that Hollywood = big business = the Republican Party. Secondly, other Capra films such as *Mr. Deeds Goes to Town, Mr. Smith Goes to Washington,* and *You Can't Take It with You* also embody the populism that was a powerful element in the New Deal. Thirdly, the situation of Columbia itself, quite apart from the beliefs of those in control, might well be seen as impelling it towards the New Deal coalition of anti-establishment forces. Despite the Academy Awards Capra collected for the studio in the 1930s it never entirely freed itself from its Poverty Row origins. Although the company bought its own studio in 1926 and in 1929 set up a national distribution organisation, at the beginning of the 1930s Columbia was still producing less than thirty features a year (to MGM's forty-three), and most of these were destined for the lower half of a double bill. Output increased steadily during the decade, but the studio was never in the same league as the majors. In 1935, for example, the total volume of business of Loew's, the parent company of MGM, was $85 million; Columbia's was $16 million. Thus Loew's had nearly 22 per cent of the total volume of business of the industry, Columbia only 4 per cent. And despite the characteristically violent swings in the film industry each year from profit to loss and back again, these relative percentages did not change for the rest of the decade. The reason why Columbia was unable to increase its share of business is that, unlike the major studios, it had no chain of theatres of its own which could serve as a secure outlet for its product. All the money it made came from the sale of its own pictures to theatres owned by other studios. MGM and the other majors could, and frequently did, recoup losses on their own films by profits on the exhibition of other companies' output.

But a potential advantage of this relative weakness was that Columbia preserved its financial independence. It had not had to borrow heavily from the banks to finance the acquisition of theatre chains, and as a result the studio was still in the control of the men who founded it, the two Cohns and Giannini. Its independence of Wall Street meant that it might well become the focus of anti-establishment forces, and that if it did it had the freedom to make films which reflected that, always providing of course that it could sell them to the theatres.

But caution is necessary even before trying to test out such a thesis. Capra in his autobiography devotes several pages to recording how charmed he was by Roosevelt's personality; yet, he says, this only made him "almost a Democrat." One might suppose that Capra, a first-generation immigrant, an Italian Catholic born in Sicily, was a natural Democrat. But the political content of his films, while embodying support for the underdog, does not attach itself to any party. His belief in the people goes hand in hand with a classically populist distrust of *all* their leaders. And other tendencies in his films, such as a pervasive anti-intellectualism and a hostility to central government, are certainly not characteristic of the New Deal.

Nevertheless there is a kind of radicalism in his films which would certainly not have commended itself to the fiercely Republican Louis B. Mayer, for example, and it therefore seems worth pursuing the thesis that Columbia might have been a focus for Roosevelt sympathisers. Harry Cohn, who controlled the production side of the company throughout the period, appears to have had no interest in politics at all. It is true that he visited Mussolini in 1933 after Columbia had released a complimentary documentary entitled *Mussolini Speaks*. But Cohn seems to have been more impressed with the intimidating lay-out of the dictator's office than with his politics. When he returned to Hollywood he rearranged his own office in imitation. Capra remarked in an interview at the National Film Theatre that Cohn didn't care what the politics of his studio's films were. His concern was with their money-making potential, which he estimated with a "foolproof device. . . . . If my fanny squirms it's bad. If my fanny doesn't squirm it's good. It's as simple as that" (quoted in *King Cohn*, p. 142). If Giannini had wanted the studio to take a pro-New-Deal stance, then it seems as though Cohn would have had no particular objections.

The only way of testing whether there was such a policy, in default of any access to whatever records of the company may still exist, is to look at the films that Columbia made during the period and to find out what one can about the people who made them. It's at this point that the sheer physical difficulties of this kind of work intrude. Taking the period 1926–41, from just before the introduction of sound to a year or so after Capra left Columbia (an arbitrary choice, but less arbitrary than some, and one which corresponds very roughly to the period of the Depression and the consequent New Deal, as far as World War II), Columbia, despite being one of the smaller studios, made on my calculations 627 feature films. (The figure may not be exact because the *Film Daily Year Book*, from which the calculation is made, lists the films of each year twice—once under each studio and once in alphabetical order for the whole industry. Titles appearing in one list don't always appear in the other.) To make those films the company employed 67 different producers, 171 directors, and 269 writers. (The figure for writers is from 1928; they are not credited in the *Year Book* before that date.) By writers is meant those credited with a screenplay. Authors of the original stories from which the films were made might amount to another two or three hundred people. There are also fifteen people whose names appear at one time or another as directors of the company, Columbia Pictures Corporation.

These are the people within the organisation whose position would have allowed them to influence the political content of the films. One might wish to argue that everyone—actors, cameramen, designers, right down to the studio policemen—had some kind of influence, however small. Melvyn Douglas, for example, who acted in many films for Columbia in the 1930s, was active in liberal causes. I have excluded these workers from consideration mainly because, given the nature of the production process, as far as one understands it, and the rigid division of labour, their control over the political content (if any) of a film would have been less. Actors didn't make up their own lines. In any case one has to stop somewhere, and it's not too easy to find out who the studio policemen were.

One is thus faced with a preliminary list of 522 people; to be precise, it is slightly less because the division of labour was not absolute and some writers directed or vice versa. But there is not much overlapping, and the total must be around 500 (this for one small studio during a mere fifteen years of its fifty-year existence). The BFI Library has a card index system which allows one to check whether the library has entries on individuals in books, in periodicals, or on microfiche. I accordingly looked up everyone who worked on more than the occasional film. Very few of these names appear in the index and when they do it is often merely a reference to a tiny cutting in *Variety* recording the person's death and giving a person/short list of the films worked on. (This is not a criticism of the state of the library but of the state of film history.)

A few things do emerge. Columbia seems to have been, in the higher echelons, a tight-knit community (one precondition perhaps of a consistent policy). One of the producers was Ralph Cohn, the son of Jack. Everett Riskin, another producer, was the older brother of Robert, who wrote several of Capra's screenplays. Sam Briskin, general manager of the studio in the early 1930s and executive in charge of production from 1938 to 1942, was the brother-in-law of Abe Schneider, treasurer of the company for most of this period. Briskin's brother, Irving, was another producer at Columbia. Yet this doesn't tell us much about an industry where the pull of family relationships was always strong and where "the son-in-law also rises" was a standard joke.

On the political affiliations of the vast majority, I found no information at all, nor even any information on their lives which would permit a guess. Some very few wrote books or had books written about them, but with the exception of Cohn and Capra their careers were peripheral to Columbia. A few more have been the subject of articles in film magazines, and from these one can glean scraps of information. Richard Maibaum, who wrote a few scripts for the studio, was the author of some anti-lynching and anti-Nazi plays before coming to Hollywood. Dore Schary, whose Democrat sympathies were well known, was also a writer at Columbia in the 1930s. So, very occasionally, were Donald Ogden Stewart, associated with left wing causes at the time, and Edward Chodorov, involved with committees for refugees from Spain and Germany and later more or less black-listed. But this scarcely amounts to much. Stewart, after all, wrote a lot of scripts for MGM.

More significant, at first sight, than the presence of liberals, is the fact that exactly half of the Hollywood Ten were actually employed at Columbia during the 1930s, namely, Edward Dmytryk, Dalton Trumbo, Herbert Biberman, John Howard Lawson, and Lester Cole. But a concerted Communist effort at the studio is hardly likely. Only Dmytryk worked there more than occasionally, and he during his time as a contract director was making routine B-feature films (musicals, horror pictures, thrillers) which, one must assume, offered little scope for the kind of social comment Dmytryk later put into *Crossfire*. There were one or two other Communists working at Columbia who testified before the House Un-American Activities Committee four years after the 1947 hearings which sent the Ten to jail. Paul Jarrico, who wrote for Columbia the screenplays of *No Time to Marry* (1938) and *The Face behind the Mask* (1941), was called before the committee in 1951 but refused to testify and pleaded the Fifth Amendment. Another called before the committee in 1951 was Sidney Buchman. One of Harry Cohn's favourite writers, Buchman specialised in comedy. Among his credits for Columbia are *Whom the Gods Destroy* (1934); *I'll Love You Always, Love Me Forever, She Married Her Boss* (1935); *The King Steps Out, Theodora Goes Wild, Adventure in Manhattan, The Music Goes Round* (1936); *Holiday* (1938); *Mr. Smith Goes to Washington* (1939); *The Howards of Virginia* (1940); and *Here Comes Mr. Jordan* (1941). Buchman admitted that he had been in the Communist Party from 1938 to 1945, but refused to supply the committee with the list of names of other members it required and was cited for contempt. He was found guilty and given a one-year suspended sentence and a $150 fine.

Buchman clearly occupied an influential position at Columbia. He was a producer as well as a writer and was associated with some of

Columbia's greatest successes in the late 1930s and early 1940s. But if *Mr. Smith* is satirical about Washington life, it retains an unswerving, even touching, faith in American political institutions, and it is difficult to see that Buchman's membership of the Communist Party had any great effect on what he wrote. Indeed many of his associates appear to have been surprised to learn that he was a Communist.

It may be that a more detailed search through such records as are available would turn up some decisive evidence. But on what has been presented so far it seems unlikely that, Dr. Giannini notwithstanding, there was any deliberate policy of favouritism to the New Deal or left causes. The same conclusion seems likely to follow from the films. Here again one is attempting generalisations based on woefully inadequate knowledge, because, apart from those directed by Capra, I have seen very few of the films Columbia made during the period. Nevertheless some impressions can be gained from looking at the records. In the late 1920s and early 1930s the staples of the studio's output were adventure and action films, comedies often mildly risqué, and the occasional exposé (one of Jack Cohn's first successes at Universal was to convince Carl Laemmle of the box office potential of *Traffic in Souls*, a sensationalist feature on the white slave trade). Westerns and thrillers made up the rest of the production schedule. Of course titles can be misleading, but a list of the films produced in 1928 probably gives a fair indication of at least the type of films being made:

> *That Certain Thing, The Wife's Relations, Lady Raffles, So This Is Love?, Woman's Way, Sporting Age, Matinee Idol, Desert Bride, Broadway Daddies, After the Storm, Golf Widows, Modern Mothers, Name the Woman, Ransom, Way of the Strong, Beware of Blondes, Say It with Sables, Virgin Lips, Scarlet Lady, Court Martial, Runaway Girls, Streets of Illusion, Sinners' Parade, Driftwood, Stool Pigeon, The Power of the Press, Nothing to Wear, Submarine, The Apache, The Lone Wolf's Daughter, Restless Youth, The Sideshow.*

Besides Capra, directors working regularly for Columbia at this time included the veteran director of serials George B. Seitz (*The Perils of Pauline*), and Erle Kenton, another veteran who had been in pictures since 1914. The policy, one guesses, was one of efficient professionalism dedicated to getting the most out of Columbia's meagre resources. Not only did Columbia make less films; it also spent less on each production than the major studios. (Few of its films at this time ran more than seventy minutes.) This would seem to leave little room for the carefully considered personal statements of the kind Capra aspired to later in the 1930s. This is not to say that there was no possibility of social or political comment, however, as the history of Warner's at the same time shows.

After Capra's astonishing success with *It Happened One Night* in 1934, which won Columbia its first Oscars and enormously increased the studio's prestige, pictures of the earlier type were supplemented by the occasional more expensive production. Though Columbia had contract players of its own (for example, Jack Holt and Ralph Bellamy or, in westerns, Buck Jones and Charles Starrett), they could not compare in box-office appeal with the stars of bigger studios. Columbia could not afford the budgets which having bigger stars would have entailed. On the other hand it could never break into the big time without them. Harry Cohn's solution to this vicious circle was to invite successful directors from other studios to make occasional pictures for Columbia, pictures which would be given larger than usual budgets and which would have stars borrowed from other studios. Careful planning permitted short production schedules and kept costs down to what Columbia could afford. Capra too was given increasingly larger budgets and outside stars. Thus a number of big-name directors came to work at Columbia during the later 1930s, often tempted by the offer of being allowed to produce their own films. Among the titles produced at Columbia during the period after *It Happened One Night* were:

> 1934: *20th Century* (dir. Howard Hawks, with John Barrymore and Carole Lombard), *The Captain Hates the Sea* (dir. Lewis Milestone, with Victor McLaglen and John Gilbert); 1935: *The Whole Town's Talking* (dir. John Ford, with Edward G. Robinson), *She Married Her Boss* (dir. Gregory La Cava, with Claudette Colbert), *She Couldn't Take It* (dir. Tay Garnett, with George Raft and Joan Bennett), *Crime and Punishment* (dir. Josef von Sternberg, with Peter Lorre); 1936: *Theodora Goes Wild* (dir. Richard Boleslavski, with Irene Dunne); 1937: *The Awful Truth* (dir. Leo McCarey, with Cary Grant and Irene Dunne); 1938: *Holiday* (dir. George Cukor, with Cary Grant and Katherine Hepburn); 1939: *Let Us Live* (dir. John Brahm, with Maureen O'Sullivan and Henry Fonda), *Only Angels Have Wings* (dir. Howard Hawks, with Cary Grant, Thomas Mitchell, and Richard Barthelmess), *Golden Boy* (dir. Rouben Mamoulian, with Barbara Stanwyck and Adolphe Menjou); 1940: *His Girl Friday* (dir. Howard Hawks, with Cary Grant and Rosalind Russell), *The Howards of Virginia* (dir. Frank Lloyd, with Cary Grant), *Angels over Broadway* (dir. Ben Hecht and Lee Garmes, with Douglas Fairbanks

Jr.), *Arizona* (dir. Wesley Ruggles, with William Holden); 1941: *Penny Serenade* (dir. George Stevens, with Cary Grant and Irene Dunne), *Texas* (dir. George Marshall, with William Holden, Glenn Ford, and Claire Trevor), *You Belong to Me* (dir. Wesley Ruggles, with Barbara Stanwyck and Henry Fonda), *The Men in Her Life* (dir. Gregory Ratoff, with Loretta Young).

But despite this sprinkling of prestige productions the basic recipe remained much the same as before. There were lots of low-budget westerns (a dozen or so in 1940) directed by Lambert Hillyer, a veteran of the Columbia lot, or Joseph H. Lewis, and starring Bill Elliott or Charles Starrett. The studio made several series: a number of films based on Blondie, the cartoon character, the Lone Wolf series of thrillers, an Ellery Queen mystery series, and so on. There were light comedies from Alexander Hall, more light comedies and musicals from Walter Lang, and plenty of crime films (a few titles at random from 1938: *Women in Prison, When G-Men Step In, Penitentiary, Highway Patrol, Reformatory, Convicted, I Am the Law, Juvenile Court, Smashing the Spy Ring*).

What is one to conclude from what emerges of Columbia's production policy in this period? Aware that a viewing of all the films might prove one wrong, it could be said that there is no evidence of Columbia's deliberately following a line favourable to the New Deal. Of course it could be objected that a similar scanning of the titles of Warner Brothers films of the same time would fail to reveal what an actual viewing of the films shows—a detectable if not pronounced leaning towards Rooseveltian attitudes. But this much seems likely: the policy of bringing in outside stars and directors (and writers too) for big-budget productions would have worked against the continuity required for a deliberate political policy. Whereas at Warners a nucleus of stars, writers, producers, and directors was built up capable of producing pictures that fused the thrills of crime with social comment, at Columbia the occasional film (such as *A Man's Castle*, directed by Frank Borzage in 1933) which took the Depression as its subject was a one-off, with the exception of Capra. And it does seem as though Capra *was* an exception. As far as one can tell, the directors who did not have his freedom at the studio did not follow him in the direction of social comment, and neither did directors brought in from outside with a similar amount of freedom. And Capra's films, after all, despite his standing within the studio, are only a tiny proportion of all the films Columbia made in the 1930s.

If one can say that the presence of Giannini on the trust controlling Columbia did not lead to films predominantly favourable to the New

Deal, then can one not also throw doubt on the assumption that control of a studio by interests favourable to the Republican Party led to films (such as *Young Mr. Lincoln* and *King Kong*) designed to make propaganda for that party? No one would argue that there was a total lack of correlation between ownership and the content of films. No studio in the 1930s would have tolerated outright Communist movies, or anything very close to that. (Nor for that matter would a fascist film have stood any chance of being made.) But within these parameters, considerable diversity was possible—a diversity, moreover, which it is dangerous to reduce by the simple expedient of labelling all the films as bourgeois. The difference in political attitudes between, say, *The Good Earth* (MGM, 1937) and *The Grapes of Wrath* (20th Century-Fox, 1940)—two films with not totally dissimilar subjects—are not negligible and relate to real political and social events of the time. But they cannot be explained simply in terms of who owned the studios or in terms only of social attitudes at the time. Any explanation would require that a number of factors be taken into account, and not least of these would be the exact nature of the institutions which produced them.

The history of the American film industry, then, forms a kind of missing link in attempts, Marxist and otherwise, to make connections between films and society. As we have seen, many of the materials needed to forge that link are missing, which is why the title of this essay, "Notes on Columbia Pictures Corporation 1926–41," is intended to imply more than the customary academic modesty. The problems of producing such a history are both practical and the result of a massive ideological prejudice, and I am aware that the information I have produced on Columbia in the 1930s amounts to very little in the way of real knowledge. But this information has been the result of a few hours in the library, not of a large-scale research programme. If one considers how much has been learned, for example, about British labour history in the nineteenth century, the possibilities for further research do not seem hopeless. As a subject it would appear equally as unpromising as the history of the film industry. Apart from newspapers there are few written sources and the people involved are all dead. The history therefore has to a great extent to be reconstructed from the material objects which survive: buildings, institutional structures, the customs and practices of a people. But full-time academics and research students have been working in the field for years. The study of the history of the American film industry has scarcely begun.

Key Workers and
the System

Richard B. Jewell

How Howard Hawks Brought *Baby* Up: An *Apologia* For The Studio System

When the merging of studios, exchanges and theaters into a few large corporations, and the extravagances of the "out-spending" era, had brought an end to the independent production, the inelastic methods of bureaucracy replaced the loose practices of democracy in picture making. Now a new idea, instead of having to win the "O.K." of one autocrat of a little kingdom, had to run the gauntlet of editorial boards, production committees, and conferences of various sorts. A multitude of alleged experts awaited the fellow with the new thought, and when his innovation had completed the circuit of the studio's intricate system there was seldom a trace of originality left in it. The sharp shears and heavy smoothing-irons of the experts had transformed the wild, crazy idea to one of the rigid patterns in favor, at the time, with the studio head and his yes-men and yes-women.
Benjamin B. Hampton, 1931[1]

From the *Journal of Popular Film and Television* 11:4 (Winter 1984), 158–65. Reprinted with permission of the author and the Helen Dwight Reid Educational Foundation. Published by Heldref Publications, 1319 Eighteenth St., NW, Washington, D.C. 20036-1802. Copyright © 1984.

Richard B. Jewell

> *Production methods under this rigid system became mechanized: the "assembly line" appeared in Hollywood. The resulting standardization of pictures caused the downfall of the most important directors during the late twenties. The various branches of production were divided and specialized so specifically and minutely that directors had a lessening opportunity to contribute to the whole. Most directors became "glorified foremen" under the producer-supervisors.*
>
> Lewis Jacobs, 1939[2]

Many books and articles dealing with the American cinema have been written since Benjamin Hampton and Lewis Jacobs completed their pioneering studies in the 1930s. Yet the basic descriptions which these two men applied to the studio system, and the general hostility which they expressed toward it, still predominate in contemporary scholarship. No fewer than six recent and major books utilize Jacobs's "factory" and "assembly-line" analogies in their discussions of Hollywood's major studios.[3] Although most qualify their assessments to some extent, the authors of these books tend to agree with Hampton and Jacobs that the studios were bureaucratic, impersonal, conservative, rigidly structured, and antagonistic to technical innovation and artistic achievement. Men and women of taste, intelligence, and imagination are often portrayed as being destroyed by this system—either squandering their talents by producing the formulaic, escapist entertainment demanded by the system, or rebelling against it, only to be crushed (e.g., Von Stroheim) by its steamrolling, assembly-line operations.

The authors often find themselves with a major predicament when they move beyond these general evaluations of the studios to more specific discussions of the filmmakers who worked for them. The writers admire the works of many of these directors, so they are faced with explaining how their favorites could make exemplary films within such a restrictive organizational structure. Here is one representative attempt to reconcile the contradiction:

> These Hollywood directors worked under studio rule, presumably as journeymen employees involved in the mass production of popular entertainment. They were assigned a script rather than choosing one. They were given a cast of performers and told by a producer to shoot the film in so many days. . . . Yet despite all these restrictions and enforced collaborations, somehow these directors, over the years, managed to make films which were stamped with their particular vision.[4]

This type of argument is wonderfully romantic. It conjures up visions of an elite cadre of auteur supermen bending an iron-clad system to their wills or, at the very least, of a slippery band of Houdinis able to wriggle out of their studio straitjackets and "be free." Unfortunately, the explanation does not provide a clue as to how the directors managed these feats of creative hocus-pocus.

The recent availability of studio records—dusty and unmagical though they may be—will help fill in many important gaps in Hollywood scholarship and provide some specific answers to the studio versus auteur dilemma. By studying the production histories of individual films, we gain a more complete understanding of how the studios actually functioned and how auteur directors managed to protect and project their styles and visions while employed by the studios.

My test case is *Bringing Up Baby*, the screwball comedy par excellence, directed by Howard Hawks and released by RKO Radio Pictures in 1938. The story of the making of *Baby* has been pieced together from files in RKO's West Coast archive.

In order to understand how this comedic treasure came to be produced, it is necessary to flash back to late 1935, when Samuel Briskin took charge of production at RKO. Briskin was brought from Columbia to RKO by Leo Spitz, the company's newly appointed corporate president. Although in receivership at the time, RKO was holding its own. *Roberta, Alice Adams, The Informer,* and *Top Hat* had been released in 1935, and each had received excellent critical notices and performed well at the box office. These films were the product of a unit production system overseen by B. B. Kahane and J. R. McDonough—two executives who allowed their staff producers to handle their pictures with minimal supervision or interference from the front office.

Despite the fine results generated by the system, Spitz followed a well-established principle of corporate management and brought in his "own man" to superintend the studio's filmmaking activities. Sam Briskin had developed a reputation as a tough, stubborn, aggressive executive at Columbia. He was, in the words of Frank Capra, a "hit-first type."[5] Highly ambitious, Briskin must have been delighted to be the top man at RKO after laboring in Harry Cohn's shadow for many years. Briskin's initial move as production chief was to do precisely what Leo Spitz had done—recruit his own staff. By mid-1936, Edward Small, Jesse Lasky, and Howard Hawks were members of the Briskin team, developing projects which he hoped would become hits and strengthen his position at RKO.

Producer-director Hawks was given an exclusive two-year contract that called for a salary of $2500 per week, plus a percentage of the profits from his pictures. The first project to interest him was *Gunga Din.* Staff producer Edward Small had brought the rights to the famous Kipling poem with him to RKO and, after some negotiations, agreed to turn the property over to Hawks for development. Hawks, in turn, interested one of the top writing teams in Hollywood, Ben Hecht and Charles Mac-Arthur, in doing the script, and all three went to New York to work on it. There the writing proceeded at a very leisurely pace; this exasperated Briskin, who periodically informed the threesome of his impatience, but he was powerless to speed them along. Hawks did inform his employer that the story would require three virile male leads, so Briskin began putting out feelers to other studios, hoping to borrow the right stars since RKO had no suitable prospects under contract.

In April 1937, the Hecht-MacArthur script was ready, but Sam Briskin was not. He had failed to convince Louis B. Mayer to lend him Clark Gable, Spencer Tracy, and Franchot Tone, and Ronald Colman had also refused to do the picture. Briskin had no choice but to put *Gunga Din* on the shelf until an appropriate cast could be secured. He, therefore, instructed Hawks to develop something else.

By this time, Howard Hawks had been working for RKO for more than a year without shooting a single frame of film. This reflected negatively on Briskin; a production head's job was to turn out a steady stream of commercially successful pictures, not to pay big salaries to directors who were not making a contribution. Although Briskin might grumble about the length of time required to complete the *Gunga Din* script, he knew that Hawks was not to blame for its postponement. Still, he needed a Hawks film and he needed a good one, for his RKO tenure was not developing as he had hoped. The films made by Briskin's other handpicked producers had, by and large, been an undistinguished and unprofitable lot.

In addition, Sam Briskin had a crucial star problem to solve. Katharine Hepburn had been considered RKO's top female performer when Briskin joined RKO. Beginning with *Sylvia Scarlett,* the studio's first release of 1936, Miss Hepburn had appeared in one flop after another, thereby tarnishing her box office image and diminishing RKO's star roster. This was much more upsetting than the Hawks situation because, compared to its major competitors, RKO was sadly lacking in star power. Since a company sold its product blocks largely by promising to deliver a certain number of films featuring public favorites, it was considered imperative to boost Hepburn back to the lofty position she had once occupied in the show business hierarchy.

Miss Hepburn did not come to mind immediately when Hawks informed Briskin in May that he wished to make a film based on a *Collier's* magazine story entitled "Bringing Up Baby." The RKO story departments had recommended "Baby" for purchase in April, and its head, Robert Sparks, had encouraged Briskin to hire the story's author, Hagar Wilde. Briskin, however, had shown no interest until Hawks made his decision.

Then everything changed. Dudley Nichols, one of RKO's top writers, went to work on the story with Hawks, Miss Wilde was brought out from the East to collaborate with the director and screenwriter, and, in short order, a decision was made to star Katharine Hepburn. The role of daffy socialite Susan Vance would be unlike any part she had played before; perhaps the public would embrace this new Hepburn persona.

The writing continued through the summer of 1937. While Nichols and Wilde developed the script, Briskin and Hawks hunted for the right male lead. Fredric March, Ray Milland, Fred MacMurray, and Leslie Howard were considered before Cary Grant won the job. Grant and Hepburn had worked together before in *Sylvia Scarlett*.

Budget was a matter of special concern to Sam Briskin. Realizing that public hostility to Katharine Hepburn was real enough, at least for the moment, he calculated that *Bringing Up Baby* had little chance of making a profit if it cost much more than a half million dollars. He told Hawks that the script should be prepared so that $600,000 would be the absolute maximum expenditure. Despite this admonition, the director and his writers gave their imaginations free rein. The first estimating script weighed in at a hefty 242 pages, the revised draft at 194 pages, and the final shooting script at 202 pages. Given a certain amount of "over-writing," this still represented a mammoth amount of material. By the time the film was ready to go before the cameras, the budget had been estimated at $767,000 for a fifty-one-day shooting schedule.

Briskin now had three apparent options. He could scrap the film altogether because of the excessive cost; postpone it until script and budget could be brought into line; or allow it to go forward, but instruct Hawks that he must prune the script so that the film would cost no more than $600,000. In reality, the latter was the only viable option. Briskin could not afford to cancel the project for several reasons, including the money that had already been invested in it (Hawks's salary, the writers' salaries, set construction costs, etc.) and the company's need to provide exhibitors with "A" pictures. He could not postpone the film either, because of the nature of the studio commitment system, which, for example, gave RKO the services of Cary Grant for a limited period of time. If Grant were not used during that time, RKO lost him but had to pay his salary anyway.

Therefore, Briskin reluctantly gave Hawks the go-ahead, hoping the director would find a way to whittle down the script and budget. Briskin had become a truly beleaguered executive by this time. His major productions (*The Woman I Love*, *New Faces of 1937*, and *The Toast of New York*) had proved to be highly disappointing, and he had had more difficulty meeting release schedules than any previous RKO production head. When a company's distribution network promised a film to its most important customers on a certain date and then failed to deliver the picture as promised, it caused shock waves throughout the entire corporate system. Publicity and advertising were disrupted, a mad scramble ensued to find an adequate filler picture, and the film in question often entered the marketplace at a less-than-opportune release time. Most important, the situation damaged the credibility of the studio itself, making exhibitors wary of buying blocks of films from the company in the future.

Briskin definitely needed a breakthrough film to release the pressure that was building against him, and he must have felt that *Bringing Up Baby* could be that film. *Baby* did not even have to be a blockbuster; it would be enough if it returned Katharine Hepburn to public favor, thus breathing life into RKO's moribund star contingent.

Howard Hawks certainly understood all this. He realized that a great deal was riding on *Bringing Up Baby*, and he also realized that, politically speaking, he occupied the true position of power. About six weeks before the film went into production, Briskin's assistant Lou Lusty sent the following memo to his boss. It serves both to confirm the basic auteur contentions about Hawks and to reveal how a cagey director could manipulate the system.

> I know, because the gentleman has said so in so many words that he's only concerned with making a picture that will be a personal credit to Mr. Hawks regardless of its cost—and your [Briskin's] telling him the other day that it would be suicidal to make a Hepburn picture for seven or eight hundred thousand dollars I know made no impression on him at all. . . . Hawks is determined in his own quiet, reserved, soft-spoken manner to have his way about the making of this picture. . . . With the

salary he's been getting he's almost indifferent to anything that might come to him on a percentage deal—that's why he doesn't give a damn about how much the picture will cost to make—and you know so well that you couldn't even break even if a Hepburn show cost eight hundred grand. All the directors in Hollywood are developing producer-director complexes and Hawks is going to be particularly difficult.[6]

Shooting commenced on September 27, 1937. In order to protect the studio's interests, Briskin assigned an associate producer to the film. The man chosen was Cliff Reid, a veteran who had worked in the same capacity on John Ford's award-winning RKO film *The Informer*. Reid's job was to "remind" Hawks that the script had to be cut and to make sure the production ran smoothly and efficiently. Reid, however, turned out to be something of a pushover. Disregarding the pressure from both Reid and Briskin, Hawks proceeded at a deliberate pace. Every day the dialogue would be rewritten on the set, causing the company to shoot less than the production department had estimated. Katharine Hepburn had some difficulty learning how to play screwball comedy, so Hawks introduced her to Walter Catlett, who tutored her throughout the rest of the production.[7] Hepburn also missed seven full days due to illness, and Hawks never got around to removing anything from the script. For these and other reasons, the picture quickly fell behind schedule. It soon became obvious that it would go beyond its projected date of completion and exceed its already excessive budget estimate.

These facts did not elude Leo Spitz or the RKO board of directors. A little over one month into the production, Briskin was forced to resign. Although certainly not the sole reason, the chronicle of *Bringing Up Baby* was a factor in Briskin's departure. Production reports indicate that the shooting pace slackened even more after Briskin left. The major question at this point is why RKO did not simply fire Hawks and turn the film over to someone else. One can only speculate, though the reasons seem obvious: the insertion of a new director, who was unfamiliar with both the story and its treatment, would have caused confusion and resentment on the part of cast and crew and, quite probably, have slowed things down even more. It might also have ruined the picture altogether.

Hawks went on working past the November date when the original schedule indicated completion, beyond the holidays and into the new year. Finally, on January 8, 1938, the shooting was completed. The original, fifty-one-day schedule had ballooned to ninety-three days, and the final budget amounted to $1,073,000.

The aftermath was fairly predictable. *Bringing Up Baby* was released to mixed critical notices and average box office business. It did not seem to do much for Katharine Hepburn's career either. Briskin proved to be right in his prediction that a Hepburn film costing more than $700,000 could not make a profit. The final RKO loss on *Baby* amounted to $365,000. It also turned out to be Hepburn's last RKO picture. After a loan-out to Columbia for *Holiday*, she returned to her home studio, refused to appear in *Mother Carey's Chickens*, and was released from her contract. The RKO braintrust were convinced that she was washed up, but she would prove them wrong at MGM, beginning in 1940.

Likewise, Hawks found himself out of a job. *Gunga Din* had been reactivated while *Bringing Up Baby* was shooting. Knowing that it would be a much more ambitious and complicated picture than *Baby*, new executive producer Pandro Berman decided to turn it over to a more reliable director: George Stevens. (Ironically, Stevens developed his own perfectionist qualities on *Gunga Din*, which went $700,000 over budget.) Hawks's brother and agent, William, was called into the studio and informed that Howard would be terminated. The director was upset by this—not because he would be giving up his $2500 weekly salary but because he would not have an opportunity to direct *Gunga Din*, which was precisely the type of male adventure saga he loved best. Nevertheless, his contract was canceled upon payment of $40,000 severance money.

It might seem that the system had prevailed over Hawks after all, since he was now branded as profligate and undependable and was out of a job. But, of course, the system was much larger than RKO Radio Pictures; within a short time, Hawks was back at work at Columbia on *Only Angels Have Wings*. It is important to note that that picture and Hawks's next effort, *His Girl Friday*, both starred Cary Grant. Hawks and Grant had obviously established a solid working relationship on *Bringing Up Baby*, which suggests that Hawks had actually increased his industry clout on *Baby*, rather than decreasing it. In addition to making memorable comedy, he had forged an alliance with a star whose career was rising rapidly. If Cary Grant wanted to work with Howard Hawks, Hawks's pictures would be made by one studio or another.

Now that we have surveyed the making of *Bringing Up Baby*, I would like to offer the following modest proposals:

The time has come to dispense with the assembly-line analogy for studio production. Although the moguls no doubt wished their operations could be as efficient and predictable as those of a Ford plant, their product mitigated against standardization.[8] It is true, of course, that the production history of *Bringing Up Baby* is not typical; the film resulted from a special set of circumstances which enabled its director to control the picture more completely than would normally have been the case. Still, the departmental structures and operating methods of studios never turned filmmaking into a conveyor-belt business. Most pictures presented special problems which could not have been solved by inflexible, factory-inspired methods.

Leo Rosten, who studied the studio system when it was at its peak, has described it very well:

> Movie making is not a systematized process in which ordered routine can prevail, or in which costs can be absolute and controlled. Too many things can and do go awry, every day, every hour, during the manufacture of a movie. Movies are made by ideas and egos, not from blueprints and not with machines. Every story offers fresh and exasperating problems; every actor, director, writer carries within him curious preferences and needs; and the omnipresent hand of a mutable public throws sudden switches in the traffic of ideas through which the making of movies flows. The movie business moves with relentless speed, change is of the essence, and Hollywood must respond to change with short-spanned flexibility.[9]

Unfortunately, most scholars have preferred the depersonalized studio characterizations of Hampton and Jacobs to the somewhat nebulous, but more accurate, depiction of Rosten.

The power and influence of the movie industry's "A"-level talent during the studio years have been seriously underestimated. The conception of the artist as corporate slave was fueled by periodic tirades against the moguls and their methods. One need only recall Frank Capra's 1939 letter to the *New York Times* in which he claimed that "80% of the directors today shoot scenes exactly as they are told to shoot them without any changes whatsoever, and . . . 90% of them have no voice in the story or in the editing"[10] or Bette Davis's well-publicized battles to prevent Jack Warner from forcing her to appear in mediocre pictures. Nevertheless, studio records contradict the impressions produced by these and other angry outbursts against the system. Most major actors and actresses could and did turn down parts they did not like (even at Warner Brothers), and it was normal for "A" directors to have considerable freedom in their choice of material, to work with writers on the preparation of the script, to have the strongest voice in casting decisions, and to be left alone when they were directing the film. These basic conventions might be breached if a picture went widely over budget or if the studio executive felt the footage was no good. Still, as in the case of *Bringing Up Baby*, a studio rarely fired a director or halted production, even if the film did run over in both time and money.

The last proposal is for an open-minded reevaluation of the system itself and of each individual studio. There is more scholarly work to be done if we are to move beyond the one-sided generalizations that prevail in the current literature. We need, first of all, to recognize the complexity of these organizations. It is wrong to lump MGM, Paramount, Warner Brothers, Twentieth Century-Fox, RKO, and, oftentimes, Columbia, Universal, and United Artists together and treat them as if they were carbon copies of one another. Each of these companies had its own special characteristics, and each underwent significant changes during the studio system era. Each was a world unto itself with its own ways of making movies and making money. It is also time that we recognize the intrinsic genius of the system. There were both sound business sense and artistic advantage in the assembling of a diverse group of specialists under one umbrella structure. These talented individuals were able to grow and learn and work together in ways that enriched them all, as well as the capitalistic organizations they served.

A modern systems analyst studying the old Hollywood studios would certainly find them grossly inefficient and honeycombed with flaws. Ironically, these very weaknesses enabled the studios' more imaginative employees to make pictures that are still studied and appreciated today. The studios have taken enough punishment; we should give them a second look, recognizing that they may represent the best system for commercial filmmaking thus far developed in world cinema.

NOTES

1. Benjamin B. Hampton, *History of the American Film Industry*, new ed. (New York: Dover Publications, 1970), pp. 416–17.

2. Lewis Jacobs, *The Rise of the American Film*, new ed. (New York: Teachers College Press, 1967), p. 296.

3. Thomas W. Bohn and Richard L. Stromgren, *Light and Shadows*, 2nd ed. (Sherman Oaks, Calif.: Alfred Publishing, 1978), pp. 199, 204–5; David Bordwell and Kristin Thompson, *Film Art: An Introduction* (Reading, Mass.: Addison-Wesley, 1979), pp. 8–9; David A. Cook, *A History of Narrative Film* (New York: W. W. Norton, 1981), pp. 265–9; Louis Giannetti, *Masters of the American Cinema* (Englewood Cliffs, N.J.: Prentice-Hall, 1981), pp. 9–13; Gerald Mast, *A Short History of the Movies*, 2nd ed.

49

(Indianapolis: Bobbs-Merrill, 1976), pp. 265–65; David Thomson, *American in the Dark* (New York: William Morrow, 1977), pp. 69–70.

4. Thomas Sobchack and Vivian C. Sobchack, *An Introduction to Film* (Boston: Little, Brown, 1980), p. 299.

5. Frank Capra, *The Name above the Title* (New York: Macmillan, 1971), p. 90.

6. Lou Lusty, memo to Sam Briskin, 10 August 1937, "Howard Hawks" file, RKO West Coast Archives, Los Angeles, California.

7. Joseph McBride, *Hawks on Hawks* (Berkeley and Los Angeles: University of California Press, 1981), p. 72.

8. Even at the "B" level, where production elements were more strictly controlled than at the "A" level, the "assembly-line" conception is inaccurate. The creative team that worked on the Val Lewton films at RKO, for example, had ample leeway to develop a new strain of psychologically penetrating horror films. Their budgets were limited, but, otherwise, their innovative efforts were unencumbered by studio policies and procedures.

9. Leo C. Rosten, *Hollywood, the Movie Colony, the Movie Makers* (New York: Harcourt, Brace, 1941), p. 255.

10. Frank Capra, letter to *New York Times*, 2 April 1939, quoted in Louis Giannetti, *Masters of the American Cinema*, p. 19.

Paul Kerr

My Name Is Joseph H. Lewis

Despite the recent publication of John Caughie's excellent anthology, *Theories of Authorship*,[1] auteurism has been conspicuously absent from the agenda of *Screen*[2] in particular and film studies in general of late. But auteurism refuses to go away. It crops up in Festival retrospectives, in the programming of repertory cinemas, as the organising principle behind cinema seasons on television, in educational syllabuses, and among the assumptions of articles in *Screen* itself. Indeed there remains, as Caughie argues, a reluctant sense in which while it is assumed that authorship (in both its traditional humanist "exception to the Hollywood rule" and its post-structuralist "subject's construction of and by a reading" guises) is an inadequate critical concept, it is difficult—if not altogether impossible—to entirely dispense with it. Caughie's anthology itself collects much of the best writing on the relation between texts and authors but is quick to acknowledge the relative absence of work on the relation between authors and contexts. Understandably dubious of the liberal extensions of auteurism to embrace non-directorial personnel and similarly sceptical about the contextualising work done on Hollywood genres and Hollywood as industry,[3] Caughie admits that his book

> has very little to say on the place of the author within institutions (industrial, cultural, academic), or on the way in which the author is constructed by and for commerce. Partly this reflects a dissatisfaction with most of what has been written, which has tended to remain within the romantic concept of the artist, with its concentration on questions of artistic freedom and industrial interference, and with its continual desire to identify the true

From *Screen* 24:4/5 (July/October 1983), 48–66. Reprinted with permission of the author and *Screen*. Deletions by request of author.

author out of the complex of creative personnel. At the same time, questions of the author's relation to institutional and commercial contexts are increasingly being recognized as crucial. . . .[4]

This article attempts to sketch out—if not yet to fill in—some of the gaps discussed by Caughie concerning the place of the author within those institutions.

The title of this piece has both a playful and a polemical purpose. Playful because it marries the title of Joseph H. Lewis's first major success, *My Name Is Julia Ross*, with an echo of the first clause of John Ford's famous statement "My name is John Ford. I make westerns." Unlike Ford, Lewis—in spite or perhaps because of the cult status of some few of his films—is not familiar enough to assume such an easy equivalence with a directorial oeuvre, let alone to conjure up a conventional genre, nor can his name even be relied upon to guarantee recognition among readers of specialist journals like *Screen*. And this, to risk repeating myself, is important. There is no obvious genre that Lewis can claim to have made his own—as Ford could modestly associate himself with the western. Lewis began and ended his career with westerns, but in between was a decade or more in which he made none at all and it is that decade, in which he essayed the musical, the comedy, the war film, and the crime thriller, with which I am primarily concerned here and in which Lewis made his name as a director. Indeed, if it can be said that Lewis made any categorisable and consistent type of film at all in those years, then the critical consensus can suggest only two coherent candidates for such continuity. First, that they are all "Lewis" films, a formulation which simply elides the problem by transforming the auteur canon itself into a virtual genre, and second, that they are all B films destined for the bottom half of Hollywood's double bills.

There is, however, a third and rather more contentious case to be made for Lewis: indeed, a number of critics have already argued that the bulk of his 1945–55 output falls into the category now known as film noir. This may, of course, be no more than a symptom of the very real difficulty auteurists have experienced attempting to define and describe these films. Nevertheless, their eccentricities, their excessiveness, their expressiveness as texts of and for their time, combined with their centrality in, their representativeness of a particular professional strategy at a specific moment and mode of the American cinema's, and indeed the American film industry's, development is what interests me now.

This article grew out of a paper I presented at the 1980 Edinburgh Film Festival, which included a pretty comprehensive retrospective of Lewis's films. That retrospective itself says a great deal about Lewis's standing in 1980, though the conclusions reached by the various contributors to the event all share the conviction that Lewis is and was something of an unsuitable case for the Edinburgh treatment. It is also significant that the Edinburgh Retrospective, unlike many of its predecessors, did not transfer to the National Film Theatre in London or inspire a tie-in publication. On the other hand, this article itself is a part of the expanding Lewis bibliography. The draft presented in Edinburgh was itself derived from an earlier article published in *Screen Education*,[5] and this case study of Lewis, however schematic, presents an opportunity for amending the more obvious weaknesses and filling in some of the more gaping omissions of that previous piece. What it does not attempt is textual analysis—not because this is not considered crucial in relocating authors in institutions but because there are several very useful examples of such analyses already available.[6]

What follows can be divided into three relatively distinct parts: first, a claim for the surprisingly continuous results of, but historically and institutionally extremely diverse reasons for, expending energy in familiarising exhibitors, audiences, and critics with Lewis's name; second, a sketch of the landmarks in the industrial terrain in which Lewis operated and a discussion of the ways in which "he" achieved some of the "effects" for which he has since been celebrated; and third, a survey of the history of attempts to construct Lewis as an author within the critical and academic institutions.

In 1942 the United States government reached a temporary settlement with the major studios in the so-called Paramount case, and, for the "big five" vertically integrated majors at least, the twin practices of block booking and blind selling were either effectively curtailed or banned outright.[7] For the first time all their products had to be sold to exhibitors individually, and this included B films, which were even, occasionally, now subject to press previews and trade shows. Relatively rapidly, B films were encouraged to become increasingly competitive, compulsorily and compulsively different, distinctive. What had previously, perhaps, been a rather static aesthetic and occupational hierarchy between B's and A's became suddenly more flexible. No longer could a company like Columbia guarantee outlets for its films in blocks—it had to sell them singly and it could consequently no longer rely on its own "trade name" to attract exhibitors or assure quality. Rather paradoxically perhaps, one of the avenues this opened up among the "ambitious B's" involved the contravention of current formulas and standard stylistic practices (too often referred to as the Classic Hollywood style), as indulgence in excess, individuality, idiosyncracy, virtuosity as if for its own sake. Within these differences, however, residues of Hollywood's cinematic standardisation remained. First, of course, the constraints within which such "experiments" took place were real and tight; second, the conventions against which such reactions were expressed remained relatively common among a large number of different film-makers wishing to "make a name for themselves"; and third, in order for a director like Lewis to differentiative his work from that of his contemporaries he would be obliged to standardise his own style wherever possible, for purposes of recognition—and reward.

Today, the naming of such directors as Fuller, Karlson, Mann, Ray, Siodmak, Tourneur, Ulmer, and so on continues for rather different reasons. At the level of British distribution and exhibition there remains a need to "authorise" Hollywood directorial retrospective repertory screenings as art in order to attract art-cinema audiences otherwise antipathetic to American cinema; film critics, meanwhile, require authors to "credit" for the films they review in columns still dominated by the methods of literary criticism. And at a more academic level, the fashion for film noir in particular and for Hollywood's post-war years in general which characterised the 1970s and early 1980s can be understood as nostalgia for a certain style, specifically a style which contravened not only the supposed standard practices of the time but also the theoretical accounts of more generalised Hollywood practices articulated in *Screen* and elsewhere. More cynically, it adds another "individual" name to the "traditional" pantheon of teachable "talents." Finally, the presence of television, historically, has not only had an arguable effect on the development of film noir but also—it is often alleged—complied readily and in an almost parodic manner with some at least of the rules of that realism which film noir has been hailed as having broken.

Attempting to locate the author, Lewis, in the place and time of Hollywood in the late forties and early fifties is far from simple. In 1974 Edward Buscombe, writing an article for another of Edinburgh's Hollywood director retrospectives—this time on Raoul Walsh—sought, by sketching out the "house style" of Warner Brothers, where Walsh worked continuously for some years, and relating it, albeit tentatively, to that studio's industrial structure, to "call into question the simple notion of

Paul Kerr

Walsh as an auteur who dictated the style and contents of his pictures."[8] Instead, Buscombe argued that

> working for a studio with as distinctive a policy and style as Warners imposed a number of constraints on any director. Yet these constraints should not be thought of as merely negative in their operation. Working for the studio meant simply that the possibilities for good work lay in certain directions rather than in others.[9]

In attempting to adapt Buscombe's approach to a specific period in the cinematic career of Joseph H. Lewis, a number of problems rapidly appear. First of all, Lewis—unlike Walsh (or, for that matter, Ford)—was never exclusively involved with a single studio for more than four or five consecutive years. From the first film he directed, in 1937, to the last, in 1958, Lewis worked at Grand National (1937), then Universal (1937–38), then Columbia (1940), then Monogram (1940–41), then PRC (1941), then Universal again (1942), back to PRC (1944), then RKO (1945), Columbia again (1945–49), then for the King Brothers (distributed by United Artists, 1950), then MGM (1950), then for United States Pictures (distributed by Warner Brothers, 1951), then back to MGM (1952–53), then for Security-Theodora Productions (distributed by Allied Artists, 1955), then for Scott-Brown (distributing through Columbia, 1955–56), and, finally, on two films for Collier Young Associates and Seltzer Films (both of which were distributed by United Artists, 1957–58). Whether this almost incessant mobility is more characteristic of the B's than of more prestigious productions or whether it is more specific to Lewis is difficult to determine. The number of companies Lewis worked for, however, together with the fact that the peak period of his career coincides with the decline (and divorce) of the vertically integrated studio system (which the presence of so many independents toward the end of the Lewis list bears out) suggests that a director/studio study is inappropriate here. Furthermore, because he was an unprestigious director, Lewis's career is relatively undocumented. In order to overcome some at least of these problems I restrict my attention here to an industrially defined (sub-) genre, the B film noir, an area in which, it has been argued, a large proportion of Lewis's 1945–55 output can comfortably be situated; this focus allows me to draw in some detail on my *Screen Education* article.

There I associated the development of the B film noir with what I called "a negotiated resistance to the realist aesthetic on the one hand and an accommodation to restricted expenditure on the other,"[10] a formula which should become clearer in the following paragraphs. Very schematically, the argument boils down to the conviction that film noir, far from being reducible to a specific sociopolitical atmosphere, an aesthetic ancestry, or a set of émigré authorial signatures, actually related to the particular conditions of its production, distribution, and exhibition. Indeed, I suggested that film noir combined an economically determined "low-budget" mode with an ideologically determined "anti-realist" mode. What I did not discuss in that article, and what I would like to briefly draw attention to here, are what Althusserians would describe as the political determinants of the genre.

Very briefly, I would suggest that the B film noir is an ambitious B, a B bidding for critical and/or commercial prestige. The Supreme Court rulings against blind selling and block booking encouraged and indeed obliged the B companies (and the B units within the majors, though perhaps here the pressures were somewhat diluted and delayed) to inject an element of expressive individuality into their products. At the same time the shift to independent production (partly accelerated by tax incentives) and the rise of the Directors Guild professionalised the directors, reaffirming the rhetoric of individuation, creativity, and differentiation. The Directors Guild, founded in 1936, succeeded in drawing up an agreement with the studios in 1939 recognising the creative function of the director, ensuring salary minimums, and safeguarding contracts.

Low-key lighting—a characteristic as common to film noir as it was rare in other contemporary genres and almost entirely absent from the thrillers of the previous decade—functioned simultaneously to conceal the meagre production values of the B film noir while itself constituting a striking style. This propensity away from realist denotation toward "expressionist" connotation was also a consequence of (and could cash in on) the constraints of the Production Code. Furthermore, the "hybrid" quality of the film noir was perhaps, at least in part, attributable to increasing studio insecurities about marketing their B product (covering all their generic options, as it were, in each and every film). The experience of directors like Lewis in companies as different as MGM and PRC and genres as distinct as spy films, horror films, musical westerns, screwball comedies, and war films—experiences denied many contemporary directors who worked only at the prestige end of the industry—may also have contributed to the curiously cross-generic quality of the B film noir. Similarly, if low-key lighting styles, for example, were more economic than their high-key alternatives, they were also dramatically and distinctively different from them, from the A films that tended to employ them, and from the new technologies of Technicolor, television, and deep focus, all of which necessitated high key.

By the end of the 1950s the studio system, the double bill, black-and-white cinematography, the Production Code, the very status of cinema as the most popular—and profitable—art were all being eroded. In their place, a shift was already taking place to independent production, single-feature programmes, colour cinematography, wide and small screens, and an audience classification system. The period of this transition, the period in which the equation between black and white on the one hand and realism on the other was at its most fragile, is that of the B film noir, the period in which Joseph H. Lewis made his name.

Between 1945 and 1955, Lewis directed twelve films; of these, one is a light comedy, one a swashbuckler, and another a (noirish) war film. The other nine are *The Falcon in San Francisco* (1945), *My Name Is Julia Ross* (1945), *So Dark the Night* (1946), *The Undercover Man* (1949), *Gun Crazy* (1950), *A Lady without Passport* (1950), *Desperate Search* (1952), *Cry of the Hunted* (1953), and *The Big Combo* (1955). The latter was his last black-and-white film and his last film noir. Lewis's career in cinema continued with four Technicolor Westerns; he then turned to television, where he continued to direct episodes of western series into the 1960s.

Before looking in any detail at the production of any of Lewis's B films noirs (all of which had running times under ninety minutes and almost all of which were made on the conventionally derisory schedules and budgets of the second feature), it is worth making a few observations about his earlier career. Lewis had worked as a director for almost ten years by this time at the smaller B companies and in the B units of the "little three" majors. Consequently he was already identified (as many B directors were) with specific series of second features, in Lewis's case the Bob Baker/Fuzzy Knight singing westerns and the Bowery Boys films. *The Falcon in San Francisco* was also one of a series of RKO Falcon films, but Lewis's employment there seems to have been on a strictly one-off contract. Perhaps the ever-fluid administration at RKO meant that for a director to exercise any consistent or coherent "creativity" there he or she needed a strong producer/production unit behind which to shelter (viz. Val Lewton). From RKO, Lewis turned to Columbia, where he was to make the film that was to bring him critical and even commercial success for the first time. At Columbia, the production unit structure seems to have exercised considerably less importance than at RKO; at Columbia, the crucial factor seems to have been the favour of Harry Cohn.

Lewis worked at Columbia from 1945 to 1949, his most pro-longed period with any company. His first film there was *My Name Is Julia Ross*, a project he claims to have chosen for himself and for which he was allocated a twelve-day shooting schedule and a $125,000 budget—limits which Lewis apparently exceeded by four or five days and $50,000, respectively.[11] Having gone considerably over both budget and schedule without severe reprimand, Lewis even managed to secure a sneak pre-view for the finished film (which ran only sixty-five minutes)—an appar-ently almost unprecedented event for a B film but presumably a part of Columbia's new "ambitious B" strategy. According to Lewis the film grossed four or five million dollars; certainly Lewis's future with Colum-bia was guaranteed and positive reviews by the likes of James Agee together with a New York Critics Award cannot have damaged the film's chances.

The little three companies (Columbia, Universal, and United Artists—so-called to distinguish them from the theatre-owning big five: Paramount, Twentieth Century-Fox, MGM, Warner Brothers, and RKO) had refused to sign the 1940 Consent Decree eliminating blind selling and block booking among the majors. Compliance with the decree obliged the majors to introduce trade shows for all their films and to opt for a maximum of five films per sales package. With their theatre chains regularly hungry for new product, the majors understandably opted for the continuation of the mass production system, which they had already operated for more than a decade. The minors, on the other hand, decided to slim down, producing fewer, better films. The little three's refusal to endorse the decree did not prevent the other majors from transforming the industry. Paramount, RKO, and Fox reduced their selling blocks to five; MGM went to blocks of ten, Warners and UA used unit sales, and Columbia and Universal stayed with full-season blocks. But the big five's transformed strategy inevitably influenced even the least flexible com-panies: selling by studio brand name became increasingly untenable, even for companies like Columbia, which still sold films in large blocks, and B competition and consequent differentiation intensified. Thus, Columbia's ambitious risk with *My Name Is Julia Ross* was reprised elsewhere, especially in the B film noir. At Universal, Siodmak's *The Killers* began as a B; at Fox, Preminger's *Laura* had similar low-budget origins and was destined for the bottom half of the bill; and at Warner Brothers, Huston's *The Maltese Falcon* was also allegedly conceived and cast as a second feature. Lewis describes in *Positif* how Columbia could not stretch to a budget for extras on *Julia Ross* (each of whom would have cost fifteen dollars a day) but forced him to create an "English" atmo-sphere through imaginative assembly of stock footage, studio streets and sets, fog, fountains, and back projection. James Agee, in the *Nation*, wrote, "The film is well planned, mostly well played, well directed and in a somewhat boomhappy way, well photographed—all around, a like-able, unpretentious, generally successful attempt to turn good trash into decently artful entertainment."[12]

At the success of *Julia Ross* Columbia encouraged Lewis to direct another "crime melodrama" (a phrase that recurs throughout the trade press reviews of Lewis's films noirs, as well as those of other directors). Based on an inexpensive *Reader's Digest* story, the script of *So Dark the Night* necessitated twenty days' shooting and a French town set, but Lewis's B budget—probably no more than for *Julia Ross*—could not meet the twenty dollars a day that Fox demanded in rent for theirs. Lewis has described in some detail how he and his art director and sketch artist walked around the Columbia back lot looking for a possible, passable location:

> We walked around that back lot which was over in the valley, I'll bet you six times, and I kept coming back to one spot. One spot. And that one spot—there was a town—they had made a war film and they bombed the hell out of it, and half a church was left. And the buildings were just demolished. And I was inspired by that steeple, that church steeple. And we walked around into a field . . . Now this is just a field—no sets, nothing—and way in the background is that steeple. And I looked at the art director and I said "if you took a bulldozer and you made a winding road here, and a dirt road that led past that steeple; and you took a thatched roof in the foreground, just a roof and a side of a building, and over here further back in perspective so you have it, you know, one in the foreground, one in the background, to cover up all the burned-out buildings and everything, and you had another flat there, and down this sliding road I saw a little donkey cart or some French villager came or an automobile came, would I give the impression of a French village?" And the art director leapt for joy, and by the time I had finished, the sketch artist had drawn a French village for me with two flats in the foreground and out of a field we made a dirt road. That's the French village. . . .
>
> When the girl is found dead, the little French guy comes running up to her mother and there's a long dialogue scene where he tells her mother the girl is dead and she screams and cries and all that. And I got on the

set and I rehearsed it and I said oh, no, no, no, impossible. How can I supply dialogue to meet this kind of situation? And so, I threw out all the dialogue . . . I put the camera outside of the house and way in the background was a big window that was cut up into about sixteen different little panes and there you saw the mother busy polishing some silverware or something. And through the scene as taken from outside the farmhouse, in runs this little Frenchman, but in extreme long shot, and he runs through the house and he disappears behind a wall and then reveals himself in front of this window. They're two tiny figures . . . in an extreme long shot and you can't hear. He's talking of course, but you can't hear it. We're shooting it, you know, without sound. And the only noise, shattering noise, that you hear [is] when she drops that silver platter or whatever it was, and that's all you see. . . .[13]

The point of reprinting these anecdotes here is not to salute the "imagination" of the director and his production team but rather to acknowledge the complex ways in which the much commented-on "Bressonian" spareness of Lewis's settings and yet the fluid "Ophulsian" manner of his shooting style both originate precisely in the industrial constraints under which the film was made. Once again Cohn and the Columbia hierarchy were happy with the result and, by way of promotion, "miscast" Lewis to direct the musical sequences in the far more prestigious and hugely successful Larry Parks vehicle *The Jolson Story*. This was followed by two further, equally uncharacteristic projects: a second Parks vehicle, *The Swordsman*, and an unsuccessful Cary Grant—style comedy about a man reincarnated as a horse, *The Return of October*. Finally, Lewis was allowed to return to the path he had begun to carve out with *Julia Ross* and directed his third crime melodrama for Columbia, *The Undercover Man*. Here again, in spite of the film's B status, Lewis was allowed unusual license, including the luxury of a three-camera set-up (quite a conventional A film technique but, because of its expense, almost unheard-of among B's), and even rehearsal time for an improvisatory dialogue scene. (Once again, censorship pressures prevented a straightforward, denotative narrative of the Capone case on which the script was based; instead, Capone's identity behind the "big fellow" could only be connoted by careful re-creation of Capone's familiar hat.) *Time* magazine commented, "Director Joseph H. Lewis has turned out a neat little job. It is more entertaining than most of the better-advertised movies it will get paired with on double feature bills. . . . It just goes to show that thoughtful direction and handsome camera work can lift a mediocre movie a long way above its humble origins."[14]

In respect of my general remarks about the industrial imperatives of film noir it is perhaps pertinent here to mention that it was in 1945, Lewis's first year at Columbia, that that company was finally formally charged with conspiracy to infringe the Anti-Trust laws; indeed, the very same issue of the *Motion Picture Herald* (November 17, 1945), which reviewed *Julia Ross*, also carried an article about the Anti-Trust suit and the probable outcome and consequences of the then imminent decision on block booking. Similarly, the same issue of the *MPH* (September 4, 1946) in which *So Dark the Night* was reviewed included news of Columbia's response to those charges and that decision. It is also worth noting that it was in 1945 that Columbia first employed Technicolor as well as the cheaper Cinecolor process. In 1949, following the Anti-Trust case conclusion, which finally outlawed the film industry's vertical integration and instructed the majors to divest themselves of their theatrical holdings, Columbia decided to discontinue the last of its B series (including crime thriller series like *Boston Blackie* and *Crime Doctor*) and concentrate its efforts on the ambitious B and modest A end of the industry; the same year it was the first of the majors to launch its own television subsidiary, Screen Gems. Much could be said about the determining role of Columbia studios as a structuring "author" of Lewis's films there in the early 1940s; similarly, it is clearly worth considering the contribution of contract cameraman Burnett Guffey, who was cinematographer on *Julia Ross, So Dark the Night,* and *The Undercover Man.* Suffice it to say here, though, that such considerations cannot displace Lewis entirely from the films that carry his credit as director.

Lewis followed *Undercover Man* by leaving Columbia (for unknown reasons) and working for the King Brothers, an independent and slightly suspect production outfit distributing through United Artists. According to Lewis, the King Brothers were extremely generous and non-interfering, and his budget and schedule were consequently increased from their Columbia levels. The King Brothers had apparently made their money installing slot machines and were anxious to legitimate themselves by going Hollywood. Based on MacKinlay Kantor's *Saturday Evening Post* story, *Gun Crazy* cost about $450,000 and took thirty days to shoot, even employing a new portable sound system for the famous two-mile location tracking shot. Contemporary critics and filmmakers apparently besieged Lewis with queries about the mysterious multiple back projection technique the sequence seemed to have demanded: they could not believe that it was actually shot from the back of a car driven down a street on location in a single take. But Lewis had learned to experiment with exceptionally long takes and unconventional location tracking shots much earlier in his career, with, for example, the celebrated ten-minute, single-take courtroom sequence in *The Silent Witness* and the polo pony–mounted cameraman in *The Spy Ring* (1938). United Artists, who had arranged to distribute *Gun Crazy*, offered the King Brothers a sum of money to take the latter's names off the film but they refused. Perhaps as a result of—or in retribution for—this conflict, UA was reluctant to push the film and it was eventually launched twice, once under an alternative title, *Deadly Is the Female*. UA had been named, along with the rest of the majors, in the 1948 Anti-Trust decision and, despite its own lack of theatres, had to adapt to meet the needs of a changing market. An administrative reshuffle in 1950 had led to a new regime and a new distribution strategy: under Krim and Benjamin the new policy involved the active pursuit of quality B's or what were considered bargain basement A's.

From the King Brothers, Lewis went to the other end of the prestige spectrum, MGM, to direct a film entitled *A Lady without Passport*. On this occasion, instead of being expected to create an atmospheric set out of virtually nothing—as at Columbia—Lewis was able to exploit MGM's extensive backlot and existing sets from previous features. The main bordertown set in *A Lady without Passport*, in fact, is a revised version of the Verona Square set on MGM's lot 2, which had been built for *Romeo and Juliet* in 1936. *A Lady without Passport* was one of the first of MGM's quasi-documentary crime cycle of second features, fictionalising the *Crime Does Not Pay* format (a 1935–48 MGM series) but expanding the two-reeler length. (Lewis complains in *Positif* that the presence of Hedy Lamarr in the cast unnecessarily glamourised the project.) In 1948, the year of the Anti-Trust decision, Dore Schary had been appointed as head of MGM's B productions and immediately set about supervising the transformation of the studio's formulaic series, serials, and spin-off properties into fewer, better B's, B's which would simultaneously "express" and "exploit" topical issues like, in this case, the plight of illegal immigrants. Lewis left MGM after *A Lady without Passport* and made a war film for Warner Brothers, *Retreat, Hell!* but returned in 1952 to make *Desperate Search* and *Cry of the Hunted* (1953). It was not until 1955, however, toward the end of the film noir period, that Lewis was to direct his last and most fully blown work in the genre. *The Big Combo* was distributed by Allied Artists, and that company's president at that time, Steve Broidy, has described the "nervous A" (as ambitious B's and modest A's were sometimes known) as an important strategy in Monogram's "premeditated attempt to upgrade our status in the industry," an attempt to achieve "a percentage deal, as opposed to the flat rental"[15] fee for the second features and the new co-features it was providing for exhibition:

> One of the big things that kept us from making as much progress as we deserved to make, at a time when we were making a fairly good run of product, was the fact that the exhibitor, in those days, bought pictures based on the precedent he had paid for product. . . . That's what led to the creation of Allied Artists. It was the same company, same personnel, same everything, but we created a totally different image by calling it Allied Artists.[16]

Thus, in 1953, Monogram changed its name. Only one of Lewis's films was ever distributed by the company, but as an example of the new strategy it is as good as any other—a gangster film for "adults," full of "sock, shock and brutality" (*Hollywood Reporter,* February 10, 1955); "grim, sordid, sexy and candid . . . likely to satisfy most adults . . . but in no sense a film for children" (*Motion Picture Herald,* February 19, 1955). Describing the torture scene, *Variety* was rather less generous, commenting that "The moronic fringe of sadists will enjoy this and all the little kiddies will be sick to their stomachs" (February 16, 1955). *The Big Combo* is undoubtedly the blackest of Lewis's films noirs; the cinematographer was John Alton, and, in *Cahiers du Cinéma,* the reviewer restricted his comments entirely to Alton's contribution. But it is, in fact, a very understated film—Robert Mundy, for instance, has remarked on the subjectively shot and recorded machine-gun sequence and the sexuality of the Jean Wallace character, both of which pushed at the Production Code but, by virtue of their very subtlety, escaped the censor's scissors.[17]

At the time, however (as well as ever since), most critics focused on a comparison between Lewis's *Big Combo* and Lang's 1953 film *The Big Heat,* generally asserting the former's indebtedness and alleged inferiority to the latter. (A similar comparison has haunted almost every article about *Gun Crazy,* which is traditionally measured up against Ray's *They Live by Night,* Lang's *You Only Live Once,* and Penn's *Bonnie and Clyde.*) Essentially, Lewis is accused of plagiarism at the levels of plot, style, and even title, but the accusation is extremely uninformed, first, because the American film industry and the American cinema both depended—as did genre cinema in general and film noir in particular—on repetitions, conventions and familiar formulas. Thus the plot of *The Big Combo* (1955), scripted by Phillip Yordan, was indeed based to some extent at least on the success of *The Big Heat*. And *The Big Heat* (1953) was scripted by Sydney Boehm, was produced by Columbia and starred Glenn Ford. Four years earlier, in 1949, Columbia had produced another film with a very similar plot-line, also scripted by Sydney Boehm and also starring Glenn Ford. The film was called *Undercover Man*, and it was directed by Joseph H. Lewis.

The point of this anecdote is not to prove Lewis somehow more original than Lang, but simply to illustrate how self-perpetuatingly the hierarchies of value within film culture (and all its institutions) function. *Undercover Man* was a B film, for all its ambitions. It was well enough received and did reasonably enough at the box office, but Lewis, unlike Lang, was never a name to put up in lights; he was not a German émigré—veteran of UFA expressionism—but a contract director—veteran of PRC. Most important, he was a B not an A director. Consequently, *Undercover Man* was not sold with the same sort of energy or expectations as accompanied *The Big Heat*. It received less press coverage, fewer prints were struck, its theatrical run was brief. All these factors put severe constraints on the possibilities for retrospectives and re-viewings (and, thus, for rejigging the pantheon). In Britain and America—though this is perhaps less true of France—the criteria employed for the selection and preservation of films in the National Archives and equivalent bodies bore (and still bear) a direct relation to their respective critical and/or commercial success. If a film is considered to be critically prestigious enough it will be acquired and preserved, budgetary constraints permitting; if, on the other hand, the film is a big box-office success and/or a big budget production then it is likely that among the large number of prints produced, one will eventually find its way into the archives, often via donation. But a film like *Undercover Man* and, by extension, not only all of Lewis's work but B films in general fit neither of these categories; they remain forever outside the self-perpetuating system of profitability and prestige which is so scrupulously guarded and guaranteed by the allocation of production finance and facilities, by Academy Awards, and so on. In the event, the print of *Undercover Man* destined for Edinburgh almost fell apart under the strain of projection.

Which brings me to the role of the cultural, academic, and critical institutions in the history of attempted "authorisations" of Lewis. Tim Pulleine, in the *Monthly Film Bulletin*,[18] has usefully traced some of the

English language perspectives on Lewis, and while what follows is certainly no more comprehensive than Pulleine's account, it does cover a longer period and a wider area. Paul Willemen, in his Edinburgh article on Lewis,[19] relates the apparent retrospective interest in Lewis to what he describes as "the phenomenon of cinephilia," which he associates with the "residues of surrealism in post-war French culture."[20] Richard Thompson, in his piece in *Cinema*, sees *Gun Crazy* as a precursor of the nouvelle vague, and elsewhere the film has been estimated as an influence on Godard in general and *A Bout de Souffle* in particular.[21] Avoiding such problematic but provocative notions, however, Willemen is undoubtedly right to point to the French and specifically the surrealists as being (among) the first serious critics to acknowledge Lewis. Ado Kyrou's *Le Surréalisme au Cinéma* (1953) describes *Gun Crazy* as "an admirable film, which alone of all cinema clearly marks the road which leads from l'amour fou to la revolte folle."[22] Two years later, the publication of Borde and Chaumeton's *Panorama du Film Noir Américain* (1955), the first book-length study of the genre, also saluted that film as deserving "a place by itself" as "a nearly unclassifiable work . . . a kind of Golden Age of American film noir."[23]

In the United States it seems that Andrew Sarris was one of the first to take Lewis seriously (perhaps through the critic's connections with the American *Cahiers*); in his book *American Cinema*, Sarris slots Lewis into a section entitled "expressive esoterica" alongside the likes of Budd Boetticher, Phil Karlson, Don Siegel, Robert Siodmak, Jacques Tourneur, and Edward G. Ulmer. Sarris saluted Lewis's "somber personality . . . revealed consistently through a complex visual style," but today Lewis remains one of the only directors so relegated to have resisted promotion.[24] In 1962 Sarris had issued a challenge in the pages of *Film Culture*, warning Lewis's admirers that "in this direction lies madness"[25]—a warning that the writer was to withdraw the following year, but which has somehow stayed alive through the terms of appraisal Lewis's critics have employed ever since, from Sarris's "expressive esoterica" to Willemen's "cinephilia." In 1971, the American magazine *Cinema* (then edited by Paul Schrader) devoted eleven pages to Lewis, comprising three articles, an interview,[26] and a filmography. If Lewis proved less than forthcoming about his "personality" there is some material about the production of a number of his films. More interesting, however, are the articles on Lewis by Schrader himself, by Thompson, and by Robert Mundy. Schrader regards *Gun Crazy* as quite simply "one of the best American films ever made"[27] but is unable to offer any explanation for the alleged excellence of the film, in the light of what he clearly considers the relative mediocrity of most of the rest of Lewis's work; indeed, he found his enthusiasm for the quality of the director decreasing in direct proportion to the quantity of his films viewed. Predictably, Schrader compares *The Big Combo* negatively to Lang's *The Big Heat* and adds that Lewis's only other strong film, *Undercover Man*, pales beside Mann's *T Men*. Mundy is more generous, though his conclusion that "Lewis's work presents a problem of classification. . . . To look at his work in genres is of little . . . use"[28] is ultimately unhelpful. Richard Thompson's rather longer consideration is less cautious, arguing that, the early work apart,

> Lewis found his metier, if not his personal vision, in the new popularity of the film noir. From *Julia Ross* on, all his successful films were either outright films noirs (*Gun Crazy, Undercover Man, Big Combo, A Lady without Passport*) or contained *maudit* elements (*Desperate Search, So Dark the Night, Cry of the Hunted, A Lawless Street, Halliday Brand, Terror in a Texas Town*). Upon these films—of varying quality, but none without interest—Lewis's reputation rests. Though it seems difficult to claim for Lewis a consistently black vision, his visual style contained several elements conducive to the genre: a taste for Bazinian depth of focus and for its temporal twin the long take; for camera movement (relativity) rather than alternating static cuts (isolated specificity); for cinematographers with dramatic, concrete styles, often harshly black and white; for naturalistic location shooting or, failing that, for modestly scaled back-lot work stressing character/environment interfaces rather than explicit spectacle.[29]

Lewis didn't rate an entry in the 1972 *International Encyclopaedia of Film*, but in 1974 Tom Flinn's article "The Big Heat and The Big Combo" appeared in *Velvet Light Trap's* special issue on the 1950s and was entirely devoted to a textual and "political" comparison between the two oft-compared films.[30] The same year, the first lengthy appreciation of Lewis, retaining Sarris's "insanity clause," appeared "Joseph H. Lewis: Tourist in the Asylum."[31] In 1975 a second interview with Lewis, this time by another American critic, Gerald Peary, appeared in the French magazine *Positif*;[32] as if to outdo *Cinema*, *Positif* provided seventeen pages for several critics to consider Lewis, but once again, the interview elicited little more than the few already familiar anecdotes and some additional production details, while the articles reprised the assertions about Lewis's alleged affinity for film noir.

In 1980 Lewis's status for "cinephiliacs" rose further still. The BFI's *Monthly Film Bulletin* ran retrospective reviews of *The Falcon in San Francisco*, *Gun Crazy*, *A Lady without Passport*, *That Gang of Mine*, *Undercover Man*, *The Big Combo*, *The Halliday Brand*, *Retreat, Hell!* and *Terror in a Texas Town* and devoted its back cover to Tim Pulleine's essay on the director.[33] These efforts composed part of the preparations for the Edinburgh Film Festival Retrospective for which the first draft of this article was written and to which Paul Willemen, Paul Taylor, and Richard Combs also contributed.[34] Unlike previous retrospectives at Edinburgh, however, there was no tie-in publication from either the Festival itself, the BFI, or *Screen*. Nor was the retrospective taken up later in London at the National Film Theatre—though a small season was mounted at a repertory cinema, Riverside Studios, some weeks before the festival.[35] More important in the British promotion of Lewis in the early eighties were the reviews run in the London listings magazine *Time Out*. The magazine then exercised a virtual monopoly on the audiences of the more adventurous repertory/independent exhibitors in the capital and the reviews duly alerted large (new?) audiences to the films. The two films that received caption reviews were, perhaps predictably, *Gun Crazy* and *The Big Combo*, though, rather less conventionally, it was *The Big Combo* which first attracted exhibitor and consequently reviewer attention in this case. It's worth printing the two reviews in full:

> Everything you always loved about American "film noir" in one sensational movie: Joseph Lewis' *The Big Combo* (Electric, from Sunday). Police lieutenant Cornel Wilde searches neurotically for evidence to pin on mobster Richard Conte—because he nurses a pathetic crush on his victim's moll Jean Wallace. Along the way, through the night and fog, he clutches at fragmentary clues (a name, a photo), goes to bed with a stripper and lovingly helps her on with her shoes, and suffers torture—by hearing aid. Sent to get him are two thugs (Lee Van Cleef and Earl Holliman), who share not only guns but also beds; their relationship provides the movie with its most tender moment. The pace is brutal, the tone is harsh, the dialogue is cruel. Almost certainly the greatest movie ever made, as heady as amyl nitrate and as compulsive as stamping on insects. (Tony Rayns)[36]
>
> From its opening moments, it's clear that *Gun Crazy* (Independents: Electric) is a B-picture classic. Directed by Joseph H. Lewis—whose later noir thriller, *The Big Combo* was also recently rediscovered by the Electric—it features an amiable but gun-crazy hero who abandons

Hometown USA to elope with the (lady) sharpshooter from a travelling circus. Deep in mutual obsession, they run out of money, patience, and time; then take to armed robbery and the road that leads (inevitably) to death. Flatly passionate, never vampish, Peggy Cummins turns in a staggering performance which threatens, singlehanded, to overthrow the cultural and sexual certainties of middle American life. Even, at the very end, this last romantic couple refuse to pay the price of their rebellion: hunted down in a misty, echoing swamp, their tormented faces express only pain and fear, never a trace of guilt or regret. Compulsive genre cinema, wearing its low budget and Freudian motifs with almost equal disdain; it simply knocks spots off senile imitations like *Bonnie and Clyde.* (Chris Auty)[37]

Also in 1980 the American Telluride Film Festival mounted an impressive film noir retrospective, which featured the attendance of Lewis himself, who was interviewed at length by Paul Schrader.

Paul Willemen's paper for Edinburgh is the latest piece on Lewis I have been able to trace—though I should repeat that my aim here is not an exhaustive bibliography but rather a schematic scrutiny of that bibliography as part of the case study of attempted "authorisations." And Willemen's article neatly opens up (and yet rather peremptorily also simultaneously closes off) that debate, noting that

> Many avowed auteurists in France, the US and Britain have attempted to claim him as an author. All have failed. Not because it would be impossible to construct a thematic coherence covering a substantial proportion of his work, but because the films appear to resist such efforts, locating their pleasure elsewhere, on a more disturbing though fascinating level.[38]

But is it indeed possible to construct such a coherence? Mundy proposes some potential significance in the recurrence of swamp scenes, the predilection for long takes, tracking shots and depth of focus, and a thematic concern for memory and its loss.[39] Thompson underlines Lewis's liaison with film noir and further notes that "Lewis seems instinctively to cast his films in the form of hunter-hunted chases" but concludes that "no consistent style of mise-en-scene is apparent, no Lewis look or Lewis POV or Lewis conceptual slant that can be spotted from film to film."[40] Myron Meisel reiterates the hunter-hunted motif and adds another recurrent item of Lewisiana in "the inseparability of individual identity from social action." He notes an irreconcilable collision between "the noir determinism of his style" and "his brief for family ties as the root of moral responsibility." Meisel goes on to unpack this assertion a little, describing how Lewis's apparent penchant for "characters (who) express themselves exclusively through their actions" makes for what he calls "good visceral cinema."[41] The former emphasis, on family ties, is repeated by Pulleine; the latter is reprised in Tom Milne's remarks on Godard's debts to Lewis.[42]

More generally, however, all the critics surveyed seem to agree: that Lewis's films are often stronger in parts than as wholes, as in Lewis's oeuvre itself; that the B film noir provides a useful way into understanding Lewis, if only so as to distinguish his films that fall outside its parameters; that his stylistic signature, however difficult to determine, did preempt some of the attributed innovations of the nouvelle vague and yet at the same time functioned as a symptom of and a valediction for a certain sort of American cinema. Finally, there seems to be a critical consensus that Lewis was unwilling and/or unable to impose his personality on his films, but that

> Picking through Lewis' diverse filmography, it is quite easy to find evidence of a director with a strong personality—and just as much evidence of one who never really found a subject. Lewis might almost embody the kind of caricatured figure that an auteurist critic would hold up as the epitome of the cult of the director: stylistic authority operating in a vacuum.[43]

Lewis clearly poses a problem for auteurism—as for genre criticism—acknowledged by almost all who have written seriously about his work (with the possible exception of Paul Willemen). But such problems do little to deter the desperate search of anachronistic auteurists, the cry of the hunters. Trying to identify a coherent, consistent "thematic core" in the Lewis oeuvre, of course, begs the too rarely raised question of just what constitutes such an oeuvre, such a core. This article has attempted to argue that neither are static but rather that both are conjunctural and are continuously being reconstructed. Nevertheless, it's interesting to note that the film which "made Lewis's name" in the industry at least, *My Name Is Julia Ross,* should have made the memorisation of a name, an identity, so central to its plot and, indeed, its title. Apparently Lewis chose this project for himself—in fact it seems to have been the first occasion on which he was able to select a script rather than simply being himself selected to direct one. And Lewis himself changed the title from the script's *Woman in Red. So Dark the Night* retains the identity/memory thematic (and was also a project selected by Lewis himself). While it may be dubious at best to make much more of this than ironic coincidence, it is worth adding that several of Lewis's films carry this idea, from the undercover identities of the detectives in *A Lady without Passport* and *Undercover Man* to the uncovered identities of the mysterious Alicia in *The Big Combo* and the fleeing Bart named by the press in *Gun Crazy*. More intriguingly, perhaps, two more films express the urgency of names and naming in their very titles, *A Lady without Passport* and *The Halliday Brand.*

It's tempting to reject Willemen's remark about Lewis's films— "the scripts are unchallenging, the acting stereotyped and haphazard, the ideologies unfailingly reactionary"—as no more than impassioned polemic against auteurist excesses. But the films are worth defending against such charges not because of any disservice such remarks may do to Lewis or his films but because of their disservice to film history and film studies. Certainly several of the scripts as well as the actors Lewis worked with were imperfect; equally certainly, however, the scripts for *My Name Is Julia Ross, A Lady without Passport, The Undercover Man, Gun Crazy, The Big Combo,* and *The Halliday Brand* were actually excellent, as were many of the performances in Lewis's films and, as a number of critics have suggested, it was Lewis who failed to match them. . . . Of all Lewis's work in the period, only *Retreat, Hell!* seems to have had an indisputably propagandist project; and in Hollywood, as elsewhere, it is essential to be wary of intentions. Labelling the entire Lewis oeuvre as reactionary seems at best impulsive and at worst critically reactionary itself—. . . . away from the kind of acknowledgement of the films' historical context, their institutional place that this article has been urging as a necessary precondition of any analysis—let alone evaluation—of cinema, from levels of writing or acting to ideology.

For Willemen, however, the present status and historical locus of Lewis's work are simply to be regretted:

> When cinephilia disappears, Lewis' films will cease to have any function, their specificity will vanish along with the spectator's inability to acknowledge a desire for cinema, the asocial, politically irresponsible joy of looking.[44]

It is hard to take this kind of combination of cultural pessimism and radical puritanism seriously as polemic, let alone as prophecy. But if Lewis's films have had a "political" role in the last three decades, then that has been their function as hiccups, indigestible exceptions to theories about the general applicability of certain propositions about Holly-wood as industry and as cinema, about genre, about the classic realist text, about authorship itself, about the impossibility of attributing essen-tial "ideologies" to texts outside of their institutional site and historical moment, about specifically the history of Hollywood's modes of produc-tion and their relation to modes of representation/signification. That mode of production actively prohibited and delimited the possibilities of individual authorship. But the moment and specific site of such produc-tions as Lewis's between 1945 and 1960 also importantly coincide with another political determinant on Hollywood, that of the HUAC [House Un-American Activities Committee] hearings and the consequent black-list. The blacklist made all too literal the cliché about the authorless anonymity of the average Hollywood film. After the first HUAC hearing (in 1947) and particularly after the first trials (in 1951) a number of film-makers were forced to work anonymously either for the B's or for the new independents. Victor Navasky's *Naming Names*, a study of the blacklist era, comments:

> Independent filmmakers . . . were by definition antagonistic to studio values. Some were independents because they were incapable of func-tioning other than on the margin (and on the cheap). And it seems fitting that one of these, the King brothers, should have made it a regular practice to employ blacklisted personnel under pseudonyms—not as a protest against repression but as a calculated risk, a shrewd economy, getting top talent for minimal money. It was the King brothers who hired Dalton Trumbo.[45]

Trumbo's first script for the Kings was apparently *Gun Crazy*. Lewis admits that the MacKinlay Kantor script was far too long; he does not, however, admit that the crediting of Millard Kaufman as co-screenwriter was simply a "front" for the "unemployable" blacklisted Trumbo.[46] Lewis had collaborated with people on the liberal left at Columbia in the late forties. In 1958 he was to be associated even more strongly with blacklistees. The script for his last film, *Terror in a Texas Town*, is attributed on the films credits to Ben L. Perry. Lewis notes in his interview with Bogdanovich that Ned Young, a blacklisted writer who also appears in the film, contributed to the script uncredited. So, accord-ing to Navasky, did another eminent blacklistee, John Howard Lawson.[47] In this light, the film's gunfight between (HUAC friendly witness) Sterling Hayden and (the blacklisted) Young takes on new charges.

To paraphrase Buscombe's formulation about Walsh and Warners, it has been the ambition of this piece to call into question the predictable—if problematic—promotion of Lewis to the auteur pantheon, to recognise that working in an industrially defined sub-genre with as distinctive a strategy and style as the B film noir imposed a number of constraints on "creativity," and to insist that such constraints should not be seen as merely negative in their operation. Working in the area of the B film noir meant simply that the opportunities for commercial and critical success lay in certain (industrial, generic) directions rather than in others. Sheila Johnston, in an article on the production context of the New German Cinema, has argued

> Not just that some highly individualistic West German films in the sixties and seventies seem to invite an auteurist reading, but that the conditions for an Autor cinema were deliberately cultivated (in conjunction with certain industrial, political and cultural developments) rather than accidentally propitious.[48]

Were Johnston's observations about German art cinema extended to Hollywood, they would go some way to meeting Caughie's suggested relation of "the author . . . to institutional and commercial contexts."[49] Indeed, I would like to suggest, by way of a conclusion, that the late forties and early fifties in Hollywood, particularly in the competitive realm of the ambitious B/nervous A picture, provided similarly decisive developments, developments which at least partially encouraged the authorial hallmarking and, indeed, the directorial "expressiveness" of people like Lewis. Countless critics have remarked on the richness of film noir and the number of familiar and unfamiliar film-makers who excelled themselves in the genre. Perhaps that genre, though never named as such at the time, was an accidentally propitious arena in which the process of "authorisation" could be played out and institutionally inscribed. In the 1970s and 1980s, on the other hand, film noir in general and the B film noir in particular have indeed been deliberately recultivated around a number of names— names like Karlson, Fuller, Siodmak, Mann, Tourneur, and Ulmer. Among them that of Joseph H. Lewis has functioned to literally re-authorise and consequently categorise a number of B films noirs in this period just as, in the 1940s and 1950s, that subgenre itself could be said to have helped to authorise Lewis.

NOTES

1. John Caughie, ed., *Theories of Authorship* (London: British Film Institute and Routledge & Kegan Paul, 1981). See also Stephen Jenkins, ed. *Fritz Lang: The Image and the Look* (London: British Film Institute, 1981). Jenkins conceives of Lang neither biographically nor structurally, since the former assumes a romantic artist behind every aspect of "his" work, while the latter "implies that such a structure exists as something to be grasped." Instead, Jenkins addresses Lang as a "space where a multiplicity of discourses intersect, an unstable, shifting configuration of discourses produced by the interaction of a specific group of films (Lang's filmography) with particular, historically and socially locatable ways of reading/viewing those films," p. 7.

2. See, however, Steve Neale's article "Authors and Genres" in *Screen* 23:2, 84–89.

3. Caughie, *Theories of Authorship,* p. 14.

4. Ibid., p. 2.

5. Paul Kerr, "Out of What Past? Notes on the B Film Noir," *Screen Education* 32/33 (Autumn/Winter 1979/80), 45–65.

6. A number of such textual analyses are referred to in the footnotes to this article. See below.

7. See Janet Staiger's overview of the shift to independent production in this issue of *Screen* 24:4–5 (July/October 1983), 68–79.

8. Edward Buscombe, "Walsh and Warner Brothers." In Phil Hardy, ed. *Raoul Walsh,* Edinburgh Film Festival, 1974. See also Steve Jenkins's article "Edgar G. Ulmer and PRC: A Detour down Poverty Row," in *Monthly Film Bulletin* (July 1982), 49:582 152.

9. Buscombe, "Walsh and Warner Brothers," p. 60. That such "constraints" and "directions" could be much more than simply stylistic is central to Buscombe's argument. While Lewis's career at Columbia is too brief to benefit from the kind of studio/director study devoted to Walsh and Warners, it is worth noting that elsewhere Buscombe has published an article on Columbia itself, "Notes on Columbia Pictures Corporation 1926–41," *Screen* 16:3 (Autumn 1975), 65–82. In this article Buscombe addressed the question of Columbia's studio style and political affiliations, asking whether or not that company's relative independence from Wall Street finance freed its film-makers politically. Buscombe's conclusion is negative, but he does point out that precisely half of the Hollywood Ten were employed at Columbia in the 1930s. Among the radicals/blacklistees that Lewis worked with at the studio were Larry Parks (who starred in *The Jolson Story* and *The Swordsman*), Sydney Buchman (who was an uncredited contributor to the script of *The Jolson Story*), Robert Rossen (who produced *Undercover Man*), and Nedrick Young (who appeared in *The Swordsman* and who worked with Lewis on and off throughout his career after they both left Columbia).

10. Kerr, "Out of What Past?" p. 45.

11. These and other figures in this article derive from Peter Bogdanovich's interview with Lewis in *Cinema* (Fall 1971), 7:1 and from Gerald Peary's interview in *Positif* 171–172 (July/August 1975). They have not been verified against the extensive Lewis material held by the Chicago Institute of Art.

12. Quoted in Doug McClelland, *The Golden Age of B Movies,* (Nashville: Bonanza Books, 1978), p. 146.

13. Lewis interviewed by Bogdanovich, *Cinema* 7:1, 48.

14. Quoted in McClelland, *The Golden Age of B Movies,* p. 186.

15. Interview with Broidy in Charles Flynn and Todd McCarthy, eds., *Kings of the Bs* (New York: E. P. Dutton, 1975), p. 271.

16. Ibid., p. 272.

17. See Robert Mundy's untitled article in *Cinema* 7:1 (Fall 1971).

18. Tim Pulleine, "Undercover Director or: The Name is Joseph H. Lewis" in *Monthly Film Bulletin* 47:554 (March 1980), 60.

19. Paul Willemen's paper is reprinted, with a new afterword, under the heading "Edinburgh–Debate," *Framework* 19, 48–50.

20. Ibid., p. 49.

21. Richard Thompson's untitled article on Lewis appeared in *Cinema* 7:1 (Fall 1971), with articles by Schrader and Mundy and an interview by Peter Bogdanovich (*Cinema* 7:1). Tom Milne has also referred to an alleged influence on Godard in his review of *Gun Crazy* in *Monthly Film Bulletin* 47:554 (March 1980), 57.

22. Quoted by *Cinema* 7:1, Thompson, 46.

23. Ibid.

24. Andrew Sarris, *The American Cinema* (New York: E. P. Dutton, 1968), pp. 132–33.

25. Andrew Sarris, "The High Forties Revisited," *Film Culture* 24 (Spring 1962), 66.

26. The interview makes a useful comparison with Bogdanovich's previously published "interview books," *Fritz Lang in America,* Movie Paperbacks, Studio Vista, 1967, and *John Ford,* Movie Paperbacks, Studio Vista, 1968.

27. Schrader in *Cinema* 7:1, 43.

28. Mundy in *Cinema* 7:1, 45.

29. Thompson in *Cinema* 7:1, 46.

30. "The Big Heat and The Big Combo–Rogue Cops & Mink-Coated Girls" in *The Velvet Light Trap* 11, 23–28.

31. Myron Meisel, "Joseph H. Lewis: Tourist in the Asylum." In Flynn and McCarthy, eds., *Kings of the Bs.*

32. *Positif*, pp. 39–55.

33. Pulleine, "Undercover Director."

34. Paul Willemen's and Richard Combs's contributions were printed in the 1980 *Edinburgh Film Festival* brochure. Paul Taylor has written on Lewis in *Time Out*, May 2–8, 1980, p. 51 and p. 53.

35. Taylor, *Time Out.*

36. *Time Out*, March 2–8, 1979, p. 43.

37. *Time Out*, September 21–27, 1979, p. 49.

38. Willemen in *Framework*, p. 49.

39. *Cinema* 7:1.

40. Ibid.

41. Meisel, "Joseph H. Lewis."

42. Milne, *Monthly Film Bulletin* 47.

43. Richard Combs's review of *Undercover Man* appeared in *Monthly Film Bulletin* 47:554, 58.

44. Willemen, *Framework*, p. 50.

45. Victor S. Navasky, *Naming Names,* (New York: Penguin, 1981), p. 155.

46. Michael Sragow, "Ghostwriting—Unraveling the Enigma of Movie Authorship," *Film Comment* 19:2 (March/April 1983), 9.

47. Navasky, *Naming Names*, p. 345.

48. Sheila Johnston, "The Author as Public Institution," *Screen Education* 32/33 (Autumn/Winter 1979/80), 68.

49. Caughie, *Theories of Authorship*, p. 2.

Thomas Schatz

"A Triumph of Bitchery": Warner Bros., Bette Davis, and *Jezebel*

The classical Hollywood cinema, by its very nature as a commercial art form, was rife with conflict and contradiction, and the production system it developed in the 1920s and 1930s contained but scarcely subdued its essential discord. It's worth suggesting in fact that the Hollywood studio system, with its factory-based mode of production and division of labor and its distinctive relations of power, not only permitted but virtually demanded a degree of struggle and negotiation in the filmmaking process.[1] Ultimate authority belonged to the owners and management executives, of course, whose primary goal was to make movies as efficiently and economically as possible. But the impulse to standardize and regulate operations was countered by various factors, especially the need for innovation and differentiation of product, the talents and personalities of key creative personnel, the growing power of labor unions and "guilds," and the intervention of federal and state government via the courts. All of these ensured that the Hollywood studio would be not only a center of production but a site of struggle as well.

Perhaps the most complex and paradoxical figure in this struggle was the movie star, whose enormous power on the screen and at the box office did not extend into the production arena. The founding of United Artists in 1919 was in one sense a declaration of independence by three

From *Wide Angle* 10:1 (1988), 16–29. Reprinted with permission of the author and Johns Hopkins University Press.

of the industry's biggest stars—Charlie Chaplin, Mary Pickford, and Douglas Fairbanks—who refused to submit to the burgeoning "studio system." But with vertical integration and centralized production, the "star system" became simply another factor in the overall equation of commercial filmmaking—an equation that was calculated by the studios and that relegated the star, whatever his or her "marquee value" and visibility, to subordinate status.

The movie star was still the industry's principal resource, particularly since each studio keyed its distinctive "house style" to specific stars and genres. This further restricted an actor's power and autonomy, however, since stardom for studio contract players so often involved heavy typecasting in formula stories. The more effectively a studio packaged and commodified its stars, the more restrictive the studio's and the public's shared perception of that star's screen persona tended to be. There were exceptions, especially among those stars who eventually became free agents and gained some control over story selection, script development, and principal cast and crew assignments. Contract stars rarely had such leverage, although in some cases a studio's casting and marketing strategies did ease the constraints. MGM, for instance, had the resources and the personnel ("all the stars in the heavens") to "off-cast" its top players and to co-star them in different combinations.

The antithesis to MGM during the studio era was Warner Bros., whose penchant for typecasting and formula filmmaking was unequaled among Hollywood's leading companies. Warner's stock in trade in the 1930s were its gangster and urban crime films with James Cagney and Edward G. Robinson, its crusading bio-pics with Paul Muni, its backstage musicals with Dick Powell, and its epic swashbucklers with Errol Flynn. Bette Davis was the only female contract player to reach stardom at Warners during the Depression, but it didn't come easily. The studio's commitment to "woman's pictures" was marginal at the time, and Kay Francis rather than Davis won most of those roles. Davis usually was relegated to co-star status in male-oriented crime films or occasionally played the lead in an urban melodrama, usually cast as a distaff version of Warner's male stars. She was perceived, as one sales executive put it, as "a female Jimmy Cagney."[2]

Davis overcame that perception and carved out a niche for herself at Warners in the late 1930s, battling the entrenched Warners system to create a star persona that was as powerful and provocative—and as distinctively feminine—as any in the movie industry. That persona finally coalesced with the 1938 release of *Jezebel*, and the trajectory of

Davis's career to that point—from contract player to studio star—is revealing not only of Warner's operations and the evolution of its house style during the 1930s but also of the contract player's role in the studio production process.

———————

Warners signed Davis in December 1931, when its studio operations and market strategy were being completely overhauled.[3] A decade of tremendous growth and risk during the 1920s had lifted Warner Bros. from second-class status to the ranks of a full-fledged integrated major, on a par with Paramount, MGM, Fox, and RKO. But the stock market crash and Depression, coming after heavy investments for sound conversion and theater acquisition, forced company president (and elder sibling) Harry Warner into a more conservative, cost-efficient strategy. Low-budget production was stepped up, budgets for A-class features were cut, and "prestige pictures" for the more lucrative and competitive first-run market were eliminated altogether.[4]

Studio boss Jack Warner and his production chief, Darryl Zanuck, cultivated a new crop of stars and genres to accommodate Harry's market strategy. Warner's emergent style shunned the high-gloss, well-lit worlds so often displayed by MGM and Paramount, as well as the cozy Americana of so many Fox features. Warners opted instead for a bleaker—and a more cost-efficient—worldview, even in its musicals. Its Depression-era pictures were fast-paced, fast-talking, socially sensitive (if not downright exploitive) treatments of contemporary life. Stories were "torn from the day's headlines" and centered on working-class stiffs and lowlifes, on society's losers and victims rather than heroic or well-heeled types. And perhaps most distinctive were a lack of native optimism in Warners pictures and a cynical distain for romantic love as either a motivating plot device or a means of narrative resolution.

Warners still had a few established high-priced stars like William Powell, Kay Francis, and Joe E. Brown on its roster, but the emerging male stars like Cagney, Robinson, and Dick Powell were better suited to Warner's more economical and genre-based approach to production. These stars were willing—at least in the early stages of their careers—to work more often and for lower salaries, and also to let the studio shape their screen roles. As Warner's new stars and genres caught on with the public, though there were inevitable struggles with its new contract players, many of whom entered contract negotiations with the same combative demeanor that they displayed on-screen. The earliest battles were with Robinson and Cagney. Robinson's breakthrough came with *Little Caesar*, released in January 1931, and Cagney's came some three months later with the release of *The Public Enemy*. The enormous success of both pictures secured the gangster film as the veritable foundation genre in Warner's Depression-era output, launching Robinson and Cagney to stardom and initiating heavy contract negotiations with both players. Because Robinson had done *Little Caesar* without signing a long-term contract, its runaway hit status gave him considerable leverage. In February 1931 he signed a two-year, six-picture deal at $40,000 per picture, although the studio balked at giving him any control of story, script, or casting.[5]

Cagney was already under a long-term contract paying him $400 per week when he did *The Public Enemy*, and he spent much of 1931 and 1932 lobbying for a new pact. Jack Warner, who handled contract negotiations and most of the important casting decisions, refused to renegotiate and put Cagney on indefinite suspension in 1932 when he refused to perform.[6] Intervention by the Motion Picture Academy resolved the dispute, and Cagney's weekly salary was raised in late 1932 to $3000 for forty weeks per year.[7] But Cagney soon realized, as had Robinson, that stardom brought a higher salary but a more narrowly defined screen persona. As their commodity value increased, the studio grew more obstinate in refusing their demands for different roles or even minimal input into decisions regarding story selection and script development. Typical of the studio's handling of such requests was a letter from Zanuck to Robinson in late 1932. "We will accept anybody's ideas or suggestions," reasoned Zanuck, "but the treatment of the subject in script form should be left largely to the judgement and intelligence of our 'system.'"[8]

Bette Davis was having an even tougher time dealing with the "judgment and intelligence" of Warner's system, since the studio put so little stock in its new crop of women players. An ill-advised talent raid on Paramount early in 1931, just before the gangster sagas hit, brought both Kay Francis and Ruth Chatterton to Warner's changing style and market strategy. Francis earned $3000 per week in 1931–32, and Chatterton a staggering $8000 per week while doing only three pictures per year.[9] Warners also had several promising ingenues under contract at the time, including Davis, Ruby Keeler, Joan Blondell, and Ginger Rogers. Davis dominated this group in terms of salary and status, but she lagged far behind her male colleagues. After signing in 1931 for $400 per week, Davis did nine pictures over the next thirteen months, none of any real note. Her option was renewed in December 1932 for $550 weekly, and again a year later for $750.[10]

By then Davis was complaining frequently to Jack Warner about both her workload and the poor quality of her roles, and in February 1934 Warner decided to placate her—and to get her off his back—by loaning her to RKO to play the ill-tempered cockney prostitute in an adaptation of Somerset Maugham's *Of Human Bondage*. It was in that RKO picture, ironically, that Davis first displayed her distinctive personality, playing an emasculating and singularly unattractive shrew whose emotional intensity and sense of self-preservation were oddly engaging for Depression-era audiences. That role did little to change the studio's perception of her abilities and her screen type, however. When Davis reported back to Warners, she was cast as a home-wrecking secretary in *Housewife* (1934) and then as Della Street in a low-budget Perry Mason thriller, *The Case of the Howling Dog* (1934). Davis refused to report for the latter project, and on June 14 the studio informed Davis that her "contract shall be considered suspended . . . for a period equivalent to the period during which such failure, refusal and neglect [to report] on your part shall continue."[11] That same day studio attorney Roy Obringer informed another of Warner's lawyers of the suspension. "As you know," he wrote, "Bette Davis has been giving us considerable trouble and appears to have the idea that she has approval of stories."[12]

All this occurred just before RKO released *Of Human Bondage*, and when that Leslie Howard–Bette Davis picture hit, Davis's fortunes took a predictable change. Movie columnist Alma Whitaker described the reversal in the Sunday edition of the *Los Angeles Times* on 22 July 1934: "When she walked out on Warner Brothers [sic] a month ago, in protest against what she calls 'dumb moll' roles, and specifically a 12-line 'dumb secretary' part, the verdict on *Of Human Bondage* was still in the lap of the gods." But when the RKO picture was released, said Whitaker, "the New York critics hailed Bette in such superlative terms" that she was "welcomed back into the [Warners] fold with embarrassing effusion."[13] Jack Warner took Davis off suspension and promised her better roles, and he came through in early August when he cast her as the adulterous, seductive Marie in *Bordertown*, a crime thriller starring Paul Muni.

Muni had more control over his career than any of Warner's new crop stars in the early 1930s. He was an established stage star when he made his movie debut in 1932, cast by independent producer Howard Hughes to star in *Scarface,* and the success of that gangster saga encouraged Jack Warner to sign Muni to a one-picture deal for *I Am a Fugitive from a Chain Gang* (1932). When that picture hit, Warner offered Muni a two-year, eight-picture deal paying him $50,000 per picture and allowing him concessions that were given to no other star on the lot. Those included approval of story, role, and script; billing as sole star both on-screen and in all advertising; loanouts only on consent, with story and role approval, and at a 50-50 split with Warners on any salary overage; definition of a "year" as twenty-one weeks, with Muni allowed "to render his services as he sees fit upon the legitimate stage" between film projects.[14]

Muni himself initiated *Bordertown* in March 1934, when he sent a copy of the recently published novel to Hal Wallis. The story was a variation on the classic gangster saga, centering on a Mexican lawyer who falls victim to his own ambitions and the wiles of an Anglo-American seductress. He abandons his people and his ideals, emulating the American success ethic and steadily degenerating into a murderous criminal. Muni wanted Carole Lombard to co-star, but once he saw *Of Human Bondage* he agreed with Jack Warner that Bette Davis would be ideal as the seductive Marie. Director Archie Mayo took *Bordertown* into production on 17 August 1934, scheduled for six weeks on a budget of $343,000.[15] It was vintage Warners: a contemporary crime saga with a veneer of social realism, long on action but short on plot development, relying mainly on the intensity of its stars and on its frantic pace to carry the narrative. And although it was very much a Paul Muni vehicle, Davis made the most of her role, especially in her descent into madness during the latter stages of the film.

Bordertown was released in January 1935, and it bolstered the image Davis had established in *Of Human Bondage* of an intense, ruthless, sexually aggressive woman who relied on her will and wits to get what she wanted. But Jack Warner and production chief Hal Wallis, who succeeded Zanuck after his departure in 1933, failed to exploit her distinctive persona, casting Davis in a second-rate woman's picture and then two routine crime thrillers after *Bordertown*. Not until late 1935 was she given anything to work with, cast as an alcoholic, self-destructive actress in *Dangerous* (1935) and an idealistic, love-struck waitress in *The Petrified Forest* (1936). *Dangerous* was released in December while Davis was doing *The Petrified Forest*, and though it brought her an Oscar nomination it scarcely improved her lot at the studio. Next Warner cast her as the femme fatale in *Satan Met a Lady* (1936), a cut-rate version of Dashiell Hammett's *The Maltese Falcon*. Davis found both the part and the picture unacceptable and she refused to report. A suspension changed her mind and she did the picture—her sixth that year and the twenty-third for Warners in four years.[16] Her next assignment, *Golden Arrow* (1936), was a role so weak that Kay Francis had taken a suspension to avoid it, and once production closed in February 1936 Davis resolved not to start another picture without a new contract and the assurance of better roles.

That was not altogether unreasonable in early 1936. The worst of the Depression was over and Warners actually turned a profit in 1935 after four straight years of heavy losses. That same year Harry Warner decided the company was ready to start competing with the other majors in the first-run market. Along with its usual slate of crime thrillers and melodramas, Warners sent a few prestige projects into production in 1935—pictures such as *Anthony Adverse, A Midsummer Night's Dream, Captain Blood,* and *The Story of Louis Pasteur.* Davis figured she warranted as much, particularly after she won an Academy Award for best actress in *Dangerous.* Jack Warner still balked at giving her a prestige vehicle, but some two weeks after production closed on *Golden Arrow,* and within days of the Academy Awards ceremony, Davis was offered the lead in RKO's *Mary of Scotland* (1936). Set to direct was John Ford, who had just won best director and best picture Oscars for RKO's *The Informer* (1935). Davis desperately wanted the role, but when Warner was informed via memo of RKO's request to borrow Davis, he returned the memo with "Not interested" scrawled across the bottom.[17]

That was the last straw so far as Davis was concerned, and she resolved to stay out of pictures altogether until her status at the studio changed. She took a six-week "layoff"—a leave without pay, though not a suspension, since the time off was not added to her contract—and traveled to New York for the Democratic convention. It was Davis's first trip East in several years, and after the recent Oscar she was big news. Always adept at manipulating the press, she took the opportunity to blast Hollywood's power brokers. The *Evening Journal* ran a story, "Film Bosses 'Headache' to Bette Davis," in which she not only criticized the Warners but stated flatly that she would not return to the studio for retakes on *Golden Arrow.*[18] That same date (25 March 1936) the *World Telegram* ran a banner heading: "'They'd Make All the Women Wed the Men,' Cries Bette Davis," in which she took on the Production Code as well as the studio.[19]

While Davis was in New York, her agent forwarded a demand to Warners for a new contract with the following terms: five years, with salaries escalating from $100,000 to $200,000 per year (she was then earning $64,000 per year); a maximum of four pictures annually; star or co-star billing with her name above the title and in equal-size type as her co-star; the services of either Tony Gaudio, Sol Polito, or Ernie Haller on camera; three consecutive months' vacation each year with the right to do one outside picture.[20] Davis refused to start her next assignment without the new pact, and Jack Warner promptly put her on indefinite suspension, resulting in weeks and then months of negotiation. By mid-summer Warner had offered her $2000 per week and a vague promise of better roles.[21] Davis rejected the offer, and in mid-August she sailed to England to discuss a contract with an independent company, Toeplitz Productions.

Warners sued to prevent Davis from signing, and the case was tried in a British court in October 1936—one of many lawsuits between Warners and its recalcitrant stars in the 1930s. In fact while the Davis case was being tried in England, Ann Dvorak was suing Warners in the California courts. Both cases centered on Warner's suspension policy, which added time to an actor's contract when he or she refused to perform, thus preventing stars from waiting out their contracts and becoming "free agents." Warners won both suits, although the studio's British attorney candidly voiced his surprise at the outcome. He counseled Jack Warner after the trial that the company "should have the right to suspend" and also "to discontinue payment of salary," but he suggested that "there should be a limit to the period which the Producer can add on to the existing period of the contract."[22]

Davis decided not to appeal the judgment, which was reported to Warner through his London attorney after Davis visited his office. The attorney wrote Warner that Davis "was very subdued and in a much more chastened spirit" and that she intended to return to work without any "modifications" of her existing contract. At the close of this report, though, the attorney relayed several "requests, as mere suggestions," intended for "the mutual benefit of [Davis] and the Company." Incredibly, Warner's own attorney began pleading Davis's case, reiterating her earlier demands for Jack's "sympathetic consideration" and even suggesting that the studio cover her court costs.[23] Jack Warner refused to yield but he got the message; Davis may have lost this skirmish but the war would go on.

Even as he fumed, however, Warner had to admire Davis's strategic shift from obstinate adversary to charming, compliant victim. Her performance for the lawyers and for Warner himself displayed a range and flexibility far beyond what she'd been able to do on-screen, and it was at that point that Warner decided to make Davis a significant peace offering. He had already lined up several routine Davis projects, starting with the lead in yet another crime thriller, *Marked Woman* (1937). But he also went after a property that he knew Davis wanted, which featured a seemingly impossible role he now believed she could pull off. Davis expressed her appreciation to Warner in a handwritten note in January 1937. "I am thrilled to death about *Jezebel*," she wrote. "I think it can be as great, if not greater, than *Gone with the Wind*—thank you for buying it."[24]

David Selznick's two-year "Search for Scarlett" was just getting under way in early 1937, and Bette Davis was a leading contender for the part. There was no real chance of her playing Scarlett O'Hara, since her improving market value only intensified Warner's opposition to letting her do any outside work. Still Davis coveted the role, and what with the lawsuit and the public response to Margaret Mitchell's best-seller, Warner was inclined to give her the chance. Selznick already owned the rights to *Gone with the Wind*, but Warner felt he had as strong a property in *Jezebel*, a play by Owen Davis that had run on Broadway in 1933–34. The story was set in the Old South and centered on Julie Marston, a spoiled Southern belle whose headstrong behavior costs her the love of her fiancé, a young Yankee banker. After he breaks their engagement and leaves New Orleans, Julie realizes her loss and connives to get him back, even after he marries someone else. The opportunity comes via an arbitrary plot device—a yellow fever epidemic—and Julie is united with her beloved after he contracts the disease, though they seem destined to a tragic end.

Actually, Warners had almost bought the property for Bette Davis back in 1935, before she won her Oscar and bolted the studio and before Mitchell's novel was published. The initial misgivings about the project were summarized in a February 1935 memo to Hal Wallis from his assistant Walter MacEwen, who recognized that the story "would provide a good role for Bette Davis, who could play the spots off the part of a little bitch of an aristocratic Southern girl." But MacEwen doubted whether "a picture built solely around her in an unsympathetic role would be so well liked." He suggested that they add "a touch of the good old regeneration through suffering," which would make her character "a wiser and more palatable person after the final fade out."[25] Wallis concurred, but a succession of writers and supervisors failed to work out a suitable adaptation, and in March 1935 Wallis decided against buying the property.[26]

The stakes had changed since then, and in January 1937 Warner bought the rights to *Jezebel* for $12,000.[27] The story problems remained, but this time around, Wallis was determined to resolve them by placing even more emphasis on Julie's suffering after her fiancé's departure and by doing away with the plague angle as a motivation for her redemption. But over the next six months a succession of writers, directors, and supervisors—including Robert Buckner, Edmund Goulding, Clements Ripley, Lou Edelman, and Abem Finkel—failed to come up with a satisfactory script. One outspoken critic of the project was Goulding, a writer-director with extensive stage experience and formerly with MGM, who had just directed Davis and Henry Fonda in *That Certain Woman* (1937). In a July 1937 memo to Wallis, Goulding described the "background and characters" of the play as "intriguing," and he felt that it was "quite possible to put a vivid picture upon the screen." But he was convinced the project was doomed because, with or without the plague and the redemptive finale, "the picture can only tell the story of the triumph of bitchery."[28]

Another six weeks of script revision only reinforced Goulding's misgivings, and in late August Warner and Hal Wallis began looking outside the studio for help. They decided to bring in William Wyler, a director under contract to independent producer Sam Goldwyn, who recently had handled such A-class projects as *These Three* and *Dodsworth* (both 1936). Still in his mid-30s, Wyler had come a long way since his apprentice years directing shorts and five-reel westerns for Universal. He had two dozen features to his credit over the last decade, and he also was touted as a capable "script doctor." Warner signed him to write and direct for fifteen weeks at $6250 per week, with instructions that *Jezebel* be ready to shoot by late October.[29] Wyler came aboard 6 September 1937, and between rewrite sessions with Finkel and Ripley (who eventually received screen credit) he worked on pre-production with associate producer Henry Blanke and various department heads. A "Final Draft Screenplay" was approved on 13 October, the same day Jack Warner closed a deal with independent producer Walter Wanger, getting the fast-rising Henry Fonda in a straight swap for Joan Blondell.[30] A start date of 25 October was set, with a seven-week shooting schedule and a 13 December closing date. Among the line items on the budget, which totaled $783,508, were the following:

—Story cost	$ 12,000
—Continuity and treatment	28,958
—Director	93,750
—Supervisor	14,700
—Cameramen	8,704
(incl. Ernie Haller—8 wks @ 500)	
—Star (Bette Davis—flat salary)	20,000
—Cast	99,762
(Henry Fonda—18,750)	
(George Brent—19,500)	
—Music	26,200
—Sets	55,590
—Props	24,351
—Wardrobe	39,319
—Film and labs	14,000
—Studio overhead	196,177[31]

Wyler realized when he took *Jezebel* into production that the script still needed work, but his and Fonda's upcoming commitments and Warner's production schedule demanded that he start the picture in late October. Wallis kept Finkel and Ripley on the project, but once Wyler started shooting he had other plans for working out the script revisions. Those plans brought a new player into the game, namely, John Huston, who was then a much traveled 30-year-old writer, actor, painter, and former prize fighter just off a theater stint in Chicago. Huston had done some writing for Universal in the early 1930s (where he met Wyler), and after deciding to take another shot at movie writing, he reworked one of his short stories, "Three Men and a Girl," and sent it out as a movie treatment.[32] "I then called Willie Wyler," Huston later recollected, "asked him to put me up for a while, took a plane to California, and sold the treatment to Warner Brothers [sic] for $5000, with a contract . . . to write the screenplay."[33]

Warners signed Huston on 18 September 1937,[34] and while staying with Wyler the two men began talking informally about *Jezebel*. Wyler was impressed with Huston's ideas and when production opened, Wyler asked Wallis to assign Huston to the picture. Wallis agreed, and on 28 October he sent a memo to Blanke explaining that he wanted Huston "to sort of represent [Wyler] in collaboration with the writers and yourself." Wallis added that Wyler "knows Huston personally, spends a great deal of time with him, and will see him at night, and he maintains that Huston knows exactly his feeling and thoughts about the script, and his views on the last half of it."[35]

Bette Davis also was getting to know Wyler personally and seeing him "at night." The two embarked on an intimate affair soon after Wyler arrived on the lot, bringing an end to Davis's troubled marriage to bandleader Ham Nelson and providing a unique opportunity for her to help shape the most important role in her career. So Wyler and Huston, with heavy input from Davis, worked evenings throughout the shoot, rewriting the script, polishing the dialogue, and blocking out each day's camera setups. Thus Davis exercised a semblance of "creative control" over the project, and John Huston, who would be vital to Warners in the coming decade, got a crash course in filmmaking and in the politics of sex and power in Hollywood. The studio bosses tolerated the affair and the unconventional writing setup, since neither threatened the project's development—on the contrary, both seemed to enhance it.

Wyler's shooting of *Jezebel* was another matter, though. From the opening weeks of production, his deliberate and seemingly excessive methods caused concern. "Possibly Wyler likes to see those big numbers on the slate," wrote Wallis to Blanke early in the shoot, "and maybe we could arrange to have them start with number '6' on each take; then it wouldn't take so long to get up to 9 or 10."[36] By late November Wallis had lost his sense of humor, and unit manager Bob Fellows was sounding the alarm almost daily. Appended to Fellows's production report of 24 November, for example, were these comments: "To date WYLER has arranged a little better than 2 [script] pages per day for 25 days. . . . I do not believe anyone is aware of just how slow Mr. WYLER is. Company delayed from 9 AM to 1130 AM changing script and rehearsing new scene with Miss DAVIS and Mr. FONDA. Picture is nine days behind schedule."[37]

Like any production manager, Fellows was basically an efficiency expert, and he was used to operating with staff directors like Mervyn LeRoy or William Dieterle, who followed the shooting script, put their actors through their paces, and brought pictures in on time and under budget. Wyler, conversely, freely reworked the script, exploited his intense personal relationship with Davis to provoke her emotions just before shooting scenes, and often called for one take after another without saying a word to the performers about what he wanted done differently. Wyler also designed intricate camera setups and elaborate movements, often using long takes, reframing, and deep-focus shooting to involve several planes of action in a given shot. This demanded meticulous preparation and performance by both cast and crew, demands that were altogether new to most Warners personnel.

Soon both Wallis and studio manager Tenny Wright were badgering Blanke about the time and money Wyler was costing the studio. An 8 January memo about one of the previous day's shots typified Wallis's attitude as the picture fell further behind schedule: "The first [take] was excellent, yet he took it 16 times. Doesn't this man know that we have closeups to break up a scene of this kind? . . . What the hell is the matter with him anyhow—is he absolutely daffy?"[38] Wallis's anger was fueled by the fact that he could do little besides fire off memos to Blanke, who as associate producer was to represent the interests of the front office but without alienating the director or disrupting the project. Blanke was equally frustrated, realizing by now that he was superfluous in a production of this kind—a first-class star vehicle in the hands of an outside director—and could do little to soothe Wallis or to enhance Wyler's efficiency.

Even with the delays and the escalating costs, though, Wyler's authority over the shoot was never directly challenged. There was a suggestion in mid-December that William Dieterle be brought in to make sure the scenes with Fonda were completed before his 17 December departure date, but Bette Davis flatly refused to work with anyone but Wyler on the production, and the issue was dropped.[39] Wyler did manage to close Fonda by the 17th, but by mid-January he had fallen so far behind schedule that John Huston was pressed into service to direct a key scene that did not include Davis: a duel between one of Davis's suitors and the younger brother of her former fiancé. The sequence was shot "on location" at the Warner's ranch,[40] thus marking Huston's directoral debut some three years before *The Maltese Falcon* (1941), his first credited work as a Warners director.

This was yet another obvious violation of the studio's authority and its standard operating procedure; Huston was, after all, an untried director and fledgling writer who had been under contract for only a few months. But Warner and Wallis permitted such violations for several basic reasons. One had to do with the peculiar division of labor in Hollywood. A studio-based director was simply another department head in an assembly-line operation, but his was one department—i.e., "principal photography"—that was sacrosanct in the filmmaking process, and his authority was usurped only in the most extreme of circumstances.

That was due largely to the director's privileged and delicate rapport with his performers, which in the case of *Jezebel* was of grave concern. Warner did not want to upset his temperamental star, and it was evident from the dailies that Wyler was getting from Davis the performance of her career. Her Julie Marston struck the perfect balance of bitchery and captivating charm, of euphoria and barely subdued hysteria, evoking both sympathy and grating irritation.

It was equally evident as the footage was assembled into a rough cut how much the picture depended on Wyler's skills as a director, which was all the more reason for Warner and Wallis to curb their interference. They were not used to making this distinction, since Warner's factory-oriented system required that staff directors be more adept as technicians and traffic cops than as narrative artists. But it was Wyler's direction, as much as the script or Davis's performance, that brought Julie Marston to life and shaped the viewer's conception of both that character and the story. This involved more than simply lighting and shot composition, although Wyler and cinematographer Ernie Haller did capture Davis's physical beauty as no previous Warners filmmakers had done. Even more important was Wyler's ability, through camerawork and cutting, to situate Julie as the governing sensibility of the story. Through the calculated use of point-of-view shots, reaction shots, glance-object cutting, and shot/reverse-shot exchanges, Wyler carefully orchestrated the viewer's identification with and sympathy for Julie, which was so essential for the story to "play."

In a medium governed by the equation "time is money," Wyler's artistry proved costly indeed. The cost on *Jezebel* climbed from $783,000 to $1,073,000 as the project fell some five weeks behind schedule, finally closing on 17 January.[41] The extent of Wyler's "inefficiency," at least by Warner's standards, can be glimpsed in the following comparison of the number of script scenes, camera setups, camera takes, and minutes of usable footage shot per day during a randomly selected week on three different Warners productions:

I Am a Fugitive from a Chain Gang (LeRoy, 1932)[32]

8/5/32	5 scenes	15 setups	36 takes	5'06"
8/6	17	15	29	7'05"
8/7	5	17	38	3'45"
8/8	12	27	53	7'25"
8/9	8	2	33	5'20"

The Life of Emile Zola (Dieterle, 1937)[43]

3/15/37	4 scenes	16 setups	37 takes	3'00"
3/16	10	25	58	5'50"
3/17	3	22	44	4'05"
3/18	21	23	47	3'45"
3/19	3	31	52	6'50"

Jezebel (Wyler, 1938)[44]

11/1/37	5 scenes	4 setups	25 takes	1'45"
11/2	1	8	57	0'20"
11/3	2	6	43	1'25'
11/4	3	4	36	1'50"
11/5	3	14	69	2'05"

LeRoy's phenomenal speed in the early 1930s was the benchmark of "productivity" for Warner's directors and a key to its house style as well. A master at translating on-set efficiency into narrative economy, LeRoy shot *I Am a Fugitive* in only five weeks for just under $200,000, creating a hell-bent crime thriller in much the same style as he had in *Little Caesar* a year earlier. By 1936–37 LeRoy himself had slowed considerably as he took on high-cost, high-gloss projects like *Anthony Adverse*, but staff directors Lloyd Bacon and William Dieterle still cranked out films at LeRoy's earlier rate. Note Dieterle's productivity on *The Life of Emile Zola*, a Paul Muni vehicle shot in early 1937. Though it was a period piece featuring Warner's highest paid star, Dieterle cranked out *Zola* in eight weeks on a budget of $699,000, and it was steeped in the traditional Warners style. Its elliptical story developed at a frantic pace, relying heavily on montages and transitions. This was countered by the minimal camerawork and cutting during individual scenes, when Dieterle framed the dramatic action in medium or medium-long shots and cut to close-ups, reaction shots, or point-of-view shots only when absolutely necessary—which was not often, given his narrative pacing and the stage-bound quality of Muni's performance.

Consequently *Zola* had much the same feel as Warner's earlier crime sagas, and viewer identification with Muni's character was of little importance as the story unfolded. The same was true of *Marked Woman*, the Davis crime thriller that Lloyd Bacon had directed earlier in 1937. Although the story relied on viewer sympathy for Davis's character—an amoral hustler who goes straight when local mobsters kill her innocent sister—neither her performance nor Bacon's direction really draws the viewer into the narrative or lifts *Marked Woman* above the ranks of Warner's routine crime thrillers. In fact its performance, production values, and narrational style seem altogether primitive compared to those of *Jezebel*, which was paced much more evenly and deliberately—never as frantic and elliptical as *Zola* or *Marked Woman* in its transitions, and never as ponderous in its dramatic sequences. And most important, to watch *Jezebel* was to be wedded to Julie Marston's consciousness, to adopt her "way of seeing" and perverse logic in making sense of her world and her plight.

Jezebel was an immediate success both commercially and critically after its March 1938 release, bringing Davis another Oscar and reinforcing Warner's growing commitment to prestige pictures, especially quality woman's pictures starring Bette Davis. In the four years following *Jezebel* she did a dozen films, including *The Sisters* (1938), *Dark Victory* (1939), *The Old Maid* (1939), *All This and Heaven Too* (1940), *The Letter* (1940), *The Great Lie* (1941), *The Little Foxes* (1941), *In This Our Life* (1942), and *Now Voyager* (1942). Clearly the "female Jimmy Cagney" rap and the urban crime thrillers were finally behind her, with the contradictory Julie Marston—both emasculating shrew and charming innocent—defining the subsequent inflections of Davis's persona. The development of that character can be traced back to earlier roles, of course, but it was *Jezebel* that confirmed the currency and marketability of that persona and that set the trajectory for her peak years as a Warners star.

Thus *Jezebel* marked a watershed in Davis's career and in Warners' house style as well, countering the studio's traditional male ethos and signalling a shift to a more classical and character-based approach to film narration. But though the studio finally had a fix on Davis's screen persona and began tailoring projects to suit her, Davis continued to battle for greater authority over her pictures and her career in general. Warners never really satisfied her demands, but still Davis stayed on at the studio long after other top stars like Cagney and Robinson had bolted for freelance status. In fact, from 1934 to 1949 she did only one picture outside Warner Bros. Davis seemed to sense that despite her struggles with the studio powers—and in some ways because of them—her personality and the Warners style were inexorably bound together, fused in that peculiar symbiosis of star and studio style that was so essential to the Hollywood cinema.

NOTES

1. See David Bordwell, Janet Staiger, and Kristin Thompson, *The Classical Holly-wood Cinema: Film Style and Mode of Production* (New York: Columbia University Press, 1985). Staiger's analysis of Hollywood's mode of production and division of labor during the studio era (1920–60) is especially illuminating.

2. Letter from Charles Einfeld, director of publicity and advertising in New York, to Jack Warner, 12 April 1937; *Jezebel* production files, Warner Bros. Archive, Doheny Library, University of Southern California, Los Angeles (hereafter "Warner Bros. Archive, USC").

3. Contract between Warner Bros. and Bette Davis, 24 December 1931; Bette Davis legal files, Warner Bros. Archive, USC.

4. For more detailed analyses of Harry Warner's market strategy in 1930–31, see Nick Roddick, *A New Deal in Entertainment: Warner Brothers in the 1930s* (London: BFI, 1983), and Douglas Gomery, *The Hollywood Studio System* (New York: St. Martin's Press, 1986).

5. Contract between Warner Bros. and Edward G. Robinson, 5 February 1931; Warner Bros. Legal Files, United Artists Collection, Wisconsin Center for Film and Theater Research, State Historical Society, Madison, Wisconsin (hereafter "UA Archive, WCFTR").

6. For an excellent survey of Cagney's ongoing battles with Warner Bros. in the 1930s and 1940s, see Kevin Hagopian, "Declarations of Independence: A History of Cagney Productions," in *Velvet Light Trap* 22 (1986), 16–32.

7. Contracts between Warner Bros. and James Cagney, 14 October 1931 and 4 October 1932; UA Archive, WCFTR.

8. Quoted in Rudy Behlmer, *Inside Warner Bros. (1935–1951)* (New York: Viking, 1985), p. 7.

9. Contracts between Warner Bros. and Kay Francis, 12 January 1931, and Warner Bros. and Ruth Chatterton, 12 January 1931; UA Archive, WCFTR.

10. Contracts between Warner Bros. and Bette Davis on 16 June 1932, 29 November 1932, and 6 December 1933; UA Archive, WCFTR.

11. Letter to Bette Davis from P. A. Chase, Assistant to Jack Warner, 14 June 1934; Bette Davis files, Warner Bros. Archive, USC.

12. Letter to Ralph Lewis from Roy Obringer, 14 June 1934; Bette Davis files, Warner Bros. Archive, USC.

13. Alma Whitaker, "Triumphant Return of Bette Davis," *Los Angeles Times* (22 July 1934).

14. Contract between Warner Bros. and Paul Muni, 28 June 1933; UA Archive, WCFTR.

15. *Bordertown* production files, Warner Bros. Archive, USC.

16. According to a summary of Davis's contractual problems prepared by studio attorney R. W. Perkins for Warner's British attorneys on 6 October 1936, Davis was suspended from 3 December to 7 December 1935 for refusing to report for *Satan Met a Lady*; Bette Davis files, Warner Bros. Archive, USC.

17. RKO's request and Warner's handwritten reply appear in a memo from Roy Obringer for Jack Warner, 2 March 1936; Bette Davis files, Warner Bros. Archive, USC.

18. "Film Bosses 'Headache' to Bette Davis," *New York Evening Journal* (25 March 1936).

19. "'They'd Make All the Women Wed the Men,' Cries Bette Davis, Assailing Film Censors," *New York World-Telegram* (25 March 1936).

20. Letter from Martin Gang, Davis's agent and attorney, to Warner Bros., 6 April 1936; Bette Davis files, Warner Bros. Archive, USC.

21. Letter from studio attorney Roy Obringer to attorney Ralph Lewis summarizing the Davis situation, 23 June 1936; Bette Davis files, Warner Bros. Archive, USC.

22. Letter to Jack Warner from Denton, Hall and Bergin, the studio's London-based law firm, 22 October 1936; Bette Davis files, Warner Bros. Archive, USC. The attorney's reservations, in fact, were the same as those expressed by the California Supreme Court in its May 1944 decision in favor of Olivia de Havilland and against Warner Bros., thus bringing to an end the studio's long-standing suspension practice and enabling disgruntled contract players to wait out their contract and become a free agent.

23. Letter to Jack Warner from Denton, Hall and Bergin, 3 November 1936; Bette Davis files, Warner Bros. Archive, USC.

24. Letter from Bette Davis to Jack Warner, 6 January 1937, in which she also asked Warner to arrange a personal loan for $14,000 to cover her legal expenses, which Warner agreed to do; Bette Davis files, Warner Bros. Archive, USC.

25. MacEwen memo to Wallis, 15 February 1935; *Jezebel* production files, Warner Bros. Archive, USC.

26. Wallis instructed Warner to have Jacob Wilk, the East Coast Story Editor, "get out of the purchase"; Wallis memo to Warner, 27 March 1935; *Jezebel* production files, Warner Bros. Archive, USC.

27. According to correspondence between MacEwen and both Warner and Wallis in December 1936, the deal was struck that month and Miriam Hopkins was being considered seriously for the lead. By the time the deal was closed in early January, Davis was penciled in for the lead. *Jezebel* production files, Warner Bros. Archive, USC.

28. Goulding memo to Wallis, 17 July 1937; *Jezebel* production files, Warner Bros. Archive, USC.

29. Warner Bros. contract with William Wyler, 25 August 1937; UA Archive, WCFTR.

30. Approved "Final Draft Screenplay" dated 13 October 1937, with revisions added through 30 December 1937; Warner Bros. Script Collection, UA Archive, WCFTR. Agreement between Warner Bros. and Walter Wanger swapping Fonda for Blondell, 13 October 1937; *Jezebel* production files, Warner Bros. Archive, WCFTR.

31. Preliminary budget and shooting schedule approved 26 October 1937; *Jezebel* production files, UA Archive, WCFTR.

32. Huston's 49-page treatment was adapted by Huston and submitted to the studio in March 1939, later revised by Huston and Howard Koch in 1943–44–45, and released in 1945 under the title *Three Strangers;* Warner Bros. Script Collection, UA Archive, WCFTR.

33. John Huston, *An Open Book* (New York: Alfred A. Knopf, 1980), p. 71.

34. Contract between Warner Bros. and John Huston, 18 September 1937; UA Archive, USC.

35. Memo from Wallis to Blanke, 28 October 1937; *Jezebel* files, Warner Bros. Archive, USC.

36. Wallis memo to Blanke (addressed to "Dear Tovarich [comrade] Blanke"), 4 November 1937; *Jezebel* files, Warner Bros. Archive, USC.

37. Memo accompanying Daily Production Report from Bob Fellows to T. C. Wright, 24 November 1937; *Jezebel* files, Warner Bros. Archive, USC.

38. Wallis memo to Blanke, 8 January 1937; *Jezebel* files, Warner Bros. Archive, USC.

39. The idea of bringing in another director was first broached in a memo from Fellows to T. C. Wright on 26 November 1937. Dieterle's name came up frequently during December and he was still being considered as late as 4 January 1938, when Fellows in his Daily Production report stated he hoped to "get some definite information" about Dieterle's status on the picture; *Jezebel* files, Warner Bros. Archive, USC.

40. On 10 January 1937 Fellows reported: "second unit with Blanke and Houston [sic] shooting, covered 1/4 pages of script and finished the SWAMP sequence in 4 setups."

The unit finished the "DUEL sequence" on 13 January 1937. *Jezebel* files, Warner Bros. Archive, USC.

41. Closing cost included in an undated revised budget; *Jezebel* files, Warner Bros. Archive, USC.

42. *I Am a Fugitive from a Chain Gang* files, Warner Bros. Archive, USC.

43. *The Life of Emile Zola* files, Warner Bros. Archive, USC.

44. *Jezebel* files, Warner Bros. Archive, USC.

David Bordwell

Deep-Focus Cinematography

Deep-focus cinematography has held a great interest for film aesthe-
ticians, and the reasons are not obscure. It is a technological development
which can be clearly correlated with stylistic consequences: the evidence
seems to be baldly there on the screen. Just as important, deep focus
seems to invite a stress upon innovation as such—André Bazin called it
"a dialectical step forward in the evolution of film language"—and upon
the individual innovators (Orson Welles, William Wyler, Gregg Toland,
et al.). The argument being made here tries to frame the central problems
somewhat differently.

First, what are we trying to explain? "Deep focus" itself requires
some definition: the "deep focus" of Lumière is not that of Renoir, and
that of Renoir is not that of Welles. Nor will a simple opposition of depth
and flatness in image composition take us very far. Most simply, we are
asking why at specific periods the classical paradigm favored certain
renditions of depth over others. Why is a shot like figure 1, with its fairly
close foreground plane and sharply focused rear plane, so rare in 1937 and
yet quite ordinary a decade later? To answer such a question, we must
not simply link technological devices to the image; we must examine
how such "deep focus" functioned within the classical paradigm. The
issue of innovation should in its turn be treated in an institutional
context. This is not to say that individual filmmakers do not count, but
the nature of their contributions will be largely defined by the ways that
the mode of production encouraged and appropriated individuals' innovations. In certain ways, deep focus extended the range of the classical

From *The Classical Hollywood Cinema: Film Style and Mode of Production to 1960*, by
David Bordwell, Janet Staiger, and Kristin Thompson (London: Routledge & Kegan Paul,
1985), pp. 341–52. Reprinted with permission of the author and Routledge & Kegan Paul.

David Bordwell

Figure 1. (*above left*). Casbah (*1948*).

Figure 2. (*above right*). The Kid Brother (*1927*).

Figure 3. (*centre left*). *Deep staging with fairly sharp focus in the rear planes:* Greed (*1924*).

Figure 4. (*centre right*). *Deep focus with a strong foreground and employing a wide-angle lens:* The Show (*1927*).

Figures 5–6. (*below*). *The hard-edged image in the late silent era:* So This Is Paris (*1926*).

paradigm. To investigate deep-focus cinematography, we will need to look at the historical role played by specific technical agencies, especially the American Society of Cinematographers (ASC).

    In discussing how films may represent depth, we must keep several distinctions in mind. Spatial depth is not simply one "thing"; it is a quality we attribute to widely different sorts of images. One distinction that must be maintained is that between mise-en-scène and cinematography. You can represent spatial depth through composition, setting, and light and shadow; and you can represent depth through choice of lens, amount of light, aperture, film stock, and optical process work. For example, Jean Renoir's films of the 1930s often produce depth by composing significant action on two planes or by using doors and windows to frame distant action; yet usually only one of these planes will be in sharp focus. Similarly, one can have every plane of a shot in sharp focus, as in Carl Theodor Dreyer's *La Passion de Jeanne d'Arc* (1928), and yet because of the ambiguous composition and the blank decor relatively little depth is demarcated. The distinction between deep-space mise-en-scène and deep-focus cinematography lets us isolate various ways that the classical Hollywood style has represented space.

A second distinction is no less important: that between device and function. It is one thing to say that *Citizen Kane* (1941), or any film, contains shots of unprecedented spatial depth; it is another thing to claim that that device functions in a new way. The innovations, sources, and first times exhumed by film historians often become less startling if placed in their functional context, within a film or within a tradition.

The Soft Style in the Sound Period

During the 1920s, the classical representation of a shot's depth obeyed a few simple principles. Typically, the principal actors performed on one or two planes only, and the surroundings (wall, road, horizon) constituted general background planes. There would usually be one plane of interest, the figure in the foreground (e.g., a close-up or medium shot of the hero) or, less often, a figure in the middle ground (e.g., the hero framed by a tree or doorway in the foreground). Great depth is more common in long shots than in closer framings. In *The Kid Brother* (1927), Harold waves goodbye to his girlfriend in the distance (figure 2), but the foreground plane is still at a considerable distance from us. Medium shots could also use marked depth, as in figures 3 and 4, but such compositions are rare in American silent films. On the whole, deep-space staging in the shot obeys a fixed rule: the greater the shot scale (that is, the closer it comes to being a long shot), the greater the potential depth; the less the shot scale, the shallower the space.

What of deep-focus cinematography? In the 1920s, the American cinema contained two distinct impulses, one toward sharp-focus filming, another toward a softer and more diffused look. Not until the second half of the 1920s did a certain photographic softness become generally accepted. By April 1928 Joseph Dubray could write: "It is acknowledged by cinematographers in general that the need of absolutely sharp definition is a thing of the past. The dramatic quality of present day cinematography demands a certain softness of contours throughout the whole image."[1] Several factors contributed to the soft look: soft-focus lenses, filters, diffusion of the light sources, different developing procedures, and the increased use of Mazda lamps. The style owed a good deal to much older trends in still photography, whereby pictures were considered "artistic" and painterly if they had a blurry softness about them. Whether the image was crisp or diffused, however, the arrangement of the players in the shot did not fundamentally differ. Compare two sets of shots (figures 5–8) from *So This Is Paris* (Lubitsch, 1926) and *Seventh Heaven* (Borzage, 1927). The cinematographic styles are significantly different (determined by differences in studio, genre, and filmmaker) but the depth of each shot's playing space is comparable: medium close-ups of a figure and a background, long shots with greater depth.

The introduction of sound modified the soft style. In certain respects, the image remained soft in focus and definition, and Patrick Ogle has pointed out how certain factors favored that quality (the supremacy of the Mazda lamp, the use of low-contrast developing solutions, the cinematographers' insistence on shooting at maximum aperture).[2] Certainly the practice of multiple-camera shooting also had an effect. The need to light the set for several camera positions created a flat illumination, while the extremely long lenses used for multiple-camera filming tended to weaken definition. Yet the softness of the early sound films is not the softness of *Sunrise* (1927), *Seventh Heaven*, or *The Tempest* (1928). In the outstanding films of the silent soft style, the blurring of edges and textures was often accompanied by dark blacks and sparkling highlights; the image shimmered. In the early sound films, the image can be said to be soft only insofar as it is grayer, with lower contrast.

The difference was due to several factors. Machine developing tended to standardize a middle-range degree of contrast in processing all shots. Moreover, early incandescent illumination simply could not produce crisp definition. In 1928, Karl Struss and Charles Rosher, two chief practitioners of the soft style, complained that with Mazdas the colors

Figures 7–8. (above). The soft style in the late silent film: Seventh Heaven *(1927).*

Figure 9. (centre left). Moby Dick *(1930).*

Figure 10. (centre right). A Midsummer Night's Dream *(1935).*

Figure 11. (below left). The Enchanted Cottage *(1945).*

Figure 12. (below right). Wide-angle distortion in Each Dawn I Die *(1939).*

blended too much: arcs could pick out wrinkles in fabrics, but Mazdas could not distinguish two black-clothed figures when they came into contact. Proponents of incandescents found this a desirable "softness," while antagonists called it "blurred, foggy composition."[3] Theater projectionists protested that they could not focus these images; the National

Carbon Company even advertised new projector carbons for "the modern soft, low key or fuzzy film."[4] Furthermore, the fact that most 1928–31 shots were filmed through a pane of glass (because the camera was in a booth or blimp) gave early talkie photography a lack of definition that one observer called "mushy."[5] (See figure 9.) Finally, the soft films not only diffused the light sources but also applied very heavy diffusion filters to the lens. (The filters were ranked from 1 to 4, the heaviest.) Sometimes the cinematographer would also set up taut sheets of mesh or other material between various planes of the shot. After the coming of sound, cinematographers avoided such heavy diffusion. Scrims were not generally used between planes, and much lighter diffusion filters (scaled from $1/2$ to beyond $1/32$) became the norm.[6] The result was a smooth and slight overall blurring that sought to be both unnoticeable and constant from shot to shot. After the early 1930s, the sparkling, heavily diffused soft style was used only to convey a fantasy atmosphere (see figures 10 and 11).

Once a modified "soft" style became the norm for the sound era, the service firms responded. The earliest panchromatic film had been relatively slow and contrasty, but in 1928 Eastman marketed a lower-contrast, more sensitive stock. In 1931, the firm introduced Super Sensitive Panchromatic, the first stock created specifically for Mazda light, low contrast, and "softer highlight rendering."[7] Proponents claimed that the film itself produced the softness that would otherwise have to be created by lighting and filters. Eastman quickly improved the Super Sensitive stock by adding an anti-halation backing that gave a brighter image with more shadow detail. Within two years, both Du Pont and Agfa had introduced similar emulsions. While other service agencies quickly adapted to the film stock—Bausch and Lomb introduced its Raytar lenses designed for fast film, and Max Factor devised appropriate make-up—cinematographers pondered exactly how to use the new panchromatic.[8]

Producers expected that the sensitive emulsions, being at least twice as fast as the old ones, would lead to a lowering of lighting levels and consequently a decrease in costs. At first, this did not happen. A 1931 Academy survey discovered that most studios using fast film did not consume less amperage.[9] Cinematographers were using the same number of lighting units and were not stopping down the lens, because "sharp photography is not artistic photography."[10] But when the ASC officially recommended the new fast films to its members, it pointed out that "with the present lightings and smaller lens openings, improved definition can be obtained without sacrifice of those qualities of softness which have always been the artistic aim of cinematographers."[11] After 1931, most cinematographers chose to keep the lens at full aperture, cut down the light levels, and save money on the set.

Cinematography in the 1930s thus became a give-and-take between the technical agencies and the cinematographers. The agencies were committed to "progress": faster and finer-grained films, faster lenses, more portable and powerful light sources. Throughout the decade, suppliers introduced a series of faster emulsions, culminating in 1938 with Agfa Supreme, Du Pont Superior II, and Eastman Plus X and Super XX. Mole-Richardson perfected an incandescent spotlight with Fresnel focusing lenses in 1935 and at the same period created a new series of lightweight and automatic-feed arc lamps. Most cinematographers in turn chose to keep a soft style. The faster films and more powerful lights were used to reduce set lighting levels, sometimes by as much as 70 percent. The arc lamp had never been completely abandoned when sound arrived, but after 1935 it was not uncommon for cameramen to mix incandescents with the improved Mole-Richardson arcs, again in the name of control, economy, and efficiency.[12] The faster films also reduced the need for modeling light. As one cinematographer put it:[13]

> The film itself [Plus X] now does half the work of separating the different planes of your picture. People stand out more clearly from their backgrounds. Even separating the planes in close shots—the little matter of keeping a coat-lapel from blending into the background of a garment—of giving an illusion of depth to faces and figures—is easier with the new film.

The speed of the new films allowed some cinematographers to rely more on spotlighting. Because dolly shots often made floor lighting cumbersome, most lights were hung above the set, but the light was often so distant from the action that only powerful spotlights could work effectively. Mole-Richardson cooperated and designed a variety of spots with controllable beam-spreads and a dimmer that regulated the intensity of light at any point.[14] In short, most cinematographers sought to maintain a balance between technological novelty and the "artistic" demand for soft images. Yet some cinematographers experimented with ways to produce harder, more sharply defined shots. What explains this penchant for innovation?

As an organization, the ASC replicated, in its own particular terms, the tension between standardization and differentiation at work in the production sector generally. On the one hand, the ASC asked the cinematographer to be a craftsman, cleanly obeying the rules. At the same time, he was expected to originate techniques. "Bert Glennon introducing new method of interior photography"; "Reverse studio lighting methods to put big night spots on the screen"; "A new viewpoint on the lighting of motion pictures"—such titles, from *American Cinematographer* and the *Journal of the Society of Motion Picture Engineers*, indicate the degree to which novelty had become institutionalized. Every article told the same story. The cinematographer encounters a particular problem on a production. He devises a mechanism or procedure to solve the problem in a way that might prove useful on other productions. The article concludes that the solution could improve quality, differentiate the product, and cut expenses. For example, when Hal Mohr devised a ball-and-socket lens mount to keep several planes in focus, *American Cinematographer* featured an article in which he explained that such shots made the scene more dramatic and easier to shoot. The article concluded that "the device can be of inestimable value in the Cinematographer's efforts to reconcile the dramatic purpose of Cinematography with the mechanical limitations of the camera."[15] Similarly, Bert Glennon was praised as "a man whose progressiveness and sincerity has kept the photographic competition moving."[16] Not only the cameraman's employer but his professional association encouraged him to innovate.

While some cinematographers sought to introduce new lighting techniques, camera supports, or filters, others experimented with the rendering of depth. Some cinematographers used lenses wider than the 50mm norm to increase depth of field. James Wong Howe (*Transatlantic* and *Viva Villa!* 1933) and Hal Mohr (*Tess of the Storm Country*, 1932) are the most famous instances, but many early sound films (e.g., *Applause, Young Sinners*) use a short focal-length lens occasionally. Mohr used his ball-and-socket mount for *Green Pastures* (1936) and *Bullets or Ballots* (1936). Bert Glennon employed a 25mm lens for *Stagecoach* (1939). In *Each Dawn I Die* (1939), Arthur Edeson made fairly close shots with a wide-angle lens (see figure 12). Tony Gaudio's "precision lighting" was an attempt to increase depth by creating strong key light with less fill. Coated lenses, which increased light transmission and enabled cameramen to stop down the aperture, began to be used in the late 1930s in films like *Tobacco Road* (1940), which Arthur Miller shot with remarkably little backlighting.[17]

Such developments in deep-focus cinematography encouraged some directors to stage more ambitiously in depth. Deep-space compositions crop up occasionally throughout the early sound era (see figures 13–15 for instances). Such shots are chiefly remarkable for placing the

Deep-Focus Cinematography

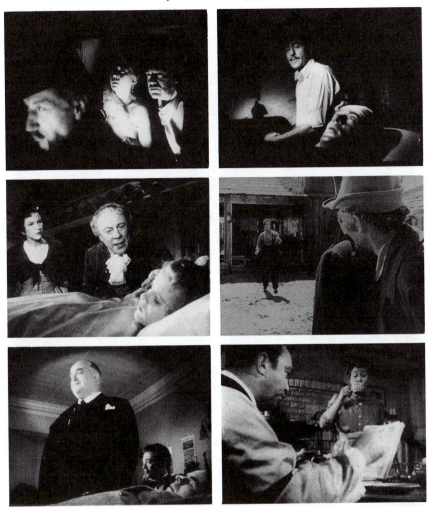

Figure 13. (above left). Bulldog Drummond *(1929).*

Figure 14. (above right). A Farewell to Arms *(1932).*

Figure 15. (centre left). Anthony Adverse *(1936).*

Figure 16. (centre right). All That Money Can Buy *(1941).*

Figure 17. (below left). The Maltese Falcon *(1941).*

Figure 18. (below right). Our Town *(1940).*

foreground plane in medium shot, even if it is not in focus. But on the whole, the 1930s cinema adhered to the staging practices of the 1920s. Not until 1940 and 1941 do films systematically place foregrounds quite close to the camera and in sharp focus. This prototypical "deep-focus" look is usually associated with *Citizen Kane,* but this film, available for industry viewing in April 1941, appeared in the midst of a string of similar efforts.

There is, for example, *The Stranger on the Third Floor* (available to the trade in September 1940), in which Boris Ingster and his cinematographer Nicholas Musuraca played and filmed courtroom scenes in considerable depth. There is William Dieterle's *All That Money Can Buy* (July 1941), shot by Joseph August, with its striking backlighting, wide-angle shots, and emphatically close foregrounds (figure 16). There is *Meet John Doe* (March 1941), in which George Barnes used wide-angle lenses and rapid rack-focusing to create great depth. There is also *The Maltese Falcon* (September 1941), whose looming ceilings, foreshortened views, and striking depth of field make Arthur Edeson's cinematography strongly akin to Toland's work (figure 17). There are, in particular, two films designed by William Cameron Menzies, *Our Town* (May 1940) and *Kings Row* (December 1941), both directed by Sam Wood. Many shots in *Our Town* are staged in remarkable depth, with looming foreground objects and great depth of focus (figure 18). *Kings Row* is no less claustrophobic, with huge foregrounds and a dense organization of actors and decor (figure 19). One of the most important exponents of deep space and deep focus, Menzies sketched each shot in advance and even specified the lens to be used.[18] Unlike Toland, who was to argue for the realism of deep space, Menzies excelled in using depth to create contorted, fantastic perspective. His set designs for *The Tempest* (1928), *Bulldog Drummond* (1929), and other films had a calculated Germanic look which exploited unusual angles for deep-space compositions (figure 20). Whether or not Menzies influenced Toland (who assisted George Barnes on *Bulldog Drummond*), his work anticipates the grotesquely monumental depth of *Citizen Kane.*

These innovations are not all that drastic. Within the context of the classical style, such depth devices were quickly assigned familiar functions. For instance, staging in depth often enhanced centering, as when the foreground figures are silhouetted or out of focus and our attention is drawn to the lighted middle ground (see figure 21). At other moments, a deep-focus composition will function as an establishing shot, especially in a cramped setting (for example, figure 22). Or the spatial

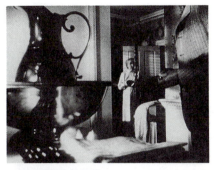

Figure 19. Kings Row *(1941).*
Figure 20. A drawing by William Cameron Menzies for Alibi *(1929).*

depth will constitute a variant on the familiar shot/reverse-shot (figures 23 and 24). Sometimes the depth is motivated generically, as in the skewed sets of a horror film like *The Bat Whispers* (1931). Stylized or "realistic," before *Citizen Kane*, staging and shooting in depth went generally unnoticed because the devices fitted comfortably into roles allotted by the classical style.

David Bordwell

Figure 21. (above left). Jezebel *(1938).*
Figure 22. (above right). Arrowsmith *(1931).*
Figures 23–24. (below). Deep space shot/reverse shot in Our Town *(1940).*

Gregg Toland and Deep Focus

The innovations of Gregg Toland should be seen not only in the context of the development of 1930s technology but also in the context of the ASC as a professional organization. Patrick Ogle has examined the ways in which Toland synthesized various innovations of the decade—wide-angle lenses, fast film, arc lighting for black and white, coated lenses, the new silenced Mitchell camera (figures 25 and 26). But Ogle assigns the cause of this to Toland's artistic desire to experiment.[19] What Ogle's purely technical account misses is the way the concept of artistic experimentation was defined by the institutions within which Toland worked. Certainly as an independent producer, Samuel Goldwyn gave Toland a strong incentive to differentiate the studio's product. The most pertinent stimulus, however, was supplied by Toland's professional organization.

The ASC articulated a contradictory task for the cameraman. He was, firstly, to be an artist. The ASC encouraged its members to think of

Figure 25. (above). Gregg Toland (far left) and Howard Hawks (far right) using the Mitchell BNC to film
    Ball of Fire *(1941).*
Figure 26. (below left). Use of a wide-angle lens in Dead End *(1937), shot by Toland for William Wyler.*
Figure 27. (below right). These Three *(1936).*

themselves as creative people, comparable to the screenwriter or director. Implicitly, then, each cinematographer's work was to have something distinctive about it. We have already seen the stress laid on individual innovations and virtuosity. But at the same time, the ethos of the craft held that the cinematographer's work must go unnoticed by the layman.

The ideal, remarked John Arnold, president of the ASC, "is to so perfectly suit the cinematography to the story that the former is imperceptible, and the latter is subtly heightened."[20] Arthur Miller claimed that the viewer should forget that he or she has seen cinematography in watching a film.[21] To avoid distracting from the story, the cinematographer's style would have to adapt itself to each film. *American Cinematographer* praised one cameraman because "The casual observer viewing these two films would hardly suspect they were photographed by the same man."[22] The model is unobtrusive artistry, innovation that does not challenge reigning norms. Gregg Toland's problematic position in the early 1940s arose from the conflicting demands of individual artistry and self-effacing professionalism.

For a few years, Toland was the most famous cinematographer in Hollywood, and indeed the world. He began very young: an assistant cameraman at age sixteen, George Barnes's assistant at twenty-two, and at twenty-seven the youngest first cameraman in Hollywood. During his work with Goldwyn, Toland was entrusted with many of the studio's most important projects, such as Eddie Cantor and Anna Sten vehicles. Toland was admitted to the ASC in 1934, when he was barely thirty. For the next six years, no cinematographer received more public attention. In the pages of *American Cinematographer*, Toland explained how he used the new Mitchell camera, shot low-key, planned every set-up, used arc lighting for black and white, and devised new photographic gadgets. He shot a string of prestigious films (*Les Misérables* [1935], *These Three* [1936], *Dead End* [1937], *Kidnapped* [1938], and *Goldwyn Follies* [1938]). After winning the Academy Award for black-and-white cinematography for *Wuthering Heights* (1939), he clinched his fame with *The Grapes of Wrath*, *The Westerner*, and *The Long Voyage Home* (all 1940). With the reputation of being a fast, efficient worker and a meticulous attender to details of laboratory work, Gregg Toland at the age of thirty-six was the most powerful cameraman in Hollywood. He had an unprecedented long-range contract with Goldwyn, which was said to include a provision that he must be allowed to direct a film.[23] (At his death, he was also one of the few stockholders in Goldwyn Productions.) No wonder, then, that *American Cinematographer* noted that most cinematographers believed that "Toland's acknowledged brilliance has placed him in the most nearly ideal position any Director of Photography has enjoyed since the halcyon days when D. W. Griffith and Billy Bitzer were between them creating the basic technique of the screen."[24]

Like many of his peers during the 1930s, Toland occasionally experimented with technical devices to give greater depth: arc lamps, faster film, lens coating, and wide-angle lenses. Many of Toland's shots display qualities common in other cinematographers' work. Sometimes the shot will have considerable spatial depth in the composition, but the foreground will be decoratively darkened or unfocused (figure 27). Sometimes a short-focal-length lens at an unusual angle will yield a shot/reverse-shot pattern (figure 28). Almost always, however, the 1920s principle holds: long shots have greater depth of field than closer shots. Even as late as *Wuthering Heights*, when a shot's foreground may be in medium close-up, one plane or another is out of focus. When Cathy is at the table, for instance, she is in focus in the middle ground, and Hindley's shoulder and the servant's hand are out of focus in the foreground. Nevertheless, Toland's work of the late 1930s deserves closer consideration. First, several of the films he worked on make a systematic use of depth of space and of focus that was generally rare at the time, and second, in some images we can find what would become Toland's individual use of deep focus.

Wuthering Heights (March 1939), shot for William Wyler at Goldwyn, employs certain aspects of the setting as motifs, and these aspects usually have to do with depth. In general, there is Wuthering Heights itself, a low, mazelike set with raked floors and low ceilings similar to those in *Stagecoach* (released February 1939). More specifically, depth is used as a motif to contrast eras within the story. When as youngsters Cathy and Heathcliff peer into the Grange, the camera tracks past them to the window to reveal the ball inside. The penetration into the room expresses Cathy's fascination with the glittering life there. Years later, with Cathy now Lockley's wife and mistress of the Grange, Heathcliff the gentleman calls on them. As the three leave the room, the camera suddenly tracks back, through the same window. The contrast of periods and the sense of change issue from the parallel camera movements into and out of depth.

Dead End (1937) is in many respects even more remarkable. The confinement to a single set and a loose unity of duration (one day) mark the film as fairly theatrical. Within these conventions, however, Toland and Wyler create a constant interplay in depth. The various lines of action are interwoven within deep space: Wyler will shift our attention from a foreground action to a new action in the background. This practice poses no great problem for depth of focus, since typically the foreground is still in long shot. But in one virtuosic framing, two hoodlums in a restaurant plan to kidnap the rich man's son (figure 29). The men are in focus in profiled close-up; outside the window, a woman wheels a baby carriage

David Bordwell

Figure 28. (above left). These Three (*1936*).

Figure 29. (above right). Dead End (*1937*).

Figure 30. (centre left). The Long Voyage Home (*1940*).

Figure 31. (centre right). Dead End (*1937*).

Figure 32. (below left). Dead End (*1937*).

Figure 33. (below right). The Long Voyage Home (*1940*).

across the street. The woman is too far away to be in focus, and her child is not the target of the scheme, but the fact that she occupies frame center and is the only moving figure in the shot gives her a symbolic salience. Here is the sort of staging in extreme depth, with a significant element in foreground close-up and a thematically important element in a distant plane, that will become familiar in *Citizen Kane.*

The Long Voyage Home (October 1940) was praised by *American Cinematographer* for Toland's memorable shots, and it is possible that it exercised considerable influence on deep-focus films of 1941. As in *Dead End*, there is little backlighting, but the sensitivity of the film stock picks out various planes. Again, the action is staged in depth, especially along the ship's deck. Since the background plane is often only a few feet beyond an extremely close foreground plane, both planes can be in sharp focus (figure 30).

Toland's late 1930s career is of interest chiefly because in the three films mentioned, a fairly rigorous use of depth becomes central to the overall construction of space. Moreover, while many shots resemble other cinematographers' explorations of deep-focus imagery at the period, certain images in *Dead End* and *The Long Voyage Home* bear the mark of Toland's distinctive treatment of deep space and deep focus. The characteristic Toland shot is lit low-key, with little fill or backlighting. There are several significant planes of depth, all in focus. There is an exaggeratedly enlarged foreground plane—usually a face. Most important, heads crowd into the frame, competing for attention by position (centered, uncentered), size, movement, glance, and aspect (profile, frontal).

An excellent example of the Toland trademark occurs in figure 31, when the Bogart character terrorizes the young boy. There are not only several planes (from the beanie in extreme lower foreground to the wall in the distance) but several distinct areas of action in the shot. A comparable zigzag of our attention operates in figure 32. In the scene of the group song from *The Long Voyage Home* (figure 33), the foreground element is not so exaggerated, but the frontality is even more marked. Furthermore, the typical Toland composition crams all the dramatically significant elements into the frame. This has the effect of making the shot notably static: all the figures are visible from only one vantage point; any camera or figure movement would impede our sightlines. Toland's densely organized compositions do not, as Bazin argued, make our perception existentially free; instead, dialogue, gesture, and figure aspect direct our attention. We must also remember that such packed shots are legible because they are carefully imbedded in an orthodox context of clear establishing shots, analytical cutting, and closeups. Such com-positions' use of deep space and deep focus will become dominant in Toland's 1941 work.

If Toland was striving, within his professional context, to distin-guish his own contribution, what do we make of *Citizen Kane* (released April 1941)? The film's stylistic features—the diagonal perspectives (with ceilings), the splitting of action into two or more distinct planes, the use of an enlarged foreground plane (close-up or even extreme close-up), the low-key lighting, and the persistent frontality—all had been seen, in fragmentary fashion, in Toland's previous work. But *Kane* enabled Toland to consolidate a unified "look" as his trademark.

In this film, deep focus is elevated to a coherent style on the basis of two principles. The first is the dramatic expanse of the sets. The *Inquirer* offices, the auditoriums and opera stages, Xanadu, even the Kane family cabin and El Rancho nightclub, are all conceived as enormous spaces, both high and deep. Here Toland's deep focus functions in traditional ways: even on these vast sets, the angles still operate within patterns of shot/reverse shot (e.g., Kane and Susan shouting across the cavernous hall in Xanadu) or of establishing shots (e.g., Gettys watching Kane's rally from a balcony). A second, more innovative principle made *Kane*'s deep focus flagrant: the use of unusually long takes. Toland claimed that in the interest of "simplification," Welles decided to avoid cuts.[25]

> We pre-planned our angles and compositions so that action which would ordinarily be shown in direct cuts would be shown in a single, longer scene—often one in which important action might take place simulta-neously in widely-separated points in extreme foreground and back-ground. . . . Welles' technique of visual simplification might combine what would conventionally be made as two separate shots—a close-up and an insert—in a single, non-dollying shot.

The important phrase here is "non-dollying." In *Kane*, the static, cramped quality of Toland's particular brand of depth is given full sway by the use of the almost unmoving long take. The most famous deep-focus shots in the film—Susan's music lesson, the scene of Kane signing away his newspapers (figure 34), Kane's firing of Leland, Susan's attempted suicide, and most of the shot in Mrs. Kane's boardinghouse—all are notably rigid and posed, relying greatly upon frontality and narrowly circumscribed figure movement. These shots call attention to themselves not only because they are so deep but also because they are so prolonged and fixed.

Citizen Kane was, then, an opportunity for Toland to make flamboyant deep focus identified with his own work. Welles had come to Hollywood with no professional film experience, and (according to Welles) Toland had sought out the *Kane* assignment. After the filming was completed, Toland was at pains to claim several innovations. For greater realism, he explained, many sets were designed with ceilings, which required him to light from the floor. Since the sets were also deep, he relied on the carrying power of arc lamps. Furthermore, since Welles and Toland had decided to stage action in depth, Toland sought great depth of focus by using Super XX film, increasing the lighting levels, and using optically coated wide-angle lenses.[26] As a result, Toland claimed to be able to stop down his lens "to apertures infinitely smaller than anything that has been used for conventional interior cinematography in many years."[27] In an era when f-2.3 and f-2.8 were the common apertures, Toland boasted that he shot all *Kane*'s interiors at f-8 or smaller apertures.[28] The result shifted the traditional limits of deep space. In yielding a depth of field that extended from about eighteen inches to infinity, Toland's "pan-focus" made it possible to have a sharp foreground plane in medium shot or even close-up and still keep very distant background planes in focus.

In justifying pan-focus for *Citizen Kane,* Toland walked the cinematographer's narrow line between artistic innovation and modest craftsmanship. Welles allowed originality full play, Toland claimed. But experimentation was controlled by certain demands. Static long takes in the name of "simplification" could be justified as a more efficient production procedure, allowing dialogue scenes to be shot more quickly. There was a stylistic demand as well, which Toland labeled "realism." Realism of space, because the eye sees in depth: "For all practical purposes it is a perfect universal-focus lens." Realism of time, because cuts call the audience's attention to "the mechanics of picture-making." In all, realism in the name of continuity and concealed artifice: "Both Welles and I . . . felt that if it was possible, the picture should be brought to the screen in such a way that the audience would feel it was looking at reality, rather than merely a movie."[29] The terms of the rationale are familiar, but "the most style-conscious cameraman of his time," as Toland was later called, did not quite get away with it.[30] The visual style of *Citizen Kane* was sensed as so unusual that the Toland "look" became famous but also came under considerable criticism within the industry.

Citizen Kane's distinctive cinematography made Toland the only Hollywood cameraman whose name was known to the general public. In 1941, Toland signed five major articles about his shooting technique, one of which appeared in *Popular Photography* and another in *Theatre Arts*. In June, *Life* ran an extensive feature about *Kane:* nominally about Welles, the article devoted most space to explaining "pan-focus" using illustrations especially prepared by Toland. Toland's name was kept in the limelight by the release of two more films in 1941, *The Little Foxes* (August) and *Ball of Fire* (December). By the end of the year, amateur enthusiasts were learning how to apply pan-focus to their home movies, and Goldwyn was reported to be offering Toland the most lucrative and prestigious contract any cinematographer had received.[31]

Toland's professional peers had a more mixed response to his work. True, he had publicized the cinematographer as a creative artist. Nonetheless, many cinematographers felt that Toland's work swerved too far from the orthodox style.[32] *Kane* was criticized for distorted perspectives and excessive shadows. Charles G. Clarke pointed out in *American Cinematographer* that although the soft style had been abused, Toland had gone too far to the other extreme. For one thing, *Kane*'s small apertures gained depth at the price of "that illusion of roundness which— fully as important as depth of definition—is a necessity in conveying the illusion of three-dimensional reality in our two-dimensional pictures."[33] Clarke went on to claim that exaggerated depth of field sacrificed selectivity—the ability to control audience attention by focusing on only the most important character. Toland was often criticized on these grounds. *American Cinematographer*'s review of *How Green Was My Valley* (December 1941) hits Toland in almost every sentence:[34]

> [Arthur] Miller makes eloquent use of the modern increased-depth technique. But he does it without lapsing into the brittle artificiality which has so often accompanied the use of this technique. His scenes have depth—often to a surprising degree—but they also have qualities of "good photography" which are all too often lost in attaining unusual depth of field. His scenes have depth, yes; but they also have a lifelike roundness, a soft plasticity of image, and a pleasing gradational range which have all too often been sacrificed in pursuit of depth.

Commentary in *American Cinematographer* about *The Little Foxes* was even more critical, complaining that simultaneous action in foreground and background created confused, scattered compositions: "The eye hardly knows where to look."[35]

Such responses to Toland's work were not simply jealousy. They were signals that Toland had developed too eccentric a style. His artistry was no longer unobtrusive. The reaction against Toland's lack of volumes and selectivity was caused by his refusal to use edge-lighting, his rigid placement of figures, his relatively undiffused close shots of women, his cramped compositions, and especially the lengthy takes that prolonged the viewer's awareness of depth.

One other factor, not mentioned at the time of *Kane*'s release, seems an important cause of the film's "brittle artificiality." So strong was the mystique surrounding Toland that his "pan-focus" lens work was given credit for shots that were not made as he had claimed. During the late 1930s, the RKO Special Effects Unit, under Vernon Walker, had become famous for its realistic matte and optical printer work.[36] In 1941, no writers acknowledged that many of *Citizen Kane*'s deep-focus effects had been created by Walker's unit. Several of the Xanadu shots, ceilings included, were mattes. The shot of Kane firing Jed Leland was done in back-projection. In 1943, Linwood Dunn, supervisor of RKO's optical printer work, claimed: "The picture was about 50% optically duped, some reels consisting of 80% to 90% of optically-printed footage. Many normal-looking scenes were optical composites of units photographed separately...."[37] (Again, William Cameron Menzies had anticipated this practice, using back-projection and mattework for depth effects in *Our Town*.) Even shots not optically treated were not necessarily strict "pan-focus." Dunn points out that Susan's suicide scene, for example, was a multiple exposure, the foreground planes of the shot being exposed separately and the focus being changed for each plane.[38] At the time, Toland did not admit that many deep-focus shots were not done in the camera. Indeed, many of the illustrations accompanying his 1941 articles and interviews are captioned as examples of pan-focus when they are actually optically printed images. In his later films, Toland had no recourse to such optical work, which explains why their depth of field is not so extreme. *Kane*'s use of special effects gave it a cartoonish look which was not greatly imitated. That Arthur Miller, not Toland, won the Academy Award for black-and-white cinematography in 1941 and that *Citizen Kane* looks not quite like any later Hollywood film suggest that Toland's extreme style had to be modified to fit classical norms.

Deep-Focus Cinematography in the 1940s and 1950s

If *Kane* was more controversial than copied, where lies Toland's significance? Even while criticizing Toland, Clarke claimed that deep focus gave the cinematographer a new tool, "a better way of meeting the requirements of any story-situation. Let us hope that if the pendulum of cinematographic style swings back again toward increased softness, we will not forget this technique."[39] Toland set a new standard for technical prowess: after him, a skilled cinematographer had to know how to use coated lenses, fast film, floor-level lights, and great depth of field. Moreover, although extreme deep focus had been attempted before, the publicity attending Toland made deep focus an active issue for the first time. Cinematographers were forced to face exactly how deep focus would be used, as Clarke put it, in particular story situations.

One of those situations was defined, following Toland, as "realism." In the 1940s a realist aesthetic somewhat modified classical practice. This was conceived as partly an "objective" verisimilitude, especially of setting and lighting. Filming on location was initially encouraged by wartime economy measures in production, and it was facilitated by the fact that military demand had resulted in the production of more portable and versatile equipment.[40]

Once the war ended, manufacturers created equipment and film stocks that helped location filming; 35mm camera design was least changed. A very few filmmakers did use Eyemos, Arriflexes, or Eclair Camerettes, but lightweight cameras were rarely used in Hollywood before the 1960s. Sometimes a cinematographer might use a combat camera, such as the Cunningham, for "realistic action scenes." More development took place in other fields. Several companies began to supply powerful portable photoflood units. After William Daniels used photofloods extensively on *Naked City* (1948), filmmakers began to take these lamps to location because they could run off house current. Photoflood lighting was also feasible because of increased film speed.[41] In 1947, Paramount and Du Pont began to use latensification to raise film speed quite considerably. (Latensification is a process which converts underexposed film to acceptable printing quality by re-exposing the film to a weak light.) By 1950 latensification was standard practice in several studios.[42]

> It is now possible to shoot location scenes in office buildings, narrow halls, alleys, etc., using only a few photofloods for illumination and, by giving the negative the latensification treatment, insure an acceptable print. Moreover, it is possible to achieve print quality in such footage that makes it no problem at all to edit it with scenes shot with normal studio lighting.

Soon after, in 1954, Eastman dramatically increased black-and-white film speed by introducing Tri-X (ASA 250 daylight, 200 tungsten). At the end of the decade, Eastman produced a sharper black-and-white stock and a color film suited for location shooting.[43]

Location shooting, taken in conjunction with low-key ("mood") lighting, helped define one distinct postwar cinematographic practice. This practice did not fundamentally violate classical principles of causal and generic motivation. We also see that this conception of "realism" also owed something to a standardization of deep-focus shooting. Certain traits became common to many "realistic" films of the 1940s and 1950s. First, there was the increased use of short focal-length lenses. The wide-angle lenses necessary for achieving deep focus were handy for cinematographers working in close quarters on location: by exaggerating distances, the short focal-length lens made actual locations, such as small rooms, seem more spacious. Moreover, in some shooting situations, full and sharply focused shots of several figures would be impossible without a lens which could expand the angle of view.

The 35mm and 30mm lenses became more common. Frank Planer, in describing his work on *Criss Cross* (1948), remarked: "To give the picture added realism through photography, we filmed every scene with the 30mm lens to carry a wire-sharp depth of focus throughout the frame."[44] Whereas the 50mm lens was considered standard until the war, by 1950, the 35mm had become the norm; by 1959, cinematographers were said to have almost completely discarded the 50mm lens.[45] Another innovation of the late 1940s, the Garutso modified lens, was designed to increase depth of field without increasing the amount of light. With the Garutso, even location filming could use fairly wide apertures and still get good depth of field.[46] Thus many films of the period retained great depth of playing space and depth of focus on location. Several films shot on location used deep-focus extensively (*Act of Violence* [1948], *Lady from Shanghai* [1948], *Johnny Belinda* [1948], *A Double Life* [1948], *Asphalt Jungle* [1950], and *Viva Zapata!* [1952]).

Furthermore, just as Toland had used the faster Eastman stocks with more light, so some cinematographers took advantage of faster films and latensification to increase depth of field. Tri-X, initially designed for television filming, could be used on location to achieve depth of field, as in *Blackboard Jungle* and *Black Tuesday* (both 1955). Similarly, latensification was praised for enabling the cinematographer to stop down for greater depth. Joe MacDonald reported that latensification enabled him

David Bordwell

Figure 34. (above left). Citizen Kane *(1941).*
Figure 35. (above right). T-Men *(1948).*
Figure 36. (centre left). Gun Crazy *(1949).*
Figure 37. (centre right). The Maltese Falcon *(1941).*
Figures 38–39. (below). Kings Row *(1941).*

to film some shots for *Viva Zapata!* (1952) at an aperture of f-22. Comparable results had already been obtained in *Sunset Boulevard* and *Asphalt Jungle* (both 1950).[47]

In some ways, then, Clarke's prophecy was fulfilled. Deep focus gave the cinematographer "a better way of meeting the requirements of any story-situation." Deep focus became one paradigmatic alternative (see figures 35 and 36). Yet it was not a drastically new one. Cinematographers continued to use diffusion filters and three-point lighting, and they sought innovations like the Garutso lens (which yielded a great depth of field without the hard, contrasty effects of stopping down the lens). Just as Hollywood had quickly lauded, then revised, the extreme low-key "Lasky lighting" in *The Cheat* (1915), so cinematographers toned down Toland's idiosyncratic style. Even in non-location films, deep focus and deep space were assimilated to existing norms of genre and decoupage. A horror film like *Hangover Square* (1945) could use bizarre low angles and depth to signify a threatening atmosphere. Other films absorbed deep focus into normal shooting and cutting patterns. If the shot was not a static long take (as in *Kane*), an occasional deep-focus composition could effectively establish or reestablish a locale (figure 37). If the deep shot was not exaggeratedly frontal, it could create a crisp over-the-shoulder reverse angle (figures 38 and 39). Toland himself used his particular brand of deep focus in such conventional ways for the comedy *Ball of Fire* (December 1941), which—although not entirely free of the rigid poses of *Kane*—does avoid the long take and fits the deep shots into orthodox shot/reverse-shot combinations or into grotesque comic juxtapositions (figure 40).

While many filmmakers of the 1940s inserted the deep-focus composition into a classical decoupage, some directors explored another possibility. For Wyler, as Bazin pointed out, the shot in depth constituted an equivalent of a normally edited breakdown of the scene. Action and reaction, cause and effect, are now shown within the same shot. But frontality, evenly spaced figures, and glances all function to guide the spectator's perception of the image. The pragmatic Wyler justified his practice as wholly traditional, creating "smooth continuity, an almost effortless flow of the scene."[48] Thus in *The Little Foxes*, when Zan glimpses her boyfriend eating with another woman, Wyler refrains from cutting in to him; but since Zan turns her back to us, our attention is driven to the background (figure 41). Other filmmakers followed the same principle, although with more open compositions; in figure 42, from *Manhandled* (1949), the detective notices the water cooler in the nearest plane, and his glance cues us to look at it. In both examples, the single shot does duty for a series of eyeline-matched close-ups. Thus filmmakers either inserted deep-focus shots into a traditional sequence or implanted the classical editing principles within the deep-focus shots themselves. Either way, the classical paradigm remained in place. Holly-

Figure 40. *(above left)*. Ball of Fire *(1941)*.
Figure 41. *(above right)*. The Little Foxes *(1941)*.
Figure 42. *(below left)*. Manhandled *(1949)*.
Figure 43. *(below right)*. The Best Years of Our Lives *(1946)*.

wood deep-focus cinematography created only what Leonard Meyer calls trended change.

Toland's own career after 1942 is a measure of the assimilation of deep focus to classical norms. After returning from the Navy, he shot *The Best Years of Our Lives* (1946) for Wyler and Goldwyn. The film has several deep-focus shots, but now Toland almost never jams many faces into the frame and never makes the foreground plane close and frontal. Compare figure 43, of Fred and Peggy in the drugstore and the manager in the distance, with the famous shot in Mrs. Kane's boarding house; or compare the intimate space of the parlor in figure 44 with the depth of the stairwell in figure 45, from *The Little Foxes*. Toland's postwar compositions are relatively spacious and open, with more recourse to reframing, and none are allowed to take on the rigidity of *Kane's* long-take tableaux. The most famous example of the new flexibility in Toland's compositions is the scene in Butch's tavern, when Al looks from

Deep-Focus Cinematography

Figure 44. (above left). The Best Years of Our Lives *(1946).*
Figure 45. (above right). The Little Foxes *(1941).*
Figures 46–47. (below). The Best Years of Our Lives *(1946).*

Homer playing the piano in the foreground to the phone booth in the
distance, where Fred is calling Peggy (figure 46). In *Kane*, our attention
would be drawn to the booth by decor, lighting, and sharply angled
perspective. Here, Wyler cuts in closer (figure 47). The scene is analyzed
for us.

Toland's professional practices changed as well. Wyler recalled
that in the postwar films Toland had recourse to a sliding diffusion screen
"to keep the sharp focus of realism, without being harsh or unflattering
to the women he photographed."[49] In interviews, Toland justified his
quest for deep focus as always subservient to the film's story. But he did
continue his experiments. Toland was associated with his trademark—
wire-sharp depth in cinematography—until his death in 1948 and thereafter. For *Roseanna McCoy* (1949), he was said to have perfected an
"ultimate-focus" lens that could stop down to f-64. He was reported to
carry in his wallet a strip of film bearing a shot with a focal depth of three
inches to infinity; in the foreground was a face.[50]

Toland, then, did not overthrow the classical style. The film that posed the most problems, *Citizen Kane,* was not typical, partly because of its reliance upon optical work, partly because of its lighting, compositions, and long takes. Nonetheless, Toland's innovations not only made his reputation; they also influenced his peers. After 1942, in good part through the activities of the ASC, Hollywood cinematography adopted a less picturesque deep-focus style better suited to the demands of classical narrative and decoupage. Long takes would be used, but not in conjunction with static deep-focus compositions. The ability to execute a shot in depth became one more mark of the expert cinematographer, but the wary professional chose not to call attention to deep focus by making it a personal trademark.

NOTES

1. Joseph Dubray, "Large Aperture Lenses in Cinematography." *Transactions of the Society of Motion Picture Engineers* 12:33 (1928), 206.

2. Patrick Ogle, "Technological and Aesthetic Influences upon the Development of Deep Focus Cinematography in the United States," *Screen Reader* 1, ed. John Ellis (London: British Film Institute, 1977), pp. 87–88. See also Peter Mole, "Will There Always Be a Need for Carbon Arcs?" *American Cinematographer* 31:2 (February 1951), 72–73; Charles W. Handley, "History of Motion Picture Studio Lighting," *A Technological History of Motion Pictures and Television,* ed. Raymond Fielding (Berkeley and Los Angeles: University of California Press, 1967), p. 122.

3. Michael Leshing, "Time and Temperature Control," *International Photographer* 16:4 (May 1944). 22; Mary Eunice McCarthy, *Hands of Hollywood* (Hollywood, Calif.: Photoplay Research Bureau, 1929), p. 60; "Projection Faults Denounced," *Academy of Motion Picture Arts and Sciences Bulletin* 13 (11 August 1928), 4; Frank Woods, "The Sound Motion Picture Situation in Hollywood," *Transactions of the Society of Motion Picture Engineers* 12:35 (1928), 626; Carl F. Gregory, "Limitations of Modern Lenses," *Cinematography* 1:2 (May 1930), 9, 29; James Wong Howe, "Lighting," *Cinematographic Annual* 2 (1931), 50–51; J. J. Finn, "The Indictment against 'Soft Lighting,'" *International Projectionist* 1:3 (December 1931), 20.

4. "Bring Them Back for More," *Motion Picture Projection* 2:9 (June 1929), 5.

5. William Stull, "Solving the 'Ice-Box' Problem,'" *American Cinematographer* 10:6 (September 1929), 7. See also Lewis W. Physioc, "Exposure Control Serious Problem," *International Photographer* 2:4 (May 1931), 6–8; Lewis W. Physioc, "Problems of the Cameraman," *Journal of the Society of Motion Picture Engineers* 17:3 (September 1931), 408–9.

6. George H. Scheibe, "Filters for Special Effects," *American Cinematographer* 14:12 (April 1934), 486; Lewis W. Physioc, "Physioc Writes of Camera Problems," *International Photographer* 3:8 (September 1931), 5–6; John Arnold, "Shooting the Movies," in *We Make the Movies,* ed. Nancy Naumburg (New York: Norton, 1937), p. 154; Lewis W. Physioc, "More about Lighting," *International Photographer* 8:7 (August 1936), 5; George Scheibe, "Soft Focus," *International Photographer* 11:3 (April 1939), 6; Charles B. Lang Jr., "The Purpose and Practice of Diffusion," *American Cinematographer* 14:5 (September 1933), 171, 193–94; John Arnold, "Cinematography—Professional," *The Com-*

plete Photographer, vol. 2, ed. Willard D. Morgan (New York: National Education Alliance, 1943), p. 765. Cf. Vladimir Nilsen, *The Cinema as a Graphic Art,* trans. Stephen Garry (New York: Hill & Wang, 1959), pp. 151, 177.

7. Emery Huse and Gordon A. Chambers, "Eastman Supersensitive Panchromatic Type Two Motion Picture Film," *Cinematographic Annual* 2 (1931), 107.

8. Oliver Marsh, "Super-Sensitive Film in Production," *American Cinematographer* 12:1 (May 1931), 11; Hal Hall, "Improvements in Motion Picture Film," *Cinematographic Annual* 2 (1931), 93–102; Charles G. Clarke, "Fast Improvements of Fast Film," *American Cinematographer* 12:3 (July 1931), 10, 40; V. B. Sease, "Du Pont's New Panchromatic Film," *American Cinematographer* 13:5 (September 1932), 17, 25; P. Arnold, "A Motion Picture Negative of Wider Usefulness," *Journal of the Society of Motion Picture Engineers* 23:3 (September 1934), 160–66; "Symposium of New Motion Picture Apparatus," *Journal of the Society of Motion Picture Engineers* 17:3 (September 1931), 387; James Barker, "Make-up for Fast Film," *American Cinematographer* 12:7 (November 1931), 11, 24.

9. Clyde DeVinna, "New Angles on Fast Film," *American Cinematographer* 12:2 (June 1931), 19, 22; Fred Westerberg, "New Negative to Improve Quality," *International Photographer* 2:4 (May 1931), 29.

10. "Quality Photography: A Measure of Superior Craftsmanship," *International Projectionist* 2:3 (May 1932), 12. See also, "Report of the Studio Lighting Committee," *Journal of the Society of Motion Picture Engineers* 17:4 (October 1931), 645–55.

11. "ASC Recommends Fast Films," *American Cinematographer* 12:3 (July 1931), 19.

12. For summary accounts of 1930s innovations, see Emery Huse and Gordon A. Chambers, "New Eastman Emulsions," *International Photographer* 10:11 (December 1938), 23–27; "Pan and Sound Put Inkies on Top," *International Photographer* 10:3 (April 1938), 43–48; Joseph Valentine, "Make-up and Set Painting Aid New Film," *American Cinematographer* 20:2 (February 1939), 54–56, 85; "Lighting the New Fast Films," *American Cinematographer* 18:12 (December 1937), 494; "Report of the Studio Lighting Committee," *Journal of the Society of Motion Picture Engineers* 33:1 (July 1939), 97–100.

13. L. W. O'Donnell, quoted in "Lighting the New Fast Films," pp. 69–70.

14. "Report of the Studio Lighting Committee," *Journal of the Society of Motion Picture Engineers* 30:3 (March 1938), 294–98; G. Gaudio, "A New Viewpoint on the Lighting of Motion Pictures," *Journal of the Society of Motion Picture Engineers* 29:2 (August 1937), 157–68.

15. Hal Mohr, "A Lens Mount for Universal Focus Effects," *American Cinematographer,* 17:9 (September 1936), 371.

16. John Castle, "Bert Glennon Introducing New Method of Interior Photography," *American Cinematographer* 20:2 (February 1939), 82.

17. James Wong Howe, "Upsetting Traditions with *Viva Villa!*" *American Cinematographer* 15:2 (June 1934), 64, 71–72; "Riddle Me This," *American Cinematographer* 13:6 (October 1932), 16; Castle, "Bert Glennon," p. 83; Gaudio, "New Viewpoint," pp. 157–68; "Lighting *Tobacco Road,*" *International Photographer* 13:1 (February 1941), 3, 7.

18. James Wong Howe, in *Hollywood Cameramen,* ed. Charles Higham (London: Thames & Hudson, 1970), p. 88. See also, "The Layout for *Bulldog Drummond,*" *Creative Art* (October 1929), 729–34, and William Cameron Menzies, "Pictorial Beauty in the Photoplay," in *Introduction to the Photoplay,* ed. John C. Tibbetts (Shawnee Mission, Kans.: National Film Society, 1977), p. 166.

19. Ogle, "Technological and Aesthetic Influences," pp. 92–93.

20. John Arnold, "Art in Cinematography," *American Cinematographer* 12:12 (April 1932), 25.

21. Quoted in Leonard Maltin, *Behind the Camera: The Cinematographer's Art* (New York: New American Library, 1971), p. 69.

David Bordwell

22. Herb A. Lightman, "Documentary Style," *American Cinematographer* 30:5 (May 1949), 176.

23. Harry Burdick, "Intense Preparation Underlies Toland's Achievements," *American Cinematographer* 16:6 (June 1935), 240, 247; Gregg Toland, "Using Arcs for Lighting Monochrome," *American Cinematographer* 22:12 (December 1941), 559; "Adjustment for Dolly Head," *American Cinematographer* 16:6 (June 1935), 246; Gregg Toland, "Practical Gadgets Expedite Camera Work," *American Cinematographer* 20:5 (May 1939), 215–18; "Toland with Twentieth's *Kidnapped* Awarded Camera Honors for July," *American Cinematographer* 19:7 (July 1938), 274; "Toland's *Dead End* Selected in Caucus One of Three Best," *American Cinematographer* 19:4 (April 1938), 141–42; "Ace Cinematographer Gregg Toland Passes," *Los Angeles Times* (29 September 1948), n.p.

24. Walter Blanchard, "Aces of the Camera XIII: Gregg Toland," *American Cinematographer* 23:1 (January 1942), 15.

25. Gregg Toland, "Realism for *Citizen Kane*," *American Cinematographer* 22:2 (February 1941), 54, 80.

26. Ibid., Gregg Toland, "I Broke the Rules in *Citizen Kane*," *Popular Photography* 8:6 (June 1941), 55, 90–91.

27. Toland, "Realism," p. 55.

28. There persists among American cinematographers the belief that Toland also used the "Waterhouse Stop" method to achieve small apertures. Joseph Walker explained:

> With the advent of sound we all had difficulty matching the exposure with different lenses, especially very short focus lenses at small apertures. Some of the diaphragms were so sloppy there could be a half-stop different at f:11, depending on whether you stopped the lens down to f:11 or opened it up to f:11. My own solution was to own four complete sets of lenses and try to match the calibrations.
>
> Gregg Toland used very short focus lenses on *Citizen Kane* and used them at small apertures. His solution, and a very practical one, was to use the "Waterhouse Stop" system, whereby a small piece of metal with an accurately drilled hole in it is inserted in a slot in the lens barrel, in place of the conventional diaphragm. A different metal strip for every stop is needed but this way the f-stop would match on all lenses that were prepared in this way.
>
> I think these lenses were shown at a meeting at the ASC.

(Letter from Joe Walker to Charles G. Clarke, 23 May 1972. In ASC files.) In his articles, Toland makes no mention of using the Waterhouse stop method, but it is possible that he did.

29. Toland, "Realism," pp. 54–55.

30. Joseph V. Mascelli, "What's Happened to Photographic Style?" *International Photographer* 30:1 (January 1958), 6.

31. Gregg Toland, "The Motion Picture Cameraman," *Theatre Arts* 25:9 (September 1941), 647–54; "Orson Welles: Once a Child Prodigy, He Has Never Quite Grown Up," *Life* 10:21 (26 May 1941), 108–16; John Mescall, "Pan-Focus for Your Home Movies," *American Cinematographer* 22:12 (December 1941), 576, 593; Blanchard, "Aces," 15, 36. See also Hal McAlpin, "Let's Shoot 'Em Sharp," *International Photographer* 15:12 (January 1943), 7–9.

32. Mescall, "Pan-Focus," p. 576; "Through the Editor's Finder," *American Cinematographer* 22:9 (September 1941), 424; "'Increased Range' System Promises to Revolutionize Photography," *International Projectionist* 16:6 (June 1941), 12; "Report of the Studio Lighting Committee," *Journal of the Society of Motion Picture Engineers* 38:3 (March 1942), 282.

33. Charles G. Clarke, "How Desirable is Extreme Focal Depth?" *American Cinematographer* 23:1 (January 1942), 14.

34. "Photography of the Month," *American Cinematographer* 23:2 (February 1942), 66.

35. "Photography of the Month: *The Little Foxes*," *American Cinematographer* 22:9 (September 1941), 425.

36. Linwood Dunn, "Optical Printer Handy Andy," *International Photographer* 10:5 (June 1938), 14–16; "Special Effects at RKO," *International Photographer* 12:11 (December 1940), 4: "First Rear Projection Specifications," *International Photographer* 11:2 (March 1939), 22.

37. Quoted in Walter Blanchard, "Unseen Camera Aces II: Linwood Dunn, ASC," *American Cinematographer* 24:7 (July 1943), 268.

38. Interview with Linwood Dunn, conducted by Kristin Thompson and David Bordwell, July 1980, Hollywood, California. See also Donald Chase, *Filmmaking: The Collaborative Art* (Boston: Little, Brown, 1975), pp. 293–97; Peter Bogdanovich, "The Kane Mutiny," *Esquire* 77:4 (October 1972), 100–101.

39. Clarke, "How Desirable," p. 36.

40. Mitchell, for instance, developed a lightweight, single-system 35mm camera for combat photography, while Art Reeves designed a field camera that used reflex viewing. RCA paralleled the advances in photography with portable sound-recording equipment. Military demand also elevated 16mm to the status of a semi-professional gauge. Hollywood studios had used 16mm occasionally for wardrobe, location, and acting tests before the war, but after 1942, the usage increased, partly because 16mm stock was not rationed as strictly as 35mm. James Wong Howe enthusiastically predicted that 16mm would soon become the production standard because it was cheaper and the equipment was more flexible. See E. J. Tiffany, "Mitchell 35mm Single System Sound Camera," *American Cinematographer* 24:9 (September 1943), 330–43; Art Reeves, "The Art Reeves Reflex Motion Picture Camera," *Journal of the Society of Motion Picture Engineers* 44:6 (June 1945), 436–42; Ainslie R. Davis, "New Light Weight Recording Equipment Serves in the War Effort," *Journal of the Society of Motion Picture Engineers* 42:6 (June 1944), 327–48; William Stull, "16mm Gains in Studio Use," *American Cinematographer* 13:10 (October 1942), 442; Ezra Goodman, "Post-war Motion Pictures," *American Cinematographer* 26:5 (May 1945), 160.

41. Ralph Lawton, *"Champion,"* *American Cinematographer* 30:6 (June 1949), 196, 218; Frederick Foster, "Economy Lighting with Photofloods," *American Cinematographer* 31:1 (January 1950), 10–11, 20.

42. Phil Tannura, "The Practical Use of Latensification," *American Cinematographer* 31:2 (February 1951), 54, 68–70. See also Leigh Allen, "New Speed for Films," *American Cinematographer* 30:12 (December 1949), 440, 456.

43. Emery Huse, "Tri-X—New Eastman High-Speed Negative Motion Picture Film," *American Cinematographer*, 35:7 (July 1954), 335, 364; Emery Huse, "Eastman Plus-X Panchromatic Negative Film (Type B)," *American Cinematographer* 37:9 (September 1956), 542, 546; Frederick Foster, "A Faster Color Negative," *American Cinematographer* 40:6 (June 1959), 364–65, 368, 370.

44. Jack Taylor, "Dynamic Realism," *International Photographer* 20:9 (September 1948), 6–7.

45. Charles L. Anderson, "Filming with Perspective Control," *American Cinematographer* 31:10 (September 1950), 313; "Choosing and Using Lenses," *American Cinematographer* 40:5 (May 1959), 296.

46. R. M. Newbold, "The Garuzo Lens in Motion Picture Photography," *American Cinematographer* 31:7 (September 1949), 320; Leigh Allen, "Deep Focus and Longer Takes," *American Cinematographer* 31:7 (July 1950), 234–35, 257; Hal Mohr, "Why I Used the Garutso Lens in Filming *The Four Poster*," *American Cinematographer* 33:11 (November 1952), 482, 500–501.

47. Stanley Cortez, "Tri-X in Feature Film Production," *American Cinematographer* 35:1 (January 1955), 33, 44–45; Herb Lightman, "The Filming of *Viva Zapata!*" *American Cinematographer* 33:4 (April 1952), 155; Herb Lightman, "Old Master, New Tricks," *American Cinematographer* 31:9 (September 1950), 318; Herb Lightman, "Realism with a Master's Touch," *American Cinematographer* 31:8 (August 1950), 286–88.

48. William Wyler, "No Magic Wand," *Screen Writer* 2:9 (February 1947), 10.

49. "A Letter from William Wyler," *Sequence* 8 (Summer 1949), 68.

50. Lester Koenig, "Gregg Toland, Film-Maker," *Screen Writer* 3:7 (December 1947), 30–31; "Gregg Toland, One of Top Lensers, Dies at 44," *Daily Variety* (29 September 1948), 6; "Letter from Wyler," 68-69.

Product Conventions

Robert C. Allen

William Fox Presents *Sunrise*

To the film historian few films are more conspicuously extraordinary than *Sunrise*. Its synchronous musical and effects track makes it a curious technological hybrid. It incorporates the efforts of, respectively, the most famous writer, director, and designer of the German "Golden Age," yet was made in Hollywood. Produced within the studio system, the *Sunrise* project was nevertheless given attention and freedom which, if not unique, were certainly highly unusual. Indeed, it is tempting to consider *Sunrise* that most fortunate of accidents, one of the few of many Hollywood extravagances which, more through happenstance than foresight, turned out to be a work of lasting cinematic art. But one sells short the historical importance of *Sunrise* if one attributes the fact of the film's production to the inexplicable whims of a movie mogul or simply to chance. As J. Douglas Gomery points out in his study of the innovation of sound in the American film industry, there was much more business planning and much less caprice at the highest levels of Hollywood during its heyday than we are generally led to believe.

It is the thesis of this paper that *Sunrise* can be viewed as an integral part of one of the most carefully orchestrated and ambitious bids for power and prestige in the history of the American cinema, and that in large measure *Sunrise*'s historical significance is to be found in its relation to other Fox films that were equally part of William Fox's truly grandiose scheme to control the movie industry.

From *Quarterly Review of Film Studies* 2:2 (August 1977), 327–38. Reprinted with permission of the author and Harwood Academic Publishers on behalf of Redgrave Publishing Co.

Production Planning

Of central importance to a historical understanding of any film made within the Hollywood studio system is a basic knowledge of studio production strategies. Hollywood executives, like television programmers of today, rarely thought in terms of a single work; each film was one component of a total schedule, each production a fraction of a yearly budget.

The Hollywood studio of the late 1920s still organized its year around the old theatrical season, beginning in September and lasting through the spring. Production planning began in the winter, with the schedule for the coming season usually finalized by March or April. The production executive staff would begin with a production budget (based on the success of the previous year and a forecast of market conditions), breaking it down into allocations for productions or groups of productions according to properties on hand, stars, and genres.[1]

The Universal production schedule for 1927–28, for example, divided a $15,000,000 production budget among sixty-six feature films, five serials, assorted shorts, and weekly newsreels, with one-third of the amount going to the nonfeature categories. The breakdown within the feature program was divided among eleven "specials," thirty-three "features," and twenty-two "thrill dramas." The specials were the prestige pictures of Universal. The particular designation of this category changed from studio to studio (Paramount, for example, called them "New World Specials"), but the category remained the same for all the major studios. Specials (using the term to signify the most expensive productions of any studio) were often based on properties with a high public-recognition factor. Among the Universal specials for 1927–28 were five popular novels and two current plays. These films also featured the studio's biggest stars and highest paid directors and were the most expensive productions in the schedule. Next came the features which were the backbone of a studio's release schedule, utilizing contract players and directors and relying upon less expensive properties: short fiction from popular magazines and original stories contributed by the studio writing staff. The thrill dramas were the cheapest category to produce and often included the bulk of the studio's western films—in the case of Universal, a genre which composed 45 percent of the studio's total output.[2]

Following initial specification of property, star, and budget, a film would be turned over to a production executive, the actual supervisor of the project. Naturally, the studio production manager or chief production executive reserved the most important productions for himself, with those at the other end of the hierarchy being given the task of cranking out seven Hoot Gibson westerns. While the major Hollywood studios (Paramount, MGM, Fox, Universal, Warner Brothers, Producer's Distributing Organization, First National) were each producing thirty-five to seventy films annually at this time, it was the top one-fifth of their feature output—the specials—which received a lion's share of the budget allocation, attention, and advertising.

The most special of the specials would be released first as road-shows: long-term engagements at a few key theatres in large cities at top prices ($1 to $2). The Cathay Circle Theatre in Los Angeles, for example, ran only four pictures during 1927: *What Price Glory, Seventh Heaven, The Loves of Carmen,* and *Sunrise.* In New York, at the Astor Theatre, *The Big Parade* ran from January 1 to September 17.[3] Other specials, features, and thrill dramas would open in first-run theatres in large cities and then move down through the exhibition system into smaller cities and towns and subsequent runs.

It is important to keep this production hierarchy in mind in considering the place of *Sunrise* in Fox's plans, for it was the special category, the most prestigious of productions, which Fox most wanted to develop—the category into which *Sunrise* certainly falls.

Fox's Position in Hollywood

In one sense William Fox is the archetypal Hollywood success: the poor son of Jewish immigrants who, through hard work and shrewd business practices, clawed his way to the top of the motion picture industry, amassing a huge personal fortune in the process. Fox's struggle is further characterized by his almost superhuman tenacity in the face of seemingly insuperable obstacles. Fox's first venture into show business came around 1905, when he was tricked into investing some $1,600, which he had saved from years of menial labor, in what he was led to believe was a prospering nickelodeon in Brooklyn but which was actually a financial disaster. Despite this most inauspicious beginning, Fox was able to build a chain of twelve vaudeville/film theatres by 1910 and initiate his own film distribution concern. It was in January of that year that the Motion Picture Patents Company attempted to extend the near monopoly control that it had over film production to include distribution as well. Fox was the only distributor to hold out against the enormous power of the industry trust, resisting all attempts to buy and coerce him out of business. For several years he survived only through the action of a court order that forced the Motion Picture Patents Company to supply his theatres with film until his legal action against them was settled. Fox and the other independents eventually won out legally and economically against the trust, and in 1913 he added film production to his distribution and exhibition activities with the formation of Box Office Attractions.[4]

The early 1920s were, in the words of a 1930 *Fortune* article, "a time of gradual but unbroken progress which had brought Mr. Fox to a prominent, but by no means dominating position." Fox films, the article goes on to say, were "not considered of major importance," but were popular and profitable.[5] This characterization is echoed by Glendon Allvine. Fox's chief publicist in the late 1920s. The Fox output, he says, was "a steady flow of unpretentious, sentimental and folksy pictures . . . without the reaching for art and biography that occasionally varied the menu at Paramount and Warner Brothers."[6]

By 1925 Fox occupied, along with First National and Warner Bros., a middle echelon within the film industry in terms of both economic power and product prestige. In both categories Hollywood was presided over by Paramount and MGM. These were the largest and most fully vertically integrated film companies, controlling not only the production and distribution of their products but exhibition as well through the hundreds of theatres in their Publix and Loew's chains. Fox, like Warner Bros. and Universal, owned few theatres in 1925. In terms of working capital, Fox was a distant third behind MGM and Paramount— his rivals had resources of $38,000,000 and $20,000,000, respectively, while Fox had $13,000,000.[7]

Product prestige can be thought of as the extent to which the films of a studio are perceived to be of "quality" by contemporary molders of public opinion about films—commentators and critics in the trade and the general press. In determining the Fox prestige factor I have examined the annual critical poll taken by the *Film Daily Yearbook* of trade paper and newspaper film critics, a total in 1925 of 104 "best films" lists. I also consulted *Photoplay*, the most influential of the fan magazines in the late 1920s, for its monthly designation of the six best films released. In 1925, the first year of *Film Daily*'s poll, of 112 films mentioned by 104 critics, only seven were Fox productions, the highest rated being John Ford's *The Iron Horse*, which was the fourteenth most often mentioned film. It was the only Fox film to be listed by more than two critics.[8] Similarly, of the seventy-two pictures singled out by *Photoplay* in 1925, only two were Fox efforts. In both lists the films of Paramount and MGM predominate.

Parenthetically, it might be noted that there is a negative correlation between heavy emphasis on thrill drama productions and studio prestige. Universal, few of whose films were praised by critics in either source, devoted 44 percent of its production schedule to Westerns alone, while MGM's Westerns output made up only 10 percent of its releases. Fox, once again, fits neatly in the middle, with 27 percent of its release schedule composed of Westerns (mostly Tom Mix and Buck Jones).

Also, Paramount and MGM were the first of the Hollywood studios to import foreign directors and producers, particularly from Germany. In 1926, for example, MGM had under contract Victor Seastrom, Benjamin Christensen, Ludwig Berger, Marcel Del Sano, and Dmitri Buchowetzi. Paramount had hired Mauritz Stiller, German producer Erich Pommer, and Europe's hottest directorial property, E. A. Dupont, whose *Variety* was a critical and financial success in the United States. Even Universal had Paul Leni. The only foreign flavor in the Fox lineup was the release of a few films directed by Alexander Korda in Germany under contract to Fox. While I am not suggesting a causal relationship between the use of foreign talent and the critical success of a studio's output, a positive correlation does exist. The relative scarcity of Westerns among the productions of Paramount and MGM combined with their importation of "artistic" foreign talent does point to an emphasis on the "special" class of productions—the category, of course, critics would be most likely to focus upon.

The Fox Move: 1925–29

Although the precise date is difficult to determine, we can say that one of the greatest expansion plans in the history of the motion picture industry was launched around June 1925. It was then that Fox Film Co. underwent reorganization, issuing common stock for the first time. In all, $6,600,000 of common stock was sold, giving William Fox the necessary capital to set up the Fox Theatre Corp. with the goal of building thirty first-run theatres of 4,000 to 5,000 seats each in key cities. A total investment of $200,000,000 was projected for theatre acquisition and construction over a four-year period.[9] These theatres would give Fox access to the crucial key markets he had not been able to control in the past and would put him in a more competitive position with Paramount and MGM. The Fox move into exhibition was stepped up in 1926–27 as he began to purchase theatres by the chain. *Moving Picture World* for April 2, 1927, announced the purchase by Fox of the premiere American picture palace, the Roxy. This acquisition on Broadway and the purchase of other Roxy theatres in the New York area was referred to in an editorial as giving Fox "a commanding position in the increasingly competitive warfare, which is the outstanding feature of this period of the film industry's development."[10] In 1927–28 Fox acquired the Poli circuit of twenty major theatres in New England, the Wesco chain of 216 theatres, one-third interest in First National Theatres, and an additional 313 theatres in New York, New Jersey, and Ohio.[11]

In 1925–26 Fox became interested in the possibilities of sound motion pictures. He supported the experiments of his engineer, Theodore Case, bought for $60,000 the rights to the Tri-Ergon sound process, and negotiated with Western Electric for the rights to its Vitaphone process. In 1926 he launched the Fox Movietone News. He lost $3,000,000 for the first five years of its existence, but during this time Fox Movietone moved "so far ahead of the four other newsreels that they never caught up."[13]

At the same time, Fox production facilities were upgraded. In January 1926, Winfield Sheehan, Fox's associate since 1913, arrived in Hollywood to supervise a studio expansion program which would cost $3,000,000 and take one year to complete.[14]

Fox was certainly not alone in expansion during the late 1920s. Warner Bros. acquired the Vitagraph studios and foreign distribution network in 1925, began to buy and build theatres, and invested in the Western Electric sound process. Paramount and MGM also acquired more theatres. But the Fox move was the most dramatic of any studio expansion effort. By the end of 1928 Fox had "risen to a position of prominence among the Big Four of Cinema."[15] His greatest coup was yet to come, however. On March 3, 1929, he bought, at above market price, one-third interest in Loews Inc. (443,000 shares), paying a total of $50,000,000. On the open market he acquired 227,000 additional shares, giving him 53 percent interest in the company. He also purchased control of British Gaumont, valuable for its distribution system and chain of important theatres in the United Kingdom. For a fleeting moment Fox was the most important and powerful film magnate in the world, controlling the production of Fox and MGM studios, Loew's Theatres, Fox's own large chain, one-third interest in First National Theatres (and its production subsidiary), British Gaumont, and assorted other holdings. The stock market crash, demands for margin payments from his bankers, and a November 1927 lawsuit against Fox for restraint of trade shattered Fox's dream. After a decade of near bankruptcy, congressional hearings, and cutthroat financial involvements, Fox wound up at Moyamensing Prison in Pennsylvania, serving a sentence of one year and a day for attempted bribery.[16]

The Fox drive for economic power in the late 1920s was paralleled by attempts to enhance the prestige of Fox productions. The first evidence of a move away from the unpretentious drama and comedy which had characterized Fox output came in the fall of 1925, when it was announced that Fox was arranging with a number of Broadway producers to finance plays with strong movie potential. For years the successful stage play had been "the most coveted of story properties to the motion picture industry." Here was a ready-made story with proven dramatic appeal and with considerable public recognition, the latter due to the advertising given a Broadway play and its usual road tours. But as the demand for successful stage properties increased during the 1920s, so did their price. *Ben Hur*, originally produced in 1899, was sold to the screen in 1921 for $1,000,000. As early as 1919, film companies began to move into theatrical finance. In return for production funds, the film company would receive the screen rights to the play.[17]

In 1925 Fox spent $150,000 in theatrical finance (a straight play could still be produced for under $10,000), a level of Hollywood involvement in Broadway which "alarmed" several observers of the American stage.[18] Fox's scheme to corner the market for film rights to Broadway successes was undone, however, in April 1926. An agreement was made between Broadway producers and playwrights that forbade film producers from securing screen rights before production of the play and required that all rights be granted on a sealed bid system, with no preference being given to the backer of the play. Fox left theatrical production after one season, the economic motivation for his move now gone.[19] But this abortive move did not by any means mark the end of Fox's attempt to bolster his special productions through the acquisition of successful stage vehicles. The January 2, 1926, issue of *Moving Picture World* contained an advertisement which set the tone for the 1926–27 Fox production plans: "For release in the new season, starting September 1926, Fox takes another great step forward through the production of the world's best stage plays and popular novels of high screen value."[20] Among the fifteen

"Fox Giant Specials" for 1926–27 were four David Belasco plays (*The Auctioneer, Return of Peter Grimm, The Grand Army Man*, and *The Music Master*); *The Cradle Snatchers*, a Broadway comedy which ran for 338 performances in 1926; *The Monkey Talks*, a stage success in London and Paris; and *What Price Glory?* the 1924 smash Broadway hit for which Fox paid $100,000.[21] In all, nine of the fifteen Fox prestige pictures for 1926–27 were adaptations of stage plays. Two others were based on novels, and the remaining four were based on short stories or were written by the Fox staff. Thus, by 1926 the strategy for the upgrading of Fox specials had begun to emerge: acquire successes in other media— stage hits, best-selling novels, etc.—rather than relying upon stars (as MGM was doing) or hiring big-name writers.

Concomitant with a new emphasis on the "Giant Specials" was a decline in importance to the Fox lineup of its "Super Westerns." As the following table shows, the portion of the Fox schedule given over to Westerns was reduced by half between 1924 and 1928.

Westerns as Percentage of Annual Output

1924	35%
1925	29%
1926	29%
1927	27%
1928	18%

In 1926 the Fox strategy began paying off. Whereas the previous year's productions had been all but ignored by critics, the 1926–27 specials fared much better, especially the stage adaptations. *What Price Glory? The Music Master, The Monkey Talks, A Holy Terror*, and *The Cradle Snatchers*, all based on Broadway hits, were among *Photoplay's* best films of the month.

The flagship production of the 1926–27 season was *What Price Glory?* the film against which future Fox productions would be measured. Fox paid $100,000 for the rights to film *What Price Glory?* guarding its investment by having Winfield Sheehan supervise its production.[22] While *What Price Glory?* was still under production in the winter of 1926, plans were being made for the next two Fox "Giant Specials": *Seventh Heaven* and *Sunrise*. In the January 2, 1926, issue of *Moving Picture World*, Fox announced that F. W. Murnau had been hired to direct several films in Hollywood for the studio. Fox publicists attempted to depict the relationship between Fox and Murnau as one of patron/artist rather than employer/employee. Murnau had been brought to America to enable him "to put . . . subjective thought on the screen, to open up the mind, the heart, the soul."[23] Fox's decision to hire Murnau clearly indicated that he wanted the Fox Film Company to be not only the most powerful studio in Hollywood, but also the most prestigious. Fox had not merely imported another German director; he had brought to America the man he believed to be "the genius of this age," the director who, in *The Last Laugh*, had made "the greatest motion picture of all time."[24] At a gala banquet honoring "Dr. Murnau" on the eve of his journey from New York to Hollywood in July, William Fox spoke to the assembled diplomats, socialites, and literati of "the growth, by mass and class, of the entertaining power of the screen." The *Moving Picture World* correspondent covering the event remarked of Fox: "It was a proud night for him. He realizes the move on which he is embarking will have a tremendous influence on pictures as an international art."[25]

The financial and artistic freedom Murnau was given in the production of *Sunrise* indicates that Fox wanted him to make "the highly artistic picture." An editorial in *Moving Picture World* describes this genre as follows:

> Often these are made with the advance realization that their making will not be followed by a great financial return. They are made with the hope that they may gross their costs or at least represent but a small loss. They are made to satisfy the comparatively limited number who appreciate the best, and produced in the hope that they will help to give tone to the general product through satisfying the minority demand.[26]

The "highly artistic picture" served several functions for the studios. First, as the editorial points out, it was an appeal to a sophisticated minority audience. Producers were, no doubt, also sensitive to charges (particularly prevalent since the Hollywood moral scandals of 1921–23) that they were pandering to the lowest of human instincts and that the Hollywood product was nothing but pap for the masses. These prestige pictures could be trotted out by the studios as evidence that in addition to providing the populace with entertainment, they were also patrons of the highest cinematic art. There was also value in attracting critical attention to these films—giving the studio publicity which, it was hoped, would rub off on the rest of the schedule.

In May of 1927, as Fox was announcing its 1927–28 lineup, *Seventh Heaven* premiered at the Cathay Circle Theatre in Los Angeles, replacing *What Price Glory?* which had played there since November.

Seventh Heaven followed the same formula as its predecessor. It was based on a successful stage play (704 performances on Broadway), was personally supervised by Winfield Sheehan, and was given an "unusually strong preliminary campaign." In April "Eloise," the French taxi used in the film, was driven to Chicago by a French war hero as an advertising stunt.[27] As with *What Price Glory?* much was made of the high production values of *Seventh Heaven.* A week before its premiere an article in *Moving Pictures World* announced that the film had cost $1.3 million and had taken a year to complete.[28] The next week this same trade paper predicted that *Seventh Heaven* would prove to be a popular as well as a critical success, saying the film "should make a wonderful record for itself" in the big cities *and* should do equally as well in "the lesser houses."[29]

This prophecy was indeed accurate, and with the success of *Seventh Heaven* Fox's bid for prestige began to be taken seriously. The lead article of the Hollywood section of *Moving Picture World* for May 14 notes "One does not have to travel very far in these parts to hear that not only is Fox product completed out here during the past six months many times better than it ever has been, but that Fox artistry and quality are second to no contemporary." And on June 18, in reviewing the progress of the new season's program, *Moving Picture World* says, "Recent Fox product has been surprisingly good."[30]

The situation, then, in the summer of 1927—the eve of *Sunrise*'s debut—is that Fox had attracted considerable notice both among critics and within the movie industry as a result of his effort to bolster his special productions. This attention had been directed at two films, *Seventh Heaven* and *What Price Glory?* Both were high-budget, carefully produced adaptations of successful plays—skillful, though in no way "artsy" vehicles which appealed both to cosmopolitan patrons of big city palaces (and hence to reviewers) and to rural audiences. In the midst of the production and release of these two films, Fox had brought to the United States the director he called the greatest in the world and given him carte blanche for his first American effort. E. Winthrop Sargent of *Moving Picture World* asked in July, "What's going to happen at the Fox offices after the release of *Seventh Heaven?*" After the release of *What Price Glory?* the Fox publicists had said, "Wait til you see *Seventh Heaven.*" Now, Sargent said, the industry waits to see *Sunrise*—a film which, he suggested, would "have to do a powerful lot of running to outstrip *Seventh Heaven.*"[31]

Anticipation began to build in March 1927 when it was announced that *Sunrise* was being titled and edited. On March 5, the

Hollywood columns of *Moving Picture World* noted that "Reports and photographs filtering through from Hollywood indicate that the distinguished German director has created an unusual picture." The article gives the term "unusual" a favorable connotation by adding that John Ford, then a contract director with Fox, had declared *Sunrise* to be the greatest picture ever produced on the basis of the rushes he had seen.[32] But given the pattern of success established by *What Price Glory?* and *Seventh Heaven,* speculation began to mount that *Sunrise* might prove to be too unusual. The prospect troubled William Fox enough to cause him to issue a statement in August, one month before the premiere of *Sunrise,* denying rumors that the film was in any way bizarre or that Murnau had been unnecessarily extravagant in its production. This apologia was necessary, said Fox, "because of the exotic and sometimes freakish character of the majority of foreign films which have been shown in this country." As if to try to squeeze *Sunrise* into the Fox prestige film mold of stage and literary adaptations, Fox reminded his exhibitor-readers in *Moving Picture World* that *Sunrise* was based on Sudermann's "well-known story."[33]

Fox's statement raises the possibility that he was responding to a backlash against German films developing immediately prior to the release of *Sunrise.* In April, E. Winthrop Sargent had chastised critics who seemed to think "nothing is good, unless it be a handful of UFA's." Seven months later James Quirk, the editor of *Photoplay,* derided the "pseudo-intellectuals" who reserved their praise for foreign works while dismissing American films.[34] It is interesting to note in this regard that while Murnau's *The Last Laugh* (released in the United States in 1925) and his *Faust* (1926) were prominent among films on "ten-best" lists, *Tartuffe,* which preceded *Sunrise* by less than one month onto Broadway, is noticeably absent. *Moving Picture World* in its review of *Tartuffe* said UFA had released it in the United States "apparently for the reason that it stars Emil Jannings, for the picture itself neither measures up to the better American production standards, nor is it a type of story that appeals to the average patron in this country."[35]

The bad omen of *Tartuffe,* rumors of *Sunrise's* "unusual" qualities, and, most important, the fact that it failed to follow the formula of *Seventh Heaven* and *What Price Glory?* in combining prestige production values with "appeal to the average patron" made *Sunrise* appear to be more of a failure to Fox than a success. Compared to the great amount of publicity given the reception of *What Price Glory?* and *Seventh Heaven,* the premieres of *Sunrise* passed almost unnoticed in the trade press.

Sargent mentions the Broadway premiere only to say that the audience applauded at the Movietone newsreel of Mussolini. In October, while *The Jazz Singer* was in its second record-breaking week on Broadway, *Seventh Heaven* doing well in its third Broadway run, *Wings* drawing standing-room-only crowds in its tenth week, and *King of Kings* in its twenty-sixth week, *Moving Picture World* reported that "Thus far the Fox talking device [Movietone News] is the drag for *Sunrise,* which is supposed to be a great film, and probably is to some audiences."[36]

    Sunrise and *Seventh Heaven/What Price Glory?* represent alternative routes to the prestige William Fox so dearly sought in the late 1920s: the art film, the daring stylistic tour de force, and the less ambitious though well-produced adaptation of successful theatrical and literary works. The former did not even give Fox the satisfaction of unanimous critical acclaim. The latter combined critical and commercial success. By December 1927 it was clear which path Fox had chosen. A *Moving Picture World* editorial says "From the coast comes word that Fox is going right along turning out products like *What Price Glory?* and *Seventh Heaven.*" The piece describes Fox as "one of the comparatively few far-visioned men in positions such as his."[37] Far visioned, yes; a philanthropist, no.

NOTES

    1. "Paramount/Famous Players Lasky Corporation," *Harvard Business Reports,* 8, 1929, 182–200.
    2. *Moving Picture World,* March 26, 1926, 376.
    3. *The Film Daily 1928 Yearbook,* p. 844.
    4. Glendon Allvine, *The Greatest Fox of Them All* (New York: Lyle Stuart, 1969), pp. 35–45.
    5. "The Case of Mr. Fox," *Fortune* May 1930, 49.
    6. Allvine, *The Greatest Fox,* p. 38.
    7. *The Film Daily 1926 Yearbook.*
    8. *The Film Daily 1926 Yearbook,* pp. 31, 417–25.
    9. *The Film Daily 1927 Yearbook,* p. 741; 1928, p. 810.
    10. *Moving Picture World,* April 2, 1927, 267.
    11. "The Case of Mr. Fox," *Fortune* May 1930, 49.
    12. Allvine, *The Greatest Fox,* p. 12.
    13. Ibid., pp. 105–12.
    14. *Moving Picture World,* June 25, 1927, 589.
    15. "The Case of Mr. Fox," p. 49.
    16. Allvine, *The Greatest Fox,* p. 157.
    17. Robert McLaughlin, *Broadway and Hollywood* (New York: Arno Press, 1974), pp. 52–59.
    18. Ibid., p. 67.
    19. Ibid., p. 80.

20. *Moving Picture World*, January 2, 1926, 5.
21. McLaughlin, *Broadway and Hollywood*, p. 56.
22. *Moving Picture World*, April 3, 1926, 332.
23. *Moving Picture World*, January 2, 1926, 69.
24. Allvine, *The Greatest Fox*, p. 98.
25. *Moving Picture World*, July 17, 1926, 151.
26. *Moving Picture World*, April 23, 1927, 719.
27. *Moving Picture World*, May 7, 1927, 36; April 23, 1927, 734.
28. *Moving Picture World*, May 21, 1927, 192.
29. *Moving Picture World*, May 28, 1927, 289.
30. *Moving Picture World*, May 14, 1927, 92; June 18, 499.
31. *Moving Picture World*, July 23, 1927, 244.
32. *Moving Picture World*, March 5, 1927, 35.
33. *Moving Picture World*, August 6, 1927, 402.
34. *Photoplay*, November 1927, 27.
35. *Moving Picture World*, September 3, 1927, 50.
36. *Moving Picture World*, October 1, 1927; October 22, 503.
37. *Moving Picture World*, December 24, 1927, 7.

Jeffrey Sconce

Narrative Authority and Social Narrativity: The Cinematic Reconstitution of Brontë's *Jane Eyre*

As of 8 May 1942, the pre-production staff of David O. Selznick Productions estimated that Charlotte Brontë's celebrated novel of 1847, *Jane Eyre*, could be brought to the screen for $831,156 (the film version was released in 1944). This budget was itself a version of *Jane Eyre*, the ledger sheets providing an outline of interpretive emphasis for the novel. The single most expensive item on the budget, for example, covered the salaries of the film's two principal stars, demonstrating that most major Hollywood films of the 1930s and 1940s, even prestigious literary adaptations of "classic" novels, were first and foremost vehicles for bankable stars.[1] For the Selznick organization, *Jane Eyre*'s contribution to Joan Fontaine's carefully constructed career was as important as Joan Fontaine's contribution to *Jane Eyre*, if not more so. The second most expensive item on the budget provided for set construction. Stars require credible and involving virtual worlds in which to operate, of course, and with a period piece such as *Jane Eyre*, such success was often a function of money. Before Brontë's *Jane Eyre* reached its final form as a screenplay, then, and long before the story ever appeared before the cameras, the novel as articulated in this budget was already firmly situated within an interpretive approach bound to a specific socio-economic moment in the

From *Wide Angle* 10:1 (1988), 46–61. Reprinted with permission of the author and Johns Hopkins University Press.

American cinema. The financial blueprint for *Jane Eyre* was at once a strategy of interpretation (how to most effectively and economically translate a written text into a visual one) as well as an emblem of the social formation that grounded the production and consumption of Hollywood films from the period (with its attendant emphasis on star and spectacle).

Perhaps the most fascinating entry on the budget, however, was for the novel itself. Within this budget of $831,156, the cash outlay for Brontë's *Jane Eyre*, referred to on the ledger under the heading of "story," was a grand total of 50 dollars.[2] This paltry sum, when weighed against the enormous expense involved in securing stars and scenery, emphasizes a tension at work in many Hollywood literary adaptations from the period, a struggle between page and screen marked by two competing varieties of capital. At 50 dollars, *Jane Eyre* was a bargain in terms of the immense mobilization of economic capital involved in translating the novel into a motion picture, and yet the novel, as a familiar, socially valued story already prominently situated within the audience targeted by the studio, possessed a cultural capital that made the property far more valuable and its adaptation far more problematic. "Prestige" films such as *Jane Eyre* were of value to a studio in that they presented pre-sold commodities, proven stories with high audience interest and an aura of "quality" ripe for exploitation. To successfully realize the cultural capital of a novel as a prestige film, however, required integrating the story within conventional cinematic narrative practice in such a manner that it signified its quality as "literature." In other words, while *Jane Eyre*, as a title in the public domain, cost virtually nothing to acquire, the narrative, as circulated in the public domain, presented a substantial challenge to a standardized system of narrative production obligated to acknowledge and accommodate the work's cultural stature.

In the dynamic between standardization and differentiation, described by Janet Staiger as controlling terms in the economic and artistic intersection of the American commercial cinema,[3] Hollywood literary adaptations represented an attempt to differentiate studio product through an "elite" quality of story material that, for both studio profit and audience comprehensibility, had to be reconciled with the dominant standardizing procedures of cinematic narrative production. A literary adaptation thus involved assigning the economic capital of the studio to convert the cultural capital of the novel back into the economic capital of a successful motion picture. This process of adaptation required more than a simple transcription of the material into a new medium and involved a complex reconciliation of the interrelated demands between fidelity to the material, practices of the medium, and expectations of the audience.

The development of the *Jane Eyre* project between 1940 and 1944 demonstrates the complex negotiation of these economic and cultural concerns. As a motion picture, *Jane Eyre* was to present a "unique" story through a conventionalized, popular medium, integrating the story's contemporary identity within the medium's contemporary structures of narrativity. The final product of this negotiation represented a specific version of the literary work, a text that encapsulated the novel as articulated both by a contemporary audience and by that audience's most familiar mode of cinematic narrative. The process of cinematic adaptation, then, can be described as an intersection of audience expectation, conventional cinematic narrative practice, critically interpretive approaches to the source material, and economic considerations of the production company. The trajectory of development in the *Jane Eyre* project is, therefore, more interesting as an articulation of a particular form of narrative practice than as a "faithful" rearticulation of a specific, literary narrative.

The merit of literary adaptation has long been a topic of discussion in film theory and criticism, and often, this debate has privileged the imagined sovereignty of the literary work over the characteristic demands of cinematic practice. Dudley Andrew has termed this the "tiresome" discussion of fidelity to the source material.[4] According to this perspective, film versions of novels are of value inasmuch as they are "true" to the novel, as if some ideal state existed where the semiotic gulf between word and image could be bridged in an isomorphic replication of the source material. As Andrew comments, "Fidelity of adaptation is conventionally treated in relation to the 'letter' and the 'spirit' of the text, as though adaptation were the rendering of an interpretation of a legal precedent."[5] Cinematic adaptations must always fail in this regard due to the fundamental irreconcilability of the film and the novel as semiotic systems.

Arguments of the aesthetic impoverishment and artistic recklessness of cinematic adaptation, however, labor under the assumption that the literary work itself is a stable, ideal entity embodying a definitive, transhistorical meaning, a "legal precedent" in Andrew's terminology. This conceptualization of an "ideal" text has recently been under attack within the field of literary criticism itself, as evidenced in the work of Jane Tompkins and Jerome McGann.[6] Novels are always unstable in meaning, not only in Bakhtin's sense that they, as products and representations of socially negotiated language, "are overpopulated with the intentions of others,"[7] but also in the sense that even as seemingly coherent, closed works of art, their identities actually change across time through their insertion into a variety of social formations. McGann and others argue persuasively that there is never an original work that circulates a definitive "meaning" in society, only a succession of texts and contexts. A literary work is a history of its textual variants as well as the history of use and thought surrounding these texts as situated in a historical succession of cultural orders. "All art," therefore, "is a social product with various, and changing, social functions to perform."[8] Each time a new text, commentary, or account of a literary work appears, including a film version, it constitutes both a reformation of the history of that work as well as a representation of the work newly formed within a specific, contemporary cultural moment.

With studio adaptations of literary material, the rearticulation of the "work" as a new "text," one consonant with the medium's dominant signifying practices, produced an adaptation that rejected the work's authoritative meaning and replaced it instead with an authoritative mode of narrativity. A transcendental meaning for the work yielded to a conventionalized form of representation in a compromise between fidelity to the material and fidelity to the medium. Cinematic narrative practice, through conventions of story construction mutually developed by the industry's history of production and the audience's history of textual consumption, thus subjected the diffuse identity of a literary work to a shared form of narrativity, harnessing the broad and socially negotiated "meaning" of the work to fuel a narrative event enjoyable to a contemporary audience.

In the case of *Jane Eyre,* all of this was stated, quite succinctly, by David O. Selznick himself in a letter to Helen Jerome, a British playwright who had adapted *Jane Eyre* for the stage and, as a self-proclaimed authority on the work's "meaning," felt qualified as the most logical choice for a screenwriter. In response to her overtures, Selznick wrote:

> I understand perfectly your adoration of the work, but I must ask you to rationally understand that this infatuation is not exclusive with you. There is no patent on a fondness for the words of the Brontës, and neither an affection for their work, nor a study of it, in themselves entitle anyone to claim association with their translation into any medium.[9]

By 1940, the meaning, popularity, and significance of Brontë's almost century old novel could not be traced back and isolated in a single authoritative text or approach, having already been diffused through a variety of identities and uses. Bringing *Jane Eyre* before the cameras in the early 1940s required a reading that captured the novel's importance and identity for a contemporary audience through a narrative form familiar to them, a task perhaps better executed by a Hollywood producer than by a devoted Brontëphile.

The development of the *Jane Eyre* project demonstrates just such a process of reading—one that attempted to balance the demands of a single narrative with a common narrativity. The many drafts of the script represented provisional compromises between Brontë's work and the projected cinematic text, each revision incorporating decisions made concerning the material, the medium, and the audience. When the film finally appeared in American theaters in 1944, it represented the summary moment in a four-year process of adaptation involving the collaborative input of hundreds of people and the resources of two major Hollywood studios.[10] From the project's initiation in Selznick's story department to its actual production on the soundstages of Twentieth Century-Fox, the controlling concern remained how to best encode Brontë's written text in sound and image so that it both signified the "work" for a contemporary audience and entertained as a self-contained motion picture. This project often required attention to more than drafting an accurate script and designing authentic sets and costumes.

In initiating the project, for example, Selznick quickly discovered that the studio had more to contend with in crafting its adaptation than the mere plot mechanics of Brontë's novel. By the summer of 1940, Selznick's research department had located no less than twenty-seven separate adaptations of *Jane Eyre* for the stage and screen. As *Variety* reported in November of 1940, "*Jane Eyre* looks to be the screen's most popular gal. Right now eight producers are standing in line to woo her."[11] In supervising a screenplay for the project, Selznick was naturally quite concerned about fitting his own version within this preexistent sea of Jane Eyres, and worried also as to the possible legal ramifications if the Selznick version should somehow overlap with a previous production. Selznick even considered authorizing a side-by-side structural comparison of these many versions, wondering, "What do we do if there is an inevitable piece of construction that would be necessary to both the play and the picture?"[12] Selznick was well aware that translating the book from the page to the screen might require certain logical choices in narrative construction specific to a visual medium, and he was eager to avoid accusations of plagiarism as well as a potential copyright infringement suit.

In addition to these explicit versions of *Jane Eyre*, the Selznick organization also had to contend with a number of novels and films significantly informed by the *Jane Eyre* story. Daphne du Maurier's *Rebecca* (1940), a subtle reworking of *Jane Eyre* set in a contemporary context, was perhaps the most famous of these. Selznick and Alfred Hitchcock had brought du Maurier's novel to the screen just prior to the *Jane Eyre* project, placing Selznick in the somewhat ironic position of having to differentiate a new adaptation of *Jane Eyre* from his own previous adaptation of another adaptation of *Jane Eyre*. "We are anxious to avoid any resemblance to *Rebecca*," he reminded John Houseman and Robert Stevenson, the picture's original screenwriters.[13] Selznick often repeated this directive in the correspondence surrounding the project, and later audience research indicated that moviegoers were indeed aware of the great similarities between the two stories. The cultural currency of the *Jane Eyre* story in American film of the 1930s and 1940s, while making the project a seemingly sure move commercially, also required adjusting the story both to reestablish its authority as the "original" version and to differentiate it from its previous reworkings.

Another aggravation for Selznick came when a rival studio scheduled a project entitled "Devotion" for production and release at the same time as *Jane Eyre*. "Devotion" was to be the screen biography of the Brontë sisters, and from accounts of the first screenplay, seems to have been modeled primarily on Charlotte Brontë's novel *Villette* (itself a reworking of the *Jane Eyre* model). Selznick realized, however, that the Brontës were known for turning their real lives into fiction and was concerned that "Devotion" would be too similar to *Jane Eyre*. At the very least, he knew "Devotion" would require an account of Charlotte's writing of *Jane Eyre*, as it was her first major success, and believed this would constitute a rival version of the story that would detract from his own. A flurry of exchanges between the two studios expressed these concerns, and, to Selznick's relief, the project was temporarily buried (although not necessarily because of Selznick's protests).

The twenty-seven versions of *Jane Eyre*, the countless displaced Jane Eyres and the "Devotion" project emphasize the difficulties encountered by Selznick Productions in developing a strategy of adaptation for this familiar, almost saturated story. Confronted with these many replications of the novel's basic story, Selznick and his writers had to identify the narrative's most important features and devise an innovative method of bringing them to the screen. To successfully mine the cultural capital of the novel, already so widely dispersed, required a definitive cinematic treatment that positioned the novel as the definitive version of this familiar story.

This process began with Barbara Keon, Selznick's scenario assistant, mapping the plot of Brontë's novel chapter by chapter and providing an analysis of the principal characters' motivations. Keon broke the novel down into a series of vital plot points and provided a summary of each character's psychological profile at different moments in the story. At the same time, other members of the staff prepared material on costumes, sets, and historical background. Researchers investigated everything from what foodstuffs might be found on a nineteenth-century country dinner table to fashions in facial hair from the period. The combined research, most of it accomplished before the first draft of the script, constituted a blueprint of the novel for cinematic construction, a plan of both selection (the best scenes and characters to use) and elaboration (how to realize certain sparsely described or poorly executed scenes in the book). Keon's preliminary work sought to identify the many potential narratives in the book in order to isolate the one that would make for the most compelling motion picture, while the historical research into the period provided a dense web of details from which to select items that would "authenticate" the film as an accurate version of Brontë's work.

As with all novels, *Jane Eyre* contained a number of potential narratives that could be mined through subtle inflections on the material. Not surprisingly, the Selznick studio chose to emphasize the story as a romance, streamlining its treatments and scripts around the story's central love story. As summarized by the story department and reduced to its basic plot points as a romance, *Jane Eyre* thus begins with Jane as an orphan child living with her Aunt Reed at Gateshead Hall. At Gateshead, she is tormented by the rest of the family, and early in the story she is locked in the "red room" as punishment for an infraction that was not her fault. Her one ally in the house is the maid, Bessie. After a conference with the severe Mr. Brocklehurst, Jane is sent away to the Lowood school, where her life is equally miserable. Conditions at Lowood are so bad that her closest friend, Helen Burns, eventually dies from maltreatment and neglect. Her only protector during this period is the kindly Dr. Lloyd. After Helen's death, eight years pass, and Jane, now a young woman, is offered a position at Lowood as a teacher. She decides instead to seek her place in the world as a governess and by posting an advertisement, gains a position at Thornfield Hall. At Thornfield, Jane gradually falls in love with the Hall's mysterious master, Edward Rochester. Though Jane is in love with Rochester, she is sure that he is destined to marry the beautiful Blanche Ingram. Interspersed with this budding romance are a number of mysterious happenings in the Hall, disturbances which Jane attributes to the servant, Grace Poole. Jane briefly returns to Gateshead to tend to the death of Aunt Reed, and when she comes back to Thornfield, Rochester proposes to her. On the day of the wedding, however, an attorney stops the ceremony and claims that Rochester has a wife still living. Rochester takes them back to Thornfield and shows them his wife, an insane woman who has been the cause of the previous mysterious occurrences in the Hall. Jane, despite Rochester's entreaties, leaves Thornfield to start life over again. She travels to the parish of St. John Rivers, who eventually sets her up in a teaching position. A year passes, and Rivers asks Jane to marry him and join him as a missionary in India, telling her she was born for "labor and not for love." An anguished cry in the night brings her back to Thornfield, however, where she discovers that the once great Hall has been destroyed in a fire. The "mad wife" has perished in the blaze, removing the obstacle to her and Rochester's marriage. She finds Rochester blind and crippled. They marry, and he regains his sight in time to see the color of his first child's eyes.

From this summary, Houseman and Stevenson began the first draft of their adaptation with an evaluation of the narrative strengths and weaknesses of Brontë's novel. In the preface of the first draft of the screenplay, dated 15 April 1940, Houseman and Stevenson offered a number of comments on Brontë's novel that described and defended the emphasis of their adaptation. They decided, for example, that Helen Burns, Jane's childhood friend who dies tragically, was "irrelevant, out of proportion and misleading." They even offered their own biographical explanation for this "flaw" in the novel, claiming that Helen would never have been included if "Miss Brontë had not been swayed by personal grief. She was too good a craftsman not to have stuck to the straightline story." Similarly, they described the St. John Rivers section of the novel as "a dull, shoddy and boring piece of writing." They acknowledged his structural importance in the novel, but announced nonetheless their intention of altering his characterization to make him more interesting and narratively useful in the film.

As a consequence of these observations, Houseman and Stevenson's first draft of *Jane Eyre* concentrated on the "straightline story" of the romance between Jane and Rochester. The Gateshead and Lowood sequences of Jane's youth were pared back to a bare minimum, so much so that the entirety of Jane's tenure at the hellish Lowood was condensed into a two-minute montage sequence covering eight years of miserable living conditions at the orphanage. Brocklehurst and Aunt Reed were the only two characters retained from the novel's depiction of Jane's youth. Bessie, Dr. Lloyd, and Helen Burns were each deleted. The imperative, clearly, was to get Jane to Thornfield and into her involvement with Rochester as soon as possible.

The long process of negotiating this adaptation began in earnest with Selznick's response to this first draft. Selznick was less than happy with a shortened version of Jane's childhood. "As for little Jane," he wrote, "the most logical thing after this opening would be to dissolve to an English jail of the period and show a hardened criminal, the result of what the child has gone through."[14] He called on the screenwriters to find out "what makes Jane tick" and argued that what happens to her as a child has a significant influence on her future relationship with Rochester. Subsequent versions of the script reflected more emphasis on Jane's childhood, indicating an increasingly complicated structure of emplotment for both the Gateshead and Lowood sections of the story. Houseman and Stevenson expanded the red room scene to be more terrifying, which allowed the audience to see Jane being unfairly persecuted by the Reed family. They added Bessie in the fourth draft, so that Jane could voice aloud her sense of injust treatment by the Reed family, and included a Dr. Lloyd figure in the same draft to perform a similar function at Lowood. Aldous Huxley, a third writer hired for the project, introduced Helen in the fourth draft and added her death scene in the fifth draft.

For screen purposes, the main narrative task of the Gateshead section was to generate sympathy for Jane, both by showing her isolation within the Reed family and by portraying the unjust punishment she receives at their hand. Additionally, the Gateshead sequence was important, serving as the introduction to the narrative, since its point was to align instantly the viewer's identification with Jane. Still, in terms of the overall construction of the film, the Gateshead section was but a prologue for the all-important romance story. Selznick thought the scenes of Jane's youth important enough to let run "two or three reels" if necessary. At the same time, however, he and his staff realized that building sets and shooting exteriors for Gateshead would involve a significant amount of money. Letting the scenes run for several reels also presented a potential problem in narrative construction for the film as a distracting delay to the story's central romance. The problem to solve, then, was one of reconciling the necessary plot and thematic exposition of this section with the material and narrative economy of the film.

During the actual production of the film, the screenwriters employed, at the last minute, a device to save both narrative time and studio money without sacrificing the necessary exposition or character development. Thus, in the final filmed version of *Jane Eyre*, the first image is a book on a table. The book is *Jane Eyre*. An anonymous hand opens the cover and we see (and hear read to us in Jane's voice) the following printed page:

CHAPTER ONE: My name is Jane Eyre. I was born in 1820, a harsh time of change in England. Money and position seemed all that mattered. Charity was a cold and disagreeable word. Religion too often wore a mask of bigotry and cruelty. There was no proper place for the poor or unfortunate. I had no father or mother, brother or sister. I lived with my Aunt, a Mrs. Reed of Gateshead Hall. I don't remember her ever speaking one kind word to me.

From this printed page, the image dissolves to a hallway where two servants stand outside of a door. They open the door and let Jane out of a closet. She is then dragged downstairs to her meeting with Mr. Brockle-hurst, after which she leaves for Lowood.

Beginning the cinematic adaptation of a novel with an opening shot of the book was not an uncommon practice in Hollywood. What is remarkable about this particular opening, however, is that the words shown on the screen are a complete invention. They do not appear anywhere in Brontë's novel, much less on the first page. This reference to a hallucinatory page of text from *Jane Eyre* was a narrational tool conjured to accomplish a number of narrative, artistic, and economic missions. First, this opening invoked the cultural capital of *Jane Eyre* as novel and legitimated the interpretive authority of the film's adaptation. The viewers were invited to partake of Brontë's story as if they were actually going to read the book. The film had the book "in hand," so to speak, and promised to serve as an authoritative guide to Brontë's work. Second, the printed page provided a convenient means of condensing a large amount of narrative exposition, and this saved both screen time and studio resources. The elaborate plotting of the red room sequence and its narrative importance as a signifier of Jane's suffering could thus be condensed into the words "I don't remember her ever speaking one kind word to me," followed by an image of Jane locked in a small closet. A red room set did not have to be constructed, nor did time have to be spent within the narrative to follow the trajectory of the entire red room sequence. Third, the "textual" introduction positioned the viewer on how to read later characters in the film, as well as the "themes" of the story. This *Jane Eyre* was introduced as a story of place and position, isolation and charity, and bigotry and cruelty, which guided subsequent introductions to Brocklehurst, Helen, and Rivers. Other invented passages appeared later in the film to perform similar functions. Each time the printed word appeared on the screen, the viewer simultaneously received a reminder that the story was "literature," a compact bundle of narrative information, and a strategy for "reading" the film. The fabricated text invoked Brontë's "real" work as disguised through the material and narrative economy of the film's construction.

While Houseman, Stevenson, and Huxley labored to compress Brontë's 400-page novel into a film of two to three hundred shots, Selznick continued to investigate the story's popularity with the public. His concern over the story's currency was so great that he even had an assistant on the East Coast monitor the circulation figures of Brontë's novel at the New York Public Library. Throughout his career, Selznick had prided himself on fashioning adaptations that captured an audience's sense of the work, even if the adaptation itself required readjustments of the source material. He often boasted of his success in this regard with *David Copperfield* (1935), *The Adventures of Tom Sawyer* (1938), and *Gone with the Wind* (1939). With *Jane Eyre*, Selznick was most concerned with the story's identity in the reading and viewing public. Who would still be interested in seeing this story, and why?

With the script still early in development, Selznick made the logical decision of asking the audience directly what it wanted out of *Jane Eyre*. On 15 March 1942, Selznick reached an agreement with the Audience Research Institute (ARI) to test the waters for a film of *Jane Eyre*. Selznick wanted to identify who had read the novel, their impressions of it, and their likelihood of viewing it if made into a motion picture. The specific agenda for this research included the following goals:

- By exposure of synopsis, to determine the audience appeal of the basic theme.
- To find out: (a) how many persons have read the book recently, (b) how many have read it sometime but not in the recent past, (c) how many recognize the title without having actually read the book.

{}

- To find out which scenes are best remembered by those who know the story.
- To find out what features of the story militate against its audience appeal.
- To find out which features increase audience appeal.[15]

Selznick would later ask which pairings of stars increased the appeal of the story, both among those who had read the novel and those who had not. Both studies were quite literally an attempt to "read" an audience, to identify its concerns and expectations in a property so that they could be integrated into an effective adaptation. The results of this survey provide an interesting account of both the changing cultural identity of a literary work and the process of its adaptation.

Incredibly, the single most remembered scene in Brontë's novel, according to the ARI survey, was an event that is only indirectly represented in the novel. The burning of Thornfield Hall was by far the most vividly remembered scene in the book, despite the fact that Jane, who serves as the novel's first-person narrator, is not present to witness the blaze. In the novel, a minor character provides disclosure of the fire through a retrospective description to Jane after she discovers the Hall in ruins. Some recollections of the novel were even more hallucinatory. As David Ogilvy, Selznick's chief contact at ARI, noted, "Memory played a queer trick on some respondents, telescoping their impressions. A few voted for the scene 'where Rochester rescues Jane from the fire.'"[16]

This brings up an interesting question in terms of commercial adaptation. If the majority of the book's readers remember a scene that does not happen, or remember it in a significantly different manner than it appears in the book, does the adaptor privilege the aberrant reading? Or follow the dramatic structure of the novel? Which best articulates the "true" identity of the work for a contemporary audience? In regard to the burning of Thornfield Hall, this issue became a major point of contention during the adaptation process. In the preface to the first draft of the script, for example, Houseman and Stevenson appended a note stating that though showing the fire on screen would be a great temptation, they agreed with Brontë's decision to allow Jane to discover "the horror and annihilation" of the once great Thornfield as a "blackened shell." Selznick initially agreed with this decision (in part because *Rebecca* does show the fire, and he was again concerned about similarities between the two productions). After reviewing the ARI survey, however, Selznick hired Keith Winter (who had scripted the rival "Devotion") to write a scene incorporating the burning of Thornfield. Whereas in the novel, Jane leaves Rochester for a year and then returns to find the devastation of the fire, in Winter's script, the fire occurs just moments after Jane leaves Thornfield. In this draft of the script, the fire scene is the only moment the viewer is away from Jane as the narrational center of the film, and it is also the only time the viewer receives narrative information that she does not.

As with the invention of the fabricated text in the Gateshead section, however, Houseman and Stevenson engineered an ingenious compromise by the time the film went into production that reconciled the demands of Brontë's story with the demands of Brontë's audience. In the film, when Jane returns and sees the devastation at Thornfield, Mrs. Fairfax, the Hall's housekeeper, is there standing in the ruins to recount the blaze. The image dissolves to a flashback as Fairfax speaks, and we see Rochester among the flames, fighting the fire and attempting to save the mad wife. The viewer thus receives both the surprise of Thornfield destroyed, as in the novel, and a vivid depiction of the fire in the flashback of Mrs. Fairfax. The adaptation served both its masters by retaining Brontë's structure for disclosure of this dramatic information and yet portraying this disclosure in a manner consonant with the dramatic expectations of the film's targeted audience.

In addition to the creative memories of the audience, Selznick and his writers also had to confront a generally hostile preview reaction from the film's potential viewers. Ogilvy reported that the concept of *Jane Eyre* tested lower than any film he could remember, and he did his best to discourage Selznick from the project. The "want-to-see" value of the story rated 11 percent below average without cast and a weak 2 percent above average with the casting of Ronald Colman and Joan Fontaine. Among men, the story placed at 52 percent below average, and rose only to minus 34 percent with the addition of Colman, a usually popular male antidote to women's pictures. Although the project did test 2 percent above average with the casting of Colman and Fontaine, Ogilvy warned that only "misinterpretation or distortion could make it possible to use them (the figures) as an argument in favor of *Jane Eyre*."[17]

Ogilvy included in his report actual audience responses "representing majority opinion," responses that made this general disinterest in the project even more immediate.

- It's pretty morbid. It would make me feel worse than I do now.
- I just refuse to see unhappiness in the movies. *Jane Eyre* would be too tragic for me to sit through.

- I don't care for such a sordid kind of a story—a married man playing around with a single girl.
- I don't think I'd like the insane woman. [Ogilvy added here that "Insanity has always emerged as a serious *minus* factor in our studies."]
- Wishy-washy tripe.
- Crap. Too slushy. No damn love picture for me.
- You wouldn't be allowed to write down what I'm thinking about the story. I'd tell them where they could store that. [Ogilvy added that this last response was from an army private.][18]

Such negative results no doubt disappointed Selznick, who had wanted to make *Jane Eyre* since at least 1934.[19] More likely, the results probably seemed incomprehensible. *Rebecca*, an almost exact replication of the *Jane Eyre* story, had, after all, been the most successful picture of 1940, garnering an Oscar for best picture. In 1941, Joan Fontaine won an Oscar for *Suspicion* (1941), yet another displaced reworking of the *Jane Eyre* story. How could such a commercially and critically proven formula be in such disfavor?

Ogilvy offered his own interpretation of *Jane Eyre*'s poor showing:

> We have accumulated some evidence to show that the majority of theatergoers do not want to see stories where either of the lovers has a husband or wife still living. Cuckoldry seems to be the most unpopular situation of all, but the reverse seems to be almost as unpopular. . . . We don't quite understand the underlying causes of these unfavorable reactions to attempted adultery—it may be that the ladies in the audience find it hard to project themselves into the heroine's shoes when they know that the hero has a wife in the background. (Pure speculation, that.)[20]

Ogilvy's analysis may have some validity, especially in explaining *Rebecca*'s popularity over *Jane Eyre*. The most significant changes in *Rebecca*, in fact, did remove both the "insanity" and "adultery" from the story. In *Rebecca*, the "mad wife" became the dead wife, conveniently disposing of both of these apparently distasteful themes. While this, of course, does not completely explain the popularity of *Rebecca* over *Jane Eyre* (respondents made it known that they would rather see a re-release of *Rebecca* than the new *Jane Eyre*), it does suggest that the du Maurier/Selznick rearticulation of the *Jane Eyre* story may have been more meaningful for a 1940s audience, or at least more palatable, than *Jane Eyre* followed to the letter could ever be.

Not all studio adaptations were able to rely on ARI surveys to form such conclusions, of course, but Selznick's use of the ARI materials provides a concrete example of an issue on the mind of any film producer working with a literary property—how to turn a historically bound story into a compelling narrative for a contemporary audience. Obviously, a literary work can enjoy a number of identities in a number of contexts. The process of adaptation involved prioritizing and balancing these identities to generate a text that was at once a composite and a compromise.

As the *Jane Eyre* project continued, the work of Selznick, his screenwriters, and his production staff began to converge toward this goal. Within this intersection of forces, the adaptation began to take its final shape. A document drawn from the story conferences of the project provides a rich example of the dynamics of this process. This memo, headed "For Discussion" and dated 25 May 1942, demonstrates concisely how the process of cinematic adaptation involved the intersection of the firm's notions of audience expectation, the conventions of cinematic narrative practice, a critically interpretive approach to the source material, and the economic concerns of the production company.

The "For Discussion" memo consisted of a list of items to be considered pertaining to the *Jane Eyre* project, and it brought together a number of opinions, suggestions, and criticisms from the various members of the Selznick organization involved in the project. These comments included, among other items, warnings on the potential cost of sets, critiques of the perceived narrative power of characters and scenes, and even references to specific responses from the ARI survey material. The document summarizes the forces constantly at work in the process of adaptation, demonstrating the overdetermination of any single narrative decision as well as the intricacy of the critical and economic negotiation intrinsic to the adaptation process.

At this stage in the script's development, for example, the story of *Jane Eyre* had been divided into five major sections: Gateshead, Lowood, Thornfield, Lowood 2, and Thornfield 2. These geographical divisions referred to periods in the heroine's story, each seen with a certain narrative mission to accomplish. The "For Discussion" document used each of these sections as a subject heading under which to gather a variety of concerns with that section of the production. The Gateshead section—that part of the film that portrays Jane's childhood—thus included the following entries:

Too much made of exterior of Gateshead—both opening and Jane's departure. Considerable unnecessary expense involved in shooting time and set construction.

KLUNE

Too much youngster stuff. Suggest opening picture, after an establishing exterior shot, with Brocklehurst visit to Gateshead.

KERN

Not sure characterization of Jane is as interesting as in the novel; she is more pitiable in novel and less able to take care of herself; particularly in childhood sequences.

KERR

Best remembered scenes: Jane's childhood and school—7% poll.

ARI poll results

Similar comments appeared under the other section headings, cataloging the Selznick studio's concurrent concerns for budget, narrative economy, strength of characterization, audience expectation, logistics of production, and even fidelity to Brontë's "intentions." Other matters discussed at this meeting included cutting an ice-skating scene because of the expense involved in renting time at a studio equipped with an ice stage, trimming melodramatic lines from characters who seem "overdrawn," and discussing strategies for depicting the fire at Thornfield. The purpose of such production meetings was precisely to prioritize and negotiate these individual viewpoints in the adaptation process in a collective "reading" that situated the story within the socially, economically, and artistically derived signifying practice of the Hollywood film. This involved a reading of the audience, a reading of the source material, and an estimation of the capabilities and limitations of the translating system itself.

Interestingly, in the midst of these complex revisions in script development and production logistics, one section of Brontë's story remained relatively unchanged. From the first draft of the script to the completed film, the scene-by-scene breakdown of Jane's unfolding romance with Rochester remained consistent except for a few minor adjustments to enhance the mysterious events at the Hall and better articulate the romantic rivalry of Blanche Ingram. Selznick was apparently very clear as to what he wanted extracted as the primary material from Brontë's novel. Framing this central romance, however, proved t

be the most difficult task in the adaptation process. The most active revisions in the script involved the beginning and end of the story, when Jane is not at Thornfield.

This problem included not only how to represent Jane's youth at Gateshead and Lowood, as discussed earlier, but also what to do with her character during the time of her separation from Thornfield before her reunion with Rochester. Stevenson voiced this concern directly to Selznick halfway through the script's development.

> I've been worrying for some time about what seems to me a flaw in our story construction. . . . The reasons for suspecting a flaw are the following: (1) The scenes of Jane's childhood, all excellent in themselves, do not seem to add up to a motivating force for the rest of the picture. . . . (2) Consequently, though I like the individual scenes enormously, the script as a whole seems to me disjointed—just the story of Thornfield plus a prologue and an epilogue.[21]

Stevenson's solution to this problem was one common to many Hollywood films of the period. "What we need," he suggested, "is a thread running through all 3 sections, tying them together and making them the story of Jane Eyre and the struggle of her soul."

Empowering a protagonist as the psychological mover of the narrative working toward a clearly defined narrative goal was a characteristic feature of many Hollywood films of the 1930s and 1940s. As David Bordwell comments, "Psychological causality, presented through defined characters acting to achieve announced goals, gives the classical film its characteristic progression."[22] Implicit to Stevenson's argument was that the three sections of *Jane Eyre* had no apparent relation to one another in terms of such psychological causality and that there was no "thread" leading toward a defined narrative goal. There was only a "prologue," the romantic center, and an "epilogue." What was needed was "a tying together" in terms of psychological causality—a unification around Jane's consciousness so that a "disjointed" story could become "the struggle of her soul."

Stevenson believed this unification could be achieved through the character of St. John Rivers, and indeed, the most significant alterations of Brontë's novel involved the Rivers character, his relationship to Jane, and his radical displacement in the narrative. These changes, while they may seem like random and arbitrary liberties taken with Brontë's material, actually represent a calculated effort to conform the *Jane Eyre* story to the characteristic demands of Hollywood narrative

practice. The continual reworking of the Rivers character through these drafts was an attempt to unify a chain of narrative cause and effect organized around Jane as the psychological center of the story.

From the beginning of the *Jane Eyre* project, the Rivers section presented a significant problem. As stated earlier, Houseman and Stevenson described this section of Brontë's novel "a shoddy piece of writing" and believed that the sooner it was over with the better. Helen Jerome, offering an analysis of the story in an attempt to gain a job as screenwriter, described Rivers as "dull," although she recognized his structural importance to the story. "Of course in the screen version," she suggested, "you may perhaps dare to simply lap dissolve and give your audience 'One Year Later'—but still don't forget there is a definite value in the conflict in Jane's soul when she nearly accepts Rivers—the terror in the audience that she will not get the fascinating Rochester after all."[23] Early drafts of the script, then, treated Rivers as an impediment to the central love story, a necessary but boring distraction before the final reunion of Jane and Rochester.

Houseman and Stevenson's initial solution to this problem was to make Rivers less of a prig and therefore a more believable romantic choice for Jane. By "improving" Rivers's character, they hoped to increase his credibility as a romantic choice for Jane and thereby heighten the suspense of his marriage proposal. Selznick's response to this idea was ambivalent.

> I think we should be careful about this. I don't think any of us are smart enough to know what are the strengths or weaknesses of a successful work. I go further and say that I don't think the original author is able to diagnose why a given work strikes a responsive chord in the minds and hearts of millions of people. . . . The formula is not as simple as that, and throwing out one component part or changing it radically may disturb the entire combination. Even though one section or one character is weak in itself, and even at the risk of annoying or boring an audience with a poorly drawn character or a dull section, it may be the better part of wisdom to leave these same weaknesses, lest the exact balance be disturbed. For example, it may be possible—I don't say likely—that the success and appeal of *Jane Eyre* might have been somewhat less if Rivers had been a better character. . . . I am still not on the side of Brontë's "boob and buffoon." But let's kick him around with care, and be damned sure that Brontë, either deliberately or through instinct, didn't do exactly the right thing with him.[24]

With this cautious mandate, the Rivers character began a long and complicated metamorphosis. Originally perceived as an extraneous distraction, Rivers was eventually expanded as a character, given additional scenes, and bestowed with the unifying function in the narrative. As with the invented pages of text and the creative burning of Thornfield, the liberal manipulation of Rivers's character and the elaboration of his narrative function represented a compromise between the authority of Brontë's novel, the narrative demands of a well-crafted Hollywood film, and the economic considerations of cinematic production.

The first three drafts of the script followed, more or less faithfully, Brontë's characterization of Rivers. He is a simple man who aids Jane when she is destitute, offering her a job teaching at the local school. This new community is pleasant, and Jane finds some degree of happiness. After a few months, Rivers announces he is going to India and asks Jane to accompany him as his wife. While mulling the decision over, Jane hears Rochester's anguished cries in the wind and decides that she must return to Thornfield. With the fourth draft, however, several significant and interrelated changes were made:

1. Helen Burns's death scene is added at Lowood.
2. Rivers and Dr. Lloyd are condensed into a single character—Dr. Rivers.
3. River's "duty" speech ("You were born for labor and not for love") is displaced and delivered to Jane as a child while next to Helen's grave rather than as a part of Rivers's marriage proposal years later.
4. After Jane leaves Thornfield, she returns to Lowood rather than traveling to a new pastoral community.
5. Dr. Rivers proposes marriage to Jane at Helen Burns's graveside.

Obviously, these final four alterations in the script are significant departures from Brontë's *Jane Eyre*. Their adoption in the script signaled an elaborate project to unify the pre- and post-Thornfield sections of the film, once again balancing the artistic and economic demands on the narrative.

On a most basic level, for example, returning Jane to Lowood rather than introducing her to a new community saved production time and studio money. With this revision, the Lowood sets could now be used for two of the three major sections of the film, saving on set construction and shortening the shooting schedule (since all of the Lowood scenes, pre- and post-Thornfield, could be shot at once). In terms of efficient narrative construction, on the other hand, collapsing Rivers and Dr. Lloyd into a single character and placing him on both sides of the Thornfield section provided a useful continuity of character and location to frame the love story. Introduced in the opening sequences of the film, Dr. Rivers and Lowood acquired meanings that could be easily reactivated in the post-Thornfield sequence. Dr. Rivers, Jane's kindly paternal figure in the first Lowood sequence, was thus once again available to be Jane's protector in the post-Thornfield scenes. Similarly, the connotations of Lowood were reactivated as well. Lowood, though always a "secure" home for Jane in adulthood, was, through its previous association with the drabness, misery, and death of Jane's youth, that which is not Thornfield. Rather than establish a new character (St. John Rivers) and a new location (the pastoral community)—narrative operations that would require valuable time and a potentially distracting shift in the audience's attention—this new script deftly made use of established character and location to construct a simple binary opposition: Rochester/not Rochester (Dr. Rivers) and Thornfield/not Thornfield (Lowood). This binary opposition simplified what was at stake for Jane's character and unified a chain of psychological cause and effect around Thornfield and Rochester as the central, desired narrative goals.

The condensation of Dr. Lloyd and Rivers reinforced this division by providing a common agent present in the pre- and post-Thornfield scenes to argue the continuity of Lowood and its association with both physical and spiritual "labor." This function is especially apparent in the relationship of the two graveyard scenes where Rivers invokes Helen as a means of appealing to Jane's sense of "duty." The two graveyard scenes bracket Jane's experience at Thornfield, the first introducing a theme of "duty" as Jane and Rivers discuss Helen's death, and the second reactivating this theme when Rivers proposes to Jane and asks her to help him at Lowood. Conference notes from this revision called for making Rivers "a man of duty" and reiterated that his greatest importance in the script was as a "direct contrast to Rochester." The graveyard scenes in the script thus became a thematic entrance and exit to the Lowood/Thornfield opposition, a convenient means of articulating the "struggle of Jane's soul" as a choice between the romantic love of Thornfield and the endless labor of Lowood.

This rearticulation of Brontë's "love versus labor" theme became so pronounced that by the time the film was made, the suspense was no longer in Rivers's proposal of marriage, which had been deleted, but was instead in the threat of Jane's having to return to Lowood in order to feed herself. In the final version of the film, Rivers served as Jane's fatherly adviser and nothing more. A final, last-minute change between script and film is particularly revealing in this respect. Whereas in the shooting script, Jane heard Rochester's voice in the wind while composing a letter to answer Rivers's marriage proposal, in the final film, Jane hears Rochester's voice just as she begins a letter of application to Mr. Brocklehurst begging to reclaim her position at Lowood. The scenes were identical except for the letter on Jane's desk and its implications. Rivers, originally a second, lesser romantic choice to follow Rochester, thus became a nonchoice for Jane, a fatherly figure that both represented and connected the drab, passionless world of Lowood. This bifurcation of Lowood and the condensation of Lloyd with Rivers provided a continuous frame for emphasizing the drama of Thornfield and thus articulated through location and character the "love vs. labor" conflict that is the "struggle of Jane's soul."

The hybrid Rivers character, like the fabricated pages of text and the embellished burning of Thornfield, was at once a narrative liberty and a narrative solution, a creative conforming of an individual story within a common narrative practice. These liberties, each devised to rehabilitate Brontë's narrative, argue that cinematic adaptation is perhaps best understood as a collaborative and overdetermined process of collective authorship—one that includes the original author, the work as a history of texts and commentaries lodged in successive social formations, a contemporary audience and its attendant narrative expectations, and a culture industry working to interpret and balance these often divergent yet mutually determining forces. The Hollywood adaptation of a literary property during the 1930s and 1940s operated as an interpretive transformation that represented both a reading of the work and a reading of the audience—a weighing of two sets of narrative demands. The process of adaptation was thus a move toward an elusive, ideal state where these conflicts between budget and ambition, audience and work, and word and image could be reconciled into a commercially and critically successful motion picture.

Hollywood adaptations of canonical novels such as *Jane Eyre*, therefore, were not inferior imitations of individual, literary masterworks but elite inflections on an audience's shared mode of contemporary cinematic narrativity. As with a Cary Grant or a Joan Crawford, the cultural stature of *Jane Eyre* provided an added incentive for an audience to once again engage itself with Hollywood's familiar narrative machinery, and as with any other star invested with a social identity, *Jane*

Eyre was expected to follow an implicit set of conventions during the film's unfolding. The primary work of adaptation, then, was not so much matching material to medium and medium to material, but involved adapting an audience to the material through the socially negotiated signifying conventions of the medium. Each decision made on the *Jane Eyre* project attempted to improve the experience of the eventual motion picture—a process of rearticulation that dissolved the authority of Brontë's narrative into the consensual narrativity of the film's audience. For those responsible for the film's development, such an adaptation was "successful" if, in addition to capturing a sense of the novel for its readers, it satisfied the demand for a well-crafted motion picture for a much larger audience of viewers. While such an adaptation might inspire a few people to return to the novel, the chief concern was that it enticed them to return to the moviehouse.

NOTES

1. The budget for star salary reflected social relations in America as well. The star portraying Jane in the story of *Jane Eyre* was to receive $50,000 while the star playing Rochester was to be paid $100,000.

2. Since *Jane Eyre* was in the public domain, there was no cost involved in acquiring the rights to it. What this 50 dollars covered is unknown, though it perhaps may have been a fee for registering the title.

3. David Bordwell, Janet Staiger, and Kristin Thompson, *The Classical Hollywood Cinema: Film Style and Mode of Production to 1960* (New York: Columbia University Press, 1985). This dynamic is discussed throughout, but most specifically in Chapter 9.

4. Dudley Andrew, *Concepts in Film Theory* (New York: Oxford University Press, 1984), p. 100.

5. Ibid.

6. See Jane Tompkins, *Sensational Designs: The Cultural Work of American Fiction, 1790–1860* (New York: Oxford University Press, 1985), and Jerome McGann, *The Beauty of Inflections: Literary Investigations in Historical Method and Theory* (Oxford: Clarendon Press, 1985).

7. Mikhail Bakhtin, *The Dialogic Imagination* (Austin: University of Texas Press, 1981), p. 294.

8. McGann, *The Beauty of Inflections*, p. 120.

9. Draft of a letter from Selznick to Helen Jerome, 19 April 1941.

10. Selznick sold the *Jane Eyre* project, along with *Claudia* (1943) and *Keys to the Kingdom* (1944), to Twentieth Century-Fox on 18 November 1942. Selznick's explanation for this deal was that he wanted to free studio resources for his immense homefront melodrama *Since You Went Away* (1944). The deal included the script as well the services of Houseman, Stevenson, Huxley, and Joan Fontaine on the production.

11. *Variety* 140:10 (13 November 1940), 5.

12. Memo from Selznick to Daniel O'Shea, 14 July 1940.

13. Letter from Selznick to John Houseman and Robert Stevenson, 21 April 1941.

14. Ibid.

15. Letter from Selznick to David Ogilvy, 18 May 1942.

16. Letter from Ogilvy to Selznick, 30 March 1942.

17. Ibid.

18. Ibid.

19. While at MGM, Selznick asked researchers on at least two occasions to research *Jane Eyre* for development. The novel was referred to in inter-office correspondence as Selznick's "pet project."

20. Ogilvy to Selznick, 30 March 1942.

21. Robert Stevenson to Selznick, 24 March 1942.

22. Bordwell et al., *The Classical Hollywood Cinema*, p. 17.

23. Helen Jerome to Selznick, 15 April 1941.

24. Selznick to Houseman and Stevenson, 21 April 1941.

Derral Cheatwood

The Tarzan Films:
An Analysis of Determinants
of Maintenance and
Change in Conventions

Between 1918 and 1970 a total of forty-one Tarzan films were made. Two of these were for made-for-TV films, and eight were silent, leaving thirty-one commercially produced sound Tarzan features between 1932 and 1968.[1] Other broader genres have lasted that long, the Western, the Romance, the Gangster film, but no motion picture series based upon one character or upon one idea has had anything close to the staying power and, I would argue, the long-term societal impact of the Tarzan films (Dowdy, 1973:9–10). For over four decades these films provided Americans with their major source of information and mis-information about Africa and Africans, and thus for a sizable portion of the population the only real sense of their native land. That this appeal was real, no matter how distorted or genuine the image, was documented by the popularity of Tarzan films among black viewers (Cripps, 1977:352).

Moreover, the Tarzan films embody wondrous stereotypes, myth structures, and archetypes of the sort which generally set the intellectual hearts of neo-Freudians, neo-Jungians and neo-Levi-Straussians aflutter. A white man, lost in a distant primal continent, alone, his parents killed, is raised by a she-ape to become a hero, master of all he surveys and the embodiment of control over his environment. Yet even with this history,

From the *Journal of Popular Culture* 16:2 (Fall 1982), 127–42. Reprinted with permission of the author and the *Journal of Popular Culture.*

this continuing impact on society, and this dramatic myth structure, surprisingly little notice is given to the Tarzan series. There is but one attempt to analyze the Tarzan myth in detail (Cowart, 1979), and most discussions of the Tarzan films regard them as B movies made primarily for children and unworthy of serious research.[2] One finds some references to authors' experiences of Tarzan in childhood (Cowart, 1979:220–223), and Gabe Essoe's book on the Tarzan film series is primarily descriptive of the major plots, characters, and personnel involved in the production of the films. Beyond relatively simple film histories, most authors mention the Tarzan films only in passing (Cripps, 1977; Dowdy, 1973; Goodman, 1961), and many, unexpectedly, do not note them at all (Bergman, 1971; Bohn and Stromgren, 1975; Jarvie, 1970; Jowett and Linton, 1980). Even those addressing the films as serious material make glaring errors or obvious misinterpretations of the material based, one must assume, on memories of the films seen in the distant past rather than on recent viewings (Opubur and Ogunbi, 1978:345).[3]

As a result there has been no serious discussion of the organization of the Tarzan series or of the mutual reciprocal influence of the Tarzan films and the society and time of which they were a part. One of the biggest mistakes commonly made in the analyses which have been attempted and in the layperson's memory of the Tarzan films is to regard the series as a unified set, with Tarzan and Jane (and often Boy) in Africa undergoing a series of exotic adventures surrounded by black natives and dangerous animals. In fact, the Tarzan series consists of four distinct sub-sets, four abstractly identifiable sub-divisions of the whole, which provide a unique and pragmatic perceptual ground for examining the questions I address.

The Four Subsets of Tarzan Films

The first Tarzan film made, perhaps the best known, and certainly the most professionally recognized was the 1932 Metro-Goldwyn-Mayer production of *Tarzan the Ape Man*, with Johnny Weissmuller and Maureen O'Sullivan. MGM was to make a total of six films starring Weissmuller, O'Sullivan, and eventually Johnny Sheffield between 1932 and 1942. Although the producers and directors of individual films changed, the stars and the studio remained a constant through this decade, and this block of films is recognizable in conventional format and in professional quality as an MGM series. This group of six films constitutes the first such identifiable sub-set.

At the same time, however, an independent producer named Sol Lesser, who was to become a major figure in the Tarzan films, was making a separate set of movies. He made two films, in 1933 and 1938, employing Buster Crabbe as Tarzan in the first, and the mortal and forgettable Glenn Morris as Tarzan in the second. Further, during these same years Edgar Rice Burroughs was involved through Burroughs-Tarzan Enterprises in the production of a serial entitled *The New Adventures of Tarzan*, starring Herman Brix. Released in 1935, the series was spliced into a motion picture, altered slightly, and re-released as *Tarzan and the Green Goddess*, starring Bruce Bennet (only the names are changed) in 1938. The films of this series have nothing in common besides the name of Tarzan. One was filmed in Guatemala, the others in California. The woman who became Tarzan's mate was named Mary in one, Eleanor in another, and was absent in the third; Boy never appeared; the same star was never used twice for Tarzan, and so on. As a result of this confusion, the public was exposed to ten films employing five different Tarzans and three different mates from four different distributors in this first decade of sound films. The second sub-set of Tarzan films consists of this early group of Lesser productions and the single Burroughs-Tarzan Enterprises film and will be called the Lesser Independent series for convenience.

Without going into depth about the machinations and problems which led to the existence of two simultaneous Tarzan series, this overlap was finally resolved in 1942, when Lesser brought Weissmuller and Sheffield into a long association with RKO studios. MGM, feeling the Tarzan series as adult entertainment had outlived its time, was willing to release all of the stars, but Maureen O'Sullivan opted to leave the jungle. At RKO, Lesser was to make eleven films from 1943 to 1953. He was to use three different stars as Tarzan, but in each case each star was to make at least three films in sequence. This continuity undoubtedly maintained a sense of consistency for the audience through the Lesser films, although he used five different stars for Jane and two for Boy. This series, maintaining a constant studio setting as in the early MGM set and a constant producer as in the early Lesser set, enables us to see the impact of these various agencies as the changes occur.

The years 1955 through 1959 were a period of transition, in which no dominant pattern, model, star, studio, director, or producer is identifiable. Four films were produced; the final Lesser RKO picture, two

Title	Year	Subset	Color	On-site	Tarzan	Jane	Boy
Tarzan the Ape Man	1932	MGM	—	—	Weissmuller	O'Sullivan	—
Tarzan the Fearless	1933	Lesser Independent	—	—	Crabbe	Wells[a]	—
Tarzan and His Mate	1936	MGM	—	—	Weissmuller	O'Sullivan	—
Tarzan's Revenge	1935	Lesser Independent	—	—	Morris	Holm[b]	—
Tarzan Escapes	1936	MGM	—	—	Weissmuller	O'Sullivan	—
Tarzan and the Green Goddess	1938	Lesser Independent	—	Yes	Bennett	—	—
Tarzan Finds a Son	1939	MGM	—	—	Weissmuller	O'Sullivan	Sheffield
Tarzan's Secret Treasure	1939	MGM	—	—	Weissmuller	O'Sullivan	Sheffield
Tarzan's New York Adventure	1942	MGM	—	—	Weissmuller	O'Sullivan	Sheffield
Tarzan Triumphs	1943	Lesser RKO	—	—	Weissmuller	—	Sheffield
Tarzan's Desert Mystery	1943	Lesser RKO	—	—	Weissmuller	—	Sheffield
Tarzan and the Amazons	1945	Lesser RKO	—	—	Weissmuller	Joyce	Sheffield
Tarzan and the Leopard Woman	1946	Lesser RKO	—	—	Weissmuller	Joyce	Sheffield
Tarzan and the Huntress	1947	Lesser RKO	—	—	Weissmuller	Joyce	Sheffield
Tarzan and the Mermaids	1948	Lesser RKO	—	Yes[c]	Weissmuller	Joyce	—
Tarzan's Magic Fountain	1949	Lesser RKO	—	—	Barker	Joyce	—
Tarzan and the Slave Girl	1950	Lesser RKO	—	—	Barker	Brown	—
Tarzan's Perils	1951	Lesser RKO	[d]	[e]	Barker	Huston	—
Tarzan's Savage Fury	1952	Lesser RKO	—	—	Barker	Hart	Carlton[f]
Tarzan and the She Devil	1953	Lesser RKO	—	—	Barker	Mac Kenzie	—
Tarzan's Hidden Jungle	1955	Lesser RKO	—	—	Scott	—	—
Tarzan and the Lost Safari	1957	Lesser at MGM	Yes	Yes	Scott	—	—
Tarzan's Fight for Life	1958	Lesser at MGM	Yes	[g]	Scott	Brent	Sorenson
Tarzan the Ape Man	1959	MGM	Yes	—	Miller	Barnes	—
Tarzan's Greatest Adventure	1959	Weintraub	Yes	Yes	Scott	—	—

The Tarzan Films

Title	Year	Subset	Color	On-site	Tarzan	Jane	Boy
Tarzan the Magnificent	1960	Weintraub	Yes	Yes	Scott	—	—
Tarzan Goes to India	1962	Weintraub	Yes	Yes	Mahoney	—	—
Tarzan's Three Challenges	1963	Weintraub	Yes	Yes	Mahoney	—	—
Tarzan and the Valley of Gold	1966	Weintraub	Yes	Yes	Henry	—	—
Tarzan and the Great River	1967	Weintraub	Yes	Yes	Henry	—	—
Tarzan and the Jungle Boy	1968	Weintraub	Yes	Yes	Henry	—	—

[a]"Jane" was named Mary Brooks in the film.

[b]"Jane" was named Eleanor in the film.

[c]Filmed in Mexico although set in Africa.

[d]First attempt to film in color failed, and the film was released in black and white.

[e]The attempt to film on location failed, and the film was finished at RKO.

[f]"Boy" was named Joey and was a jungle orphan.

[g]Some African scenes from earlier filmings were spliced in.

Lesser films for MGM of a very different character than either of his earlier films or the earlier MGM series, and one Al Zimbalist MGM remake of the original *Tarzan the Ape Man*. These films are considered transitional and are not identifiable as a sub-unit.

Finally, in 1958 Sol Lesser, using his own translation of the handwriting on the wall, sold his rights to the Tarzan films to Sy Weintraub and Harvey Hayutin (Essoe, 1968:148). From 1959 until the last of the "Hollywood" films was made in 1968, Sy Weintraub produced seven Tarzan films using three different Tarzans. In this final bloc—the Weintraub sub-set—each picture was filmed on location and in color and used no character for Jane or Boy. I will discuss these facts, along with the conventional characteristics of the set, later.

In review, then, the Tarzan films consist of an MGM series from 1932 through 1942, a simultaneous Lesser Independent series, a Lesser RKO series from 1942 until 1955, a period of transition, and a Weintraub series from 1957 until 1968. These periods both grew out of initial observations of the conventional presentational modes in the films and then were clarified and more clearly defined and delineated with the sophistication of the analysis of the conventions. It is these conventions to which we now turn.

Conventional Structures Used in Analysis

It would be redundant to discuss conventions again in this volume. For purposes of ensuring a clarity or consistency of use, let me remark that the starting ground for such analysis in sociology has been Howard S. Becker's (1974) discussion of conventions and the extensions of this work by others (Mukerji, 1976; Rosenblum, 1978). His focus, however, was primarily upon the social actions themselves, the particular actions of people as they occurred. These activities, however, become evident—visual, audio, or sensed in some way by an audience—in the product of the action. In some cases this product is temporary, as the notes actually produced by a symphony or a specific line in a play, or more permanent, as a sculpture or a film. But in each case there is a physical reality which is both a product and a reflection of the conventional sets of activities which went into its creation.

Where these conventional production activities and the decisions involved are unavailable we must rely on the products themselves and our interpretations of those products. There is no way to know the sets of decisions and activities which went into the production of thirty-one films, not in any sufficient detail to enable us to abstract, organize, and understand the relationship of these activities to the social structure and society in which they were a part. We do have, however, the final products following from the negotiations among all participants which allowed those products to become public. These examples are also systems of conventional elements, and it is the complex relationship of process and product underlying interactionist theory which unites this complex and enables us to accept both the product and the process as enactments of one phenomenon. In my use of convention in this manuscript, then, I am discussing only the products of social activity, the films which were actually produced and distributed, rather than the detailed activities and decisions which went into their makeup. But throughout we must remain aware that these products are merely one aspect of the reality of the conventional organization of art worlds and their relationship to the larger society.

Of the multitude of visual stimuli which produce a motion picture, I became interested in five abstract classifications for analysis from the Tarzan films: those conventions of cultural, racial or ethnic, geographic, contextual, and production matters.

Cultural conventions are those visual and verbal standardized formats which are used to convey the sense of location, exotic flavor, and foreign nature of the film. They involve not only the ways, manners, and occupations of the individuals and cultures depicted but also the display of the cultural products of that society. The major visual aspects of such a display include the architecture of the villages and houses shown, the clothing of the individuals displayed, and, to a lesser degree, the activities of the extras in the motion picture as seen in passing. These behaviors include the occupational and leisure activities presented as characteristic of the people inhabiting the fictional internal culture of the film.

Racial or ethnic conventions, at their simplest, display the factual or stereotypical racial characteristics of the individuals involved. To the degree that color sets apart the races presented, color provides for an easy discrimination. However, in the majority of the Tarzan films the natives involved are something other than black, most often white actors in some swarthy-tone body makeup. Their appearance ranges, given the skill of the studio, from individuals appearing to be Mid-Eastern or South American to individuals appearing to be bit players in a local production who put on their own makeup. In addition, verbal cues are sometimes provided in the accents given the actors. Usually such accents are identifiable as the Hollywood stereotype of South or Central American or Mid-Eastern, specifically Arabic, but some are unidentifiable or at best vaguely reminiscent of Transylvanian Gypsy. The visual and verbal racial and ethnic conventions in concert with the cultural conventions employed make it possible to arrive at educated guesses as to the cultural and racial types intended in any particular film. However, this should not be taken to mean that the race or ethnicity of the people playing the parts, or more directly of the people inhabiting the area in which the action is presumed or indicated to take place, is accurate. In some scenes the cultural and racial conventions were contradictory, and quite often either the cultural or the racial conventions, or both, were out of context as established by the geographical display.

Geographical conventions are any and all presentational methods by which a location is established and maintained in a film, most often by way of four major processes or cues. First, in some of the films there is a direct statement of the geographic location of the action, either with a voice-over at the beginning or with movement of the camera "into" a map to establish location. Second, a major sense of geographical location is given through the use of terrain features, predominantly plains and jungles. Third, location is indicated through the use of readily identifiable animals with limited habitats. And fourth, through the use of botanical features in the film, the more readily and commonly identifiable the plants, animals, and terrain features, the more readily the proper geography or the geography intended can be established. As a result, those items most widely associated with exotic climes and most colloquially identifiable as such are more widely used. Since animals are generally more identifiable than plants, one finds extensive use of lions, giraffes, rhinoceroses, hippopotamuses, and the like for this purpose.

Contextual conventions are more difficult to define since they are in fact a combination of more observable or empirical visual and audio items. Generally, they relate to the standard ways of establishing tone or framing plot within the film and in respects overlap more common forms of analysis having to do with theme, plot, and formula (cf. Cawelti, 1976:5–36). Although all of the Tarzan films have adventure themes, it is quite accurate to speak of particular films as employing western formula and plot devices, variations of the family film plot, and so on.

Maintenance and Change in Conventions

As it is widely used, "formula" denotes the particular stable or relatively recurrent set of conventions employed in a cultural work (Cawelti, 1976:5). As we will be using it, conventional change will involve both the changes of particular conventional frames within a formula set or sub-set of the Tarzan films and the larger changes that occur when one set of films changes in kind or in formula to another set.

In production activities involving numbers of people, as contrasted with a novel which traditionally requires one person to produce but large numbers to distribute, we must consider the question of which of the persons or structures involved is the dominant factor in the determination of conventions or formula. At the simplest, we are aware of the fact that every individual on a set will harbor a different idea, no matter how slight, of what conventions are to be used and how they are to be used in a film (Mukerji, 1976). Our concerns as sociologists in this volume are with the processes by which the final decision is reached as to what conventions are used and how, and with the products of those decisions. Further, I am concerned here with the maintenance of conventional patterns and with the major internal or external factors which promote change in those conventions.

In the attempt to determine the major influence on convention decisions scholars have traditionally turned to directors, somewhat less to studios or major producers, and even less to independent producers or stars. My analysis of the Tarzan films indicates quite clearly that in the case of this series it is the production agency—usually one producer, though in the MGM series the studio—that is clearly the tone setter. Investigating the films abstractly divided by star, studio, or director produced few recognizable and consistent conventional patterns. Only when the films were divided by the agent of production—essentially the agent of final financial control—did clear patterns emerge. Certainly there is nothing new in discovering that the person holding the production purse strings can be in control. What is unique, however, is seeing it so clearly and consistently in a single series over such a long period of time.

The MGM Series: The Family Grows

The six films which MGM released in the decade 1932–42 have a set of clear characteristics. All are set initially in the same location—a semi-jungle area in the midhorn of Africa. Tarzan is a family man, with Jane being in every picture and Johnny Sheffield appearing as Boy in the fourth, fifth, and sixth films to round out the family.

The influence of a major studio's abilities with makeup, special effects, sets, and the general professionalism of MGM in the 1930s is apparent. Overall, production conventions are difficult to analyze because many of them consist of the ongoing agreements behind the scenes. There are, however, at least three which are readily available, visual, and amenable to direct observation. First is the use of color as against black and white. Second is the use of on-site location filming and the location of this site. Third is the sophistication of the sets, makeup, color matching, and special effects as well as all of the minor details which go to identify the quality and indirectly the intended audience of the performance. All of the MGM films were made in the United States, and all were made in black and white.

As near as one can tell from the introduction, the Mutea escarpment which appears on no maps and on which Tarzan makes his home is located geographically in the horn of East Africa, somewhere near the current nations of southern Sudan or Uganda. Tarzan's home is in a heavy forest rather than a rain forest or a jungle, reflecting in part the greater ease with which the set department could construct an accurate-looking forest rather than a heavily overgrown and moist jungle or rain forest. In the scenes in which outsiders move in from the coast, most of the travel is also through a jungle-like forest, whereas in fact most of this area of Africa is arid grasslands or agricultural lands. It is also implied that some travelers arrive via the Congo, which runs to the west coast some 1,800 miles distant. The animals displayed are generally characteristic of the area, but there is the paradox again in that they are not characteristic of the vegetation of the area. One observes lions, elephants, monkeys of all types, rhinoceroses, hippopotamuses, ostriches, alligators, zebras, apes, giraffes, wildebeests, and other animals in Tarzan's jungle forest. In addition, there are large iguana-like monsters in a mud and lava cave in one film and an octopus in another, and in a third Jane asks Tarzan to get some caviar out of their refrigerator (spring house), leaving one to ponder where the nearest sturgeon spawn.

The cultural and racial conventions in the earliest of these films are strikingly accurate for Hollywood, particularly when compared to the Lesser Independent films and the later Lesser RKO films. This may be in part due to the fact that MGM had a higher budget per film, was envisioning a more mature audience, and apparently employed native Africans as advisors. Edmund Carpenter writes, "To avoid offending African governments, MGM insisted that no film on Africa resemble Africa. Prince Modupe's task was purely creative: Design buildings, songs, shields, dances, masks, even 'languages,' all of which Americans would accept as authentically African but which no African would recognize as his" (Carpenter, 1972:78–89).

The racial conventions in the MGM series are particularly interesting. Until the final film, *Tarzan's New York Adventure,* the MGM sub-set is the most racially honest of the series as a whole prior to 1960. Unlike the Lesser series, the natives in this sub-set are black. The portrayal of the natives is in one of two modes which corresponds closely to the strange schizophrenic view of blacks held by white Americans. Many of them are subservient, child-like, frightened porters who shuffle and bow to the whites. There are also tribes who are proud, independent, fierce, and fully capable of defending their lands. As was noted in the films, even Tarzan respected their territory and did not cross into it lightly.

The cultural conventions, although not accurate in a formal sense, are what I have come to call Hollywood Accurate. They are at least roughly representative of the geographic, temporal, and cultural location they are intended to represent, and the presentation of such cultural items as shields, native dress, and architecture is close enough to represent a stylization of these items for that time and place. The shields, for example, are approximations of Zulu shields in shape, size, and design, and the native huts are closer to accurate regional architecture than the mosques, castles, and Polynesian temples which were to appear later.

Contextually, the films are adventure films dependent upon Africa and the unique geographic, botanical, and zoological features of that continent for their excitement, plot line, and development. Over time, the family component of the Tarzan films became predominant as well, and in the last film Tarzan is sent to New York, where he wears a coat and tie and swings between buildings in order to free Boy from kidnappers. This last film of the MGM series is quite different from the others—the least believable, most racist, and most clearly directed at juvenile audiences. The change from MGM to RKO involved a noticeable shift from adult audience fare and a major "adult" studio, to a primarily juvenile audience and a studio with that interest.

To broadly characterize the MGM series, then, I would put forth the following. The racial and cultural conventions strive toward accuracy from Hollywood's perspective, yet they also reflect the attitudes, ambivalence, and perceptions of the general population. The geographic conventions tend to be moderately accurate as to location, animals, and racial cultures of the area, but they are more inaccurate regarding the ecological or botanical system. The contextual conventions deal strongly with the family theme and the adventure theme, with an emphasis on African adventure. The films as a whole are made with the expertise of a major studio for an adult audience.

In 1941 MGM released the rights to the Tarzan films and the stars of those films for economic reasons. Within the studio the Tarzan movies were progressively seen as children's fare and non-characteristic of the tone or maturity of the earlier films. Externally, World War II caused the loss of foreign markets, which had made up around 50 percent of the market for these films (Essoe, 1968:112). The impact of this conflagration not only affected studio profits, thereby prompting MGM's decision to sell, but also precipitated changes in racial and ethnic conventions in the succeeding series.

For the first time, then, we see the pattern which appeared in each change of series and each new pattern of conventions. A phenomenon which was primarily external and impacted directly upon the economics of the Tarzan films as these films were envisioned by the current production agent fostered the decision to sell those rights to the series to another producer. Whether through sheer luck or the clever design of each subsequent producer, the history of the series indicates that the new producer in each case was able to understand the effects of the economic reality leading to the sale. He then conformed the conventional patterns of the films to the demands of that reality and thus to the demands of the audience. It was the movement of the series among producers and the changes in conventional formats which these engendered which, ironically, preserved the Tarzan series for over fifty years.

The Lesser Independent Series: Everybody Tarzan, You Mary or Eleanor, Nobody Jane

Both the Lesser Independent Series and the Lesser RKO series are characterized by a completely casual approach to accuracy. The major distinction between the early independent series and the later RKO sub-set can be found in the continuation of the star for the Tarzan character and the ability to create a consistent family theme as well as a consistent formula of the sort needed to appeal to the B movie trade in the RKO series.

The dominant tone of the series through the 1940s and the 1950s, a reflection of Lesser's control, is even more pronounced in the three independent films of the 1930s. There is no accurate sense of cultural, racial, or geographical reality to the films, nor is there any apparent desire to appear accurate. The creation of the sense of exotic is achieved through exclusion of familiar items rather than inclusion of accurate items. In other words, so long as the people, places, and things displayed are not readily identifiable as Western European or North American, they are acceptable. The films display to a bizarre degree the conceptions of the Universal Oriental and the Non-European-Exotic. The Universal Oriental, a term borrowed from Jerry M. Lewis, is anyone who is not a white Anglo-Saxon.[4] In the Tarzan films it applies not simply to Orientals, but to blacks and other peoples as well. This is an expansion of the concept which does some injustice to the use of Oriental, but maintains the sense of the phrase itself and cogently conveys the meaning involved. Broadly, it takes in Orientals, blacks, Latin Americans, Pacific Islanders, Arabs, and any other "exotic" cultural group. Non-European-Exotic is the corollary applying to places and things. Any place that is not "like Europe" or anything that European or European-immigrant populations do is fair game to create the sense of distant, different, and exotic climes. It is, of course, of no consequence that there are deserts and forests in Europe and the western United States or that much of Africa is arid savanna similar to the western United States or parts of Russia. In fact, many geographic and botanical features of the horn of Africa are similar to European and North American features. Those features which are similar, no matter how accurate, are avoided. The instances of this occurring are far too numerous to mention, and it is impossible to discover any consistent pattern to the cultures or peoples used beyond observing that there was simply another place, another culture, or another people in mind.

Let me offer a few examples from the films. In the first film of the Lesser Independent series, *Tarzan the Fearless*, the safari looking for Mary's father (Lesser has taken the liberty of changing Jane's name to Mary Brooks) chops its way through heavy jungle on its way from the east coast of the horn of Africa to Uganda country. The head of the natives on the safari is named Abdul, and he is clearly not black, but Arabic-nomadic, with the tent, coloring, features, and clothing of that culture. He has with him a woman wearing a gypsy costume and a gun bearer who wears a fez. The bearers themselves are black, and at one point we find them sitting around the nomadic tents (pitched in the jungle) while the rest of Abdul's men, also Arabic, ride in on their horses. These horses later come in handy in the jungle when Tarzan rescues Mary from a horse stampede. Where are these people going? To the room of the God of Emerald Fingers, an Egyptian god with the traditional rod and headpiece, guarded by men with Egyptian features and coloring, wearing Egyptian-like headdress and carrying a small round shield and a halberd from the late Middle Ages. These same guards later use drums to command black natives to attack Tarzan. It appears Lesser conceived of the global village long before McLuhan.

The second film, made in Guatemala, was produced through E. R. Burroughs's organization. While the voice-over is noting that Guatemala contains "man-eating lions, lakes infested with alligator and crocodile natives deadly to white men," we see pictures of open plains with giraffe, hippopotamuses, rhinoceroses, lions, and large-eared elephants. The third film was worse than the first two. Clearly, the production and contextual conventions of these films revolved around a vague, amorphous search for the right combination, identity, and format for the Tarzan series. Made with three stars at three locations in two countries, nothing remained the same, including the name of Tarzan's mate. In the first film Tarzan did not speak at all, in the second he was fully literate, and in the third, with Glenn Morris in the lead, it was hard to tell which was the case.

Finally, with the advent of World War II, the loss of overseas markets, and the decision that there was no place for adult-audience Tarzan movies at MGM, Lesser had an opportunity to correct the major drawbacks in his series. He purchased the rights to future Tarzan films and bought the contracts of Johnny Weissmuller, who had been playing Tarzan at MGM, and Johnny Sheffield, who had been playing Boy. Further, he arranged with RKO studios to produce and distribute through its facilities. Thus we find the combination of a regular studio setting and organization, a stable and accepted star, and a consistent producer leading to the third and most extensive sub-set of the series.

The Lesser RKO Series: From Tarzan's Ersatz Family to the Advent of Television

Even with the stability brought by the union of Lesser, Weissmuller, Sheffield, and RKO, the films made by Lesser remained fundamentally inaccurate. In the Lesser RKO series the dominant formula involved Tarzan and some member of his family in an adventure context, and although all were set in Africa the unique character of Central-Eastern Africa became increasingly irrelevant. The facilities and technicians of the RKO studio imparted a more professional quality to such staples as makeup and sets than had been present in the independent series. In general, the tone of the films was in keeping with the reputation of RKO and the apparent design of Lesser from the beginning. They were simply good, solid, juvenile B fare.

The contextual conventions of the films came increasingly to revolve around the Tarzan family and exotic adventures away from the escarpment which had served as Tarzan's home and the setting of the initial MGM films. Jane, Boy, or both appear in all but one of the Lesser RKO films, a fact which is of importance in contrast to the later

Weintraub series. The plots increasingly came to rely on standardized B formulas, and borrowing from such related genres as the Western is common. In *Tarzan and the Leopard Woman*, a wounded safari member rides into town on the back of an elephant. He falls off in front of the governor's house and gasps "ambush" before he dies in the arms of the local magistrate. Robert Faulkner has described this as *Stagecoach* with elephants.

One other item in the contextual conventions of this series stands out. Of the twelve Lesser RKO films, three have a magic or mystery motif (with titles like *Magic Fountain, Desert Mystery,* and *Hidden Jungle*),[5] and six, half the total, have female villains or cultures involved (*Tarzan and the Amazons, The Leopard Woman, The Huntress, The Mermaids, The Slave Girl,* and *The She Devil*). There seems to be little doubt that some causative or correlative factor is operative here, and the time of the appearance of these films through the mid-1950s corresponds to a similar pattern found in films about females in prison (Cheatwood, 1981). Unfortunately, no one has definitely stated what those factors are.[6]

The cultural, racial, and geographic conventions in the RKO series remained similar to those in the independent series. There was some stability initiated with the consistency of the players. Johnny Weissmuller played Tarzan in six films from 1943 to 1948, Lex Barker was Tarzan in five films from 1949 to 1953, and Gordon Scott played in the last RKO film as the first of his Tarzan roles in five films from 1955 to 1960. Johnny Sheffield appeared as Boy in five films, and Brenda Joyce played Jane in five films from 1945 to 1949. Further, each of the films began in or near Tarzan's African home and then moved to some exotic location. Tarzan traveled to deserts, lost cities, hidden valleys, or the coast of the continent—always within Africa but increasingly in unusual or fantasy-like locations. There was, given the lack of commitment to accuracy, no need to move him off the continent. Lost cities were populated with white Amazon-like women, Latin cultures abounded, and Polynesian peoples were encountered. In short, any culture, any danger, or any adventure Sol Lesser wanted Tarzan to encounter could be found around Tarzan's Africa as represented in the back lots of RKO.

Again, one example should suffice. In *Tarzan and the Mermaids*, a letter is brought to Tarzan by Benji, the river mailman who floats in a dugout skiff while playing a gourd-like guitar, wearing a straw hat and cutoffs, speaking with a Spanish accent, and playing calypso. As the movie develops, Tarzan goes to help the people of Acquitania who live on the coast. They are white, wear sarongs, live on sandy beaches in round grass huts, fish using outrigger canoes, and dive for pearls in a cave defended by a giant octopus or, as the voice-over notes, "in waters alive with monsters of the deep." Why do they dive for pearls? To give to their god who lives in a Mayan or Incan pyramid and is named Balu. Actually, Balu is the creation of the two villains, both white, one of whom speaks with a German accent. The music was composed by Dimitri Tiomkin and sounds rather like the Mormon Tabernacle Choir doing the greatest hits of Desi Arnaz as dozens of natives sing "Balu, Balu," to the accompaniment of drums and brass. In this film, as in at least six of the RKO films, there are no blacks. There are numerous natives presented on the African continent, but they are Arabic, Indian, Polynesian, South American, Central American, or Caribbean—never black.

The Transition Films: The Electronic Revolution and Confusion

Each instance of the change of production agent in the series occurred as the prior producer felt that the Tarzan movies had reached their profitable end. In a sense, each producer was correct, for he or the studio had a distinct conception of the series, and in each case the evaluation that their type of Tarzan was finished was accurate. However, it was never the character of Tarzan or the adventure format per se that was no longer viable for audiences, but instead the producer's image or conception of the hero. Thus, when MGM finished its last Tarzan with Weissmuller in 1942, it believed that the adult-level adventure series it had been making was over and the decline of foreign markets caused by the war made continuation of the series impractical, so it sold to Sol Lesser. Lesser took Weissmuller and Sheffield, created a new Jane, and transformed the series into a younger B set which was viable and profitable for another thirteen years. From 1955 to 1959, however, four films were made which clearly indicate that the series was coming to an end as Lesser had envisioned and produced it. Moreover, these transition films reflect the overwhelming changes in the visual entertainment industry which were occurring during this time. The confusion wrought is apparent in the films. In Andrew Dowdy's wonderful phrase, "Hollywood wobbled into the fifties wondering where everybody had gone" (Dowdy, 1973).

Three of the four films were made by Sol Lesser, all starring Gordon Scott as Tarzan. One of these films was made at RKO without

Jane or Boy, one at MGM without Jane or Boy, and the third also at MGM but now with both Jane and Boy. The fourth film, reflecting MGM's belated, baffling, and disastrous decision that there was still money to be made in these films, was the Al Zimbalist remake of the original *Tarzan the Ape Man* with Denny Miller. It is not only probably the least effective and most laughable movie of the series, but quite possibly one of the least effective films ever to come out of MGM. By 1959 both MGM and Lesser were convinced the long Tarzan reign was at an end and they sold to a new producer, Sy Weintraub.

There was a good reason for Lesser to feel the way he did. By 1959 every other major motion picture series had disappeared, from Abbott and Costello, who had moved to television, to Andy Hardy, who had simply grown up and succumbed to television. It is the growth of the great electronic apocalypse, television, that correlates with the decline of the Lesser model of Tarzan, the appearance of the Weintraub style, and the eventual demise of that style in 1968. With the exception of the first sale from MGM to Lesser, the major external correlate of large-scale conventional and formulaic change in the Tarzan series is television.

The first major impact was the spreading presence of the media per se, and the pivotal year was 1959. In that year, for the first time since record keeping began in 1917, the motion picture industry in the United States released fewer than 200 American-made films. As recently as 1954 the industry released fewer than 300 films for the first time in its history. At the same time, data reveal that 1959 was the first year in which there was more than one television set in use per household in the United States. Although it was not an overnight revolution, this figure reflects the astounding speed with which the change had taken place. In 1949 there had been one TV set for every 10.55 households in the country. In 1950 that figure had risen to one set per 4.15 households, and by 1959 there were more sets in use than households using them (Standard and Poor's). The increase in television usage fostered the movie industry's response of bigger and better movies and the improvement of quality as reflected in color, panorama, bigger stars, and "better" plots. In the Tarzan series, however, there was a clear shift not only in quantity and quality, but in style and formula as well.

The Tarzan series, in fact, is the only one of the various movie series to emerge from the forties and fifties intact (Dowdy, 1973:9–10). It did so not by becoming better or bigger, but by accepting and adapting to two new exigencies. First, it accepted color and on-site photography, and second, it abandoned the family format which had been its staple from

1932 to 1953. Jane appears in only two films after 1953, one of which is the disastrous MGM remake. Overall, the family series disappeared from the movies as we grew accustomed to the weekly familiarity of television friends. We forgot Dagwood and Blondie as we became neighbors with Ozzie and Harriet, new friends that we saw every week taking the place of the old family we used to visit once a year, just as old friends fade and new friends grow when we move to a new neighborhood. We ignored Andy Hardy as our Little Margie became a pal. Tarzan films survived in part by dropping the family wholeheartedly and without reservation. There was no explanation, no justification; Jane and Boy simply disappeared by 1959.

The change into the Weintraub films was clear and unequivocal. After 1959 neither Jane nor any other mate, nor Boy, nor any other continuing youngster appeared in the seven films made. Prior to 1955 only one of the twenty Tarzan films was made on location, and none was made in color; after 1959 every film was shot on location and every film was made in color.[7] This pattern of pre-1955 (pre-television) black-and-white Hollywood-made Tarzan family films and post-1959 (post-television) color, on-site, Tarzan-alone films is the clearest and sharpest distinction in the series.

The Weintraub Series: From the Tarzan Travelogue to Color TV

The final sub-set of the Tarzan movies is, in many ways, the most coherent and consistent of them all. This is quite probably due to the fact that the production conventions changed dramatically and the form and format of the films changed with it. In a clear manner the production conventions of color and location came to determine the nature of the films overall. The Weintraub series, seven films with three Tarzans, is visually interesting, colorful, and characterized by accuracy determined by on-site shooting. Although the particular sites are not strictly African, they are usually explained away through the now familiar device of Tarzan's traveling to some other exotic clime for a variety of reasons. In this series, cultural or racial differences or inaccuracies are not noticeable to the extent found in the MGM or either of the Lesser series. The difficulties of producing a rain forest, arid savanna, or accurate jungle which are encountered in studio locations were not problematic in location filming. Likewise, local natives were used as extras.

Although the plots still tended to stress the adventure and foreign drama of Tarzan, there was no more need to create the sense of exotic mystery which had led to the bizarre features found in the Lesser series. It was this sense of the exotic on which we relied for our fascination with Tarzan, both our early fascination with lands and peoples which we had never before seen and our grown-up fascination with colorful scenes of real lands and real people. When we found those lands and people in full color on the screen in our living room, we forgot the host who had taken us there in the theatres.

The change to the Weintraub series and the success of that series correlated with the first impact of television upon the audience common to Tarzan films and the new medium of TV. Weintraub's ability to use location and color outweighed television's capabilities in those respects. Then, as television attained those technological capabilities, the Weintraub series passed from the motion picture screen.

Between 1968 and 1970 three phenomena brought the Tarzan movie series to its (relatively) final end. First, in 1970 the Sony Portapak became the first readily portable commercial video unit (television camera) widely available. With that innovation, on-site filming became not only possible, but convenient and inexpensive. We came to expect both our international and our local news to be immediate and "real," and almost overnight the ghettos across the tracks and the jungles of Thailand became familiar sights on our TV screens.

Second, in 1968 the Tarzan series began on television. Any fascination with the Tarzan character or desire to see that particular set of characters could now be satisfied within the home. Familiarity may not breed contempt, but neither does it support the exotic. Like so many other heroes in the decade of the 1960s, Tarzan did not survive the dimmed lights of television and the bright glare of that exposure.

Third, and most important, in 1968 color televisions became the norm rather than the exception. Data from the Standard and Poor's Industry surveys are decisively revealing on this point. In 1961 only 147,000 color television sets were sold compared to 6,155,000 monochrome sets. In 1964, only three years later, over 1,000,000 color sets were sold compared to 8,028,000 monochrome sets. In 1965 over 2.5 million color sets were sold, and in 1966 over 5 million. In 1967, for the first time in the industry, more color sets were sold—5,563,000—than monochrome sets—5,290,000. In every year since, color sets have outsold black-and-white units (Standard and Poors, 1973; 1980).

By 1968 there was nothing left for the Tarzan series in films. Two other films were released in 1970, but they were made from the television series and starred Ron Ely, TV's Tarzan. Each of the facets which had made the series survive through the decades had been co-opted: the wonder of the exotic, the drama of foreign adventure, the familiarity of family, the interest of color, and the fascination of on-location photography. Tarzan symbolized the individual's ability to conquer the technology which he has produced, but not even that character could survive the reality of the technological media on which he relied for existence.

But the final chapter on Tarzan has yet to be written. MGM is developing a script to remake *Tarzan the Ape Man* a third time. The plot will be very close to the original; it will be in color and it will be on-site. So, if what I have argued is correct, what would the average vice-president feel the film could offer beyond the fare that can be brought into the home via television? I believe the only answer available to date supports my prior arguments emphatically. Only one role has been firmly cast to date, and it is not Tarzan. Bo Derek will play Jane. The producer of the film is her husband, John Derek.

It is possible that by finding the combination which is workable for this time and place Tarzan will survive one more remake. Given Hollywood, there can be some doubts.

NOTES

1. The thirty-one films made as talkies include one which was made as a serial in 1935 starring Herman Brix entitled *The New Adventures of Tarzan*. This was later re-released as a feature film in 1938, retitled *Tarzan and the Green Goddess* with the star renamed Bruce Bennet. These films were treated as one, and the 1938 version used in analysis. In this manuscript, any reference to Tarzan movies will, by definition, mean those films produced and released as sound films.

2. As one distinguished colleague noted, one can only wonder about a sociologist whose height of intellectual interest is watching Tarzan movies on a Sunday.

3. I hope that I have avoided some of these errors through my methodology. During 1979 I watched every Tarzan movie made from 1932 through 1970 and took what one could consider field notes on each film. These notes, when transcribed, were coded using the categories of conventions discussed in the body of the paper.

4. I am pleased that this is the first time this jewel of cultural description has appeared in print.

5. In the films involved I have often shortened the title by the deletion of *Tarzan and the* . . . which usually appears as the first section of the Tarzan film title.

6. Others feel that fewer films about women were made in the 1950s (Haskell, 1973:270). I do not know if this is a verified fact if one considers B fare as well, but it is most certainly true that fewer top-quality films with women were produced. Rosen's chapter "Suspicion Stalks," concerning the women-victim films of the 1940s, beyond its overdrawn and distressing comparisons, does not provide any really satisfactory answer.

7. The location of the films is of interest. The two films shot on location prior to 1955 were made in Mexico and Guatemala. Of the seven films made on location after 1959 only two were made in Africa. One was made in Thailand, one in India, two in Brazil, and one in Mexico. Again, this lends support to the earlier arguments of the Ubiquitous Oriental and the Non-European-Exotic.

REFERENCES

Becker, Howard S. "Art as Collective Action." *American Sociological Review* 39 (1974), 767–76.

Bergman, Andrew. *We're in the Money* (New York: Harper Colophon Books, 1971).

Bohn, Thomas W., and Richard L. Stromgren, *Light and Shadows: A History of Motion Pictures* (Port Washington, N.Y.: Alfred Publishing, 1975).

Carpenter, Edmund. *Oh, What a Blow That Phantom Gave Me* (New York: Holt, Rinehart and Winston, 1972).

Cawelti, John G. *Adventure, Mystery and Romance: Formula Stores as Art and Popular Culture* (Chicago: University of Chicago Press, 1976).

Cheatwood, Derral. "The Prison Movie, Correctional Practice and Pristine Theory: Who Listens to Whom?" Paper presented at the Academy of Criminal Justice Sciences, March 1981.

Cowart, David. "The Tarzan Myth and Jung's Genesis of the Self." *Journal of American Culture* 2 (1979), 220–30.

Cripps, Thomas. *Slow Fade to Black* (New York: Oxford University Press, 1977).

Dowdy, Andrew. *The Films of the Fifties: The American State of Mind* (New York: Morrow, 1973).

Essoe, Gabe. *Tarzan of the Movies* (Secaucus, N.J.: Citadel Press, 1968).

Goodman, Ezra. *The Fifty-Year Decline and Fall of Hollywood* (New York: Simon & Schuster, 1961).

Haskell, Molly. *From Reverence to Rape: The Treatment of Women in the Movies* (Baltimore: Penguin Books, 1973).

Jarvie, I. C. *Movies and Society* (New York: Basic Books, 1970).

Jowett, Garth, and James M. Linton. *Movies as Mass Communication* (Beverly Hills, Calif.: Sage, 1980).

Mukerji, Chandra. "Having the Authority to Know." *Sociology of Work and Occupations* 3 (1973), 63–87.

Opubur, Alfred E., and Adebayo Ogunbi. "Ooga Booga: The African Image in American Films." In Robin W. Winks, ed., *Other Voices, Other Views: An International Collection of Essays from the Bicentennial* (Westport, Conn.: Greenwood Press, 1978).

Rosen, Marjorie. *Popcorn Venus* (New York: Avon Books, 1973).

Rosenblum, Barbara. "Style as Social Process." *American Sociological Review* 43 (1978) 422–38.

Standard and Poors. *Industry Surveys* (New York: Standard and Poors, 1973), April, vol. I:E30.

Standard and Poors. *Industry Surveys* (New York: Standard and Poors, 1980), April, vol. 1:E30.

Middle-Line Workers
and the System

Martin F. Norden

Women in the
Early Film Industry

The history of women's involvement in the film industry before World War I has remained a largely unexplored area. After reading the few volumes on the subject, one may be tempted to conclude that women's roles in the film business were limited to acting, screenwriting, and occasional directing. Yet women had found their way into all tiers of the industry, from production through distribution to exhibition. Indeed, industry-watcher Robert Grau was moved to remark in 1915 that, "In no line of endeavor has woman made so emphatic an impress than in the amazing film industry, which has created in its infant stage a new and compelling art wherein the gentler sex is now so active a factor that one may not name a single vocation in either the artistic or business side of its progress in which women are not conspicuously engaged. In the theaters, in the studios and even in the exchanges where film productions are marketed and released to exhibitors, the fair sex is represented as in no other calling to which women have harkened in the early years of the twentieth century."[1] In the interest of shedding some light on the professional activities of these women who, though relatively low in number, helped shape the new industry, this article examines their representative contributions in and to the field (as reflected primarily in the major trade journal of the time, *Moving Picture World* [hereafter *MPW*]) along with possible explanations for their successes and failures.

The film production tier of the industry is the area most frequently examined by historians attempting to discern women's involve-

From *Wide Angle* 6:3 (1985), 58–67. Reprinted with permission of the author and Johns Hopkins University Press.

ment in the earliest days of the medium, and it comes as no surprise to learn that, within that tier, women directors have garnered the most attention. Indeed, so much has already been written on the two doyennes of early directing, Alice Guy Blaché and Lois Weber, that further discussion of them here would seem redundant.[2] Anthony Slide's brief but dense *Early Women Directors* has been particularly useful for bringing to light their careers, noting that "There were more women directors at work in the American film industry prior to 1920 than during any period of its history."[3]

Actually, most silent-age female directorial careers—including those of Cleo Madison, Lule Warrenton, Ruth Stonehouse, Elsie Jane Wilson, Ruth Ann Baldwin, and Ida May Park, all of whom, along with Lois Weber, were alumnae of Carl Laemmle's Universal Pictures—were launched in the years immediately following World War I and thus fall outside the scope of this paper. The conditions which led to their ascendancy as directors are very much within the parameters of this article, however, and will be examined shortly along with several films directed by Blaché and Weber.

Of course, other roles in the film production field existed besides directing and many women found their way into these positions. Anthony Slide has reported that at least three camerawomen, one female assistant director, and four female studio managers were pursuing their respective careers by the midteens, though unfortunately little is known of their work today.[4] Better remembered are the women screenwriters, who quickly dominated that section of the business during the medium's earliest years. Anita Loos, Frances Marion, and Beulah Marie Dix remain the best known (primarily through biographies, auto- and otherwise), but scores of other women made their mark. For instance, Gene Gauntier, identified by *MPW* as the "very first of the women writers," penned many one-reel drama scripts, but is perhaps best remembered for writing the script for *From the Manger to the Cross*, an early five-part Kalem hit that was revived on every Christian holiday for years. Lois Weber was another prolific writer, reportedly turning out one script per week during her tenure with Universal's Rex subsidiary.[5]

Another prominent screenwriter of the time was Carolyn Wells of the Edison company. *MPW* was effusive in its praise for a 1909 Wells-authored film entitled *Ethel's Luncheon*, a comedy about a clubman, his fiancée, his male friend, and the pranks of two madcap women. *MPW* lauded the film for rising above the usual type of slapstick so common during the time, arguing that it "demonstrates that a comedy above the rough house type will make a successful picture. And this is worth much to the motion picture world. . . . This Edison picture is different in that the comedy is delicate and clean and leaves a pleasant impression. It is scarcely too much to say that this comedy has introduced a new type of motion picture and the producers deserve the heartiest encouragement in their laudable efforts to improve the character of purely amusement pictures." Though historians have traditionally regarded the Edison concern as stodgy and conservative, due to its founder and his leadership of the monopolistic-minded Motion Picture Patents Company, it was quite progressive on the issue of women writers. It invited many of its actresses to write screenplays, and they eagerly responded. As *MPW* noted in 1914, "If we started to list the Edison players who are also writers, we would have to give the complete roster."[6]

Several women extended their scriptwriting careers by becoming the heads of the production companies' scenario departments. The best known of these was Louella Parsons, better remembered along with Hedda Hopper as Hollywood's premier gossip columnists. In the years before World War I, Parsons was the head of scripts at the Essanay company. Though she actually wrote few screenplays herself, she developed a reputation for being very helpful to tyros trying to break into the scriptwriting business via the mail. In fact, she was so helpful that she became swamped with requests for critical remarks on scripts and had to issue several public announcements stating her reluctance to continue that service.[7]

Another head of a scenario department faced with a similar problem was a woman unfortunately identified by *MPW* only as "Mrs. Brandon." As the chief script editor for the American branch of the Eclair company, Brandon was inundated with poorly written screenplays by beginners. To cope with the deluge, she began accepting scripts written only by writers who had at least three produced films to their credit.[8]

One of the first women writers to form her own film production company was Eleanor Gates, well-known at the time as an author of short stories, novels, and screenplays. The first releases of the Eleanor Gates Photo-Play Company were three- and four-reelers of her stories which had appeared in the *Saturday Evening Post*.[9]

Women also made inroads into the field of editing, an area which to this day remains a female stronghold in the film industry. As Anthony Slide has noted, countless numbers of anonymous women served as film cutters and as frame-tinters on early color productions. One may grasp a sense of this fact in an *MPW* news story reporting a fire which swept through the Hollywood cutting rooms of the Universal studios in January 1914. The journal noted in passing that the only employees in the rooms, who assisted in saving many valuable negatives, were women.[10]

A number of women held jobs that combined editing with other aspects of film production. For example, Mary O'Connor was photoplay editor as well as a script reader and a publicity manager for the Vitagraph company in 1914, while Hetty Gray Baker was both an editor and a scriptwriter for the Bosworth company; her specialty was adapting the works of Jack London into screenplays. Beta Breuil, former Vitagraph editor, became the "Artistic Manager" of the North American Films Corporation in early 1914. The position was above those of editor and production manager, and she was responsible for overseeing all creative elements that went into the films produced by that concern. *MPW* waxed enthusiastic over her appointment, suggesting that she would bring "to her work the valuable knowledge gained through her previous connections, but here her genius for devising effects and working out ideas will have an absolutely unlimited scope, for she will have no one between herself and the heads of the company." Breuil brought in Catherine Carr and Peggy O'Neill, other alumnae of Vitagraph, along with Marie Jacobs to assist her in overseeing the creative aspects of every film produced by that company.[11]

Women had a far more difficult time breaking into the financial side of film production. Indeed, it appears only one woman ever became involved in production money matters during the pre–World War I era: Agnes Egan Cobb, sales manager for Union Features, Features Ideal, and the Eclair company's American wing. *MPW* noted her prosperity in that position: "In her capacity of sales manager for these feature concerns, Mrs. Cobb has been exceptionally successful. She has been able to hold up the price of the product she handles in a crowded market and to sell a reasonable quantity." In noting the difficulty of such a job, *MPW* inadvertently revealed the reason for women's lack of access to such positions: the dominant belief that women were ill equipped to cope with financial matters. The journal wrote that Cobb's position "is essentially a man's job so, when we see a woman tackling the selling end of the business *and getting away with it* our hats must come off to that woman"[12] [my emphasis].

For similar reasons, women found themselves hard-pressed to break into the higher echelons of the distribution and exhibition sides of the industry. Those that did often found their accomplishments trumpeted in the trade press. For example, *MPW* noted the emergence of Frida

Klug within the distribution area with an article that bore the screaming headline, "A WOMAN INVADES THE AMERICAN MOVING PICTURE FIELD." Klug was the U.S. representative for the August Schultze film of Turin, Italy, the distribution agency for the Italian-based Helios, Roato, Roma, and Pasquali filmmaking companies. Klug, whom *MPW* described as "the only lady so far to our knowledge to grapple with the intricacies of the film importing and renting business," had worked as a distribution agent in London, Paris, Budapest, and other European cities. As a representative of the Schultze concern, the peripatetic Klug visited such major eastern U.S. cities as New York, Philadelphia, and Pittsburgh to promote that company's offerings. Klug was not hesitant to criticize American films and film theaters; in an interview with *MPW*, she stated she was very unimpressed with both and claimed they lagged far behind European standards.[13]

Another woman involved in the distribution end of the business was E. M. Murphy. Murphy was the chief administrator for the Troy, New York office of the United Film Company and was extremely knowledgeable of the film industry, according to *MPW*. In detailing her duties, the journal underscored the rarity of a woman holding an executive position such as this one in the film field: "It is not very often that you run across a young lady assuming the entire charge of a live film exchange, getting new customers, taking care of their wants and superintending the bookings, etc."[14]

In terms of the sheer numbers of reported instances, women exhibitors seemed to fare better than their distribution counterparts. Women who owned and managed moving-picture theaters found particular success in a number of cities east of the Mississippi River. For example, Ida Mayer was manager of a film theater in Jamaica, Long Island, while Evelyn Corbett became the Chicago representative of the Colonial Theater Company, a theater-chain operator in Illinois and Indiana, after working in the Chicago office of the Motion Picture Screen Company. In Cincinnati, F. J. Lotz ran the 1,150-seat Norwood theater, while her daughters Freda and Martha operated the smaller Nemo theater, which boasted a 500-seat airdome used during the summer.[15]

Boston also seemed to offer a favorable environment for women exhibitors; not only did Lotta Crabtree own the Savoy theater in that city, but also another woman, unfortunately identified solely by *MPW* as "Mrs. Clement," managed the B. F. Keith Bijou theater there. Clement insisted on offering a wide range of entertainment for her patrons. In addition to films, her theater presented lantern-slide shows (which she called "camera chats") and sundry live performances. As an admiring *MPW* noted, "A cultured woman like Mrs. Clement perceives the absolute necessity of supplementing the pictures with these camera talks, one-act plays and music." A tough-minded, efficient administrator, Clement strongly questioned the film-selection system followed by the film exchanges. As an independent exhibitor, she found she was denied access to the productions created by Pathé Frères, Essanay, Lubin, and the other members of the Motion Picture Patents Company. She clearly advocated an "open market" system, in which exhibitors could rent films produced by any concern.[16]

On the educational front, Katherine F. Carter was the head of the General Film Company's education division before quitting in mid-1914 to found the Katherine F. Carter Educational and Motion Picture Service Bureau in New York. This company leased film projection equipment to schools, churches, clubs, and hotels, in addition to scheduling films to be shown to these organizations.[17]

Lest I fall into a variant of the "Great Person" pitfall of historical research, I should point out that hundreds of other women occupied less prominent positions in the exhibition field, primarily as pianists who performed mood music to accompany the films. Sadly, these women were often the targets of ridicule by others in the industry. In a wondrously subtle 1911 article entitled "Jackass Music," *MPW* columnist Louis Reeves Harrison attempted to satirize the female pianists, whom he collectively labeled "Lily Limpwrist." The article featured several cartoons depicting the lamentable LL engaging in such inappropriate actions as ignoring an action scene of a film and primping and playing a lively tune during a death scene.[18] Later that same year, *MPW* published an "ode" to the female pianist, entitled "Lizzie Plays for the Pictures," parts of which are reproduced below:

> With a tum-te-tum and an aching thumb
> She keeps the time with her chewing gum,
> She chews and chaws without a pause,
> With a ragtime twist to her busy jaws,
> And her fingers fly as the hours go by;
> She pounds the keys with a languid ease
> Till the folks go home and the pictures cease;
> But Lizzie plays like a grim machine,
> And she never thinks what the measures mean,
> For she's played them oft and the notes don't waft

Any thought to her that is sweet and soft;
There's a wrangling chime as her fingers climb
Up the yellowed keys as she beats the time,
For the show that costs but half-a-dime.
And she chaws and chews as she seems to muse
On the flying films and the flitting views,
And her hands jump here and her hands jump there,
While betimes with one she will fix her hair,
But she keeps right on with the other hand
In a ragtime tune that is simply grand
And a burst of bass when she whacks her thumb
On the lower keys, and a sudden frown
As she jabs the loud, loud pedal down.[19]

One could argue that such seemingly innocuous bits of whimsy reflected to some degree the conflicting male attitudes toward women's involvement in the early film industry, and it is worth attempting to explain how these and other factors led to women's prominence in some areas of the film business and eventual decline in others. Why, for example, were women's most memorable achievements in the fields of acting, writing, and editing, but in few other areas of the field? After all, the medium was still quite young, and as Marjorie Rosen has suggested, "before it became a powerful elitist operation, the industry's hunger for material and moviemakers left little room for sexual prejudice."[20] The remainder of this essay will be devoted to pursuing and developing theories which might help explain the roles that women played—and did not play—in the pre–World War I film industry and immediately thereafter.

The cultural phenomenon most responsible for encouraging the tide of women entering the business was the suffrage movement, then under way in several countries. Though nominally limited to women's voting rights, the suffrage movement became synonymous with women's overall rights, and *MPW*, always prepared to laud women in the film industry work force, was quick to perceive its influence; in a 1913 article on a woman who sold posters to movie companies for a living, the journal observed: "In these days of the militant suffragette, we are prepared for almost anything in the way of womanly activity." In addition, the industry as a whole, which was never known for resisting the temptation to exploit current social issues, made dozens if not hundreds of films dealing with suffragists and other progressive women, Molly Haskell's claim that suffragists never found their way into films notwithstanding.[21]

Yet many women had a hard time overcoming legacies of the Victorian age that took the form of male biases against them. While pondering the shortage of women directors, Alice Guy Blaché acknowledged "that a woman's success in many lines of endeavor is still made very difficult by a strong prejudice against one of her sex doing work that has been done only by men for hundreds of years." Another bias is easily detectable in this bit of 1910 enlightenment concerning alleged reasons for many women's attraction to acting: "Nothing appeals to the feminine heart so much as the wearing of nice dresses and the opportunity of displaying them on the stage or elsewhere. Where there is the possibility of a girl being photographed in a moving picture and her portrait shown to millions of moving picture patrons, what wonder that the feminine heart aspires to have the opportunity? Here we are striking at the very root of feminine human nature: the love of finery, the love of display, the love of admiration. So it goes. So it will always go."[22]

If this notion is a reasonably accurate reflection of the then-prevalent male attitude toward women, it should come as no surprise to learn that women's most visible presence in the business emerged in the acting field, into which women bent on a film career were often shunted. It is doubtless true that a successful acting career was the major goal for many women entering the film field; indeed, they were fortunate even to have the opportunity to pursue that career prior to 1909, since most female roles at that time were played by men. Yet other women who might have had visions of finding challenging work behind the scenes often had little choice. Another pundit of the times offered this penetrating insight into those things that interest men and women: "Experts say that whatever appeals to the heart draws women, and that whatever appeals to the head draws men."[23] Again, if this observation, based on some "definitive authority" lost to the ages, is close to the dominant sentiments of the day, then there is little wonder why women in general were initially excluded from the major decision-making positions such as producing and directing in favor of acting, where pleasing personalities and equally pleasing bone structures were the going concern and where women would be in a position to exert minimal authority.

But what about scriptwriting? Why did this area come to be strongly associated with women's involvement in film? The answers seem to reside in the fact that it represented a field in which women's nonacting creative talents could be easily exploited. As suggested in a recent *Wide Angle* essay, the Hollywood writer has always been treated rather like the bastard of the industry,[24] and one may argue that this attitude began forming when women were developing a strong foothold in the writing field. It is worth noting that the scripts were often written by women who lived far away from the production centers of the industry. For example, Katharine Boland Clemens, who won a scenario contest sponsored by Carl Laemmle's Imp Company with a tragic romance set against the Spanish-American war entitled *The Double*, lived in St. Louis. Two prominent screenwriters of the time, Lillian Sweetser and Bettie Fitzgerald, lived respectively in Maine and Alabama.[25] All of the major production companies had their own scenario departments, many of which solicited screenplays by mail. This situation represented an attractive opportunity for many women, trapped in the stay-at-home life expected of them, to pursue more creative experiences and even modest careers.

Yet, as all screenwriters know, their resulting scripts cease to belong to them once the works have moved into the hands of the directors and the other production people. The directors of the pre–World War I period could easily change around any elements of the screenplays from which they worked, knowing full well they would encounter minimal resistance from the scripts' authors, who probably lived hundreds if not thousands of miles away. Thus, those women who wrote screenplays at home were at an enormous disadvantage; they may have put considerable creativity into their works but were poorly paid and in no position to exert veto power over any script changes that might arise. They often failed to receive credit for their efforts, as in the case of Grace Adele Pierce, who wrote the script for D. W. Griffith's early epic *Judith of Bethulia* (1913) and who asked the League of American Pen women to help screenwriters gain rights.[26] Given our society's long-standing abuse and disparagement of people not in positions of power (including the still-widespread belief that women trivialize any occupations or skills they master), it is not difficult to see the origins of the condescending, even hostile, attitudes toward screenwriters.

As for women's involvement in editing, it is reasonably clear that the cutter positions, widely held by women, were initially regarded as menial; cutters merely carried out the dictates of others with regard to the length and order of the shots in a film. Yet many women worked hard at their craft and helped elevate it to greater executive and creative status. One such woman was Katherine Eggleston, a then-famous magazine and newspaper writer hired in late 1913 by the Mutual Film Corporation as a "picture editor." In describing her duties, *MPW* wrote that she "views the different scenes of the picture after it is completed and arranges them with an eye to clearness of story-construction and dramatic value, establishing sequence and ridding the picture of all that does not contribute to its effectiveness."[27] Such a position, with all the creativity and decision making it entailed, was a far cry from the earliest cutting jobs.

The industry further demonstrated its ambivalence toward working women by the ways it depicted women, progressive and otherwise, in the films produced then. As many feminist film critics have pointed out, the silent-film industry heavily favored women's roles that were little more than the basic stereotypes of mothers, ingenues, soubrettes, and vamps, in other words, roles defined mainly in terms of relationships with others. (One can easily get a sense of this from the titles of such representative films of the time as *A Widow and Her Child, The Fickle Fiancée, His Friend's Wife,* and *For Her Brother's Sake.*) Yet with the suffrage movement well under way during the pre–World War I era, the international film industry began making movies which depicted women in situations other than exclusively familial or romantic ones.

Unfortunately, but predictably, these earliest efforts to portray the "New Woman" were almost always comedies which lampooned or belittled women's attempts to pursue interests outside the home.[28] Suffragists in particular received the full force of the industry's satiric jabs and were frequently characterized as either men-haters, ugly spinsters, or wives whose attempts to liberate themselves proved futile if not ridiculous. A handful of later silent films did treat suffrage with seriousness (virtually all of which were independently produced under the auspices of various suffrage organizations), but the majority of the suffrage films could be summed up in *MPW*'s description of *The Man Suffragette for the Abolition of Work for Women* (1910): "a comedy which will keep the audience roaring, and is, in reality, a good travesty upon the suffragette movement."[29]

Though few if any of such "travesties" were written or directed by women, the films they did make were hardly supportive of progressive women, at least at first. Indeed, their films initially tended to be rather conventional romantic/familial dramas. Precious little of the pre–World War I output of such women as Alice Guy Blaché, Lois Weber, and Anita Loos could be labeled "feminist" or "progressive" with fairness. For example, little of the 1910 Edison film *History Repeats Itself*, written by Carolyn Wells, could be called even mildly progressive; the film dealt with two young lovers enjoying their first kiss, who, after being interrupted by her mother, convince the older woman that their romance was but a repetition of her own.[30] If these women had any feminist tendencies, they kept them in check, perhaps believing their careers might be jeopardized if they did not.

Both Lois Weber and Alice Guy Blaché eventually veered from the straight and narrow, however, by occasionally exploring vampish themes. Consider, for example, *The Spider and Her Web* (1914), written and co-directed by Lois Weber. This movie starred Weber as "Madame DuBarry," a "spider" who caused good men to commit crimes. *MPW* defined a spider as a woman "who is dazzlingly beautiful, who has a fascinating personality and who has everything that a woman should have except a heart." This film was matched by Alice Guy Blaché's *The Woman of Mystery* (1914), a four-reeler about a Hindu princess who created a Jekyll/Hyde personality in an American male detective, using "the uncanny psychic powers developed to such an astonishing degree in the Far East." Of equal interest was Blaché's *The Dream Woman* (1914), about the weirdness that ensued after a man, who dreamed he was murdered on his birthday by his as-yet-unmet wife, actually encountered the woman in real life.[31] Though vamp stories proved popular at the box office, the male-dominated industry may have viewed such films with growing concern; it may have believed that such women-directed films featuring the destruction of men were sending out the wrong signals to the rest of society. Such films may have contributed to women's eventual near-exclusion from directorial positions in Hollywood.

In sum: the years prior to World War I held much promise for women entering all fields of the film industry, with many women directors and writers—Lois Weber, Frances Marion, Anita Loos, Jeanie MacPherson, and Bess Meredyth, to name a few—reaching their greatest successes in the years immediately following the war. Yet these women were not feminists, or if they were, they kept such tendencies under wraps. As suggested by Molly Haskell, "These women, businesswomen and artists, were not 'political,' that is, they were less the expression of a feminist movement (except indirectly, as examples of successful women professionals) than a reflection of the general female orientation of the film industry and the specific popularity of women's themes as subjects."[32] As the industry matured into a vertically integrated oligopoly bent on outmaneuvering the remaining independent factions at every turn, and as interest in women's themes declined, women found themselves squeezed out of many substantive positions in all levels of the business. These actions on the part of a nervous, newly solidified, male-dominated industry may have been due to a belief that women were not as strongly profit-minded or business-oriented as men, and that some women-directed films were mildly subversive. Only recently have we seen women in the industry in numbers comparable to those during that early glowing era in film history.

NOTES

1. Robert Grau, "Woman's Conquest in Filmdom," *Motion Picture Supplement* 1 (September 1915), 41.

2. For example, see Marjorie Rosen, *Popcorn Venus: Women, Movies & the American Dream* (New York: Coward, McCann & Geoghegan, 1973), pp. 367–74; Sharon Smith, *Women Who Make Movies* (New York: Hopkinson & Blake, 1975), pp. 1–19; Francis Lacassin, "Out of Oblivion: Alice Guy Blaché," in Patricia Erens, ed., *Sexual Stratagems: The World of Women in Film* (New York: Horizon Press, 1979), pp. 168–78; Molly Haskell, *From Reverence to Rape: The Treatment of Women in the Movies* (New York: Holt, Rinehart & Winston, 1974); and Anthony Slide, *Early Women Directors* (New York: A. S. Barnes, 1977).

3. Slide, *Early Women Directors*, p. 9.

4. Slide, *Early Women Directors*, p. 10.

5. *Moving Picture World* (hereafter *MPW*), 11 July 1914, 202; 21 February 1914, 975.

6. *MPW*, 18 September 1909, 377; 11 July 1914, 202.

7. *MPW*, 31 January 1914, 537; 22 March 1914, 1674; 11 July 1914, 202.

8. *MPW*, 6 December 1913, 1143; 29 December 1913, 1537.

9. *MPW*, 30 May 1914, 1269.

10. Slide, *Early Women Directors*, pp. 10–11; *MPW*, 24 January 1914, 398.

11. *MPW*, 2 May 1914, 829; 11 July 1914, 202; 3 January 1914, 40.

12. *MPW*, 20 December 1913, 1414; 25 April 1914, 529.

13. *MPW*, 13 November 1909, 680.

14. *MPW*, 19 August 1911, 460.

15. *MPW*, 2 September 1911, 615; 8 October 1910, 808; 14 February 1914, 812.

16. *MPW*, 29 October 1910, 1001; 15 October 1910, 859.

17. *MPW*, 11 April 1914, 200; 2 May 1914, 657.

18. *MPW*, 21 January 1911, 124.

19. *MPW*, 2 September 1911, 618.

20. Rosen, *Popcorn Venus*, p. 367.

21. *MPW*, 8 November 1913, 620; Haskell, *From Reverence to Rape*, p. 44.

22. Cited in MPW, 11 July 1914, 195; 19 March 1910, 420.

23. *MPW*, 24 December 1910, 1463.

24. Robert Holkeboer, "Sex and the Screenwriter," *Wide Angle* 5:1 (1982), 28–33.

25. *MPW*, 12 November 1910, 1088; 11 July 1914, 202.

26. *MPW*, 23 May 1914, 1109.

27. *MPW*, 20 December 1913, 1415.

28. Several films of this kind included *She Would Be a Business Man* (1910), about a housewife who swapped jobs with her husband and who, in the words of *MPW*, "returns, humiliated and repentant, and acknowledges her mistake;" *The Lady Barbers* (1910), which featured local townwomen running the title characters out of the village after their menfolk had been lining up for two and three haircuts a day; and *Baseball and Bloomers* (1911), in which a women's baseball team was hopelessly outclassed by a male team until

two macho-types disguised themselves as women and, as pitcher and catcher, mowed down the opposing members with strikes. As *MPW* noted, "The other members of the 'Girl Team' have nothing to do except look pretty." See *MPW*, 16 July 1910, 144; 12 November 1910, 1127, and 7 January 1911, 44.

29. Consider the exemplar film *When Women Win* (1909), which anticipated women's activities after they won the right to vote and, in *MPW*'s words, "do other mannish things." The film featured postwomen who used their own judgment in the delivery of the mails, business meetings which were turned into afternoon teas, and even a physician who told a "waiting wife that it is a boy and that father and child are both doing very nicely, thank you." Another film, *Fire! Fire! Fire!* (1911), presented the story of suffragettes taking over a fire department. As *MPW* described it: "The first fire alarm and its disastrous results convince the women that charge of a city department is not all their fancy painted it, and they return to their homes wetter and wiser." A final example may be found in the form of *The Reformation of the Suffragettes* (1911), in which the women of a village ostracized their fishing-obsessed men. *MPW* described the women's attitudes at the film's conclusion in these terms: "After many ludicrous attempts to do without the tyrant men, they find it impossible and rejoice in the return of their erstwhile hated oppressors." See *MPW*, 27 November 1909, 769, 771; 28 January 1911, 194, and 25 February 1911, 434. The review of *The Man Suffragette* may be found in *MPW*, 9 July 1910, 86.

30. *MPW*, 21 May 1910, 833.

31. *MPW*, 21 March 1914, 1538; 16 May 1914, 983; 21 March 1914, 1508.

32. Haskell, *From Reverence to Rape*, p. 74.

James Lastra

Standards and Practices: Aesthetic Norm and Technological Innovation in the American Cinema

One of the most important characteristics of the classical cinema is surely its stability over time. Scholars such as David Bordwell, Janet Staiger, and Kristin Thompson[1] have striven to demonstrate how a paradigm of bounded and hierarchically ordered formal options structured filmmaking during the classical period, how the dominance of a particular form of efficiently conveyed—and profitable—narrative ensured the paradigm's hegemony, and how the structure of industrial production ensured an interchangeability of personnel and therefore a kind of stability regarding the practical aspects of filmmaking. Few, however, have attempted to explain how the paradigm came to be internalized by those workers whose everyday task it was to produce the representations that Hollywood thrived on. While in the abstract it is easy to understand why the economic success of clearly told stories of goal-oriented, heterosexual, middle-class protagonists mandated the paradigm's primacy in a profit-seeking capitalist corporation and that the formal conventions of what came to be known as classical continuity cinema were especially (if not uniquely) suited to this form, it is more difficult to explain how the representational assumptions and norms necessary to this style of filmmaking came to form the instinctive or obvious solutions to the myriad representational problems raised by any particular script.

Our attempts to describe these formal conventions as, for example, a collection of arbitrary codes have more often than not led us away from the kinds of analyses that would explain how the classical paradigm actually came to regulate aesthetic practice on the set. Teach a group of students the rules or codes of continuity cinema, and they will be able to dissect any number of scenes from any number of Hollywood films, but chances are they will not be able to *make* a film whose spatial constructions and match-on-action cuts have the fluidity and clarity of a Hollywood film. It is not a question of understanding these films and their norms per se, but rather of internalizing them as a material form of practice—a job, if you will—carried out by innumerable workers whose livelihood required them to make the right decisions about lighting, framing, miking, and editing from 9 to 5, six days a week.

Indeed, the norms of classical continuity construction *were* internalized by workers in the studio system in the form of what one sociologist calls a "durably installed generative principle of regulated improvisations,"[2] or, more simply, as a consistent and coherent set of predispositions toward practice. Workers do not consciously devise these norms, these ways of doing, nor do they exhibit a conscious mastery over them. This is because the practices arise out of preexisting, objective, material conditions of the social world. As a result, these practices have an objective significance that outstrips the conscious intentions of the practitioners, yet the practices cannot simply be reduced to those objective conditions. Instead, they exhibit a regularity and consistency, perhaps even a structure, that is *compatible* with the conditions that produced them. The dispositions toward practice characteristic of Hollywood technicians are

> the universalizing mediation which causes an individual agent's practices, without explicit reason or signifying intent, to be nonetheless 'sensible' and 'reasonable.' That part of practices which remains obscure in the eyes of their own producers is the aspect by which they are objectively adjusted to other practices and to the structures of which the principle of their production is itself a product.[3]

By arguing this, I do not mean to suggest that technicians do not consciously try to conform to the conventions of continuity or to norms of beauty or that they do not work with an eye toward the significance of their decisions. On the contrary, I believe this consciousness, indeed self-consciousness, is an integral part of the modus operandi of the Hollywood professional. Further, much of the character of classical films can, in fact, be explained in terms of conscious attempts to adhere to these widely recognized norms. What I do mean to suggest, however, is that even these intentional choices are structured in advance by conditions of which the worker is necessarily unaware. While the shooting angles selected by a cinematographer may be explained by an adherence to, for example, the 180-degree rule, the specific formal character of those shots, the implicit values shaping the decision to shoot the faces, the norms of lighting, the range of different possible ways to shoot a shot/ reverse-shot sequence, or, most simply, the very bounds of the obvious, the reasonable, the possible, and so on, all of those things that go without saying are not consciously or intentionally decided on. To be sure, they are all compatible with the articulated principles of filmic construction, but not fully explainable by them.

Although this introduction may seem general and abstract, the analysis to follow will concentrate on a very concrete and particular moment within the history of the American cinema: Hollywood's transition to sound film production. The period from 1926 to 1934 saw the film industry undergo the most extensive transformations in technology, personnel, formal conventions, and mode of production in its history. As several scholars have pointed out, however, the classical continuity system emerged at the far end of this transformation relatively unscathed.[4] Nevertheless, I will argue that this apparent lack of change does not permit us to ignore the processes by which a new technology and a different set of representational standards were integrated into an existing industrial mode of production. The transition period is especially enlightening because the intersection of two major representational industries—Hollywood and the phonography/telephony businesses—allows us to highlight the otherwise occulted norms guiding representational practice in both fields. The clash between competing norms of representation as embodied in technicians' differing standards of correct practice forced an explicit examination of the logic underlying each industry's assumptions regarding the obviousness of its own ideals. The self-evidence of these norms comes under serious scrutiny as the two groups struggle to articulate their own rationale for conventions of practice and justification for maintaining them in the face of myriad pressures to change.

As each group attempts to clarify and legitimize the norms that define it professionally, we may also examine the role that informal theory—which we might even term aesthetics—plays in the regulation, justification, and reproduction of workplace practices. We may thus begin to describe the extent to which these articulated goals and standards neither match nor fully account for the variety of practices they ostensibly authorize. In addition, we can see how ideas of professional identity are complexly imbricated with allegiance to a particular aesthetic, and I might argue further, technicians' misrecognition of themselves in the ideals it represents. The technicians' misrecognition is by no means a result of their ignorance, but rather of the historical relationship established among science, engineering, corporate capitalism, industrial forms of research and production, and labor relations. As a result, I will imply larger claims about the role played by aesthetics in science, in basic research, in the structuring of representational industries, and in the development, implementation, and normalization of representational technologies. Ultimately, it is less the devices that define the cultural and historical impact of a technology than the practices that regulate, define, and determine it that are of utmost importance.

Theory and Practice

During Hollywood's transition to sound, technicians' duties often seem to have been split almost evenly between working on the set and theorizing about sound representation. Rarely has the technical community been so forthcoming with its opinions on the logic and conceptual bases of filmic construction, and even more rarely has the theoretical arena seemed so central to Hollywood filmmaking. Page after page in scientific and industry journals emphatically promote various aesthetic models, but why? What function did the *articulation* of aesthetic standards and norms play? Far from being incidental, technicians often seem nearly obsessed with discussing their positions on questions of representational illusion, accuracy, propriety, and validity, and, almost uniformly, the standards they assert are justified in terms of a transparent realism. That is, techniques of sound recording and reproduction are explained by reference to a standard apparently justified by its obviously literal faithfulness. Put more complexly, each technician naturalizes the ideals of practice by demonstrating those ideals' compatibility with a particular notion of representation that is described as obvious *and* as scientific and that comes to stand as the paradigm for *all* acts of representation, no matter how diverse. Realism of a very particular sort thus served both to structure technical and aesthetic debates and simultaneously (if circularly) to measure the validity of practices by masquerading as a universal category of evaluation.

The importance of realism as a category of analysis and evaluation was not restricted to the field of aesthetics, but infiltrated and shaped the course of industrial research and the development of techniques. Bordwell and Staiger, for example, have pointed out that realism was explicitly adopted as an industrial goal, but they add this proviso: "As for realism . . . this too was rationally adopted as an engineering aim—but wholly within the framework of *Hollywood's conception of 'realism.'*"[5] In fact, it is precisely because of a conflict between Hollywood realism and the realism advanced by sound engineers coming from the radio and telephone industries that the transition from silent to sound cinema is so complex and interesting. We might even go so far as to say that the dominant model of realism in each community was so at odds with the other that effective collaboration between them seemed almost ruled out from the start. Moreover, the sound engineers' professional identity was so completely bound up with their notion of perfect representation that the compromises between them and their Hollywood counterparts necessary for an efficient system of sound film production required complex negotiations. In other words, labor relations needed to be worked out, in part, within the field of aesthetic theory.

The relationships established in this period between the theoretical and practical realms, and between the sorts of statements appropriate to each, are indicative of a shift in the technician's social, economic, and professional position. To demonstrate this, I will open up the category of realism so central to both the representational practices of the period and to current ideological critiques of Hollywood and will show the category to be multiple, contradictory, and internally contested. Rather than a stable term of bourgeois ideology, realism is one of the prime sites of cultural struggle and appropriation. In short, two understandings of realism in sound representation embody different conceptions of the epistemological and referential properties believed to be constitutive of good sound representational practice in general. Theory, which could easily be understood as secondary to the real relations and functionings of the social world, is in fact precisely the terrain upon which certain important cultural and political struggles are fought out. If nothing else, the debates over realism set the boundaries for the manner in which a recorded sound could be understood to refer to the audible world, and they therefore authorized a circumscribed range of "legitimate" under-standings, uses, and practices.

The historical development of the American recording industries and the rise of a particular sort of engineer within these industries almost required that the debate over proper representation take center stage because the theories implicitly held by those engineers helped to struc-ture the entire field of aesthetic options and goals, as well as the course of technological development, in specific ways. Thus, the connection between sound theory and a professional identity is far from arbitrary. Ultimately, the changing contour of the sound representation debate also indicates the changing nature of the engineer's perceived role. As engi-neers from nonfilm corporations came to perceive their own identity as tied to the corporate success of Hollywood studios rather than, say, personal achievements or to the success of Bell Labs, they became sound men rather than engineers.[6] Concurrent with, required by, and to some extent constitutive of this shift is a transformation in their standards and expectations for sound representations. By investigating the contradic-tions between initial theory and ultimate practice, we can, perhaps, reimagine the link between social structure, text, and subject posited by ideological critiques[7] without having to resort to the vague pressure of an ideological demand for realism. The link between social relations and representational norms is, I believe, far more material and demonstrable.

The Invisible Auditor

What exactly were the competing representational models for sound? An early and representative statement of one theory comes from Bell Tele-phone researcher Joseph P. Maxfield in a 1926 article on sound recording:

> Phonographic reproduction may be termed perfect when the compo-nents of the reproduced sound reaching the ears of the actual listener have the same relative intensity and phase relation as the sound reaching the ears *of an imaginary listener* to the original performance would have had.[8]

This is the invisible auditor approach to realistic sound representation. As late as 1934, and in spite of years of practical experience to the contrary, Harry Olson and Frank Massa of RKO claimed that the ideal recording/reproducing situation would involve placing dummies with microphones for ears in different places around the set and recording multiple tracks. Theatrical playback would require multiple stereo tracks, with each signal routed to the seat in the audience corresponding to the literal position of its respective dummy at the original performance on the set![9] Beyond its extraordinary technical complexity (and cost), several startling beliefs underlie this model. Among other things, the writers assume, first, that movies work by offering discrete individuals something like a theatrical experience of each shot or action; second, that spectators identify their individual position with that of the mike/camera; and third, that movies are a succession of discrete, autonomous, and perceptually specific observations. Perhaps most significant, these engineers assume that the film spectator/auditor is literally a part of the same space as the original performance. This further implies that the space and acoustic quality of the *set* are identical with those of the represented world.

One practical result of this aesthetic of absolute fidelity is that each take begins to be treated as a unique and autonomous event rather than a part of a more or less homogeneous series. Hence, the acoustic quality of every take was assumed to be a function of its unique conditions of production and thus not necessarily related to the quality of the preceding or the following take. The basic representational unit of coherence for the invisible auditor model was therefore the shot (understood as a discrete perceptual experience) rather than the scene.

To put this yet another way, the specificity of each performance—the actual space, the actual distance of the camera/mike from the actor, and so forth—provided the principle of representational unity for each take. In practical terms, the invisible auditor, or situated-audience-member, approach manifested itself in a variety of concepts and techniques, including often-expressed desires for scale matching and for sound perspective. Although the practice of systematically matching long shots with distant miking and close-ups with their acoustic counterparts seems never to have been actually practiced, some technical literature continually stressed scale matching as an obvious goal. For example, in 1930, John L. Cass, an RCA engineer, decries the use of multiple microphones for a single shot, since the resulting sound record represents the sound as "heard by a man with five or six very long ears."[10] Likewise, in 1931, Carl Dreher suggests that "good reproduction requires a loudness level approximately equal to what a normal auditor would expect on the basis of his experience."[11] Although reasonably referring his standard to auditor expectations, Dreher neglects to point out against which experience to measure the appropriate volume of, say, romantic conversations between couples we have never met.[12] Again, Maxfield offers one more restatement of this basic assumption in a 1930 essay in the *Journal of the Society of Motion Picture Engineers*. "The problem to be solved is that of obtaining a sound record which correlates with the picture in such a manner that a member of the audience is given the illusion of being an actual spectator in the scene."[13]

Of course, this particular version of the theoretically ubiquitous invisible observer, which assumed a literally situated relationship to the performance, was terribly ill suited to narrative feature films. Pairing the mike and camera in close-up gave great prominence to the dialogue, but a cut to a long shot would introduce an enormous amount of reverberation while simultaneously risking dialogue intelligibility. Sudden changes in sound texture created by this approach were clearly inappropriate to the more homogeneous character of classical representation and narration that assumed compromises. Indeed, as early as 1929, mike booms had been developed to follow actors around the set, negating in practice the theoretically dominant auditor principle.[14] The use of directional mikes and soundproofing also put the lie to the utterly faithful model of sound duplication. So why did the articulation of it persist well into the 1930s? What did it offer?

Perhaps the best answer is that scale matching offered a coherent set of tools and predispositions for conceptualizing, describing, ordering, and evaluating representational practices. So, for example, when attempting to explain the concept, Wesley C. Miller of MGM tells his readers:

> The amplification of the sound must be just enough to fit the picture size. Probably the best way to express this is to say that any combination of picture and sound must be so proportioned that the latter sounds natural coming from the artificial person on the screen.[15]

Although here offering a description of an effect in the guise of a cause, Miller expresses a concern shared by dozens of other engineers trying to describe the effects of classical narration. Given a particular problem for which his aesthetic is unsuited, he reconceives the necessary representational modifications through the intellectual, perceptual, and cognitive categories readily available to him. Although another set of categories would not have been beyond his grasp, those that were ready-to-hand, and ingrained as habits and basic dispositions, were far more comfortable and familiar. Thus, the invisible auditor model of cinematic narration offered a convenient logic of day-to-day practice, which was consistent, logical, practical, and simple and which ordered the almost infinite possibilities of sound representation into a small group of probable and good techniques while excluding the rest as improbable or simply bad. Its universal application allowed theoretical explanations for qualitative judgments—it gave aesthetic evaluations a quasi-scientific basis. Simply put, it offered mental equipment, mental habits, and a standard for the profession.

Aesthetics and Basic Research

Now any number of norms or aesthetics could have performed this function. Why the fidelity model to the exclusion of others? In retrospect, this "mistake" seems tightly bound to the engineer's status in institutions like Bell Labs and, later, in the studios. The storied conflicts between sound engineers and virtually every other worker on the set bear witness to struggles over professional identity and responsibility and over the representational standards developed over time within the competing technical and industrial cultures. The very fabric of these professions is woven out of the aesthetic norms and theories held by its members and implicitly respected in their day-to-day practice, and these norms not only shaped the evaluation of devices and techniques, but also helped set the agendas for corporate investment and research.

The representational norms characteristic of engineers within the sound industries were partially, but definitively, determined by the economic situation of the larger corporation. By setting the objective conditions for research, development, and implementation, those corporations determined in a practical sense the limits of the reasonable, the thinkable, and the possible for its employees. Even though the research agendas of sound researchers at other institutions might, in fact, have differed little from those at, say, Bell Labs, the latter company wielded enormous power in setting these agendas. Bell researchers did not skew their research to suit some arbitrary needs of their employers, but

> because the dispositions durably inculcated by objective conditions . . . engender aspirations and practices objectively compatible with those objective requirements, the most improbable practices are excluded . . . as *unthinkable,* or at the cost of a *double negation* which inclines agents

to make a virtue of a necessity, that is, to refuse what is anyway refused and to love the inevitable.[16]

The bulk of research and commercial development in the sound industry was carried out in firms like Bell Labs and its subsidiary, Western Electric, where economic interest in all phases of sound technology, from mikes to amplifiers, to disks, to loudspeakers, encouraged certain forms of commercial exploitation while it downplayed other options. Given that early research into both recording and reproducing was geared primarily toward music, the heuristic of the invisible auditor was a fairly obvious one. It made perfect sense in phonography to duplicate as closely as possible the experience of an auditor in a concert hall, sensitive to all nuances of tone, performance, reverberation, and volume. So important a criterion was the concert model that advances in recording technology were often praised for allowing the recording situation to approximate more closely the concert situation in physical and acoustic terms.[17] This standard meant that the represented event, acoustic space, timbre, and so on should duplicate the original and that the auditor was conceptually and practically a part of the space of representation—literally, a witness to the performance. Thus, the demands of one social practice of sound production and reception—those typical of serious concert music—shaped the theorization of a whole range of sonic phenomena.

The dominance of the concert listener as the standard had quite a number of practical implications. Yet from the outset, engineers seemed to ignore that standard in the face of specific practical exigencies. For example, Maxfield notes that the reverberation long considered appropriate for piano performance seemed excessive when recorded and therefore suggests that some manipulations of the original space of performance "can simulate to a considerable degree *in the reproduced music,* the *effective* space relationships of the original."[18] Two significant contingencies are introduced here. First, we are forced to recognize that we are dealing with a highly conventionalized and constructed original event. We might say that this is sound produced for representation—that is, with a certain representational, rather than prophonographic,[19] effect in mind. In other words, the original sound around which the theory of correct representation is built is itself manipulated in order to ensure a certain representational effect and is therefore in no simple way a pure original that can be either faithfully reproduced or distorted by recording. Secondly, it is the effective space relationships that are now being preserved rather than actual ones. Of particular importance is an implicit acknowledgment that certain representational standards of accuracy or correctness can be derived only by reference to relations established within a given representation, rather than by way of some actual original performance. It further suggests that representational effects are not necessarily a function of that original and that they are conventional, signifying relationships—not absolute ones. Thus no absolutely transcendental categories of evaluation determine effective fidelity.

Of course, in spite of phonography and film profits, Bell's primary investment lay in telephony, which obviously had acoustic requirements different from those of music recording. There a different practice ensued. Implicitly recognizing the social *use* of sound, engineers felt entirely comfortable sacrificing 60 percent of the voice's acoustic energy (the lower frequencies), because they lost only 2 percent intelligibility in the bargain. The functional primacy of intelligibility enabled telephone systems to reduce drastically the amount of power required for transmission while retaining the ability to transmit speech with acceptable clarity. Nevertheless, the sort of research that allowed such compromises to be made—basic inquiries into the nature of sound and hearing in the abstract, as they had been defined by science—encouraged engineers and technicians to conceive of *all* forms of sonic representation as involving actual, attentive listeners, uniformly sensitive to all measurable aspects of the sound event and situated generally and characteristically as audience members.

In other words, telephones and sound reproduction engineers assumed that all sound representations must take into account the physical and physiological circumstances of an ideally defined listening situation—more or less that of the educated symphony listener—and attempt to replicate those conditions in all their complexity (binaurality, perception of source position through reverberation, phase and volume differences between ears positioned a fixed distance apart on an unchanging head, etc.—i.e., the scientific definition of the relevant parameters) in order to achieve a satisfactory simulation of actual presence at the original production of the sound. All this despite the fact that millions of people every day were listening to telephones with one ear, on instruments with severely restricted frequency characteristics, with no complaints, and constrained—in one researcher's words—by "a loss of naturalness."[20] The lab that could measure speech intelligibility in percentages was restrained by the very unscientific concept of naturalness, which not even they could quantify.

The use of so fuzzy a term as "naturalness" in a highly technical engineering journal indicates not so much a failure on anyone's part, but rather the extent to which implicit and even explicit standards of representational accuracy, legitimacy, or simply goodness guide the most scientific of attempts at objective evaluation. Technicians' ingrained and relatively unexamined beliefs about what constitutes either a good representation or the acceptable limits of deviation from that ideal profoundly shape both the character of the representations they create and the representational devices they design. As we see in the case of the telephone (although this is just as true of the microphone, the amplifier, and the speaker), the very design and application of devices are constrained by the sort of norms deemed obvious by the representational model in dominance.

The competing models of representation implied by phonography and telephony could or perhaps should have suggested that representational ideals were based in part on a sound's social or cultural function, but telephony was nevertheless routinely considered a special-case deviation from the ideal. So, rather than offering a competing paradigm centered on a communication or information model, the telephone was subsumed under the duplicative aesthetic, with the result that the norm went, effectively, unchallenged. Other cracks, however, began to appear in the invisible auditor model, as when Maxfield counseled engineers to change the characteristics of the original space in order to obtain an acceptable record, that is, to manipulate the original or prophonographic space in order to produce the effect of listening in the "proper" space. Here adequate representational space is possible only by disguising the characteristics of the actual space, and the implied correspondence between actual and represented space is decisively severed. Likewise, all around Hollywood, carpenters were busy deadening sound stages to eliminate extraneous, but altogether natural, sounds that a fidelity-based model would, ideally, wish to preserve. These deviations from the ideal were not thought to be impositions on proper technique despite being acoustic manipulations as overt as multiple miking. I would suggest that by restricting their definition of *representation* to the act of inscription, engineers could comfortably maintain a certain adherence to the fidelity model while still allowing manipulations to the set and therefore to the final product. They were, after all, faithfully recording the resulting sonic event that they had improved in advance. Thus, Maxfield could continue his insistence on a fidelity model long into the 1950s, when stereo musical recordings emerged.

A variety of justifications of this sort helped to make the invisible auditor norm a bit more flexible in practice while never really challenging it. Since professional representational standards assumed that the engineer was an operator of equipment, or simply a recordist, the various processes of representation could easily be reduced in theory to the simple act of technological inscription. Although the auditor model assumes no prioritizing activity on the part of the recordist, the sonic hierarchy characteristic of an orchestral performance in a concert hall offered the recordist an event that was already strictly ordered so that a simple recording sufficed to achieve the desired effect. A soundproofed set completely lacking in reverberation achieved a similar ordering of the sonic realm in the movies. Thus, engineers could simply delimit their own field of responsibility to the act of recording, thus assigning professional jurisdiction over the set to carpenters and designers (while nevertheless exerting decisive control over their work), and still adhere to their own ideal of proper practice. While this approach allowed engineers to achieve Hollywood's characteristic sonic hierarchy without altering their presumed standards, it did not result in the most flexible or efficient system possible. That system would await a redefinition of the relation between the profilmic event and the represented event. Crudely put, technicians needed to escape the equation of unique profilmic event and unique representation and recognize instead that the represented world need not correspond to any actual world, nor need the individual shot remain the basic representational unit. In classical film, the diegetic unity of a multishot ensemble typically takes precedence over the literal fidelity of any single shot. In short, engineers needed to redefine their function as representational rather than duplicative.

Aesthetic Norm and Professional Identity

When engineers arrived in Hollywood, however, a steadfast adherence to the norms they brought from phonography, radio, and telephony quickly placed them in conflict with other technicians, especially cinematographers and editors. Frank Lawrence, then president of the editors' union, described this war as a kind of Armageddon caused by "sound experts" who were "hopelessly ignorant of the existing public demands and high artistic standards of the motion picture production world." He amplifies his claim thus:

> Every blooming sound expert in the entire world is at present convinced
> that the only way to make satisfying sound pictures is to sacrifice every
> other feature of value in Filmland to the proper recording of sound . . .
> [the] more experienced divisions of motion picture production [should
> not] permit such rot . . . sound experts will have to get in step with the
> motion picture fraternity.[21]

In other words, while such practitioners might legitimately be thought
of as experts in their field, they had not yet realized that their field had
changed or that the norms appropriate to one representational culture
might be inappropriate to another, which had its own equally coherent
set of standards and assumptions. Although sound engineers considered
their own standards to be objective and universal because those standards
were scientific, they neglected the extent to which even their scientific
categories were imbricated with representational assumptions and were
anything but transcendental and neutral. Thus engineers' strict adherence to their self-imposed and undoubtedly high standards confirmed
them as experts of a certain type, but it hobbled them when they moved
to a new sonic culture.

Almost in response to Lawrence, L. E. Clark addresses the
conflict over aesthetics and technique explicitly in terms of professional
standing. After noting that sound recordists were typically denied screen
credit and that their low esteem enforced a cycle of degenerative neglect,
he locates the root of the dilemma in the differing technical cultures to
which cinematographers and engineers belong:

> Very few of us were originally from the studios; we came from the
> electrical laboratories, from the telephone companies, from radio broad-
> casting studios and chains, and from engineering colleges. We knew
> little or nothing of the conditions within the motion picture industry—
> and cared little about them. We were engineers—and proud of it. Our
> business was to install and operate the recording equipment, not to
> make pictures per se. . . . the sound man, [simply] places his microphone,
> and adjusts his circuits to get a good, commercial record—and lets it go
> at that.[22]

He argues in conclusion that such soundmen exhibit an "apathetic
attitude toward the artistic phases of picture making."[23] Here I part with
his view of the situation, although not with his basic statement of the
problem. Another possible explanation for the slowness with which
sound engineers integrated themselves into the Hollywood system

avoids assigning blame or labeling one group or another as less than professional, while it still accords with the evidence. Perhaps sound technicians' stubborn maintenance of engineering standards can be better understood as a strategy for protecting the quality of their work and thus their professional standing. Such apparent intransigence might then seem instead a refusal to perform work in a less than professional manner. Indeed, a wealth of evidence suggests that the sound engineers believed themselves professionally under siege.

A cartoon in the August 1929 issue of *American Cinematographer*, entitled "The Age of Alibi,"[24] humorously portrays the perceptions shared by all technicians that the new combination of sound and image was causing movie quality to suffer and that someone would be required to play the scapegoat. Professional standing and even careers were clearly at stake over the issue, as was, not incidentally, the continued profitability of the industry. The cartoon's second panel shows a soundman next to a cactus in the desert proclaiming "AT LAST—the ideal place for my microphone."[25]

In response to the discord each group struggled to maintain its self-defined standards of quality by taking every opportunity to shape the conditions of the workplace and the techniques practiced there. In order to avoid further conflict and loss of profits, both the American Society of Cinematographers (ASC) and the Academy of Motion Picture Arts and Sciences (AMPAS) created forums for debate and reconciliation. AMPAS went so far as to set up a special Producers-Technicians Committee headed by none other than producer Irving Thalberg and engineer Nugent H. Slaughter. In order to ensure that everyone on the set worked from roughly the same set of assumptions about sound recording, AMPAS also established a series of courses on principles of sound recording and reproducing that were open to personnel from all parts of the industry, from writers to cinematographers. Working through the Continuing Education Program at the University of Southern California, at least 900 employees completed the course in approximately two years. One of the chief merits of the program as far as academy executive Lester Cowan was concerned was the opportunity to train current studio employees to become soundmen instead of importing the latter from other industries.[26]

Such classes and forums for discussion did much to alleviate tensions and delays on the set, but given the entrenched norms and practices of the studios, it was ultimately the engineers rather than the actors, directors, or cinematographers who would compromise the most. While I have argued that the engineer's intransigence or refusal to play by the rules can be sympathetically understood as a purposeful attempt to maintain a craft standard of work in a factory environment, and thus as a form of workplace resistance to Hollywood's particular form of mass production, in the end, the engineer had to capitulate and, as it were, make a virtue of necessity. The phonographic assumptions shared by so many engineers were based on an inappropriately literal notion of realistic duplication and thus could not serve as a model for sound representation in general or for film sound specifically. The processes by which engineers negotiated the adjustment of their own standards to the reigning model is thus important to an understanding of the power of the classical paradigm, indicating not only how it functions in a positive fashion by encouraging certain norms but also how it necessarily effects and maintains a certain exclusion and thus ensures its own regularity.

Negotiation, Reconciliation, Redefinition

In a 1929 article, Carl Dreher, as one of the sound field's elder statesmen, points out that unlike actors and directors in the field of broadcasting, their motion picture counterparts had not yet adopted the "broadcast viewpoint." Radio personnel, he recounts, after similarly taking the demands of the sound engineer as a kind of professional affront (they, too, had professional performance standards to protect), gradually learned to "modify their execution for the sake of the microphone."[27] In other words, performers adjusted their techniques to the standards of the sound engineer, thereby ensuring that the representation, if not the (unheard) "original," was up to snuff.

In Hollywood, however, the situation was apparently quite different. Unlike radio, motion pictures do not rely solely on sound technologies for their existence, and therefore the engineer could not automatically assume the most powerful and authoritative role on the set. Rather than suggest that the various professionals on the set each adapt to each other's needs, Dreher argues that sound engineers capitulated early and that they too willingly allowed themselves to be forced again and again into impossible microphone placements in deference to camera technique. The resulting sound quality was poor and became a source of criticism of the particular sound engineer involved and, by extension, of sound engineers in general. As a result, the status of soundmen in Hollywood was much lower than it should have been, and that hampered their ability to negotiate on the set.

Bolstering his arguments, Dreher points to an apparently widespread tendency to blame sound technicians for all of the delays and inefficiencies on the set, regardless of whether they had actually caused them. To avoid such unwarranted criticism, he suggests careful note keeping in order to later defend oneself and one's professional standing.[28] In other words, conflicting professional and representational standards were perceived as causing such extensive disruptions that the groups of workers with less institutional power were required to expend a great deal of energy simply avoiding the twin losses of prestige and workplace autonomy.

The various contemporary technical journals consistently point to the connection between these struggles within the competing technical cultures. To suggest that theory is in part constitutive of the technician's identity is not, however, to suggest that technicians necessarily spent a substantial part of their time theorizing or that they engaged in explicit debate over the nature of representation in general. It does suggest that something recognizable as theory shaped the standards and practices by which groups and individuals evaluated the worth of devices, techniques, research programs, and individual representations. From this perspective, it becomes clear that Hollywood conflicts between art and science or between cinematographers, or motion picture men, and so-called sound experts or mere technicians were in fact complex processes of give-and-take and jurisdictional renegotiation between professional groups and individuals each unwilling to compromise their own standards unless convinced by a compelling argument or result—and then only if the new standard could be justified as a practical or artistic deviation.[29] If Dreher's conflicts were to be resolved, then the opposing groups would need to jointly retheorize their basic representational ideals of the Hollywood film.

The notion that a single ideal might serve as a universal standard for all forms of representational practice is not restricted to technicians by any means. David Bordwell, for example, argues that transition-era technicians in pursuit of sound perspective would try to match the acoustic qualities of sound to the scale of the image. "Engineers debated how to convey 'natural' sound while granting that strictly realistic sound recording was unsuitable."[30] As a result, engineers compromised by moving mikes to follow dialogue, by dubbing sound after principal recording, and the like. As evidently correct as this may be, a rather peculiar assumption is in play here. What, after all, does *strictly realistic sound recording* mean? A growing number of Hollywood technicians began to acknowledge the impossibility of having a single standard—"realism"—for all sound work, noting as early as 1929 that one should adjust the recording style to the type of performance being represented. For example, Wesley C. Miller argues that a vaudeville performer could be recorded more "intimately" and therefore louder than another style of performer "because of the nature of his act."[31] Eavesdropping on a quiet conversation, however, better suits the demands and expectations of the movie audience. Whether these specific examples are correct is less important than the implied recognition that in a practical sense, no single standard should govern all recording situations. In addition, by including audience expectations in his equation of representational correctness, Miller points out that different modes of address shape both performance style and recording procedure; that is, different sounds have different rhetorical functions.

Less than a year later, T. E. Shea notes that "[sound] requires not only much new apparatus, but new talent and technical training, new care and habits," adding that far from being a neutral site whose acoustic particularities must be respected, the "original" space should rather be understood as the first acoustic device for manipulating the recorded sound whose alteration "depends on the sound and scene to be recorded."[32] Another commentator writing in 1933 asserts:

> The importance of having the dialogue always clearly understandable goes without saying. Great care must be exercised at all times to have the sound effects recorded with the proper level to make the finished picture as realistic as possible. In an effort to *create realism*, we have used as many as sixteen separate sound tracks, [and] each [is] carefully controlled as to level, perspective and quality, to make a pleasing composite track.[33]

Although still measuring his success against a largely undefined concept of realism, this is a realism that is created and therefore attributable to the representation and neither to the performance nor to the act of recording. Also deserving closer examination is the presumption that the primacy of dialogue intelligibility now goes without saying. Although from our historical vantage point this claim seems almost self-evident, the standard of realism most frequently articulated by technicians assumed that if an actor really moved away from the mike and was really unintelligible, a realistic recording would duly record that. The shift in priorities evinced by the foregoing quotation indicates further recognition of the rhetorical and enunciative specificity of different modes of sound production and the types of realism appropriate to each. Thus, an alternative ideal—one of rhetorical function—competed with the invisible auditor model.

While this might indicate that the "gut reaction"[34] of the average technician was in the process of changing, the mere recognition that one might at times do something other than what was suggested by the invisible auditor notion of correct practice did not mean that there had yet emerged a consistent statement of the logic behind these deviations. The soundmen did not want to believe they were applying different standards willy-nilly, so in order to validate the transformation of standards and practices, they needed a new conceptual justification and logic of representation that agreed with both their new instincts and their new corporate responsibilities. This they found in another professional society—the ASC. In a 1934 article entitled "Getting Good Sound Is an Art," Harold Lewis draws a parallel between the photographer who purposely overexposes or underexposes a shot—therefore departing from the straightforward commercial ideal—and the sound recordist charged with recording film sound.

> Dramatic sound-recording must in the same way often depart from the standard of the commercially ideal recording. Like the cinematographer, the Recording Engineer must vary the key of his recording to suit the dramatic needs of the story and scene.[35]

That this needed to be stated explicitly indicates that even in 1934, the commercially ideal recording (i.e., the fidelity, or auditor, model) still exerted its force over the professional standards of sound recordists. In contrast to the musical recordist who always seeks to record the nuances of specific spaces and performances, the film recordist "must know how each scene fits into the pattern of the picture as a whole, what precedes it and what follows, so that he can give it the best and most dramatically expressive aural treatment possible."[36] These particular quotations carry an extra importance, for the writer was at the time the president of the newly formed Society of Sound Engineers, a group whose aim was to bring the goals of sound engineers and the film industry into accord and enhance the engineer's prestige within Hollywood, much as the ASC had done for its members.

The importance accorded to knowing "how each scene fits into the pattern of the picture as a whole" implies that engineers had begun to recognize that the classical film is better understood as a "pluri-punctual"[37] unity—a combination of fragments whose unity is constituted primarily at the level of their combination rather than as a collection of individual, essentially discrete, and autonomous units. An aesthetic that preaches the absolute duplication of perceptually discrete, profilmic events will place far too much emphasis on the texture and idiosyncrasies of the individual shot, by giving primacy to the pre-representational event rather than its diegetic representation.

The ideal of perceptual duplication presupposes, as I've argued, that the acoustic specificities of the original space and performance are necessarily and directly related to those of the finished representation, so that there is, conceptually at least, no distinction between the spaces of representation and reception: the ultimate movie audience is implicitly present on the set, and the finished film attempts to duplicate the experience of that observer. Yet, as we know, the classical cinema institutes a decisive break between these spaces, with the result that the represented space and time may have almost nothing in common with the actualities of production. The lack of sonic hierarchy that the invisible auditor model implies assumes that the movie audience is, in essence, a collection of neutral observers with no preferences or expectations with regard to image and sound priority—that they are simply witnesses to an untampered reality. That set of assumptions makes the connection of shots into larger units extremely difficult, however, because the volume and quality of sounds may vary in any way between successive shots. Classical film, in contrast, thrives on the continual foregrounding of narratively important elements against a background of less important, but generally realistic, elements.[38]

Without the sort of sonic hierarchy implied by the desires to keep dialogue intelligible[39] and to minimize the perception of changing relations to each shot when images are edited together, it would be difficult to construct a transparent continuous, multiunit whole. Indeed, an excessively faithful recording can render continuity nearly impossible, since any scene with a continuous background sound will appear discontinuous if cut together out of different takes. Such difficulties encouraged technicians to record only the dialogue on the set, with a mike near the actors, adding characteristic sounds later. This allowed continuity across cuts in the overall construction of films because discontinuous lines of dialogue (or other foreground elements) would nevertheless exhibit a consistent volume and intelligibility from take to take, thereby allowing them to be placed within an artificial, dubbed, continuous background.

This granted the ensemble a feeling of wholeness and uniformity despite actual discontinuities of production. In other words, the integrity and therefore the idiosyncrasies of the actual performance were usually sacrificed in the service of a higher level of rhetorical continuity.

Now, while concerns for continuity and the adjustments of technique they would require might be acceptable to, say, a cinematographer, they flew in the face of the established norms and standards of sound engineers. Indeed, modifying the microphone technique by, for example, moving it on a boom to follow an actor around the set (which soon became the norm in Hollywood) cannot readily be reconciled with the practices of symphonic recording or an invisible witness model. Falsifying the acoustics of the set or creating an imaginary acoustic space does not at all accord with the principal understanding of realism that shapes the engineer's self-designated technical brief: to record as accurately and with as much nuance as possible, a sonic event from a stationary, audiencelike position.

Now, in point of fact, sound technicians did precisely falsify things again and again. As Maxfield, to cite just one example, pointed out on several occasions, it did not seem a professional imposition to alter the acoustics of the set through the use of sound-absorbing materials in order to produce, through the taking of a good commercial record, in accordance with professional norms, a recording that had the characteristics (in terms of reverberation, for example) desired by filmmakers. If a space really had acoustics that were deleterious to speech intelligibility, it was deemed acceptable to change the acoustics so that a "normal" recording remained intelligible. Perhaps because set construction was not obviously the responsibility of the recordist, it was easier to justify what might legitimately be called a deviation from the ideal.[38]

Of course, such foregrounding or prioritizing techniques were commonplace in concert hall architecture and thus already within the realm of acceptable practice. Why concert halls were not considered acoustic modifications is obvious enough: Concert halls are the normal and natural spaces within which we experience music. The fact that concert halls are acoustically unlike any other spaces (aside from theaters) and are therefore reasonably considered acoustic devices seems not to enter the equation, because such spaces are an integral aspect of music as a social and cultural practice. The assumption that film sound is not a similarly social use of sound, however, seems implicit in the application of a severe model of fidelity to it. Had it been made explicit from the outset that acoustics were simply another instrument in the sound-recording chain and had not the bulk of acoustic research and practice been guided by the heuristic of the real, situated listener, perhaps it would not have seemed at first a deviation to shape film sound representations in other ways.

Given two recorded sounds with essentially the same acoustic characteristics, it would be impossible to determine whether an absence of background noises behind, for example, a voice were the result of elaborate soundproofing or of closely miking the actor with a movable boom. Thus, the finished products might be absolutely interchangeable. However, engineering standards of fidelity and representational correctness admitted one technique but not the other. Recording a sound event that was already hierarchically ordered according to a particular social function allowed the engineers to maintain a hands-off descriptive aesthetic, which eschewed any overtly narrational or rhetorical use of the sound apparatus while nevertheless achieving rhetorical effects. The untampered original was itself already rhetorical.

The emphasis on recording or inscription did not completely solve the problem and was in fact something of a hindrance. Sound technicians repeatedly needed to reconcile themselves to a mode of production based not on the collection of real events but rather on the construction of carefully hierarchized events whose realism is a function of their plausibility and their compatibility with conventions of narrative function rather than literal, perceptual duplication. Part of the difficulty in recognizing these by now somewhat banal observations is the widespread tendency to delimit arbitrarily the processes of representation to the simple act of recording, as our sound engineers had. Commentators from many different perspectives shared a tendency to treat the effects of filmic representations as if they were its causes or as if they were conditions that existed independent of the processes of representation. A. Lindsley Lane describes his understanding of the ultimate goals of cinematic representation—through the notion of the camera's omniscience—and suggests that motion picture technique should as much as possible efface itself, because a picture that

> gives self-evidence of its making is not a good picture artistically and holds the chemistry of dissolution within its own structure, drawing the audience's attention away from its story-experience purpose; is, in other words, destructive to intactness of the "illusion of occurrence," which illusion is the psychological key to a successful motion picture–percipient experience.[40]

Lane here recognizes that the goal of cinematic representation is to create the "illusion of occurrence," that is, the represented effect of an event that seems to exist independent of and prior to the act of recording—an event that seems simply to occur and be captured. This contrasts with the writings of, say, Maxfield, who, seeking the same effects, takes the idea of capturing (or recording objectively) as a necessarily actual process and therefore (like those early cinema producers who manufactured "real" occurrences) manipulates the original through staging in order that it *can* be simply captured. Lane sees the effect of the captured as precisely that—an effect. His insight seems not to have been shared by many of his contemporaries, though. Those commentators, however, should not be considered naive. In our day, the belief that there is such an all-important, independent, prerepresentational event manifests itself, as I have argued elsewhere,[41] in the privileging of the original sound in academic sound theory. Such tendencies in both informal and formal theory tend to neglect the extent to which *all* aspects of scenography can and should be understood as participating in narration—not just the aspects of filming and editing.

The role of the cinematographer as a model for the sound engineer therefore takes on even more importance, because cinematographers' prestige in Hollywood was unargued and their standards and practices perfectly suited to studio needs. By reimagining their role as akin to the cinematographer's, sound engineers ultimately jettisoned the all-defining "original sound" and the aesthetic of duplication it entailed, and for better or worse, they set about the business of manufacturing sonic worlds whose parameters were judged mainly in terms of their internal coherence—their representational functions.

Thus, by adopting the justifications for manipulating images and ultimately the prestige of the cinematographer's artistic deviations, engineers shifted their emphasis from the production of a series of discrete and autonomous units to an emphasis based on the shots' place within a larger series of representations whose unity and continuity took precedence over individual representation. The norm of invisible auditor gave way to the ideal auditor. Coincident with this shift came redefinition of the standards held to be constitutive of professional technique. By redefining the requirements of professional identity, sound technicians accommodated themselves to the reigning norms of the Hollywood film industry and thus not only retained their standing as good engineers but also paved the way for their acceptance and advancement within that industry. So, what might otherwise seem a rather marginal debate over representational theory can be understood as a crucial element in the transformation of a large, capitalist industry. Only after sound technicians came to equate their standards and their sense of professional identity and success with those necessary to the success of their new corporate employers could sound engineering become an integral part of the Hollywood system. Representational theory as articulated by these professionals was the primary ground upon which that realignment, redefinition, and integration occurred.

NOTES

1. David Bordwell, Janet Staiger, and Kristin Thompson, eds., *The Classical Hollywood Cinema: Film Style and Mode of Production to 1960* (New York: Columbia University Press, 1985).

2. Pierre Bourdieu, *Outline of a Theory of Practice*, trans. Richard Nice (Cambridge and New York: Cambridge University Press, 1977), p. 78.

3. Ibid., p. 79.

4. Bordwell, "The Introduction of Sound," in *The Classical Hollywood Cinema*, pp. 298–307; Douglas Gomery, *The Coming of Sound to the American Film Industry: A History of the Transformation of an Industry*, Ph.D. dissertation, University of Wisconsin, Madison, 1975; Alan Williams, "Historical and Theoretical Issues in the Coming of Recorded Sound to the Cinema," in Rick Altman, ed., *Sound Theory/Sound Practice* (New York and London: Routledge, AFI, 1992), pp. 126–37.

5. David Bordwell and Janet Staiger, "Technology, Style and Mode of Production," in *The Classical Hollywood Cinema*, p. 258.

6. On this point, see David Noble, *America by Design* (New York: Knopf, 1977).

7. I refer most specifically to the tradition of apparatus theory, which sought to develop a critique of the ideological work embodied in and performed by the basic apparatuses of film. Most famously this involved a critique of the notion of the bourgeois subject necessarily implied, and in fact produced, by the use of lenses ground to create so-called Renaissance perspective. While doubtless there are strong connections between the rise of this subject and the form and ideology of Hollywood films, this critique seems overly reductive and ultimately ahistorical. For a good and sympathetic introduction, see Philip Rosen, ed., *Narrative, Apparatus, Ideology: A Film Theory Reader* (New York: Columbia University Press, 1986), pp. 281–85 and 286–372, and, generally, the editor's introductions to the issues addressed by the text as a whole.

8. Joseph P. Maxfield and H. C. Harrison, "A Method of High Quality Recording and Reproducing Based on Telephone Research." *Bell System Technical Journal* 5:3 (1926), 494–95.

9. Harry F. Olson and Frank Massa, "On the Realistic Reproduction of Sound with Particular Reference to Sound Motion Pictures." *Journal of the Society of Motion Picture Engineers* (hereafter *JSMPE*) 23:2 (August 1934), 64–65.

10. John L. Cass, "The Illusion of Sound and Picture." *JSMPE* 14:3 (March 1930), 325.

11. Carl Dreher, "Recording, Re-recording, and Editing of Sound." *JSMPE* 16:6 (June 1931), 757.

12. Dreher, in fact, offers this example in an article entitled "This Matter of Volume Control." *Motion Picture Projectionist* (February 1929), 11. Although written earlier, he

here expresses more concern for the continuity of the sound take as a whole, complaining about abrupt volume changes between shots.

13. Joseph P. Maxfield, "Acoustic Control of Recording for Talking Motion Pictures." *JSMPE* 14:1 (January 1930), 85.

14. Elmer C. Richardson, "A microphone boom." *JSMPE* 15:1 (July 1930), 41–45.

15. Wesley C. Miller, "Sound Pictures: The Successful Production of Illusion." *American Cinematographer* 10:9 (December 1929), 5–6.

16. Bourdieu, *Outline of a Theory of Practice*, p. 77. Bourdieu is not talking about engineers here, and perhaps he states his point too emphatically. Nevertheless, as his work on norms of photography illustrates, these basic ideas are applicable to representational practice as well. See Pierre Bourdieu, et al., *Un Art Moyen* (Paris: Éditions de Minuit, 1965).

17. Maxfield and Harrison, *A Method of High Quality Recording*, pp. 498–99.

18. Ibid., p. 495 (my emphasis).

19. A term designed to recall the term *profilmic* meaning the realm and/or event as it exists before the camera/microphone.

20. W. H. Martin and C. H. G. Gray, "Master Reference System for Telephone Transmission." *Bell System Technical Journal* (July 1929), 536.

21. Frank Lawrence, "The War of the Talkies." *American Cinematographer* (January 1929), 11.

22. L. E. Clark, "Sound Recording: Art or Trade?" *American Cinematographer* (June 1932), 17, 32.

23. L. E. Clark, "Enter the Audiographer." *American Cinematographer* (July 1932), 10.

24. Glenn R. Kershner, "The Age of Alibi." *American Cinematographer* 10:5 (August 1929), 11.

25. The cartoon refers to actual remarks reported in a survey. See "Sound Men and Cinematographers Discuss Their Mutual Problems." *American Cinematographer* 10:5 (August 1929), 8.

26. For a reprint of the lectures delivered at the Sound School, see *Recording Sound for Motion Pictures*, ed. Lester Cowan, for the AMPAS, 1st ed. (New York and London: McGraw-Hill, 1931), for the first version of the class, and see *Motion Picture Sound Engineering, a Series of Lectures Presented to the Classes Enrolled in the Courses in Sound Engineering Given by the Research Council of the AMPAS, Hollywood, California* (New York: Van Nostrand, 1938) for the revamped version given in 1938. On the Academy's plans for the school, see, for example, *AMPAS Bulletin* 24 (15 August 29), *AMPAS Bulletin* (25 September 29), and the Academy library's special collections files on the Producers-Technicians group," see especially boxes 39 and 43 and the general files. On the history of the Academy generally, see Pierre Norman Sands, *A Historical Study of the Academy of Motion Picture Arts and Sciences, 1927–1947* (New York: Arno Press, 1977).

27. Carl Dreher, "Stage Technique in the Talkies." *American Cinematographer* 10:9 (December 1929), 2.

28. Dreher, "Stage Technique," p. 3.

29. See Rick Altman, "Le son contre l'image, ou la bataille des techniciens," *Hollywood 1927–41*, ed. Alain Masson (Paris: Éditions Autrement, 1991), pp. 74–86.

30. David Bordwell, "Space in the Classical Film," in *The Classical Hollywood Cinema*, p. 53.

31. Wesley C. Miller, "Sound Pictures: The Successful Production of Illusion." *American Cinematographer 10:9 (December 1929)*, 5–6.

32. T. E. Shea, "Recording the Sound Picture." *Bell Laboratories Record* 8:8 (1930), 356, 357, 358.

33. Nathan Levinson, "Re-recording, Dubbing, or Duping." *American Cinematographer* (March 1933), 12 (my emphasis).

34. Altman, "Sound Space," in *Sound Theory/Sound Practice,* pp. 54–55, makes essentially the same point.

35. Harold Lewis, "Getting Good Sound Is an Art." *American Cinematographer* (June 1934), 65.

36. The term suggested by André Gaudreault to describe films composed of more than one shot.

37. See Altman, "Sound Space," generally.

38. See Altman's "Le son contre l'image," pp. 74–86.

39. A. Lindsley Lane, "The Camera's Omniscient Eye." *American Cinematographer* (March 1935), 95. Effacement of cinematic technique was a well-articulated and widespread goal among technicians and was adopted as an industrial goal. One need only point to the assumption expressed again and again in technical journals that it was self-evident that microphones should not be seen on camera.

40. James Lastra, "Reading, Writing, and Representing Sound," in *Sound Theory/Sound Practice,* pp. 65–86.

Denise Hartsough

Crime Pays: The Studios' Labor Deals in the 1930s

The glitter and glamour of Hollywood's Golden Age hide a shameful secret. The bold, clever entrepreneurs who built the studio system publicized their outrageous expenditures for lavish productions and fed the gossip columnists news of clashes among strong-willed personalities. The motion picture moguls did not, however, advertise the fact that in the mid-1930s they began making payments to a union run by the Chicago syndicate.

Allegations and investigations in the late 1930s suggested a connection between Hollywood and the organization formerly run by Al Capone; court proceedings in the 1940s revealed that industry executives had indeed given over $2.5 million to union and syndicate leaders.[1] Industry heads claimed that the union (International Alliance of Theatrical Stage Employees—IATSE, or IA) had extorted the money from them by threatening to have union projectionists strike at theaters across the country. This argument convinced most commentators and seems plausible when one recalls the importance of theater revenue to the vertically integrated majors.

I argue, however, that executives of the major motion picture firms as a group chose the syndicate-run IATSE for their labor partner. The oligopolistic structure of the motion picture industry gave those executives enough power to channel the course of Hollywood labor relations in directions that best suited their own interests—the long-

From *Velvet Light Trap* 23 (March 1989), 49–63. Reprinted with permission of the author and the University of Texas Press.

term, relatively risk-free growth of their companies.[2] With regard to labor, this meant a ready supply of qualified workers at as low a price as possible. The IA benefited the major companies by keeping labor costs relatively low, undermining labor solidarity at the studios, and insisting on union scale for independent producers, thus weakening their ability to compete with the majors.

Myth: Executives Subjected to Extortion

Despite racketeering charges against the IA in court and in print during the late 1930s,[3] motion picture executives continued to deal with the union. The industry cared very much about public opinion, having hired Will Hays in 1922 to upgrade the industry's image and thus prevent government intervention.[4] However, the industry's apparently questionable role in IA dealings was easily explained as that of helpless extortion victim. Journalists, academics, studio workers, and producers themselves maintained that the IA's threat to have projectionists walk out of theaters across the nation forced industry executives to comply with the IA's demands.

Prior to a 1941 trial that exposed many of the payments producers made to IA leaders William Bioff and George Browne, observers both within and outside the industry rationalized the IA's prominence in the studios as the result of an IA projectionist strike threat. Samuel Lipkowitz's 1939 master's thesis on collective bargaining in Hollywood attributes the first labor-management agreement covering motion picture production workers—the 1926 Studio Basic Agreement (SBA)—primarily to the IA's threat to close down theaters. Lipkowitz calls the threat of a strike against studios and theaters the "major cause" of the producers' signing the SBA because "the strength of the Musicians and the IATSE in theaters made this threat very potent." Lipkowitz also regards the IA's closed shop agreement to be the result of a "threat of general strike in theaters."[5] *Variety*'s account of the events surrounding the 1935 closed shop agreement bolsters Lipkowitz's statement.[6] Similarly, articles in *Films* and the *Nation* invoked the IA projectionist strike threat to explain the Screen Actors Guild's sudden withdrawal of support for the Federated Motion Picture Crafts (FMPC) strike in 1937.[7]

Hollywood workers themselves voiced a belief in the power of an IA threat to strike the nation's theaters. A veteran MGM carpenter told the California Assembly Capital-Labor Investigating Committee in November 1937 that the committee would have no impact on the IA because "there isn't a producer in Hollywood who would dare produce a picture without the IA jurisdiction over it, for it wouldn't be shown in any theatre in the country."[8]

Nicholas Schenck, brother to Joseph and president of Loew's (MGM), testified in 1941 at his brother's tax evasion trial that he bowed to IA demands for fear that the union would "ruin the industry" by having projectionists strike. Writers of markedly different political persuasions accepted Schenck's portrayal of the situation. A fiercely anti-Communist, pro-IA article in "America's Leading Liberal Labor Weekly" states, "The producers listen to the IA's demands because of its ability to pull the projectionists and literally close almost every theatre in the country." Openly Communist screenwriter Lester Cole condemns the IA but claims similarly that the IA's "control over the projectionists was its unbreakable power over the Hollywood industry."[9]

Even after the tax evasion and racketeering trials of the 1940s, academic analysts accepted the strike threat theory. Murray Ross, author of a book devoted to Hollywood unions, explains in a 1947 article how the IA gained power: "[The IA] entrenched itself in the projection booths of motion picture houses, and by the end of 1935 it threatened to tie up all the major theatres if the producers failed to grant its demands for a closed shop in the studios. Since the box office is the pulse of the motion picture industry, the producers succumbed without a fight."[10] Labor union historian Walter Galenson concurs. According to him, the syndicate helped Browne and Bioff gain control of the IA. They then "proceeded to extort money from the large movie chains by threatening to harass them with strikes."[11]

If the IA's control over projectionists at the majors' theaters accounts for motion picture executives' willingness to deal with the IA in Hollywood, then one would expect the union's strength or weakness in Hollywood to coincide with its strength or weakness in theaters. With one exception, the IA has played a leading role in Hollywood labor relations since 1926, when it was one of only five unions recognized in the SBA.[12] Only between 1933 and 1935 did the IA's power in Hollywood diminish. After the union lost a studio strike in 1933, its Hollywood membership dropped from nine thousand to less than two hundred, and industry executives refused to renew the SBA with the IA.[13] Then suddenly, in December 1935, producers and IA officials announced that as of January 1936 the union would reenter the SBA and enjoy closed shop in the studios.

The vicissitudes of IA strength in theaters do not clearly parallel those of IA influence in Hollywood. IA projectionists weathered well the transition to sound in the late 1920s, but theater closings in 1931 and 1932 hurt employment and encouraged unionized theaters still operating to seek concessions.[14] However, *Variety* noted late in 1933 "a literal [theater] reopening epidemic, which brings the grand total of lighted houses back to a near prosperous 15,000." In both 1933 and 1939 approximately 40 percent of the nation's theaters hired IA projectionists, suggesting that the IA's fortune at the studios fluctuated independently of the IA's strength in exhibition.[15]

Theater revenue was indeed important for the major motion picture companies—those that produced, distributed, and exhibited films.[16] Mae Huettig's 1944 study of the industry's finances reveals that in the 1930s, exhibition involved over 90 percent of the industry's invested capital and generated approximately two-thirds of all income. Huettig concludes that "the principal concern of the men who run the major companies is their theatres."[17]

However, in the 1930s the IA's threats to pull its projectionists from the majors' theaters seem to have been empty. During the IA studio strike of 1933, IA International Representative Dick Green announced that he would call for a national strike of projectionists and stagehands at the majors' theaters "if the situation becomes more acute." The IA lost the strike without enlisting support from its members in the exhibition branch. IA Vice President Harland Holmden notified producers on September 11, 1937, that within a week every film had to bear the IA emblem "to insure projection of the prints throughout the country by our projectionist-members of the IATSE." Industry leaders promised to meet with IA President Browne on the matter, and the deadline passed without incident. In April 1939 Browne threatened the majors with a projectionist strike, and again the producers' promise of negotiations relieved Browne from having to make good his pledge.[18]

If the IA's threat of a projectionist strike against the majors' theaters does not account for the syndicate-run union's prominence in Hollywood, then perhaps motion picture executives coerced the union into representing studio workers. This seems unlikely considering union history (the IA, like most unions, sought to represent as many workers as possible) and the vast sums the industry paid to IA officials. If industry leaders could force the IA to do their bidding, why would they have bothered to pay? I argue for a third alternative: when the Chicago syndicate gained control of the IA and sought increased income from

Hollywood, the majors welcomed the opportunity to pay for studio labor relations that served their interests.

Reality: Executives Control the Labor Force

During the 1920s and 1930s, film industry leaders deployed their collective power to guide studio labor relations in directions useful for the majors. Motion picture executives sought control over Hollywood workers not because their wages constituted a large portion of production costs (they did not) but because a shortage of qualified workers could raise costs indirectly. Company heads usually could keep labor costs low (12 to 22 percent of yearly production costs)[19] by hiring workers on a short-term basis and raising wage rates only for selected groups. However, studio workers could drive up labor costs by lengthening production time or withholding the skills necessary for a picture's completion. Industry heads sought to curb this power. As the majors' needs changed in 1926, 1933, and 1935, industry executives strove for and attained correspondingly different arrangements to curb studio workers' power.

Goal: Keep Variable Cost Low

Most craftworkers and technicians worked on a call basis (without regular, long-term employment), and thus their earnings depended not only on wage rates but also on the amount of time worked. As industrial relations scholars Hugh Lovell and Tasile Carter point out, motion picture studio management granted wage increases "with relative ease . . . for [their] impact . . . on total cost could be reduced by more efficient methods which lessened shooting time."[20] Industry executives controlled the length and conditions of production, in addition to the hiring, firing, and assignment of workers. Ross noted in 1941 that the SBA said nothing about seniority or union response to technological change and that union efforts to set minimum crew requirements had met with little success.[21]

Motion picture executives generally tried to avoid increased labor costs. They attempted to escape paying overtime to production workers—which was mandated under the Fair Labor Standards Act—by classifying personnel as professionals. Under the act, which became effective on October 24, 1938, nonprofessional workers who put in over forty-four hours per week earned overtime pay. Current studio labor contracts called for sixty-hour workweeks. The majors' labor relations staff tried frantically to classify as professionals as many of the 25,000 studio workers as possible. Giving up on this scheme, they appealed to federal authorities for special treatment. *Variety* reported that the federal officials refused, finding the classification idea "distasteful" and shedding few tears over the high wages the industry paid to studio workers. The following spring, industry attorneys tentatively agreed that studio workers should be paid for a minimum of six hours per call. Company executives hurriedly vetoed the proposition, claiming it would cost nearly $2 million every year.[22]

By contrast, when motion picture industry management did choose to raise labor costs, it did so through increased wages (which it could contain to some extent by shortening production time) for strategically selected groups of workers. To weaken the power of the Federated Motion Picture Crafts (FMPC) in 1937, Motion Picture Producers and Distributors of America (MPPDA) labor negotiator Pat Casey offered to deal separately with the costumers' local, a non-SBA union sympathetic to the FMPC strike. Delaying a membership vote on affiliation with the FMPC, the 217 costumers settled for wage increases and a four-year contract with the majors. Seamstresses, for example, received pay increases of from 8 to 12 percent under the agreement. The costumers did not gain SBA status but had to sign a contract with each individual company.[23]

A shortage of qualified craftworkers or technicians could raise costs indirectly by prolonging or spoiling production. Since studios hired most of these workers only as necessary to work on particular pictures and paid them by the week, day, or hour, their wages entered producers' balance sheets as a variable cost. Thus, as Lovell and Carter note, the length of production determined the amount spent on those workers' wages, so that "even minor work stoppages or delays may have an almost catastrophic effect on costs."[24] In July 1933, for example, when IATSE locals struck eleven studios, the walkout affected 27,000 employees and a weekly studio payroll of $1.35 million.[25]

A protracted studio work stoppage could also interfere with distribution and exhibition. With a strike by the FMPC imminent in May 1937, distribution heads and theater operators worried that producers would not be able to honor their contracts for the season's schedule of releases. The anxious managers noted that the majors rarely tied up capital by stockpiling feature films, and that although three-fourths of the releasing season had passed, studios had yet to produce one-third of the season's films.[26]

The absence of skilled workers, or their presence as strikers, could drive up variable costs. During the 1933 IA strike, *Variety* reported that in eight days, crews at Universal had completed only two scenes of *Only Yesterday*, that a forty-piece orchestra at Warner's had had to rehearse for three days to make an acceptable recording for a *Footlight Parade* song, and that an RKO comedy had met its demise at the lab. Paramount postponed location work on three films, wanting to "take no chances of possible interference from strike sympathizers."[27]

The structure of the motion picture industry gave executives of the major companies enough power to guide Hollywood labor relations in directions useful for the majors. The manner in which the five vertically integrated companies monopolized the industry allowed those companies to enforce policies among themselves and to impose them on smaller companies. The majors' mode of financing added to the power of their executives, allowing them to take high salaries from company earnings. In addition, government agencies placed no major obstacles in company heads' paths.[28]

1926: The Studio Basic Agreement

Prior to the 1926 SBA, producers refused to recognize the unions with members among studio workers. Taking advantage of competing jurisdictional claims by three unions, executives had a ready supply of replacement workers (scabs) to defeat strikes for recognition or higher wages.[29] By 1926, the motion picture industry needed to regularize its relations with labor. Throughout the decade, the major companies bought land and built theaters at a furious rate, but not until 1926 did banks and investment firms decide that the industry had proven its worth as a good risk. After only a year and a half of this boom in investment financing, banker Attilio H. Giannini reported that investors had sunk approximately $1.5 billion into the film industry.[30] The year 1926 also marked the debut of two Warner's films with sound effects and the first Hays Office examination of scripts for items of dubious moral quality.[31] Ready to enter the high-priced sound era, motion picture executives needed to make their profits as predictable as possible.

Whether forced by a threatened projectionist strike, as Joseph Kennedy claimed, or unable to match the united power of the three main Hollywood unions (the IA, Carpenters, and Electricians reached jurisdictional agreements in 1925 and early 1926), motion picture executives signed the SBA in November 1926.[32] Whatever its genesis, the SBA served the executives well, for it maintained an open shop,[33] centralized labor negotiations, and divided Hollywood unions into two ranks—those signatory to the SBA and those excluded from it.

Under the SBA, studios continued the open shop policy they had pursued from the start. By signing the SBA, industry executives recognized five unions as representatives of some Hollywood workers but did not promise to hire only union members. The companies gained cooperation from the five largest Hollywood unions without having to guarantee work for those unions' members.[34]

The SBA centralized the power to negotiate. The SBA stipulated that the presidents of the five signatory international unions meet with a committee of five motion picture industry representatives to consider wages, hours, and working conditions. This group convened every couple of years in New York City at the Broadway office of Pat Casey to settle terms for renewal of the SBA. Each committee of five had a secretary, who, as Ross noted in 1947, was "the sole [medium] through which workers and studio managers [could] voice their complaints."[35] As industrial relations specialist Richard Lester points out, high union officials tend to share with management an interest in stability. To guarantee stability, union leaders must enforce "agreements . . . even though that means disciplining malcontented elements [sic] within the union membership."[36] So long as international union leaders could hold the rank and file to SBA contracts, industry executives benefited by dealing with fewer, and more sympathetic, unionists.

The SBA divided studio workers into two groups: those whose unions the producers officially recognized and negotiated with and those without recognition. This allowed the majors to grant raises to a few large unions while refusing even to negotiate with other workers. The 1926 agreement included the IA, Carpenters, Electricians, Painters, and Musicians. The same five international unions renewed the SBA with industry executives in 1928 for three more years. At talks in 1931, executives objected to union efforts to expand their memberships by bringing additional groups of workers into the SBA. The IA wanted the SBA to cover IA locals of lab workers and sound technicians, and the Painters called for inclusion of art department personnel as members of the Painters union. By the time management and union heads met again to discuss renewal of the SBA in 1933, the Teamsters had newly joined the ranks of recognized unions, but neither of the unions that had agitated for larger jurisdiction remained party to the SBA—the Painters dropped out in 1932, and industry leaders excluded the IA after its disastrous 1933 strike. Other workers still without recognition in 1933 included cutters, assistant directors, script clerks, costumers, art directors, scenic artists, set designers, makeup artists, and hairdressers.[37]

1933: IA out of Hollywood

Just as the SBA answered the majors' needs in 1926, the IA's virtual disappearance from Hollywood between 1933 and 1935 served industry executives' interests during those years. Plagued by a lack of working capital in the early 1930s, motion picture companies cut back production and slashed pay scales. When IA locals (including crucial camera, lab, and sound technicians) refused to cooperate, executives broke their power by supporting their jurisdictional rival, the International Brotherhood of Electrical Workers (IBEW).

Motion picture industry spending and profits remained relatively stable during the Depression, but during the early 1930s the industry experienced a drop in available working capital. Theater attendance and revenue fell during the years 1931 to 1934. This reduction in earnings hit motion picture companies especially hard because they had incurred heavy long-term debts during the 1920s theater acquisition and construction boom. In 1933 Paramount declared bankruptcy, while Wesco (a Fox theater subsidiary), RKO, and Universal's chain of theaters all went into receivership.[38]

In response to cash shortages and the lowered return from current films, the motion picture industry decreased production levels and sought reduced production costs. During the national bank moratorium of March 1933, industry executives cut an expenditure conveniently available—the pay of studio employees. Initially, the Academy of Motion Picture Arts and Sciences Committee that handled the pay cut recommended a two-month, 50 percent reduction for all workers. The committee soon modified its plan so that lower-paid workers gave up nothing or smaller percentages of their pay. However, IA studio locals refused to cooperate. They rejected any cut, holding studios to their wage agreements under the SBA.[39]

During this period, IA leaders lost control of locals and thus failed to provide the security and convenience formerly achieved through the SBA structure of centralized negotiations.[40] The rebellious IA locals included the workers least easily replaced. Studios needed large numbers of painters, carpenters, and electricians to construct soundstages and sets, but craftsworkers with those skills could be found fairly readily, for they also worked in areas other than motion picture production. On the other hand, studio executives considered sound engineers, camera operators, and lab workers most difficult to replace, since those jobs required specialized knowledge and lengthy training. The absence of these workers during the July 1933 IA strike hindered production. Studios held off sending exposed negatives to labs, not trusting the handiwork of inexperienced scabs. The shortage of qualified production workers, according to *Variety*, "brought out an avalanche of temperamental displays among players and directors caused by petty delays and the necessity of reshooting scenes numerous times."[41]

Although industry executives feigned disinterest in July 1933, terming the strike a jurisdictional dispute between the IA and IBEW, only a few months later *Variety* reported:

> One producer admitted at the end of the strike that it had cost the major companies at least $2,000,000 to battle the IA, but the producers would recoup many times this amount during the next few years through cuts in salaries and crews, besides breaking the domination of the unions for all time in the production field. . . .
>
> The refusal of IATSE members to take any salary slashes during the emergency period last March was one of the determining factors . . . [motivating] the producers to break the control of the IA among studio crafts.[42]

At every turn, the studios promoted the IBEW over the IA. Instead of negotiating with IA representatives, producers replaced striking IA workers with IBEW members, sound research personnel, and studio telephone and radio workers. Newspaper and radio advertisements brought over three hundred applicants to supplement the in-house scab labor force. Although IA members picketed peacefully, some studios increased their police forces and offered on-site room and board to scabs who might be afraid to cross picket lines. Then, in early August, industry heads officially recognized the IBEW as the representative not only for studio sound technicians but also for lamp operators, who currently held IA cards. For added measure, studio managers allowed IBEW organizers to sign up members inside the studios, a concession at that time unprecedented in Hollywood labor history.[43]

1935: Industry Leaders Bring the IA Back

After two years of curtailed production, the major companies of the motion picture industry prepared in 1935 to expand production once again. The majors had restructured their debts, giving them a greater margin of working capital to sink into production.[44] However, a piece of New Deal legislation posed a potential threat to the majors' plans. In 1935 Congress passed a law recognizing employees' right to organize and collectively make demands on their employers (National Labor Relations Act—NLRA, or Wagner Act). Since the motion picture industry desired to remain in the government's good graces, it could hardly ignore Hollywood's tradition of craft unionism and attempt to operate on a nonunion basis. The decision by the National Labor Relations Board (NLRB) to allow motion picture companies to bargain as a unit encouraged the majors to look as a group for a union to solve their potential labor problem.[45]

The majors found in the revamped IA a union willing and able to provide a subdued, plentiful work force—for a price. Following the example set by a theater chain and the IA stagehand local in Chicago, the majors paid IA leaders to prevent demands other than periodic wage increases from reaching the bargaining table and to guarantee a supply of labor uninterrupted by strikes. Once motion picture company executives had purchased their low-risk labor supply from the IA, they tried to protect their partner against challenges, both from within and outside the union.

Deals struck in the early 1930s between the most influential Chicago theater chain and the city's stagehand local paved the way for later agreements between executives of the motion picture industry and leaders of the syndicate-dominated IA. The Balaban and Katz theater group, controlled since 1926 by Paramount through its Publix Theatres company, monopolized the first-run market in Chicago for nearly three decades. IA Local 2, which supplied the stagehands for the live shows accompanying film screenings, claimed as members close to 100 percent of Chicago stagehands.[46]

Early in 1934, Local 2's business agent, George Browne, and his partner, William Bioff, decided to work with, rather than against, Balaban and Katz. Barney Balaban refused to restore a "temporary" 25 percent pay cut for stagehands at his theaters on the agreed-upon date; instead he offered to fund the IA soup kitchen for unemployed stagehands and pay Browne $150 per week to overlook the permanence of the "temporary" wage reduction.[47] Browne and Bioff agreed to do business. They demanded a one-time payment of $50,000, which haggling with Balaban's attorney Leo Spitz reduced to $20,000. Neither party lacked experience in such dealings. Balaban currently paid Tommy Maloy of Chicago IA projectionist Local 110 $150 per week for "insurance," and Browne had his own schemes. For example, in 1932 or 1933, the owner of a burlesque house paid $150 per week for Browne's guarantee that any competition opening up in the neighborhood would receive a bad deal from Local 2.[48]

Browne and Bioff celebrated their entrance into big-time racketeering at a nightclub run by Nick Circella. Circella alerted Frank Nitti, heir to the Capone organization, of the labor leaders' windfall. Since Prohibition had ended in December 1933, the syndicate sought new areas of development. Nitti notified Browne and Bioff that henceforth his group would take half the gains from their deals. To up the stakes, Nitti and his cohorts from New York and New Jersey arranged to have the 1934 IA convention elect Browne as president of the entire union. After unknown assailants machine-gunned Tommy Maloy to death in February 1935, Nitti ordered Browne and Bioff to take over IA projectionist Local 110.[49]

Browne and Bioff flexed their newly acquired muscle in 1935. In Chicago they cashed in on Maloy's former racket. The IA usually required two projectionists per booth for safety and high employment, but Maloy had waived that for theater circuits which paid him. By threatening to reinstate the requirement, Bioff received a total of $100,000: $60,000 from Balaban and Katz, $30,000 from Warner Bros., and $10,000 from Essanay. Browne and Bioff dutifully turned over half the amount to Nitti and split the rest. Pleased at the return on his investment, Nitti increased the syndicate's share to two-thirds for future deals. He did not have long to wait. In the fall of 1935 Nicholas Schenck, president of Loew's, Inc. (the theater chain that owned MGM), and Major Leslie Thompson of RKO gave Browne and Bioff $150,000 for Browne's promise to veto a strike vote by IA Local 306 (New York projectionists), which wanted a wage cut restored. As International president, Browne had constitutional authority to bestow or withhold sanction and financial support for strikes by IA locals.[50]

Early in December 1935, industry executives and the syndicate-run IA extended the scope of their dealings from stagehands and projectionists to include studio craftworkers and technicians. Officials from the largest motion picture companies met at MPPDA headquarters in New York with heads of the IA, IBEW, and American Federation of Labor. A few of the executives in attendance had participated directly in prior payoffs to the IA. Nicholas Schenck had purchased "labor peace" for New York theaters only a couple of months earlier. Leo Spitz of RKO, in his former capacity as Barney Balaban's attorney, had arranged for the $20,000 payment to Browne and Bioff in 1934.[51]

After an eight-hour meeting, the labor and industry leaders announced that as of January 2, 1936, the IA would have jurisdiction over studio camera operators, lab workers, grips, stage carpenters, property people, lamp operators, and sound technicians. The IBEW retained jurisdiction over sound technicians not involved with actual production. Industry executives not only gave jurisdiction over studio workers to the IA at the IBEW's expense but also welcomed the IA back into the SBA and granted closed shop to the five international unions signatory to the SBA.[52] The IA metamorphosed suddenly from nearly extinct outcast in Hollywood to large, powerful, leading union, the first ever to gain closed shop at the studios.

Motion picture firms strictly enforced the 1935 closed shop agreement, which increased IA leaders' ability to resist challenges from the IA rank and file. Although studio heads retained control of hiring,[53] closed shop restricted the labor pool to union members. Studio management allowed stewards from IA locals to enter the lots to check IA workers' dues cards. Unless members behind in their dues brought them up to date within a specified period, the studio refused to offer them jobs. When the efforts of IA members to reform their union from within aggravated IA officials, studios obliged by firing the vocal protestors. Twentieth Century-Fox discharged two IA propmakers within a week after they signed the complaint in a 1937 suit for their local's autonomy from the international IA. One of the men had worked in the industry since 1920. Neither could find work again for several years. At Bioff's request, Warners fired a "troublemaker" who protested the IA's 2 percent assessment on his earnings. An MGM carpenter likewise lost his job after complaining about the assessment.[54]

After 1935, industry heads also helped the IA resist challenges from other unions. When the Painters led the FMPC out on strike for recognition in 1937 and contested IA jurisdiction over makeup artists, studios hired scabs, whom Bioff immediately signed up as IA members. Six weeks prior to a hotly contested NLRB representation election between the IA and United Studio Technicians Guild in September 1939, motion picture executives signed a five-year contract with the IA. Browne had withdrawn IA studio locals from the SBA and thus from closed shop protection in January 1939. In early August, industry executives revived the closed shop agreement, and by the end

of the month required all workers on lucrative location shooting assignments to hold a paid-up IA card.[55]

Perhaps studio executives justified their actions by regarding
them as protection of an investment, for the major motion picture firms
paid enormous sums to IA leaders after welcoming the union back to
Hollywood in 1935–36. At the April 1936 SBA meeting in New York,
Browne and Bioff demanded $2 million from the film companies. Leo
Spitz facilitated negotiations between Bioff and Nicholas Schenck, who
settled on yearly payments of $50,000 from each major and $25,000 from
each smaller studio. The next day, Schenck brought $50,000 for Loew's
(MGM) and Sidney Kent $25,000 on behalf of Twentieth Century-Fox.
Paramount delivered $50,000 in small amounts through Austin Keough
in Chicago. Harry Warner paid up in December 1937 ($20,000) and
January 1938 ($80,000). Louis B. Mayer set up an elaborate scheme to
meet MGM's ongoing obligation. From June 1937 until early 1939, he
had officials of a raw film distribution company pay Bioff's brother-in-
law. Of the $500 to $900 per week the brother-in-law received officially
as commissions on sales of film stock to MGM, he kept only $125 and
passed on the rest to Bioff.[56]

The Payoff

Motion picture executives received services in return for their large
payments to Browne, Bioff, and the Nitti syndicate. IA international
heads held down Hollywood labor costs by curbing studio workers'
efforts to bargain collectively and directly with their employers and
by inhibiting solidarity among Hollywood unions, guilds, and unorga-
nized employees. These actions checked the potential power of the
Hollywood labor movement, allowing the majors to make deals, rather
than engage in genuine collective bargaining, and to pay members of
a few unions highly while refusing to recognize others. IA leaders
served the majors by insisting that only international union representatives negotiate with management, by fighting union locals' attempts
to act autonomously of their international union and by splintering
Hollywood labor coalitions. In addition, the IA tightened the majors'
oligopolistic grip on the industry by forcing up independent producers'
labor costs.

IA Squelches Worker Agitaton

IA leaders prevented workers from pressuring industry executives about wages, working conditions, or seasonal unemployment by allowing only top union officials to "negotiate" with management. IA International President Browne endorsed industry executives' refusal to deal directly with local union representatives. When members of IA Local 659 (camera operators) protested the terms Browne had set for the IA's trimphant reentry into the SBA, Browne cleared a nuanced agreement with management, then presented the revised terms to the local as a fait accompli.[57] During the 1937 FMPC strike, Pat Casey spoke longingly of the years (1926 to 1932) when the International Painters still belonged to the SBA, when "it was understood that the local Studio Painters' Unions were to be the medium through which the International Union would carry out the terms of the [SBA]." Browne soon took steps to revive Casey's golden past. The IA president announced that he would settle the FMPC strike only with an international officer of the Painters, not with Charles Lessing, leader of the FMPC, and not with Rudy Kohl, studio painters' business representative.[58]

IA International officers prevented IA members from voicing complaints between the years 1936 to 1939 by suspending the autonomy of IA studio locals. Since 1924, by-laws to the IA constitution had promised local unions "home rule"—control of wages and working conditions within a local's jurisdiction. However, the IA constitution also granted the International president "in case of any emergency the power to suspend any law or laws of the [IA] or of any local union, provided he obtains the unanimous consent of the members of the General Executive Board."[59] Browne declared a state of emergency for the Hollywood locals in 1935, subjecting them to direct control by his personal representatives, who included Willie Bioff. Under International rule, the locals elected no local officers or delegates to the International convention. Browne brought a few of the IA locals' business agents along to SBA talks but only to answer questions that might arise. After Browne signed contracts for the locals, he provided no stewards on the lots to enforce the agreements.[60]

When some IA members protested in 1937 against International supervision, Browne allowed the studio locals to vote on the issue. Appearing in person at the locals' meetings late in the year, Browne suggested that a vote for autonomy would bring reduced wages and poor working conditions, similar to those suffered between 1933 and 1935. A month before the vote, Casey had testified at a California State Assembly's committee hearing that the majors would consider the restoration of local autonomy a breach of the SBA. All four IA Hollywood locals voted overwhelmingly against autonomy.[61]

IA Keeps Labor Costs Down

IA leaders in the post-1935 era helped industry executives carry out their strategy of awarding wage increases selectively to avoid greater expenditures. IA studio locals did receive four wage increases of at least 10 percent each between 1936 and 1939. However, work remained sporadic and seasonal. In the summer of 1938, shortly before a mass meeting on studio unemployment, Browne paid lip service to the goal of guaranteed, year-round employment: "Of course, to spread employment and salaries over a yearly period is the desire of us all, and something that most certainly will be discussed at the coming [SBA] conferences. I sincerely trust a satisfactory solution will be found then to this perplexing problem."[62] The SBA talks yielded no such solution.

In a manner similar to management's treatment of the costumers, the IA undermined utility and other workers' support for the FMPC by offering them wage increases. As soon as the Studio Utility Employees (SUE) joined the FMPC strike, IA representatives offered SUE members IA work cards, free initiation, and a raise from 60 to 82.5 cents per hour. The officials told SUE members they had to have an IA work card within a few days or would lose their job. The IA claimed to have initiated over 300 former SUE workers after issuing this "invitation." The IA also offered work permits and wage increases to painters, makeup artists, and hairdressers who would cross picket lines and join the IA. According to *Variety*, this tactic worked especially well at Twentieth Century-Fox and MGM. As the trade journal noted, the IA "was cooperating with producers to keep production moving."[63]

The IA cooperated by keeping studio locals from negotiating directly with management or running their own affairs and by selectively raising wages to prevent the potentially higher cost of solidarity among Hollywood workers. This cooperation saved the motion picture industry much money. John Cogley reports studio executives testified during the 1940s that by dealing with Browne and Bioff they saved approximately $15 million. Attorney and journalist Carey McWilliams estimated in 1941 that had MPPDA members not paid $500,000 or so to IA heads, they might have had to pay up to ten times that in higher wages. Writing in

1981, screenwriter Lester Cole figured that if 25,000 to 30,000 studio employees had managed to bargain raises of $10 per week every two to three years, the total would have come to an additional $250,000 to $350,000 per week. Cole concluded that the motion picture industry got a "very generous deal" from the IA.[64]

IA Weakens Independent Producers

By holding smaller motion picture companies to union wage scales and crew requirements, the IA strengthened the majors' oligopoly. Michael Conant explains how the majors erected strong barriers to entry through long-term contracts with talent, the MPPDA censorship system, and control of first-run theaters.[65] Conant could have added to his list the cost of studio labor.

During the 1930s the IA unionized smaller companies and held them to the same wage scales and working conditions as prevailed at the majors' studios. Early in 1933 IA President William Elliott and Pat Casey conferred on a campaign to bring United Artists, Columbia, and Hal Roach into the SBA. The majors promised the IA that they would extend SBA coverage to a few minor crafts if the three smaller companies joined and adopted union wage scales. After gaining closed shop from the majors in 1935–36, the IA demanded that independent production firms pay union scale to IA members working for them. Despite pleas from the independents, the IA refused to grant lower rates for low-budget films or flat rates on a per-picture basis.[66]

In a few cases, the IA struck to enforce union standards. In November 1937, four hundred IA members walked off the Columbia lot, and IA projectionists around the nation reportedly waited for word not to show Columbia films. The studio had failed to observe crew requirements: although shooting three films, the studio had only one makeup artist in addition to the department head and had ordered actors to do their own makeup. Harry Cohn, according to *Variety*, wanted to "try and out-maneuver the union," but Louis Mayer and executives from other studios convinced him to settle immediately. After the one-day strike three makeup artists created faces for Columbia's three films, and all strikers received full pay for their one day off the job. Similarly, the IA struck for half a day at Selznick-International two years later to force implementation of the 10 percent wage increase Bioff had negotiated after the representation election.[67]

Conclusion

Given the opportunity by Browne, Bioff, and the Nitti syndicate, motion picture industry executives chose to purchase from 1935 until 1940 a relatively cheap and steady supply of qualified labor rather than to bargain collectively with their employees. Individual company officers may have refused to cooperate, but, as a group, officials of the major firms bought their stable labor force from the syndicate-run IA. By virtue of the motion picture industry's vertically integrated, oligopolistic structure, relatively free from government intervention, industry leaders had the power to deal with a syndicate-led union. As the presiding judge at the 1948 Nitti tax trial put it: "The payers [industry heads] knowingly and willingly paid over the funds sought to be here taxed, and in a sense lent encouragement, and participated with full knowledge of the facts in the activities of Browne and the Nitti group."[68]

Industry leaders' decision to deal with the IA (and the syndicate) during the late 1930s fits the pattern of labor relations established in preceding years. When capital investment increased in the late 1920s, motion picture executives recognized the largest Hollywood unions and gained labor stability without having to guarantee employment to union members. When business slowed and IA locals disrupted labor-management relations in the early 1930s, industry heads found it convenient to deal with a union more cooperative, although more limited in jurisdiction (the IBEW). When the business upturn of the mid-1930s coincided with the IA's offer to provide a broad range of workers tightly controlled by their International representatives, industry leaders granted closed shop and helped the IA expand its jurisdiction. Not the victims of extortion for five years, motion picture executives were, I argue, "smart" shoppers who selected the "bargain" in labor that best fit their current needs.

NOTES

Thanks to Matthew Bernstein for comments and suggestions on this article.

(In the endnotes, *AMPAS* refers to the United Studio Technicians Guild folder [unless another folder is indicated] at the Margaret Herrick Library at the Academy of Motion Picture Arts and Sciences in Beverly Hills, California. *UAC* indicates the Screen Cartoonist Guild collection, leaflets 1937–39, at the Motion Picture Urban Archives Center at California State University, Northridge, California, *Variety* refers to *Weekly Variety*.)

Denise Hartsough

1. For example, see Harold Seidman, *Labor Czars: A History of Labor Racketeering* (New York: Liveright, 1938), pp. 173–82 and 243–45; "Rats Raided," *Time,* 21 August 1939, 12; Carey McWilliams, "Racketeers and Movie Makers," *New Republic,* 27 October 1941, 533–35. The *New York Times* reported in detail the testimony at trials in 1941 and 1943 concerning racketeering in the motion picture industry. For example, see "Bioff, Browne Guilty; Facing 30-Year Terms," *New York Times,* 7 November 1941, 1, 14; "Bioff Describes Gang Rule of Union," *New York Times,* 7 October 1943, 25, 28. On the 1948 tax trial, see James Doherty, "U.S. to Fight Today for Tax Owed by Nitti," *Chicago Tribune,* 27 September 1948, 20.

2. I use *executives* to mean officers and directors of the companies. See Mae Huettig, *Economic Control of the Motion Picture Industry* (Philadelphia: University of Pennsylvania, 1944), p. 101. Those managers seek "the general growth of the firm rather than high dividends . . . [which involves] long-term planning and stability . . . steady supplies of raw materials, provisions for capital, and minimization of risks." See David Bordwell, Janet Staiger, and Kristin Thompson, *The Classical Hollywood Cinema: Film Style and Mode of Production to 1960* (New York: Columbia University Press, 1985), p. 316.

3. I use the terms *racket* and *racketeering* as defined in the *American Heritage Dictionary of the English Language* (Boston: American Heritage Publishing and Houghton Mifflin, 1973), p. 1075: a racket is "a business that obtains money through fraud or extortion" or "an illegal or dishonest practice," and *racketeering* means "engagement in a racket." (As slang, *racket* refers to "any business or job.")

4. See Robert Sklar, *Movie-Made America* (New York: Vintage, 1976), pp. 82–83, and Tino Balio, ed., *The American Film Industry* (Madison: University of Wisconsin Press, 1976), p. 125.

5. Samuel Lipkowitz, "Collective Bargaining in Motion Picture Production," M.A. thesis, American University, 1939, pp. 22, 31, 101.

6. *Variety,* 4 December 1935, 5.

7. Robert Joseph, "Re: Unions in Hollywood," *Films* (Summer 1940), 40; Morrie Ryskind, "It Happened One Night," *Nation,* 15 May 1937, 563.

8. Edmond W. Wentworth quoted in Florabel Muir, "All Right, Gentlemen, Do We Get the Money?" *Saturday Evening Post,* 27 January 1940, 84.

9. Nicholas Schenck quoted in McWilliams, "Racketeers," p. 535; [Sol Davison], "The Motion Picture Studio Strike," *New Leader,* 29 June 1946, 9; Lester Cole, *Hollywood Red* (Palo Alto, Calif.: Ramparts Press, 1981), pp. 215–16.

10. Murray Ross, *Stars and Strikes: Unionization of Hollywood* (New York: Columbia University Press, 1941).

11. Murray Ross, "Labor Relations in Hollywood." *Annals of the American Academy of Political and Social Science* (November 1947), 62; Walter Galenson, *The CIO Challenge to the AFL: A History of the American Labor Movement, 1935–1941* (Cambridge, Mass.: Harvard University Press, 1960), p. 622. See also Ross, *Stars and Strikes,* p. 13.

12. The five unions included in the 1926 SBA were IATSE, United Brotherhood of Carpenters and Joiners of America, International Brotherhood of Electrical Workers, American Federation of Musicians, and International Brotherhood of Painters, Decorators and Paperhangers of America.

13. Louis B. and Richard S. Perry, *A History of the Los Angeles Labor Movement, 1911–1941* (Berkeley and Los Angeles: University of California Press, 1963), p. 329; *Variety,* 20 March 1934, 4.

14. Robert Osborne Baker, "The International Alliance of Theatrical Stage Employees and Moving Picture Machine Operators of the United States and Canada," Ph.D.

dissertation, University of Kansas, 1933, p. 70. On closings, see *Variety*, 5 July 1932, 1. On concessions, see Baker, pp. 71–72; *Variety*, 20 December 1932, 23.

15. *Variety*, 7 November 1933, 4. For percentages of unionized theaters, see *Variety*, 17 October 1933, 25; *Variety*, 29 November 1939, 3.

16. The majors were Paramount, Loew's (Metro-Goldwyn-Mayer), Warner Bros., RKO and Fox (merged in 1935 to become Twentieth Century-Fox).

17. Huettig, *Economic Control*, pp. 61, 69.

18. Dick Green quoted in *Variety*, 25 July 1933, 5; Harland Holmden quoted in *Variety*, 15 September 1937, 5, 23; *Variety*, 22 September 1937, 7; *Variety*, 19 April 1939, 5; *Variety*, 26 April 1939, 16.

19. Figures from Jack Alicoate, ed., *Film Daily Yearbook of Motion Pictures*, vol. 20 (New York: Film Daily, 1938), p. 41, indicate that close to 12 percent of production costs in 1937 went for camera and crew, lighting, makeup, hairstyling, teachers, laborers, costumes and designers, cutters, and sound engineering. *Variety*, 29 June 1938, 2, printed statistics from Joseph Schenck that attributed 17.4 percent of production costs to the categories "technical" and "sets and studio." Leo Rosten, *The Movie Colony, the Movie Makers* (New York: Harcourt, Brace, 1941), p. 375, reports that 22 percent of production costs in 1939 paid wage workers at the studios (includes all wage earners, not just craftsworkers and technicians).

20. Hugh Lovell and Tasile Carter, *Collective Bargaining in the Motion Picture Industry* (Berkeley, Calif.: Institute of Industrial Relations, 1955), p. 6.

21. Ross, *Stars and Strikes*, pp. 19–20. On the broad power of the industry executives, see Huettig, *Economic Control*, pp. 59–60, and Rosten, *Movie Colony*, p. 261.

22. On overtime, see *Variety*, 14 September 1938, 19; *Variety*, 26 October 1938, 3; *Variety*, 2 November 1938, 5. On minimum call, see *Variety*, 12 April 1939, 5.

23. *Variety*, 5 May 1937, 2; *Variety*, 19 May 1937, 2. Industry heads also made strategic payments in the exhibition end of the business. Michael Conant claims that distributors paid adjustments on film rentals to independent exhibitors if a film showed a loss, because distributors "having arbitrarily assigned independent theatres to later runs, were desirous of keeping them from showing losses that might lead them to file antitrust actions to challenge the distributors' system of control." Michael Conant, *Antitrust in the Motion Picture Industry: Economic and Legal Analysis* (Berkeley and Los Angeles: University of California Press, 1960), p. 75.

24. Lovell and Carter, *Collective Bargaining*, p. 6.

25. *Variety*, 25 July 1933, 5.

26. *Variety*, 5 May 1937, 3, 46.

27. *Variety*, 8 August 1933, 7, 42.

28. For full discussions of industry structure and financing, see Huettig, *Economic Control*, and Conant, *Antitrust*. On unusually high executive compensation, see Douglas Gomery, *The Hollywood Studio System* (New York: St. Martin's Press, 1986), p. 7. On the government and the motion picture industry, see Conant, *Antitrust*, and Douglas Gomery, "Hollywood, the National Recovery Administration and the Question of Monopoly Power," *Journal of the University Film Association* (Spring 1979), 47–52.

29. See Michael C. Nielsen, "Towards a Workers' History of the U.S. Film Industry," in Vincent Mosco and Janet Wasko, eds., *Critical Communications Review*, vol. 1 (Norwood, N.J.: Ablex Publishing, 1983), pp. 54, 55; Perry and Perry, *History*, pp. 322–24; Ross, *Stars and Strikes*, pp. 7, 10.

30. Huettig, *Economic Control*, p. 50; Attilio H. Gianini in Joseph Kennedy, ed., *The Story of the Films* (Chicago: A. W. Shaw, 1927), p. 91.

31. Conant, *Antitrust*, pp. 29, 40.

32. Kennedy, *Story*, p. 24; Ross, *Stars and Strikes*, pp. 12–13; Lipkowitz, "Collective Bargaining," pp. 30–31. I question the impact of the strike threat, for Kennedy, *Story*, p.

24, says producers signed the SBA after workers "served notice that if we did not accept a closed shop in Hollywood, they would call a strike in the theatres." However, no strike occurred, despite the fact that the SBA did not grant closed shop; it only recognized five unions.

33. *Open shop* means that management hires non-union workers if it so desires. In contrast, *closed shop* limits the pool of labor to union members, and *union shop* may mean that newly hired workers must join the union after a certain time or that a set percentage of employees must be union members.

34. Ross, "Labor Relations in Hollywood," p. 58.

35. Raymond Moley, *The Hays Office* (New York: Bobbs-Merrill, 1945), pp. 195–97; Ross, "Labor Relations in Hollywood," p. 59. For the text of the 1926 SBA, see Michael C. Nielsen, "Motion Picture Craft Workers and Craft Unions in Hollywood: The Studio Era, 1912–1948," Ph.D. dissertation, University of Illinois, 1985, pp. 427–28. The group renewed the SBA for terms of from two to five years but met annually to renegotiate wages.

36. Richard Lester, *As Unions Mature: An Analysis of the Evolution of American Unionism* (Princeton, N.J.: Princeton University Press, 1958), pp. 28–29, 48, 65–66, 109.

37. See Perry and Perry, *History*, pp. 325–30; *Variety*, 8 December 1931, 11; *Variety*, 25 July 1933, 27. Studio executives set up the Academy of Motion Picture Arts and Sciences in 1927 for talent workers (actors, writers, directors—membership by invitation only) in an effort to forestall organization into actual unions or guilds. The Academy's influence diminished greatly in 1933. Its administration of pay cuts in March 1933 alienated many members; later that year, it lost a bid to represent all talent groups under the NRA. Writers left AMPAS in April to revive their guild, and actors in October to form theirs. See Ross, *Stars and Strikes*, pp. 27–29, 63, 94–105.

38. Donald L. Perry, "An Analysis of the Financial Plans of the Motion Picture Industry for the Period 1929 to 1962," Ph.D. dissertation, University of Illinois, 1966, pp. 62, 71–72; Conant, *Antitrust*, p. 31.

39. Perry, "Analysis," p. 59; Lipkowitz, "Collective Bargaining," p. 15; Ross, *Stars and Strikes*," pp. 18, 44–47; Cole, *Hollywood Red*, p. 120.

40. See *Variety*, 15 December 1931, 6; *Variety*, 1 August 1933, 48; *Variety*, 3 October 1933, 5; *Variety*, 24 October 1933, 6; *Variety*, 7 November 1933, 6; *Variety*, 15 May 1934, 25.

41. *Variety*, 5 November 1930, 12; *Variety*, 8 January 1930, 91; *Variety*, 15 May 1934, 25.

42. *Variety*, 25 July 1933, 2; *Variety*, 3 October 1933, 11. Joseph, "Re: Unions in Hollywood," pp. 44–45, says the IA's refusal to lower wages in March 1933 "marked the technicians for eventual ousting and destruction, and bad blood existed between producers and workers."

43. *Variety*, 25 July 1933, 27; *Variety*, 8 August 1933, 3; *Variety*, 29 August 1933, 56.

44. Perry, "Analysis," pp. 59, 180. Biennial statistics on the number of "wage earners" (craftworkers and labworkers) indicate that the intensity of Hollywood motion picture production did indeed change markedly around 1926, 1933, and 1935. Up to 1925, approximately 6,000 wage earners worked at the studios every year. That number had begun to increase by 1927 and leveled off around 10,800 from 1929 to 1933 (no data for 1931). In 1935, the number of wage earners jumped by nearly 40 percent, to close to 15,000. The number kept increasing in 1937 and 1939 but at a lower rate (30 percent and then 24 percent, respectively). See U.S. Department of Commerce, Bureau of the Census, *Sixteenth Census of the United States, 1940*, vol. 2, *Manufacturers, 1939*, pt. 2, p. 656.

45. Doris E. Pullman and L. Reed Tripp, "Collective Bargaining Developments," in Milton Derber and Edwin Young, eds., *Labor and the New Deal* (Madison: University of Wisconsin Press, 1957), p. 330.

46. On Balaban and Katz, see Adolph Zukor in Kennedy, *Story*, p. 75; Conant,

Antitrust, pp. 25, 85–86, 154–55; Gertrude Jobes, *Motion Picture Empire* (Hamden, Conn.: Archon Books, 1966), pp. 252–53. On Local 2, see C. Lawrence Christenson, *Collective Bargaining in Chicago, 1929–1930* (Chicago: University of Chicago Press, 1933), p. 200. Christenson, p. 201, argues that the coming of sound worked to Local 2's advantage, for the larger chain theaters staged more elaborate live shows, and scene shifters got the job of placing horns behind the screen.

47. Barney Balaban became president of Paramount in June 1936 and continued to run the company until 1964. See Gomery, *Hollywood Studio System*, pp. 33–35.

48. George H. Dunne, *Hollywood Labor Dispute: A Study in Immorality* (Los Angeles: Conference Publishing, 1950), pp. 8–9, 43. Father Dunne began researching the mob's connections to the IA and motion picture industry in 1946, when *Commonweal* asked him to write an article on Hollywood labor. Dunne's primary source on the topic is the record of a 1948 hearing in the U.S. Tax Court at Chicago on Frank Nitti's estate, at which hearing Browne and Bioff testified. Jobes, *Motion Picture Empire*, p. 355, quotes Bioff, speaking from prison in the 1940s, on the $20,000: "We didn't get it all. The soup kitchen got a few cases of canned goods outta it."

49. Dunne, *Hollywood*, pp. 5–6, 10–12. On the mob and Prohibition, see Gus Tyler, ed., *Organized Crime in America* (Ann Arbor: University of Michigan Press, 1962), p. 152. *New York Times*, 20 March 1943, 30, cites rumors attributing Maloy's death to his unwillingness to "share [his] spoils with the 'syndicate.'"

50. Dunne, *Hollywood*, pp. 6, 13–14.

51. *Variety*, 11 December 1935, p. 12. Western Electric and Chase National Bank, which gained controlling interest in Loew's around 1930, both sold their Loew's stock in 1935, just before Loew's President Schenck struck the IA deal. See Janet Wasko, *Movies and Money: Financing the American Film Industry* (Norwood, N.J.: Ablex, 1982), pp. 74–76. The shift in control may help explain Schenck's ability to make a pact with the syndicate-led union.

52. *Variety*, 11 December 1933, 5; *Variety*, 8 January 1936, 7.

53. Ross, *Stars and Strikes*, p. 20.

54. McWilliams, "Racketeers," pp. 533–34; Muir, "All Right, Gentlemen," p. 84.

55. On FMPC strike scabbing, see *Variety*, 5 May 1937, 2; Muir, "All Right, Gentlemen," 82. On studios favoring the IA in 1939, see *Variety*, 16 August 1939, 7; *Variety*, 20 September 1939, 25. The United Studio Technicians Guild (USTG) questioned the security provided by the closed shop contract, which allowed any party to withdraw by giving ten days' notice. "Extra! Labor Board Orders USTG-IA Election," USTG leaflet, August 1939, p. 1, AMPAS. NLRB policy discounted labor-management agreements made with a union prior to its victory in a representation election. Walter Galenson, *Rival Unionism in the United States* (New York: American Council on Public Affairs, 1940), p. 257.

56. Dunne, *Hollywood*, pp. 14–16; Jobes, *Motion Picture Empire*, pp. 353–55; Cole, *Hollywood Red*, p. 215; Malcolm Johnson, *Crime on the Labor Front* (New York: McGraw-Hill, 1950), pp. 29–30. Dunne, *Hollywood*, p. 16, reports that two companies (Columbia and RKO) did not pay their $25,000 per year but suffered no reprisals.

57. The original 1935–36 agreement excluded first camera operators (cinematographers) from Local 659 and thus from protection under the SBA. In March 1936, Browne and Casey secured approval from major studio managers for the addition of a clause to the SBA, so that the IA would have jurisdiction over cinematographers at least 25 percent of their working time. See *Variety*, 15 January 1936, 5; *Variety*, 4 March 1936, 37.

58. *Variety*, 5 May 1937, 23; *Variety*, 26 May 1937, 2.

59. Quoted in Baker, "International Alliance," p. 15; see also pp. 18, 43, 45, 83.

60. Ross, "C.I.O. Loses Hollywood," *Nation*, 7 October 1939, 375; *Variety*, 31 May 1939, 39; *Variety*, 18 March 1936, 25; Ted Pierce, "A Study of the Position of the

Independent Talent Guilds of the Motion Picture Industry," undated mimeo [1938–1939], p. 4, UAC. Unlike the IA studio locals, Los Angeles stagehand and projectionist locals negotiated their own contracts with management. See *Variety*, 1 February 1939, 5.

61. *Variety*, 29 December 1937, p. 11; *Variety*, 24 November 1937, p. 20; *Variety*, 12 January 1938, p. 7.

62. George Browne, quoted in *Variety*, 6 July 1938, 8. Casual employment (lack of job security for individual workers) strengthens the union, for the union "become[s] responsible for supplying competent workers as they are needed." See Lovell and Carter, *Collective Bargaining*, p. 5.

63. *Variety*, 5 May 1937, 2.

64. John Cogley, *Report on Blacklisting: I. Movies* (New York: Arno Press and the *New York Times*, 1972, orig. New York: Fund for the Republic, 1956), p. 52; McWilliams, "Racketeers," p. 535; Cole, *Hollywood Red*, p. 216.

65. Conant, *Antitrust*, p. 37. Minor companies produced and distributed films; independents just produced.

66. *Variety*, 28 February 1933, 27; *Variety*, 1 July 1936, 7. The independents who pleaded for lower scales included I. E. Chadwick, Harry Webb, B. B. Ray, Alexander Brothers, William Berke, and A. W. Hackle.

67. *Variety*, 10 November 1937, 7; *Variety*, 15 November 1939, 24.

68. Judge Kern quoted in Dunne, *Hollywood*, p. 7.

External Determinations and the System

Richard Maltby

"Baby Face" or How Joe Breen Made Barbara Stanwyck Atone for Causing the Wall Street Crash

In order to ensure the appearance of legitimacy for its actions, censorship is obliged to imagine an audience for the text it is censoring and to assess that audience's cumulative response to its various discourses. In this activity of imagining audiences, if not in the motivation for it, the behaviour of censorship resembles that of criticism. It is, indeed, at this point of correspondence that the examination of censorship procedures may prove useful to that critical activity which calls itself theory. Obviously, the institution of censorship is not independent of other social forces; the censorship procedures established by the Motion Picture Producers and Distributors of America, Inc. (MPPDA), during the 1920s and 1930s integrated "self-regulation" within the larger institution of cinema production, distribution, and exhibition. Under the supervision of the Studio Relations Committee (SRC), the application of the Production Code preceded the pro-filmic event and was in part justified to the producers in terms of the financial savings incurred by not shooting unusable material. Primary documentation regarding the procedures of censorship might be expected to reveal, with greater accuracy than, say, the reminiscences of directors, how the institution of cinema intended and expected its products to be received.

From *Screen* 27:2 (March-April 1986), 22–45. Reprinted with permission of the author and *Screen*.

Such a documented guide to expected meaning may be of particular use in considering potentially subversive readings of Hollywood texts. The production of a subversive reading can be described as a process by which the critic constitutes himself or herself as the subject of a text in some way other than that which the text proposes. Necessarily, the subversive reading must claim knowledge of a preferred reading. It is evident from the extent of critical disagreement over, for example, the preferred reading of *Blonde Venus* or *She Done Him Wrong* that particular periods and representations present problems of ambiguity in establishing what constitutes a preferred reading.

In an account of *Dance, Girl, Dance* as a critique of patriarchy, Claire Johnston privileges "Dorothy Arzner" as an agency of extra-cinematic intention identifiable from within the realm of the cinematic.[1] In her analysis of *Blonde Venus*, E. Ann Kaplan goes a stage further in distinguishing between the intentions of Dietrich in her performance and those of Von Sternberg in his direction of that performance:

> [Dietrich's] understanding of the extra-cinematic discourse she is being placed in permits a certain distance from what is being done to her, providing a gap through which the female spectator can glimpse her construction in patriarchy.[2]

As the subject of creative play among the discourses of the text, the critic may feel able to move at will between the realms of the cinematic and the extra-cinematic, and the privileging of specific elements of the extra-cinematic may be further justified in the name of polemic. However, if the critic-as-subject is restrained only by the subjectivity of the critic, the limits of permissible reading become difficult to establish. As the above examples indicate, constructing a purely cinematic criticism which only engages "what results from the cinematic apparatus"[3] is extraordinarily difficult and also necessarily ahistorical. Such criticism can discuss ideology only if it presupposes that the ideology it discusses is stable and unchanging.

Like censorship itself, history intrudes upon the playful critic as a machine for the repression of subversive meaning, providing among other things tools for the examination of intent. As such, it operates antithetically to structuralist and psychoanalytic approaches. It may, however, be employed dialectically in the hope of generating a synthesis which educates the text both from itself and from its historical specificity. There would seem to be at least potential fruitfulness in combining an analytical framework with an historical contextualisation, which, while not determining a single reading, suggests limits to the range of meanings available at the moment of production.

I
———

In what has become the standard textbook for American film history courses, Robert Sklar argues that

> In the first half decade of the Great Depression, Hollywood's movie-makers perpetrated one of the most remarkable challenges to traditional values in the history of mass commercial entertainment. The movies called into question sexual propriety, social decorum and the institutions of law and order.[4]

Sklar implies an element of intent on the part of "Hollywood's movie-makers" and also that the censorship procedures adopted by the industry in February 1930 were inadequate to prevent producers' resorting to the more explicit depiction of sex and violence as a means of holding on to a declining audience. Taking their cue primarily from Raymond Moley's paean of praise to business self-regulation, *The Hays Office*, most accounts of the period suggest that

> The years 1930–1933 passed without a notable improvement in the quality of pictures and without the elimination of those objectionable themes and treatments which had brought about the creation and adoption of the Code.[5]

Revisionist historians have interpreted the "official" account of the limited effectiveness of censorship as opening up the possibility of Hollywood's producing "subversive" films.

> Suppose for the sake of argument that scarcely any Hollywood films of the 1930s were actively hostile to capitalism in a direct political sense. One could nevertheless make a case for saying that Hollywood was in certain ways strongly subversive of the dominant sexual ideology. How else can one explain the outrage of groups such as the League [*sic*] of Decency and Hollywood's attempts to censor itself through the adoption of the Motion Picture Production Code.[6]

The case for Hollywood's subversion of dominant sexual ideology is made in Molly Haskell's *From Reverence to Rape*, where she suggests that

It was really in the early 30s that the revolutionary 20s spirit, at least the questioning of marriage and conventional morality, took hold.[7]

Sklar refers to "the Golden Age of Turbulence" between 1930 and 1934 as "an aberration, a surprise even to Hollywood itself."[8] The aberration may, however, lie more in the interpretation than in the event. If the movies of the early 1930s were declaring their proclaimed sexual and other radicalism, they would constitute an aberration in terms of both the general trend in popular culture during the early Depression years and the movies' ideological behaviour during the rest of their history. While such behaviour is possible, it is unlikely enough to require substantial critical proof.

The textual evidence for Hollywood's "challenge to traditional values" is conventionally provided by readings of a group of films invariably including three gangster movies, *I Am a Fugitive from a Chain Gang*, Mae West, the Marx Brothers, and seldom totalling more than twenty movies, or less than 1 percent of Hollywood's feature film output during the period 1930–34. It is too small and too familiar a sample on which to base so substantial a conclusion as that the film-makers of Hollywood were fomenting social or moral disorder, particularly when the list does not correspond very closely with those films with which the censors themselves—both inside and outside the Hays Office—were most concerned.

However, it is clear enough that many movies of the period contain symptoms of a cultural crisis within patriarchal capitalism: in crime films, the recurring motif of the death of the father and the inadequacy of a figure who seeks to speak in the name of the father; the frequent depiction of a "distaste for the nuclear family," which Kaplan identifies in *Blonde Venus*.[9] It is equally clear, though much less re-marked upon, that a significant number of the films of the early 1930s, including many of those discussed within conventional histories, were themselves accounts of the events of the previous decade and, in common with much other cultural production of the period, reflected on how the events of that decade had led to the Crash.[10] It is in this broader context of capitalism's representation of itself at a particular moment of crisis that patriarchy's distinctive representation of woman and female sexuality during this period can best be placed.

The decade after the First World War was witness to the exten-sive development of a mass consumer culture in America, marked most strongly by the growth of advertising. Elements of this culture found themselves in strenuous conflict with the cultural and social patterns of Victorian patriarchal sensibility, a conflict indicated by the widespread image of generational antagonism that pervaded much of the period's popular culture. Much of the conflict was oriented around a revision of prevailing codes of sexuality; as advertising promoted the act of consumption as therapeutic process, it encouraged, in its imagery, a reevaluation of the cultural place of the erotic. Movies participated in this process in two distinct realms: narrative and spectacle. In narrative terms, as Lary May[11] has documented, movies told stories in which an exuberant American female sexuality was revealed to be monogamous and innocent. The De Mille films of the early 1920s were comedies of remarriage, in which a sexuality discovered outside the conventions of Victorian patriarchy was relocated within a revised version of the institution. Acts of consumption were crucial to this process; by providing novelty through a change of appearances, they offered the means to preserve monogamy. The culture of consumption promoted fashion as a mechanism of change that in itself not only increased the obligation to consume but provided a substitute for other, more politically active, forms of change. The pre-war energies of middle-class feminism proved particularly vulnerable to such recuperative diversion.

> The emphasis on self-realization through emotional fulfillment, the devaluation of public life in favor of a leisure world of intense private experience, the need to construct a pleasing "self" by purchasing consumer goods—these therapeutic imperatives helped to domesticate the drive toward female emancipation. With great fanfare, advertisers offered women the freedom to smoke Lucky Strikes or buy "natural" corsets. They promised fake liberation through consumption, and many women accepted this new version of male hegemony.[12]

By offering themselves to their audiences as idols of consumption both within the movies themselves and through the secondary industries of publicity, stars took a significant role in advertising the therapeutic pleasures of the intense life.

> All the adventure, all the romance, all the excitement you lack in your daily life are in—Pictures. They take you completely out of yourself into a wonderful new world. . . . Out of the cage of everyday existence! If only for an afternoon or an evening—escape![13]

The generalised advertising of American consumer goods was one of the ways in which Will Hays, President of the MPPDA, insisted that "The Movies Are Helping America."

> In pictures orderly and effective home-keeping equipment for sweeping, scrubbing, washing, stirring, mixing, sewing, made their appearance, and gradually it became plain that these things freed woman from enervating toil. From the picture to the fact was an inevitable procedure. Gradually these things liberated woman to express herself in terms more befitting her dignity.[14]

The culture of consumption described the newly dignified woman as "manager" of her home, but in the movies she celebrated her liberation from domestic drudgery through an anxious concern with appearance, in preparation for erotic activity. Both the advertising industry and the movies "engaged in a therapeutic renovation of sensuality . . . locating eroticism in settings characterized by affluence, respectability, and, above all, health."[15]

Their promotion of consumer culture constructed and revealed the contradiction of its representation of woman as object but not subject of desire. Female sexuality was recuperated in narrative terms within the constraints of monogamy, but it pervaded the culture as spectacle—a spectacle publicly directed at women, and overtly representing a new realisation of the female self. In De Mille's bath scenes and advertisements for toiletries sensuality was cleansed of "Victorian associations with poverty, disease, and dirt."[16] A recurring image showed women observing themselves in mirrors.

> I saw my body. I saw my legs, my torso, my long, long arms. . . . I had never looked at my body as a piece of statuary. . . . I had this marvelous feeling. I can still feel the chills all over my body.[17]

Stuart Ewen's analysis of cosmetic advertisements focuses more explicitly on auto-erotic perception.

> Though the victorious heroines . . . always got their man, they did so out of a commodity defined *self-fetishization* which made that man and themselves almost irrelevant to the quality of their victory. Their romantic triumphs were ultimately commercially defined versions of the auto-erotic ones of Alban Berg's prostitute, Lulu, who declares that "When I looked at myself in the mirror I wished I were a man—a man married to me."[18]

As in pornography, the auto-eroticism of the gaze in the mirror ratifies the voyeurism of the male gaze. However, the cinematic representation also established an irreconcilable contradiction between the indiscriminate availability of woman as an object of scopophilic desire and the narrative insistence on the constriction of her permitted sexuality within monogamy. This contradiction, and its apparent resolution around voyeuristic/narcissistic identification within contemporary psychoanalytic theory, is historically more specific than theorists of patriarchy sometimes imply. It depends on the appearance of permissive, auto-erotic images of female sexuality, and while these were a staple of visual pornography, such images only began to proliferate in the culture through advertising and the movies in the 1920s. It was precisely the spread of such images that the reform groups were criticising.

II

The film industry had been a substantial beneficiary of progressive reform and Prohibition, but reformers maintained a wary concern over the possible deleterious effects—both physical and moral—of movies on their audiences. Throughout the 1920s the MPPDA managed to contain this concern through an elaborate public relations exercise which co-opted potentially troublesome organisations, such as the General Federation of Women's Clubs and the International Federation of Catholic Alumnae, into its "Open Door" programmes to promote "better movies," and isolated the demand for governmental supervision of the industry as extremist. A number of events at the end of the decade rendered Hays' coalition of "responsible groups" increasingly unstable. In late 1929 the leading Episcopalian newspaper, *The Churchman*, began a campaign against the MPPDA culminating in allegations that it had "retained" officials of the Federal Council of Churches of Christ in America in exchange for favourable opinions on movies. These disclosures initiated widespread criticism of the industry throughout the Protestant religious press from 1930 onwards, and the resultant publicity focused the attention of educationalists, parent-teacher groups, and other organisations on the issue. A loose alliance between these interests and independent exhibitors to the MPPDA as an instrument of monopoly developed to support legislation linking control of movie content to federal regulation of monopoly practices such as block booking, which exhibitors and reformers argued prohibited community supervision of movie standards.

This argument was taking place amidst a general reaction among white Protestants to the apparent permissiveness of the postwar decade— a reaction evident before 1929, but greatly exacerbated by the Crash. Throughout the culture there were attempts to explain and account for the failure of the system couched in terms seeking to preserve the economic base.[19] Victorian patriarchy strove to reassert itself by identifying the alleged permissiveness of the Jazz Age as the scapegoat for the collapse of the economy.[20]

The demands for movie reform should thus be seen as part of a broader reaffirmation of traditional patriarchal values at a moment of cultural crisis. This reaffirmation, itself a displaced expression of anxiety for the economic system among the middle class, focused primarily on a concern that the family unit was in danger of disintegrating.[21] Motherhood, which had "virtually disappeared from films as the main aspiration for a woman,"[22] underwent a strenuous revival. Periodicals aimed at middle-class women ran articles extolling the fulfilment to be derived from domesticity, recantations from ex-feminists, and proposals that women who did not need to work should return to the home.[23] The overt concern of movie reform groups with the deleterious effect of movies on children aligned them with the larger trend, while the underlying anxieties of white Protestants regarding their declining control of the culture were reflected in the overt anti-urbanism and implicit anti-Semitism of the campaign.

One consequence of this public concern was an increase in the activity of the state and municipal censor boards and in the unpredictability of that activity. The industry required a mechanism to safeguard its products from such uncertainties—particularly given the costs of re-editing early sound films. The officials administering the Production Code acknowledged the industry's obligation to defend "the accepted standards of the American family"[24] and "the sanctity of marriage which . . . is the very foundation of society,"[25] but much of the early work of the Studio Relations Committee involved monitoring and codifying the activities of the state boards in order to advise the studios about probable deletions. In the first years of its operation the accuracy of its predictions was vital to the establishment of its credibility with the studio heads of production.

The behaviour of the state boards varied between states and over time. Cuts made in movies between 1930 and 1934 show a pattern of increasingly rigorous control, one manifestation of this pattern being the frequency with which officials of the board wrote to Hays or Colonel Jason Joy, the first director of the SRC, complaining about current standards. One inference from such complaints is that movies were becoming ever more "daring" in their presentation of sexuality and crime. Such a claim is extremely difficult to measure in any absolute terms, but the impression of a continuous "decline" of moral standards during the early 1930s is a simplified view of a complex situation in which the general cultural climate was moving towards an increased moral conservatism.

The debate among the institutions of censorship over what the SRC described as "social problem" pictures was centred on the efficacy of narrative recuperation in contradicting scopophilic pleasure, expressed in terms of the extent to which a film's morality was to be assessed on the basis of "the effect of the whole"[26] or on the details of its depiction. Until March 1933, code officials continued to argue the producers' case that "pictures that leave a certain final moral lesson" should be permitted a dramatic licence to include "details that give the audience the opportunity to contrast good and evil." The censors were not inclined to accept the argument.[27] Dealing with an already completed product, they were primarily concerned with the elimination of detail; outright rejection of entire films was rare, and invariably began a process of negotiation to discover what deletions would make the film acceptable. While the SRC sought to persuade the censors that the code provided an adequate alternative to their statutes, most of its negotiations with the studios had to do with ensuring that it could defend a narrative through the interpretation of a code principle such as "Sympathy with a person who sins is not the same as sympathy with the sin or crime of which he is guilty."[28]

The reform lobby ignored such sophistry by insisting that the manner of presentation led audiences to identify with the sinners and hence sympathise with the sin. "We feel justified in the complaint that our most competent stars are guilty of endowing unchastity with glamour."[29] Their concern was primarily with detail, because it was the details of behaviour in the movies that children, in particular, remembered and imitated.

> They pay little attention to film morals or retribution, and the idea that a moral at the end cancels out in the child's mind unwholesome material that he has seen earlier in the picture is utterly mistaken.[30]

A second issue between the MPPDA and the censor boards was the industry's predilection for the crude but reliable market mechanism of rushing imitations of profitable pictures into production, generating seasonal cycles. When such cycles provoked controversy, the takings of individual movies were undoubtedly increased, but they provided the reform lobby with evidence of the industry's lack of social responsibility. On occasion, Hays invoked the powers of the MPPDA Board of Directors to control production—most notably, in September 1931, when the board resolved to cease production of gangster pictures.[31] The solution of one problem, however, provoked another:

> With crime practically denied them, with box-office figures down, with high-pressure methods being employed back home to spur the studios to get in a little more cash, it was almost inevitable that sex, as the nearest thing at hand and pretty generally sure-fire, would be seized upon. It was.[32]

By the end of February 1932, Colonel Joy was complaining to Hays that a cycle of "kept woman" films, inaugurated in mid-1931 with *Possessed* and *Back Street,* was becoming a major problem. He clearly saw this cycle as comparable to the gangster films.

> In the gangster picture the gangster was not a hero. . . . And yet, because he was the central figure, because he achieved power, money, and a certain notoriety, our critics complained that an inevitable attractiveness resulted. . . . They said we killed him off, but that we made him glamorous before we shot him. This is what you are apt to be charged with in this case. While the red-headed woman is a common little creature from over the tracks who steals other women's husbands and who uses her sex attractiveness to do it, she is the central figure and it will be contended that a certain glamor surrounds her. . . . I have a real fear not only of what the censors may do to the picture, but what the public itself will say.[33]

The controversy over the "kept woman" cycle grew with the release of MGM's *Red-Headed Woman* in June 1932. Written by Anita Loos, it was a comedy in which Jean Harlow progressed up the social and material ladder by a series of affairs.

> Essentially it is an exposition of the theory that the wages of sin are wealth, luxury and social position, the only desiderata being physical charm and the willingness to accept the proffered prices.[34]

What distinguished *Red-Headed Woman* from previous examples of the cycle was that the film made comedy out of what had previously been exclusively the material for melodrama and moreover provided a comic rather than a melodramatic conclusion: the film ends with Harlow living in luxury in Paris.

The ammunition it gave to the reform lobby was only part of the problem. In July 1932 Joy wrote despairingly to New York, "probably right now half of the other companies are trying to figure out ways of topping this particular picture."[35] Paramount's response, orchestrated by its new head of production, Emmanuel Cohen, included the purchase of William Faulkner's *Sanctuary* and the signing of a contract with Mae West. Both actions caused Hays and his officials considerable anxiety because, as Hays told Adolph Zukor, Paramount's behaviour "disturbs the other companies and the whole inter-company relationship."[36] Hays' fear was that the other studios would feel themselves obliged to imitate and outdo each other in competing for the sensational element of the urban trade, and in the process destroy the remains of his and the association's credibility with the "Open Door" coalition whose support he needed to resist the reform lobby. Protesting the news that Paramount was planning to film West's stage play *Diamond Lil*, Harry Warner implied that his company would, indeed, resort to such tactics.[37] Within three weeks, his head of production had produced an outline for *Baby Face*.

III

Darryl Zanuck's short story[38] is clearly borrowed from the Harlow film: it refers to the "psychology of the 'red-headed woman'" and similarly tells a story of social climbing through sexual adventure—one which is, however, unrelieved by comedy. It represents an escalation in explicitness from the comparable plots of the working-girl/Cinderella stories of the previous decade (*Love 'em and Leave 'em*, Famous Players–Lasky, 1926; *It*, Famous Players–Lasky, 1927) by transforming the flirtatiousness of the Clara Bow/Louise Brooks flapper into an overt exploitation of female sexuality. Baby Face's predatory allure comes through her capacity to convince men of her innocence as she seduces them, but the mercenary nature of her motivation is explicit: "All men wanted was her body, so she had given it to the highest bidder." It also shifts the plot's locale from the site of consumption, a department store, to the site of contemporary financial crisis, a bank.

Escaping from the Depression landscape of a Pennsylvania steel town, Baby Face goes to "the City," where, by way of a series of affairs with her immediate bosses, she progresses up the hierarchy of the Mercantile Trust Company, eventually transferring her affections from one of its managers to his fiancée's father, a director of the bank. When the younger man discovers this liaison, he shoots the director and then commits suicide. After a decent interval in Paris she takes up with the playboy president of the bank, having convinced him of her innocence. In due course she marries him, and he lavishes furs, jewels, and securities on her. The bank suffers a collapse, for which he is held responsible. He asks her to return his gifts to pay his bail, but she refuses. Just before she sails for Europe, she realises that she really loves him. She returns to discover he has killed himself.

Haskell suggests that in most of her films, Harlow "was no friend to her own sex,"[39] but her misogyny was usually relieved by its comic context. Baby Face "hates women"[40] and in her attitude to men evidences signs of a return to the original Theda Bara Vampire of *A Fool There Was* (Fox, 1915). Bara herself described the character as "the vengeance of my sex upon its exploiters,"[41] while Sumiko Higashi identifies a salient characteristic of Bara's which Baby Face shares:

> Although the Vampire represented the full unleashing of the male's sexual instinct, she herself was always in control. She had not enough feeling to lose herself and was coldly calculating instead. It might even be construed that as a supernatural version of the whore, she was frigid.[42]

Baby Face enacts this role for most of the story, but at the end she succumbs to the conventional fate of the later, less powerful figure of the vamp, losing her power by falling victim to the very weakness she has previously exploited—romantic love, which, as a result of her previous behaviour, is available to her only in its tragic form of loss. The story describes a moral landscape of mutual exploitation, but does so within a narrative firmly constructed around the premise that such behaviour, was itself immoral and not to be emulated.

Studio writers Gene Markey and Kathryn Scola produced a story outline on November 21, 1932. It begins with Lily Powers (Baby Face) the explicit victim of patriarchy. Her father exploits her to the point of trading her sexual services to a local politician in exchange for protection for his beer flat. Lily's refusal of the politician's advances is indirectly responsible for her father's death when his still explodes. The writers also introduced a supplementary character, Kragg, the town cobbler, as an alternative father-figure. Their outline[43] describes him as

> a gnarled, twisted, old German, a cripple—with a bitter resentment of the world . . . he reads Nietzsche, and he is steeped in the philosophy of nature—contempt for the weak. . . . Old Kragg is a sort of Mephistopheles. Through this girl he can get his revenge on society.

In a "brief but poignant scene" after the funeral of her father, he explains to her,

> that she has been the victim of men—whereas she should make men her victims. That, just as a man can make use of men to rise in the world—even more easily can she, using her own weapon—sex!

The introduction of Kragg has two, contradictory, effects. It provides a philosophical justification, referred to at several points in the script, for Lily's behaviour towards men. In one of her encounters with Stevens, the younger bank manager, the outline suggests

> we establish her tremendous sex attraction for him. (We go as far in this scene as the censors will allow). . . . She resents—and rightfully—his coming to her for only one purpose, after he has spent the evening with his fiancee and his fashionable friends. Moreover, she resents the fiancee—because, with her Nietzschean ideal, she wants to be the one woman. . . . (At this point the audience will sympathize with Lily—because it is made plain that Stevens' only feeling toward her is wanting to sleep with her).

By both Kragg's description and the outline's representation of the male-dominated world, Lily's behaviour is rendered explicable and even at times sympathetic. On the other hand, Kragg's misanthropy is emphasised, while the plot denies everyone, particularly Lily, happiness. The outline depicts a world in which morality is unreliable, suggesting that Lily's "Nietzschean" assertion of the self is encouraged by such unreliability, but also revealing that these conditions produce only turmoil and personal misery. In most respects, Lily's story mirrors the rise and fall of the gangster: her "illegal" progress is iconographically charted by the acquisition of clothes and furnishings; her abrupt fall is marked by a moment of self-recognition, although in this case it occurs at the death of the object of her love rather than her own. A connection is made to the economic sphere through the image of Lily's literal progress up "the gigantic forty-story skyscraper of the Old Manhattan Trust Company."[44] Lily's distraction of Trenholm, the bank's director, is identified as being the cause of the bank's failure, which occurs immediately after their marriage. This sequence of events imposes a causality on the narrative implying a quite different ideological charge to that conventionally identified in gangster movies: less a left-handed version of the American success story with a moralising ending appended for the benefit of the censors than a demonstration of the social failure provoked by the excesses of the previous decade.

Over the next four weeks Markey and Scola wrote a script which broadly followed the story outline. In Lily's rejection of her father, immediately prior to his death, she makes clear the perversity of the nuclear family she has been raised in. Declaring that her mother was right to leave him and is "better off dead—than livin' with a thing like you!" Lily

> turns on him fiercely—all the pent-up bitterness of the years loosened in a sudden flood of rage.
>
> *LILY:* Yes, I'm a tramp! An' who's to blame?
> (looking at him with terrible loathing)
> My father! A swell start *you* gave me! Ever since I was fourteen—what's it been? Men!
> (screaming at him)
> Dirty, rotten men! An' you're lower than any of 'em!
> (her voice breaks hysterically)
> I'll hate you as long as I live![45]

Later, the presentation of an idyllic view of family life becomes the occasion for a restatement of Kragg's philosophy. Alone on Christmas afternoon, Lily sees the family in the apartment next to hers gathered around their Christmas tree, father and children playing together. In her apartment she discovers a present from Kragg: Nietzsche's *Thoughts out of Season*. A passage is marked:

> "Face life as you find it—defiantly and unafraid. Waste no energy yearning for the moon. Crush out all sentiment." . . . She looks up and stares into the fire. . . . Her eyes are somber—bitter. When she came in this Christmas afternoon she was feeling sorry for herself. But now— from her friend, Kragg—this gospel of Nietzsche has brought her back to her hard point of view. Survival of the fittest![46]

Kragg's function is to supply strength and purpose at precisely those moments when Lily's exclusion from family is announced. He offers an alternative patriarchy not simply in his plot location as substitute father, but explicitly in terms of his critique of the existing social structure as false consciousness.

With Trenholm, the bank president and the only man to see through her "act" as the innocent victim of male sexual aggression, Lily reverts to conventional sexual mores in refusing to sleep with him until they marry.

> I'm just a little disappointed. . . . I was hoping you *wouldn't* be just like everybody else. . . . Silly of me, wasn't it?[47]

In these scenes it remains unclear as to how manipulative—of Trenholm and the audience—is Lily's attempt to revise the movie as a romance. When she refuses to return the money, her action is shown as uncertain, as if she is trying to convince herself:

> I have to think about myself! I've gone through a lot to get these things! My life's been miserable and hard! I'm not like other women—all the gentleness and kindness in me has been killed! All I've got are *these* things!
> (she hugs the case close to her breast)
> Without them I'd be nothing—I'd have to go back to what I was!
> (then with bitter fury)
> *No. I won't give them up!*[48]

All her subsequent actions demonstrate her inability to enact her philosophy; her inability, in fact, to reject her prescribed role as woman. The script leaves the process of her self-revelation ambiguous, only confirming it in her final discovery of Trenholm, still alive at Lily's return, in order that he may hear her declaration of love. Lily is finally redeemed/recuperated at the moment that she is also made to suffer through the recognition of her loss; she is accepted into the structures of patriarchy at the same time that she is punished for her earlier transgression of them. Kragg and Nietzsche have conveniently disappeared from the film's final reassertion of patriarchal romance. Lily, who began the movie in humourless imitation of Harlow's Red-Headed Woman, ends it in imitation of Garbo's Susan Lennox.

The script of *Baby Face* shows "the work that narrative and thematic organization performs to accommodate and recuperate developments like the independent woman stereotype."[49] In doing so, it kept to the letter of the Production Code, as it was then being interpreted. The script was submitted to the Studio Relations Committee in the second week of December 1932.

> . . . it presents a problem, and a rather serious one from the censorship standpoint. With regard to the Code there is nothing we can find in it which is in violation, despite the fact that the theme is sordid and of a troublesome nature. However, we will do our best to clean it up as much as possible, and the fact that Barbara Stanwyck is destined for the leading role will probably mitigate some of the dangers in view of her sincere and restrained acting.[50]

After some internal discussion at the SRC, Dr. James Wingate wrote to Zanuck on January 3, 1933. Remarking that it was hard to judge "a story of this type" from the script alone, he expressed a naive confidence in Zanuck's supplying "such moral values as may seem necessary to counterbalance the story, which without them might seem to stress to too great a degree the element of sex." He reinforced the point by reminding Zanuck that *Red-Headed Woman* had been banned in several Canadian provinces and severely cut by the U.S. state boards. He suggested Warner's emphasise the moral lesson by so revising the ending,

> as to indicate that in losing Trenholm she not only loses the one person whom she now loves, but that her money also will be lost. That is, if Lily is shown at the end to be no better off than she was when she left the steel town, you may lessen the chances of drastic censorship action, by thus strengthening the moral value of the story.

The draconian morality which insisted that female sexuality could not be shown to be profitable affected not only the scale of Lily's final punishment, but also her earlier conduct:

> . . . you ought to avoid making the facts of each relationship too explicit. This can be done by never really showing through dialogue or action that the man in each case is really paying for the apartment and supplying Lily with money and clothes in return for her affection.[51]

Wingate's letter made further detailed suggestions for deletions or changes in dialogue or action, premissed, as SRC recommendations then were, by the comment that such material would be eliminated by state censor boards. Infractions of the code were largely limited to specifically prohibited profanities, and the tone of this letter was typical in being advisory rather than demanding.

Production was completed in February 1933, and Wingate discussed it with Zanuck on February 28. Wingate was particularly concerned about removing elements from the opening scene which implied that Lily's father was selling his daughter to the politician "for immoral purposes." Zanuck appeared, for once, to be co-operative, and Wingate emerged from their conference enthusiastic enough to write to Hays that Zanuck appreciated the problem created by sex pictures, and would not make them were it not for pressure from the sales department, which had ordered 20 percent of its product to be "women's pictures, which inevitably means sex pictures."[52]

IV

The early months of 1933 comprised the low point of the industry's fortunes in the Depression. In late January Paramount and RKO were placed in receivership; Sidney Kent, president of Fox, was engaged in a legal battle with several members of his board of directors to avoid the same fate. The crisis was primarily one of liquidity, with the companies failing to generate sufficient box-office revenues to sustain payments on the debts they had incurred in expanding in the late 1920s. In the atmosphere of uncertainty that preceded Roosevelt's inauguration, there was widespread fear that the entire industry was virtually bankrupt, and the immediate crisis deepened with the declaration of a bank holiday on March 5. Box-office receipts were reported to have fallen by 45 percent,[53] and weekly attendance was estimated to be as low as 28 million, a figure which supplied only 20 percent of the income needed to defray weekly production costs.[54]

The possibility of imminent economic collapse was not, however, the only problem the industry faced in early March. The exact nature of Roosevelt's proposals for government control of industry were not as yet clear, but bills hostile to the monopoly power of the major companies were to be presented to Congress, including a proposal by Representative Sirovich of New York for a wide-ranging congressional investigation of the industry. State and municipal legislatures throughout the country were proposing a variety of local taxes on the movies as a readily available source of income. Hollywood's image of extravagance made it an acutely vulnerable financial target under such circumstances, and the reform lobby's growing ability to gain press coverage substantially increased that vulnerability. The first synopses of the Payne Fund Studies had been serialised in the September, October, and November 1932 issues of *McCall's*, and the claim that they would provide irrefutable scientific evidence of the detrimental effect of movies on children added considerably to the demands for governmental control.

The behaviour of the new Congress, and the extent to which it might regard such proposals sympathetically, was highly uncertain. There was a not unfounded fear that new members might believe that "riding the movies is a profitable and tenable political position"[55] given the combination of moral disapproval occasioned by reports of the industry's financial dealings[56] and the untimely success of Mae West's first film, *She Done Him Wrong*. The election of Roosevelt meant that Hays, who had supervised Warren Harding's presidential campaign in 1920, had lost his personal contacts with the administration; since the election there had been widespread rumours that he would be replaced by a Democrat. To add to the sense of alarm, there were reports that representatives of the various censor boards were planning a conference designed to produce a uniform policy on censorship.[57] Equally serious was the discontented presence in Hollywood of Martin Quigley, owner of *Motion Picture Herald*, instigator of the Production Code, and a key figure in Hays's vital alliance with Catholic organisations.

> Q. is very much discouraged about the whole Code business. He feels that our folks here . . . continue to ignore it. . . . He feels that the staff which succeeded Col. Joy is not a good one. . . . I never saw him so down in the mouth about anything.[58]

Quigley's disaffection might have resulted in Catholic withdrawal from co-operation with the MPPDA, and that in turn might have led to a legislative victory for the Protestant-dominated reform groups.

An emergency meeting of the MPPDA Board of Directors was held on the evening of March 5, primarily to consider measures to deal with the bank holiday. Hays, however, made it clear that more than economic action was required to deal with the crisis. A more rigid enforcement of the code, he argued, was absolutely necessary if the industry was to maintain any public sympathy and to stand any chance of resisting the pressure for federal intervention not merely over its content policies but also over its financial operations. He persuaded the board of directors to sign a Reaffirmation of Objectives that stated

Not only is a continuous supply of motion picture entertainment doubly essential in these times of confusion and distress, but the tendency toward confused thinking and slackening of standards everywhere re-emphasizes the importance of the progressively effective process of self-discipline by which the moral and artistic standards of motion picture production have been steadily raised during the past eleven years. . . . It is inevitable that during a period such as we now face, disintegrating influences should threaten the standards of production, standards of quality, standards of business practice, built up and maintained by cooperation. . . . We realize the fact that whether American industry will be rebuilt after the depression on a higher or lower plane depends entirely upon the maintenance or destruction of the higher business standards developed through years of cooperative effort.[59]

The Reaffirmation became the implement with which Hays began to reorganise the code administration. It was not made public at the time, because it would amount to a public acknowledgement that the industry had violated the code, but Hays immediately wrote to Wingate instructing him to tighten up the application of the code not only on new scripts but also on pictures in production and those about to be finished.[60] Joe Breen, who had previously been supervising the application of the Advertising Code, was drafted in to assist Wingate where necessary. At the same time, company heads wrote to their heads of production in Hollywood, informing them of the new policy.

During March, Hays constructed a five-point programme for the "organized solution on a co-operative scale of many of the problems of readjustment," covering ways in which the MPPDA member companies could pool facilities and hence reduce costs at the same time as they strengthened their operational hold on the industry. The association's annual meeting on March 27 ratified the programme, although one of its elements, a temporary 25–50 percent salary cut throughout the industry to meet the immediate cash crisis, had provoked strike threats by the Hollywood craft unions. The crisis had been somewhat alleviated by the partial restoration of confidence by the end of the month, and on April 6 Hays and the entire MPPDA board entrained for California to put the production branch straight on the need for stringent economies and a more vigorous application of the code. In addressing the producers on April 20, Hays was insistent:

The failure to maintain the clear promises the industry has made to the public for the protection of American family standards in motion picture

theatres will jeopardize any permanent investment in the motion picture industry. . . . The result most disastrous of the violations is the
legislative retaliation . . . peaking in this Sirovich investigation, the way
they get sore because of what is in the pictures, in the advertising, and
they take it out on us in this tax and other confiscatory measures. . . .
To meet this emergency, and as a prime matter of economy and cost
reduction, we have found it necessary to reaffirm our resolutions and
strictly enforce them.[61]

If the producers ignored his "cleanup" campaign, Hays threatened, "their
superiors in New York would find a group who would obey orders."[62] If
the studios continued to evade the SRC, he would take the issue first to
the company heads in New York, and then to the bankers and stockholders, and finally to the public. He insisted that the release of one censorable
picture

could force the entire Industry to submit to Federal censorship, which
would mean—to use his own words—that "the Industry would be placed
in a straight jacket so far as censorship is concerned—and only be able
to produce 'Jack and the Bean Stalk' and fairy tales" . . . They are going
to be more rigid with the enforcement of the Code. This attitude is
already evidenced in the letters we are now receiving from them on
scripts. Prior to this time, we were told "it is recommended, etc.," but
recently letters definitely state, "it is inadmissible, etc." or something
equally definite.[63]

Although little of this action was made public, the firmness of
Hays's stance was communicated to congressmen through the MPPDA's
highly efficient lobby operation in Washington[64] and undoubtedly played
a significant part in defeating the Sirovich resolution on May 12.

V

The first two victims of the new policy were *The Story of Temple Drake*
and *Baby Face,* both of which completed production in late February.
Negotiations between Wingate and Zanuck during March had led to
some further deletions in the Warner film, and a "more wholesome and
a brighter finish"[65] was added, in which the lovers were reconciled.
However, an alarm bell had obviously been sounded by Wingate's
mentioning that the cobbler preaches to Stanwyck "the philosophy of

Nietzsche to the effect that she should use the power that she has over men to rise in the world."[66] By the end of March the revised film had arrived in New York, where it was unofficially rejected by the New York Censor Board.

On April 1, Hays received an assurance from Harry Warner that, in accordance with the Reaffirmation, no attempt would be made to release the film until further consultations over it had taken place.[67]

Modifications to *Baby Face* needed to go beyond simply the deletion of material or the substitution of "protection shots," which most studios were by 1933 in the habit of taking on potentially dubious sequences. To bring it within the "spirit of the code," new scenes supplying "the voice of morality" were required, and their provision was complicated by the fact that Stanwyck was unavailable for retakes. The solution, encapsulated in a letter Wingate sent Jack Warner on May 11, was actually worked out by Joe Breen, who already occupied an important role in the censorship procedure.

> the greatest lack of the picture now . . . is the fact that nowhere . . . is the heroine denounced for her brazen method of using men to promote herself financially. . . . This may seem to create the impression that her mode of living and course of action are condoned. . . . We would suggest an attempt to use the cobbler in a few added scenes as the spokesman of morality.[68]

Breen was able to do what Wingate apparently could not: provide a practical solution to the studio's problem, and protect its investment. Wingate's universal unpopularity with the studio heads derived largely from his merely proposing deletions rather than suggesting improvements. The SRC, in the person of Hays and Wingate, insisted that the cobbler as Nietzschean philosopher of the immoral way be removed from the film. The SRC, in the person of Breen, put him back in with new dialogue. His initial advice:

> A woman—young, beautiful—like you—can get anything she wants in the world! Because you have power over men! . . . But you must *use* men, not let them use *you*! You must be a *master*, not a *slave*! Look! Here! Nietzsche says, "All life, no matter how we idealize it, is nothing more or less than exploitation!" That's what I'm telling you! Exploit yourself! Go to some big city where you can find opportunities. . . . Be strong—defiant! *Use men—to get the things you want!*[69]

became:

A woman—young, beautiful—like you, can get anything she wants in the world! But there is the right and wrong way—remember the price of the wrong way is too great. Go to some big city where you will find opportunities. But don't let people mislead you, you must be a *master*, not a *slave*. Keep clean, be strong—defiant! And you will be a success.[70]

Breen suggested that the book Kragg sends Lily should be *Self Help*, "because the title lends itself to broad interpretation."[71] While this suggestion was not taken up, his idea of substituting the quotation with a letter was. It read:

Dear Lily; from your letters I can tell that my advice was for nothing. You have chosen the wrong way. You are still a coward. Life will defeat you unless you fight back and regain your self-respect. I send you this book hoping that you will allow it to guide you right.[72]

All this remodelling was completed in a week, and on May 20 Wingate wrote to Hays

As the picture appears now there is no evidence of any Nietzsche philosophy. On the other hand, as you will note, all the advice of the cobbler has been on the side of morality. . . . The affair with the office boy is cut in such a manner that he has no affair with her. All the men with whom she has affairs come to destruction. One loses his job, one is shot, another shoots himself, etc. The end of the picture has been changed so that it now closes with a picture of the board of directors showing that all of Lily's money had been repaid to the bank and that they haven't a cent and that Trenholm, the former president of the bank, is working as a laborer in the steel mills.[73]

On June 8, Breen wrote to Hays that the film now conformed to the Production Code, and he suggested that Hays take the opportunity to congratulate the studio on

the splendid spirit of helpfulness which the Warners have displayed in this matter and the promptness with which they set about to clean up a very bad picture and succeeded very well.

Nevertheless, Breen reminded Hays the film's theme was still questionable and "suggests a kind, or type, of picture which ought not to be encouraged."[74] His endorsement did not, in any case, save the picture from minor cuts of dialogue and action by state censor boards, nor from a complete ban by five of the eight Canadian states.

VI

There is nothing particularly exceptional about what happened to *Baby Face*. *Temple Drake* and other "kept woman" pictures in production at the time were subjected to comparable treatment, and a year later the same fate befell a number of other films caught between two dispensations of the Code, including Mae West's *It Ain't No Sin*. The example of *Baby Face* does, however, serve to illustrate the extent of code activity at an earlier period, where it is commonly supposed that little censorship activity took place. It also provides a case study of the balance between elements in the code's moral accountancy. The narrative always presented a patriarchal moral, in which Lily's aberrant expression of her sexuality resulted in her punishment. The crime of which the narrative found her guilty was patricide, but the form of her punishment was changed from what had previously been the melodramatic fate of characters in comparable positions—deprivation, denial, and exclusion from society—to a more inclusive and perverse form of patriarchal revenge, by which she was returned to the world from which she had attempted to escape.

In this transformation, the character of Kragg retained the same narrative function as donor, but his ideological role shifted from that of alternative patriarch to true patriarch, to whose moral world Lily is returned at the film's conclusion. Where the script version offered only a pessimistic critique of the social consequences of the culture of consumption, the film's ending provided a reassertion of traditional Protestant values, in which Lily and Trenholm were announced to be *"working out their happiness together."*[75] The realignment of Kragg's role to a point where, at the end of the movie, he becomes ideologically indistinguishable from the director of the bank, who decrees Trenholm's return to the steel town, locates the film in an ideological context which Nick Roddick describes as

> a *fundamentally* just society which offered the individual, even under the most extreme circumstances, the chance to re-establish himself (rarely, if ever, herself)

The fact that the final version of the film was located in that context, however, has less to do with "the studio's ideological commitment . . . to the nascent policies of the New Deal," as Roddick argues,[76] than to external pressures on the studio and the industry to revise their product into a closer conformity with the expected norms of a culture in recession. What makes *Baby Face* so appropriate an example of the processes of ideological repression is the way in which the cinematic inverts the causality of the extra-cinematic: the Crash, represented by the failure of the bank, is caused—which is to say, explained—by Lily's effect on men. The film exposes the contradictions inherent in patriarchy's bifurcated representation of woman, by which she is narratively punished for her existence as a spectacle of desire: it is accidental (in that it resulted from Stanwyck's unavailability for retakes), but it is entirely appropriate to the movie's optical politics that the revised ending cannot show Lily in the prison of working-class domesticity to which it has returned her.

Father Gerard Donnelly, S.J., editor of the Catholic periodical *America* and an influential figure in the organisation of the Legion of Decency, rejected the theories of more extreme critics of the movies which historians have subsequently adopted when he commented that

> it would be absurd to claim that producers are deliberately trying to destroy the traditional teachings of the pulpit.[77]

The movies of the early Depression represented the crisis of the period, but they did so within the parameters of their own systems of convention, which were themselves products of the industry's complex interaction with the culture and economy of which it was a dynamic part. Those conventions revealed the crisis in patriarchal ideology which accompanied the crisis in the institutions of capitalism. The extent to which patriarchy's contradictions were exposed was indicated by a Hays Office comment on Mae West:

> The very man who will guffaw at Mae West's performance as a reminder of the ribald days of his past will resent her effect upon the young, when his daughter imitates the Mae West wiggle before her boyfriends and mouths "Come up and see me sometime."[78]

In an economic moment when the possibilities for consumption were sharply restricted, the contradictions contained within this image of woman became more apparent than they had been during its formulation over the previous decade. The image of fetishised sexuality as consumerist pleasure became more threatening for a culture in recesson, and the potential subversiveness of the image brought forth louder calls for its repression. In that sense it may be argued that the campaign to repress the image of female sexuality was concerned with its threatened exposure of the contradictions within patriarchal capitalism, but the contradiction arose not around the representation of independent woman—a figure who was continuously contained, recuperated, and repressed within narrative—but around the representation of woman as an object of consumption/desire. The Depression interrupted the smooth development of a culture of consumption and caused a temporary reconsideration of the iconography it had promulgated. The demand for the imposition of censorship was a rebellion against images of consumption, and it gained public credibility because those images had become too detached from the available reality. A recurrent criticism of both Hollywood and the previous decade was that they were guilty of the sin of excess. In the widespread criticism of Hollywood's "excessive" salaries, the idols of consumption were represented as objects of idolatry to be condemned and punished. The "kept woman" cycle was a vehicle for this condemnation, in two senses: it provided a target for it, and it also, with increasing vehemence, enacted it in the punishments it meted out to its heroines. To read *Baby Face* as an account of the conflicts of the previous decade is consistent with its existence as a text and an historical object. Judging whether audiences perceived it in these terms is rather more difficult because relatively few people were given the opportunity to see the film. Its reputation within the industry ensured a limited release, and, in common with the majority of films which provoked controversy during this period, it was prohibited from reissue in February 1935.

NOTES

Research for this article was made possible by the award of a Fellowship in American Studies from the American Council of Learned Societies. I am grateful to all the librarians and archivists who helped me immeasurably in locating documents, in particular Maxine Fleckner at the Wisconsin Center for Film and Theater Research; Sam Gill and Barbara Hall at the Library of the Academy of Motion Picture Arts and Sciences, Los Angeles; Ned Comstock of the Department of Special Collections, University of Southern California; John Hall of the RKO Archive, Los Angeles; and Karen Rench of the Department of Special Collections, Indiana State Library, and to the Motion Picture Association of America, in particular James Bouras, for allowing me to peruse documents in its New York Archive.

1. "Towards the end of the film Arzner brings about her tour de force, cracking open the entire fabric of the film and exposing the workings of the ideology in the construction of the stereotype of woman." Claire Johnston, "Woman's Cinema as Counter Cinema," in Patricia Erens, ed., *Sexual Stratagems: The World of Women in Film* (New York: Horizon Press, 1979), p. 141.

2. E. Ann Kaplan, *Women and Film: Both Sides of the Camera* (London and New York: Methuen, 1983), p. 52.

Richard Maltby

3. Ibid., p. 20.

4. Robert Sklar, *Movie-Made America* (New York: Random House, 1975), p. 175.

5. Raymond Moley, *The Hays Office* (New York: Bobbs-Merrill, 1946), p. 75.

6. Edward Buscombe, "Bread and Circuses: Economics and the Cinema," in Patricia Mellencamp and Philip Rosen, eds., *Cinema Histories, Cinema Practices* (Los Angeles: American Film Institute, 1984), p. 8.

7. Molly Haskell, *From Reverence to Rape: The Treatment of Women in the Movies* (New York: Holt, Rinehart & Winston, 1974), p. 45.

8. Sklar, *Movie-Made America,* p. 176.

9. Kaplan, *Women and Film,* p. 56.

10. E.g., *I Am a Fugitive from a Chain Gang, Public Enemy.*

11. Lary May, *Screening Out the Past: The Birth of Mass Culture and the Motion Picture Industry* (New York: Oxford University Press, 1980), p. 211.

12. T. J. Jackson Lears, "From Salvation to Self-Realization: Advertising and the Therapeutic Roots of the Consumer Culture, 1880–1930," in Richard Wrightman Fox and T. J. Jackson Lears, eds., *The Culture of Consumption: Critical Essays in American History, 1880–1980* (New York: Pantheon Books, 1983), p. 27.

13. Advertisement in the *Saturday Evening Post* quoted in Robert S. Lynd and Helen Merrell Lynd, *Middletown: A Study in Modern American Culture* (New York: Harcourt, Brace and World, 1929), p. 265.

14. Will H. Hays, "The Movies Are Helping America," *Good Housekeeping,* January 1933, 45, 130.

15. Lears, "From Salvation to Self-Realization," p. 28.

16. Ibid.

17. Actress Betty Blythe, in Kevin Brownlow, *The Parade's Gone By,* p. 436, quoted in May, *Screening Out the Past,* p. 230.

18. Stuart Ewen, *Captains of Consciousness: Advertising and the Social Roots of the Consumer Culture* (New York: McGraw-Hill, 1976), p. 48.

19. E.g., Harold J. Laski, "Can Business Be Civilized?" *Harper's,* January 1930, 170–79.

20. E.g., Harold de Wolf Fuller, "The Myth of Modern Youth," *North American Review,* June 1929; G. Murray, "The Crisis in Morals," *Harper's,* January 1930; Mary Roberts Rinehart, "The Chaotic Decade," *Ladies' Home Journal,* May 1930.

21. E.g., Floyd H. Allport, "Must We Scrap the Family?" *Harper's,* July 1930.

22. May, *Screening Out the Past,* p. 212.

23. E.g., Elizabeth Cook, "The Kitchen-Sink Complex," *Ladies' Home Journal,* September 1931; Worth Tuttle, "Autobiography of an Ex-Feminist," *Atlantic Monthly,* December 1933; Rita S. Halle, "Do You Need Your Job?" *Good Housekeeping,* September 1932.

24. Lamar Trotti, memo, July 23, 1931, Production Code Administration (PCA) *Back Street* Case File, at the Library of the Academy of Motion Picture Arts and Sciences, Los Angeles, California.

25. Joseph Breen to Dr. James Wingate, then director of the New York State censor board, May 5, 1933, RKO Production File, *Ann Vickers,* RKO Archives, Los Angeles.

26. Joy to Wingate, February 5, 1931, PCA *Little Caesar* Case File.

27. E.g., Wingate to Joy, February 11, 1931, PCA *Little Caesar* Case File.

28. "The Reasons Supporting Preamble of the Code," reproduced in Moley, *The Hays Office,* pp. 245–46.

29. Gerard B. Donnelly, S. J., "An Open Letter to Dr. Wingate," *America,* October 29, 1932, pp. 85–86.

30. "Children and the Movies," editorial reporting an address on the Payne Fund Studies by William H. Short, Director of the Motion Picture Research Council, to the

Spring 1933 meeting of the Society of Motion Picture Engineers, *America*, May 6, 1933, p. 100.

31. Wingate to Hays, June 5, 1931, PCA *The Big Brain* Case File.

32. Joy to Breen, December 15, 1931, PCA *Possessed* Case File.

33. Joy to William Orr, MGM New York, June 14, 1932 (unsent) PCA *Red-Headed Woman* Case File.

34. Martin Quigley, *Decency in Motion Pictures* (New York: Macmillan, 1937), p. 38.

35. Joy to Carl Milliken, July 7, 1932, PCA *Red-Headed Woman* Case File.

36. Hays to Adolph Zukor, November 16, 1932, PCA *She Done Him Wrong* Case File.

37. H. M. Warner to Hays, October 19, 1932, PCA *She Done Him Wrong* Case File.

38. *Baby Face*, Short Story, no author shown (screen credits identify the author as Mark Canfield, one of Darryl Zanuck's pseudonyms), November 9, 1932, 8 pp., at the Warner Library of the Wisconsin Center for Film and Theater Research, Madison, Wisconsin.

39. Haskell, *From Reverence to Rape*, p. 114.

40. *Baby Face*, Short Story, p. 1.

41. Quoted by Sumiko Higashi, *Virgins, Vamps and Flappers: The American Silent Movie Heroine* (St. Albans, Vt.: Eden Press Women's Publications, 1978), p. 61.

42. Ibid., p. 59–60.

43. *Baby Face*, Story Outline, November 21, 1932, at the Warner Library, Wisconsin Center for Film and Theater Research.

44. Ibid., p. 9.

45. *Baby Face*, Final Script, December 17, 1932, at the Warner Library, Wisconsin Center for Film and Theater Research, pp. 20–21.

46. Ibid., p. 82.

47. Ibid., pp. 117–18.

48. Ibid., pp. 131–32.

49. Christine Gledhill, "Developments in Feminist Film Criticism," in Mary Ann Doane, Patricia Mellencamp, and Linda Williams, eds., *Re-Vision: Essays in Feminist Film Criticism* (Los Angeles: American Film Institute, 1984), p. 40.

50. Wingate to Hays, December 20, 1932, PCA *Baby Face* Case File.

51. Wingate to Zanuck, January 3, 1933, PCA *Baby Face* Case File.

52. Wingate to Hays, February 28, 1933, PCA *Baby Face* Case File.

53. *Time*, March 20, 1933, 41.

54. C. F. Morgan, "Climax of the Movie Tragedy Approaches," *Magazine of Wall Street*, April 15, 1933, 670.

55. Lupton A. Wilkinson to Hays, October 29, 1932, Will H. Hays Archive, Department of Special Collections, Indiana State Library, Indianapolis.

56. *Upton Sinclair Presents William Fox* was published in early 1933, and free copies were distributed to every member of the new Congress.

57. Richmond, Virginia, *Times-Dispatch*, February 7, 1933.

58. Breen to Hays, March 2, 1933, Hays Archive.

59. Reaffirmation of the Members of the MPPDA, signed March 7, 1933, quoted in Moley, *The Hays Office*, pp. 250–51.

60. Hays to Wingate, March 10, 1933, 1933 Production Code File, Motion Picture Association of America Archive, New York.

61. 1933 Production Code File, MPAA Archive.

62. *Motion Picture Herald*, April 29, 1933, 9.

63. Harry Zehner, memo to producers and writers, May 26, 1933, in Universal Studios Censorship file, USC Special Collections Box 778.

64. Cf. John Callan O'Laughlin to Hays, April 10, 1933, Hays Archive.

65. Zanuck to Wingate, March 29, 1933, PCA *Baby Face* Case File.

66. Wingate to Hays, March 2, 1933, PCA *Baby Face* Case File.

67. Hays to Harry Warner, April 14, 1933, PCA *Baby Face* Case File.

68. Wingate to J. L. Warner, May 11, 1933, *Baby Face* Case File. Although the letter was signed by Wingate, it was undoubtedly written by Breen. All studio correspondence from the SRC was signed by its director, but it was normal practice for letters to be written by officers.

69. *Baby Face,* Final Script, pp. 26–27.

70. Dialogue transcribed from print of *Baby Face* at the Warner Library, Wisconsin Center for Film and Theater Research. See also H. J. McCord to Wingate, May 19, 1933, PCA *Baby Face* Case File.

71. Wingate to J. L. Warner, May 11, 1933, PCA *Baby Face* Case File.

72. Transcribed from print at Warner Library, Wisconsin Center for Film and Theater Research. See also H. J. McCord to Wingate, May 13, 1933, PCA *Baby Face* Case File.

73. Wingate to Hays, May 20, 1933, PCA *Baby Face* Case File.

74. Breen to Hays, June 8, 1933, PCA *Baby Face* Case File.

75. Dialogue transcribed from print of *Baby Face* at the Warner Library, Wisconsin Center for Film and Theater Research, my italics.

76. Nick Roddick, *A New Deal in Entertainment: Warner Brothers in the 1930s* (London: British Film Institute, 1983), p. 126.

77. Gerard B. Donnelly, S. J., "An Open Letter to Dr. Wingate," *America,* October 29, 1932, pp. 85–86.

78. Internal MPPDA memorandum, Ray Norr to Hays, October 18, 1933, 1933 Production Code File, MPAA Archive.

Clayton R. Koppes and Gregory D. Black

What to Show the World: The Office of War Information and Hollywood, 1942–1945

The uneasy relationship between propaganda and democracy proved especially troublesome during World War II. Interpreting the war as a worldwide crusade, liberals in the Office of War Information (OWI) won unprecedented control over the content of American motion pictures. An understanding of the interaction between OWI and Hollywood sheds light on both the objectives and methods of the nation's propaganda campaign and the content of wartime entertainment films. This episode, all but ignored by historians, offers insights into America's war ideology and the intersection of politics and mass culture in wartime. Moreover, it raises the question of whether the Roosevelt administration's propaganda strategy helped undermine some of its avowed war aims.[1]

OWI, the chief government propaganda agency during World War II, was formed by an executive order on June 13, 1942, that consolidated several prewar information agencies. OWI's domestic branch handled the home front; its overseas branch supervised all United States foreign propaganda activities, except in Latin America, which remained the preserve of the coordinator of inter-American affairs, Nelson Rockefeller. Franklin D. Roosevelt instructed OWI to implement a program through the press, radio, and motion pictures to enhance public understanding of the war, to coordinate the war information activities of all federal

From the *Journal of American History* 64 (June 1977), 87–105. Reprinted with permission of the authors and the *Journal of American History.*

agencies, and to act as the intermediary between federal agencies and the radio and motion picture industries. OWI director Elmer Davis, a liberal radio commentator, insisted that the agency's policy was to tell the truth. But information could not be separated from interpretation, and OWI told the truth by degrees and with particular bias. In all important respects, OWI met the criterion of a propaganda agency. It was an organization designed not only to disseminate information and to clarify issues but also to arouse support for particular symbols and ideas. "The easiest way to inject a propaganda idea into most people's minds," said Davis, "is to let it go in through the medium of an entertainment picture when they do not realize that they are being propagandized."[2]

Around Davis clustered a liberal staff that gave OWI one of the highest percentages of interventionist New Dealers of any wartime agency. Two assistant directors, Pulitzer prize writers Archibald MacLeish and Robert Sherwood, were enthusiastic New Dealers; another assistant director, Milton S. Eisenhower, though fiscally more cautious, was a New Deal veteran. The only assistant director who held the New Deal at some distance was Gardner Cowles, Jr., a moderate Republican publisher who had been recruited to give OWI an air of bipartisanship. Liberals of various hues permeated the second and third levels of the agency and included such figures as historians Arthur M. Schlesinger, Jr., and Henry Pringle; former Henry A. Wallace speech writer Jack Fleming; novelist Leo Rosten; journalists Joseph Barnes and Alan Cranston; financier James Warburg; and "China hand" Owen

The Bureau of Motion Pictures (BMP) in OWI was a New Deal stronghold. Its chief, Lowell Mellett, a former Scripps-Howard newspaper editor who had been a Roosevelt aide since 1939, had headed the first prewar information agency, the Office of Government Reports (OGR). "OGRE" and "Mellett's Madhouse" to conservative critics, OGR supervised the government film program. In response to the movie industry's offer of support in December 1941, Roosevelt told Mellett to advise Hollywood how it could further the war effort. Mellett established a liaison office in Hollywood and appointed as its head Nelson Poynter, a Scripps-Howard colleague. Poynter did not follow movies, but he shared Mellett's enthusiasms. Assisting Poynter was a staunchly liberal reviewing staff headed by Dorothy Jones, a former research assistant for Harold Lasswell and a pioneer in film content analysis.[4]

The Hollywood office became part of OWI domestic operations in June 1942 and began one of the agency's more important and controversial activities. The motion picture, said Davis, could be "the most powerful instrument of propaganda in the world, whether it tries to be or not." Roosevelt believed movies were among the most effective means of reaching the American public. The motion picture industry experienced far fewer wartime restrictions on output than most industries. Hollywood turned out nearly 500 pictures annually during the war and drew 80 million paid admissions per week, well above the prewar peak. Hollywood's international influence far exceeded that of American radio and the press; foreign audiences, which also reached 80 million per week, often determined whether a film made a profit. BMP believed that every film enhanced or diminished America's reputation abroad and hence affected the nation's power.[5]

The movie industry shared OWI's perhaps exaggerated idea of its products' power, but how effectively it would cooperate remained unclear. From the mid-1930s to the eve of World War II the industry was isolated from national intellectual, artistic, and political life. When Benito Mussolini's army invaded Ethiopia in 1935, an agitated friend asked a producer, "Have you heard any late news?" The excited mogul replied, "Italy just banned *Marie Antoinette!*" Conservative businessmen and their bankers ran the studios. Louis B. Mayer of Metro-Goldwyn-Mayer, the single most influential man in Hollywood, decorated his desk with portraits of Herbert Hoover, Francis Cardinal Spellman, and Douglas MacArthur. The artistic, more liberal side of the industry—the directors and particularly the writers—felt squelched. The industry avoided message films in favor of romances, musicals, murder mysteries, and westerns—"pure entertainment" in Hollywood parlance. Stereotypes flourished; accuracy was incidental. Since 1934 the Hays Office had censored sex and profanity and taught that sin was always punished; the movies' ideal world was an adolescent perception of middle-class America. Although international themes increased between 1939 and 1941, social awareness remained dim. "Most movies are made in the evident assumption that the audience is passive and wants to remain passive," noted the film critic James Agee; "every effort is made to do all the work—the seeing, the explaining, the understanding, even the feeling."[6]

Hollywood preferred to avoid issues; OWI demanded affirmation of New Deal liberalism for America and the world. When Poynter arrived in the movie capital he found the industry doing little to promote the larger issues of the war. In the summer of 1942 Hollywood had under consideration or in production 213 films that dealt with the war in some manner. Forty percent of those focused on the armed forces, usually in combat. Less than 20 percent dealt with the enemy, and most of those portrayed spies and saboteurs. Other categories—the war issues, the United Nations, and the home front—received minimal attention. Even more disturbing to OWI, Hollywood had simply grafted the war to conventional mystery and action plots or appropriated it as a backdrop for frothy musicals and flippant comedies. Interpretation of the war remained at a rudimentary level: the United States was fighting because it had been attacked, and it would win.[7]

To help the industry raise its sights, Poynter and his staff wrote a *Manual for the Motion-Picture Industry* in June 1942 that they intended as a guide for moviemakers in future projects. The manual ranks as probably the most comprehensive statement of OWI's interpretation of the war. OWI believed the war was not merely a struggle for survival but a people's war between fascism and democracy, the crusade of Vice President Henry A. Wallace's Century of the Common Man. The United States fought for a new democratic world based on the Four Freedoms— freedom of speech and religion and freedom from want and fear. The war was a people's struggle, BMP emphasized, "not a national, class or race war." Every person in the world had a concrete stake in the outcome; an Allied victory promised to all a decent standard of living, including a job, good housing, recreation, and health, unemployment, and old-age insurance—a world New Deal. The average citizen would also enjoy the right to participate in government, which suggested OWI's anti-imperialist stance. American minorities had not entered utopia, the bureau conceded, but progress was possible only under democracy, and the wartime gains of blacks, women, and other minorities would be preserved. A nation of united average citizens, who believed deeply in the cause of freedom and sacrificed willingly to promote victory, was the hallmark of BMP's democracy.[8]

The enemy was fascism. The enemy was not the Axis leadership or all of the Axis-led peoples but fascist supporters anywhere, at home as well as abroad. "Any form of racial discrimination or religious intolerance, special privileges of any citizen are manifestations of Fascism, and should be exposed as such," the manual advised. A fascist victory would entail racial discrimination, destruction of political rights, eradication of the rights of labor, and "complete regimentation of the personal life" of the common man. "There can be no peace until militarism and fascism are completely wiped out," BMP warned. When victory came, the United Nations, eschewing national interest and balance-of-power politics, would build a new world expressive of the collective will. The manual enjoyed wide distribution in Hollywood; some studios reproduced the entire contents for their personnel, and many writers welcomed the bureau's interpretation.[9]

The manual reflected the intellectual ferment of the 1930s. Many intellectuals had put a premium on commitment to some large ideal or movement; a predetermined response, not an examination of experience in its many facets, was all-important. The quest for commitment converged in the late 1930s with the search for America; the war seemed to offer that unifying commitment, and it reduced intellectual content to an uncritical adulation of America and Allies. Thus, BMP reviewers in 1942 objected to the depiction of Spanish Loyalist violence in Paramount's *For Whom the Bell Tolls,* "particularly at this time when we *must* believe in the rightness of our cause." The bureau continued:

> Now it is necessary that we see the democratic fascist battle as a whole and recognize that what the Loyalists were fighting for is essentially the same thing that we are. To focus too much attention on the chinks in our allies' armor is just what our enemies might wish. Perhaps it is realistic, but it is also going to be confusing to American audiences.[10]

To OWI the reality of experience threatened response.

Before the manual could have much effect, however, the bureau faced some immediate problems. Metro-Goldwyn-Mayer (MGM) wanted to re-release the 1939 film *The Real Glory,* which dealt with the United States army's suppression of the turn-of-the-century Moro rebellion, but now billed as war between American and Japanese troops. Philippine President Manuel Quezon protested vigorously, and Mellett convinced producer Sam Goldwyn to withdraw the picture. The bureau's patriotic appeals also staved off re-release of two glorifications of British imperialism, RKO's *Gunga Din* and MGM's *Kim.* When Columbia sought BMP advice on its proposed "Trans-Sahara," Mellett cautioned that American policy in Africa was not yet clear, and the studio dropped the project.[11]

But suggestions and patriotic persuasion had limits, OWI discovered in July 1942 when it screened Twentieth Century-Fox's *Little Tokio, U.S.A.* The film grafted a fifth-column theme to a conventional murder mystery and portrayed the Japanese-Americans—"this Oriental bund"—as bent on sabotage and trying to take over California. The hero-detective bullied his way into a home without a search warrant, and the police beat up Japanese "spies" they had arrested and disarmed. These Gestapo methods dismayed the reviewers, who asked, "Did somebody mention that we are presumably fighting for the preservation of the Bill of Rights?" By the end of the film, the Japanese-Americans were marched off to detention camps, and the detective's sweetheart, converted from isolationism, appeasement, and tolerance for Japanese-Americans, implored patriots to save America. "Invitation to the Witch Hunt," cried BMP.

Poynter appealed to the producer, Colonel Jason Joy, to make enough changes to "take most of the curse off." But Joy accused Poynter of going soft on the Japanese and gave OWI an ultimatum: *Little Tokio, U.S.A.* would go out as it stood or it could be killed if it contradicted government policy. Poynter capitulated. Twentieth Century-Fox had received army approval for the film and had rushed camera crews to Little Tokio in Los Angeles to shoot footage of the actual evacuation.[12]

OWI now recognized that to inject its propaganda ideas into feature films, the Hollywood bureau had to influence the studios while films were being produced; moreover, since the army was interested mainly in security not ideology, the bureau had to be the sole point of contact between the government and the industry. Accordingly, Poynter asked the studios to submit their scripts to his office for review. While he had no direct power to demand scripts, Poynter achieved some limited cooperation. He had taken an unprecedented step. The Committee on Public Information (Creel Committee) of World War I had allowed films to go abroad only if the committee's shorts went with them, but George Creel apparently had not attempted to influence the content of entertainment films directly.[13]

As studios hesitantly began submitting scripts, OWI encountered problems. Particularly sensitive was the depiction of home-front race relations. MGM's "Man on America's Conscience" refurbished Andrew Johnson as the hero of Reconstruction; vulture-like Thaddeus Stevens fulfilled the need for a heavy. OWI passed the script to Walter White, executive secretary of the National Association for the Advancement of Colored People, who, with the black press, the *Daily Worker,* and a group of Hollywood luminaries, raised a chorus of protest. Mayer dismissed the outcry as the work of what he called "the communist cell" at MGM. When Mellett appealed to national unity, the studio at last agreed to delete the inflammatory references to slavery and to change Stevens into a sincere, if still misguided, figure. The film, released in December 1942 as *Tennessee Johnson,* did not entirely please OWI, but it demonstrated nonetheless the influence the bureau could wield by reading scripts.[14]

Poynter seized that opportunity with one of the few scripts Paramount submitted, *So Proudly We Hail,* a $2-million epic of the seige of Bataan. He suggested that one of the army nurses headed for martyrdom might say: "Why are we dying? Why are we suffering? We thought we . . . could not be affected by all the pestiferous, political spots elsewhere in the world. We have learned a lot about epidemics and disease. . . . when a political plague broke out there [in Manchuria] by invasion, we would not have been willing to do something about it. We had to wait until this plague spread out further and further until it hit Pearl Harbor." He also outlined a Christmas sermon that traced the cause of democracy from Jesus Christ through the Century of the Common Man. The studio wrote in some of Poynter's ideas, though not in his exact words, and OWI ranked it among the best of the war films.[15]

Combat films reflected OWI's influence probably as much as any type. In the bureau's ideal combat movie, an ethnically and geographically diverse group of Americans would articulate what they were fighting for, pay due regard to the role of the Allies, and battle an enemy who was formidable but not a superman. In RKO's *Bombardiers* a pacifist-influenced bombardier worried about bombing innocent civilians. At OWI's suggestion, the revised script introduced the concept of a just war and explained that the enemy's targets were everywhere while the Americans', although admittedly not surgically precise, were limited to military targets. Occasionally the studios became too bold for the bureau. "War *is* horrible," BMP acknowledged, but it nevertheless asked the studio to "minimize the more bloody aspects" in *Corregidor*. OWI liked reality but not too much of it, which reinforced Hollywood's inclination toward avoidance. This, even more than OWI's sermonettes, vitiated the impact of many combat pictures. *So Proudly We Hail* remained chiefly a cheesecake-studded story of love on the troop carriers and in the foxholes. And "the most sincere thing Paramount's young women did," said Agee, "was to alter their make-up to favor exhaustion (and not too much of it) over prettiness (and not too little of that). . . ." Few feature films approached the impact of combat documentaries, such as John Huston's *Battle of San Pietro* and especially the British *Desert Victory*.[16]

By the fall of 1942, films in all categories were showing OWI's imprint, whether through script review or application of the manual for the industry. The motion picture bureau praised two films released in 1942 for filling in gaps on the home front. MGM's *Keeper of the Flame* dramatized native fascism. A wealthy American wanted to institute anti-labor, anti-Negro, anti-Semitic, and anti-Catholic campaigns and to exploit the people of the United States for members of his class. Universal Pictures made *Pittsburgh* to show the home front geared for war. A tempestuous love triangle composed of John Wayne, Randolph Scott, and

Marlene Dietrich was resolved when labor and management united behind something greater than themselves—the war effort. Some of the speeches had been culled directly from the OWI manual, the bureau observed, "and might have been improved by translation into terms more directly and simply relating to the characters . . . in this particular film." But OWI Hollywood reviewers urged Mellett not to miss *Pittsburgh* or *Keeper of the Flame.*[17]

If the studios chose to ignore OWI, however, they could turn out what Poynter termed "ill-conceived atrocities." Preston Sturges's giddy Paramount comedy *Palm Beach Story* carried on the Hollywood tradition of satirizing the idle rich. But the BMP feared that this "libel on America at war," with its blithe disregard of wartime hardships, would offend the American allies. Another Hollywood staple that disturbed OWI was the gangster film, of which Paramount's *Lucky Jordan* was representative. The hero tried to dodge the draft and swindle the army, but when the Nazi agents beat up a gin-swilling, panhandling grandmother who had befriended him, he converted to the American cause, helped round up the Axis spy ring, and meekly returned to the army. His turnabout dramatized in specific, human terms the reality of fascism. Yet his individualistic commitment suggested to OWI reviewers that the United States had nothing ideological against Adolf Hitler; as the hero put it, Americans just did not like the way Nazis pushed people around. OWI wanted the hero to undergo a more profound intellectual awakening and to announce it explicitly. BMP feared, moreover, that gangster films' cynicism and lawlessness, while not particularly harmful at home, tended to support Axis propaganda abroad. The bureau asked the Office of Censorship to bar from export *Palm Beach Story, Lucky Jordan,* and other films it disliked. The censorship code was limited mainly to security information, however, and since these films hardly contained military secrets, the censor granted them export licenses. The censor, ironically, was more lenient than the advocates of free speech.[18]

Hearing increasingly bad reports on the effect of American films abroad, Davis looked for a way to keep Hollywood from putting across "day in and day out, the most outrageous caricature of the American character." Mellett proposed that a representative of OWI's overseas branch join BMP's Hollywood office; this official could more credibly object that certain films harmed foreign relations and could carry OWI's case to the censor. "It would hurt like hell" if a picture were withheld from foreign distribution, Mellett pointed out. Davis agreed and appointed one of Sherwood's chief aides, Ulric Bell, as the overseas arm's representative to Hollywood. A former Washington bureau chief for the Louisville *Courier-Journal*, Bell possessed impeccable New Deal credentials and had been one of the key figures in the prewar interventionist movement. Arriving in Hollywood in November 1942, he shared Poynter's reviewing staff. Bell's influence soon exceeded what Mellett and Poynter had dreamed of or, indeed, thought proper.[19]

OWI then tried to cut in on the chummy relationship between Hollywood and the more glamorous armed forces in early December 1942. The war and navy departments furnished men, equipment, and advice to the compliant industry. The military branches scrutinized scripts and films mainly for security and seldom cooperated with OWI. Davis asked the war and navy departments to channel all of their contacts with the movie industry through OWI's Hollywood office. The military flatly declined.[20]

At the same time Mellett dispatched a hotly controversial letter to the studios. He advised the industry to submit routinely treatments and synopses of projected films, as well as finished scripts, to Poynter's office. Mellett also asked the producers to submit all films to his Hollywood outpost in the long cut—the last stage before final prints were made. While little new material could be added then, OWI could still recommend that harmful scenes be snipped out. Moreover, all contacts between the studios and federal agencies, including the military services, should be channeled through BMP. "Censors Sharpen Axes," bannered *Variety*. Mellett wanted "complete censorship over the policy and content of our pictures," said Bill Goetz, vice president of Twentieth Century, reflecting the attitude of nearly all studio heads. The magnates wanted an in-house censor, such as Mayer or Y. Frank Freeman, the conservative head of Paramount.[21]

Shocked by the industry's furious reaction, Mellett and Davis tried to soothe the executives. Studios remained free to make any picture they wanted without consulting anybody, and, short of violating treason statutes, they could distribute any picture in the United States. The main purpose of the letter, Mellett and Davis insisted, had been to clarify the relationship between OWI and the armed forces for the industry. Privately Mellett told Poynter to pull back. Suggesting dialogue for *So Proudly We Hail* had been a mistake, Mellett said; Poynter agreed. The Hollywood-office pride in *Pittsburgh* and *Keeper of the Flame* could "only result from the appearance of your own stuff in those two pictures," BMP's chief continued. "The propaganda sticks out disturbingly." "Great things" had already been accomplished, but Mellett warned Poynter to modify his operation in whatever ways necessary until the storm subsided.[22]

In fact, BMP reviewers acknowledged decided improvement in the treatment of OWI themes in late 1942 and early 1943. Hollywood tried to redeem its prewar condescension toward foreigners by stressing the Resistance. BMP liked the 1942 Academy Award winner *Casablanca* for its depiction of the valiant underground, the United States as the haven of the oppressed, and the subordination of personal desires to the greater cause of the war—although they would have preferred that the hero had verbalized the reasons for his conversion. As OWI suggested, Fritz Lang's story of Lidice, *Hangmen Also Die,* showed a united Czechoslovakia resisting German barbarism. *This Land Is Mine,* the work of Jean Renoir and Dudley Nichols, seemed to OWI a "superb" picture of the French resistance, capped by the "vital" oration of the once cowardly schoolmaster defying occupation authorities. Yet, as critics such as Leo Braudy noted, the teacher, for all his passion, remained "a man orating in a locked room." Even in the talented hands of Renoir and Nichols, the message overwhelmed the creation of believable characters and real situations.[23]

Such problems, among others, counteracted OWI-approved efforts to reverse Hollywood's negative prewar image of the Soviet Union. The idea of filming Ambassador Joseph E. Davies's *Mission to Moscow* apparently did not originate with OWI, but BMP reviewers made some relatively minor suggestions when they read the script, which followed the book all too faithfully. Beneath a giant world map, the prescient Davies chatted amiably with an avuncular Joseph Stalin, illustrating how Americans and Russians were all brothers under the skin in the global struggle. Bell termed the picture "a socko job on the isolationists and appeasers—the boldest thing yet done by Hollywood." Bold perhaps, but its cosmetic treatment of the occupation of Finland, whitewash of the Moscow purge trials, and abnormally simplistic formula evidently convinced few viewers. *Mission to Moscow* was "mishmash," said Manny Farber of *New Republic.* "A great glad two-million-dollar bowl of canned borscht . . . ," sighed Agee.[24]

Brotherhood usually meant Americanization. Lillian Hellman's script for Goldwyn's *North Star* had good possibilities, particularly in its semi-documentary approach to ordinary Russians. But director Lewis Milestone turned the Bessarabian cooperative into an American prairie town, and the handsome peasants sang and danced as if they had strayed from a Broadway musical. "War has put Hollywood's traditional conception of the Muscovites through the wringer," observed *Variety*, "and they have come out shaved, washed, sober, good to their families, Rotarians, brother Elks, and 33rd Degree Mason."[25]

The motion picture bureau also recorded success in reorienting the portrayal of the home front. *One Destiny* told how Pearl Harbor changed the lives and affections of various persons in an Iowa farm community. The bureau persuaded Twentieth Century-Fox to change the original script's emphasis on ill feeling between an enlisted man and a man who stayed on the farm to an understanding of how the war effort needed various talents in many places. King Vidor's *An American Romance* originally recounted the rags-to-riches saga of a Slavic immigrant who became a great automobile manufacturer, sold out, and then returned to manufacture aircraft for the war effort. The individualistic, Henry Ford–inspired hero troubled OWI, but bureau-induced changes softened the picture sufficiently for OWI approval. Blacks, who in the first script had been nice but definitely kept in their place, were eliminated. The depiction of labor unions as radical, violent conspiracies—"a fascist tactic pure and simple," said OWI—was altered. For OWI and outside reviewers alike, the strength of *An American Romance* lay in its documentary-style celebration of United States geography that conveyed "the greatness of America."[26]

Despite BMP's influence on movie content, Bell began campaigning to curb pictures he felt were still undesirable. The Office of Censorship issued a new code on December 11, 1942, that helped Bell immensely. The new index banned from export films that showed rationing or other economic preparations for a long war, scenes of lawlessness in which order was not restored and the offenders punished (this aimed primarily at gangster films), and portrayals of labor or class conflict in the United States since 1917. Bell wanted the code tightened even more. Poynter vehemently disagreed, especially with the restrictions on post-1917 America. If OWI's strategy was to tell the truth, he argued, it should "make a sacrifice hit now and then." Films should admit the United States had problems, as foreigners knew, but should show how democracy solved them. "Fascist methods need not be used to defeat the common enemy of Fascism," he told Bell. Poynter predicted that the new code would make studios shy away from significant war themes.[27]

Bell nevertheless pressed the censor, particularly as a means of trapping B movies that were often shot without scripts and of thwarting studios that tried to parlay military or FBI approval into an export license. *They Came to Blow Up America*, which dealt with the seven saboteurs who landed on Long Island in 1942, was a case in point. The Federal Bureau of Investigation saw nothing wrong with the script, but Bell thought the sabotage was exaggerated and FBI was shown as inefficient. "Even the FBI's approval does not make it suitable for overseas presentation," he said. The censor passed it anyway. Bell enlisted Davis's help in February 1943 for a test case—Republic's quickie B feature, *London Blackout Murders.* This picture implied the British government would accept a negotiated peace, took some mild swipes at Lend Lease, and showed an overworked doctor accidentally cutting off a woman's head during a blackout instead of amputating her leg. Censorship director Byron Price could not agree that "suppression should go the lengths Bell has suggested." America's allies could "take it," Price said, "and the enemy would find ways to distort developments anyway." RKO hid from Bell its low-budget picture *I Walked with a Zombie* until the censor granted an export license. In similar fashion other films, including the Bob Hope–Dorothy Lamour picaresque *Road to Morocco,* which Eisenhower had said "simply must not reach North Africa," were spirited out of the country.[28]

In mid-summer 1943, however, Bell triumphed. Congress's anti–New Deal axe chopped OWI's domestic branch to a fraction of its former size. Mellett and Poynter left BMP, Paramount executive Stanton Griffis took charge of what little remained of BMP's own productions, and Bell inherited the Hollywood review staff. Freed of Poynter's restraints, Bell convinced West Coast censor Watterson Rothacker to adopt his approach. In quick succession Rothacker denied foreign audiences *Fugitive from a Prison Camp, The Great Swindle, The Batman, Hillbilly Blitzkrieg, Sleepy Lagoon,* and *Secret Service in Darkest Africa.* By fall 1943 the censor followed OWI's recommendations in almost all cases. Films such as *Lucky Jordan,* Bell said, almost certainly would be barred from export now. The major remaining difference between OWI and the censor concerned westerns such as *Buffalo Bill,* which dramatized whites' mistreatment of Indians. The film had a factual basis, Rothacker observed, and since it was set before 1917 he could not touch it. OWI had become the censor's advance guard. Hollywood could still make any film it chose, but as the *Motion Picture Herald* pointed out, no one would produce a picture "known in advance to be doomed to domestic exhibition exclusively."[29]

BMP's increasing influence over a Hollywood willing to cooperate was apparent in movies about the home front, especially juvenile delinquency. *Where Are Your Children?* appalled BMP reviewers with its "sensational portrayal of a young girl's downfall, youthful drunkenness, orgiastic dancing and necking, a seduction resulting in pregnancy, a stolen car, a joy ride, a murder, an attempted suicide and the repentant older generation." While the film promised something for everyone, OWI told Monogram Pictures to tone it down if it wanted foreign release. The studio's cuts did not satisfy OWI. Following BMP recommendations closely, Rothacker ordered 508 feet cut from the film before he approved it for export. RKO's contribution to delinquency was a film whose progression of titles suggested its modification under OWI pressure: *Youth Runs Wild* became *Are These Our Children?* then *The Dangerous Age*, which was released as *Look to Your Children*, whose conclusion assembled a series of "stock shots showing how the Boy Scouts, 4-H Clubs, city playgrounds and similar institutions are combatting juvenile problems." Like sin punished in the end, democracy solving its problems was ruled suitable for export.[30]

Almost all the major OWI themes converged in the most expensive picture made up to that time, Darryl Zanuck's hagiographic *Wilson*, released in August 1944. BMP persuaded screenwriter Lamar Trotti to balance machine politicians by emphasizing the people's power. The studio excised a line to which BMP objected: "With Wilson now firmly in the saddle and riding herd on a docile Congress. . . ." While the original script had dwelled on the failure of the League of Nations, the revised version stressed hope. A few obstructive men could not kill the League, Woodrow Wilson said; "the dream of a world united against the awful wastes of war is too deeply imbedded in the hearts of men everywhere." OWI recommended *Wilson* for special distribution in liberated areas, not merely because its theme was "so vital to the psychological warfare of the United Nations" but because of the picture's "rare entertainment value." Despite good intentions and a $5.2-million budget, however, Hollywood and OWI reduced a character worthy of William Shakespeare to a cardboard prig and his ideas to primer simplicity. As history it was a travesty; as entertainment, a bore; as box-office, a bust.[31]

Wilson was one of the last major films to deal significantly with OWI themes. Combat pictures, such as *Thirty Seconds over Tokyo*, held steady, and pictures about the home front, such as *Pride of the Marines*, which fulfilled OWI's desire for films about returning veterans, showed a slight increase. But the other OWI categories showed sharp declines. The 1944 Academy Award winner, Bing Crosby's *Going My Way*, reflected the shift to non-ideological, frequently religious, entertainment pictures in which war and rumors of war seldom intruded. Several reasons contributed to this shift, among them increasing war weariness and a sense that the war would end soon. But another important cause of the decline was what Poynter had predicted: the alliance between OWI and the censor made the studios shy away from significant themes.[32]

By the fall of 1943 Bell had convinced every studio except Paramount to let OWI read all their scripts instead of certain selected ones, and even Paramount agreed to discuss its scripts with OWI in general terms. In 1943 OWI read 466 scripts; in 1944, 744. The 1,210 scripts reviewed in those two years represented almost three-fourths of the 1,652 scripts the Hollywood office read between May 1942 and its demise in August 1945. From September 1943 through August 1944, BMP analyzed eighty-four scripts with American lawlessness or corruption as a main theme; forty-seven were corrected to its satisfaction. Racial problems were corrected or eliminated in twenty of twenty-four instances, distortions of military or political facts in forty-four of fifty-nine cases. Fifty-nine of the eighty scripts that portrayed Americans oblivious to the war were improved. During this period OWI managed to have 277 of the 390 cases of objectionable material corrected, a success ratio of 71 percent. Yet these statistics understate OWI's influence. Many scripts already showed the influence of the "Manual for the Motion Picture Industry" when they reached OWI readers, making alterations unnecessary. Complete statistics are not available, but from January through August 1943—before Bell's agreement with the censor had much effect—BMP induced the industry to drop twenty-nine scheduled productions and, particularly noteworthy, to rework parts of five films already approved by the censor. Bell closed the remaining gaps in the line established by Mellett and Poynter. From mid-1943 until the end of the war, OWI exerted an influence over an American mass medium never equaled before or since by a government agency.[33] The content of World War II motion pictures is inexplicable without reference to the bureau.

Hollywood had proved to be remarkably compliant. The industry found that its sincere desire to help the war effort need not interfere with business that was better than usual. Freedom of the screen had never been Hollywood's long suit: an industry that had feared being "enslaved" by Mellett was already in thrall to Will Hays. As the studios learned that OWI wanted "only to be helpful, their attitudes change[d] miraculously," observed Robert Riskin, a Sherwood aide who had been one of Hollywood's highest-paid writers. In "brutal honesty," Riskin continued, the industry's "unprecedented profits" had encouraged cooperation that surprised even the "movie moguls." The studios let BMP know what stories they were considering for production—some of the hottest secrets in movieland—so that the bureau could steer them into less crowded areas and thus smooth out the picture cycle. OWI's international role was especially important. Hollywood films hit the beaches right behind the American troops, provided they had OWI approval; the agency charged admission and held the money in trust for the studios. United States filmmakers were planning a large-scale invasion of the foreign market after the war, and OWI established indispensable beachheads. Indeed, Riskin lamented in mid-1944: "An unsavory opinion seems to prevail within OWI that the Motion Picture Bureau is unduly concerned with considerations for commercial interests."[34]

Although OWI and Hollywood first seemed to conflict, they eventually developed excellent rapport, for their aims and approaches were essentially compatible. The "chief function of mass culture," Robert Warshow has observed, "is to relieve one of the necessity of experiencing one's life directly." Hollywood, conceiving of its audience as passive, emphasized entertainment and avoidance of issues. OWI encouraged Hollywood to treat more social issues and to move beyond national and racial stereotypes. However, since OWI was interested mainly in response, it stressed ideology and affirmation; it raised social issues only to have democracy wash them away. Here the seemingly divergent paths of Hollywood and OWI joined: avoidance and affirmation both led to evasion of experience. Instead of opening realms of understanding by confronting experience, OWI—the propaganda agency—and Hollywood—the dream factory—joined hands to deny realities. However laudable the goals of propaganda, Jaques Ellul has suggested that it creates a person "who is not at ease except when integrated in the mass, who rejects critical judgments, choices, and differentiations because he clings to clear certainties."[35] Through their influence over motion pictures, the OWI's liberals undermined the liberation for which they said they fought.

NOTES

1. Film historians such as Lewis Jacobs and Paul Rotha and Richard Griffith recognize the heavy ideological emphasis of World War II movies, but do not realize the influence of the Office of War Information (OWI). Lewis Jacobs, "World War II and the American Film," *Cinema Journal* VII (Winter 1967–68), 1–21, and Paul Rotha and Richard Griffith, *The Film Till Now: A Survey of World Cinema* (London: Spring Books, 1967), pp. 464–67. The most complete history of OWI restricts its film coverage to the Bureau of Intelligence. Allan M. Winkler, "Politics and Propaganda: The Office of War Information, 1942–1945," doctoral dissertation, Yale University, 1974. John Morton Blum accepts OWI's contention that producers should use their own judgment about wartime movie

content and concludes that "with few exceptions, *Wilson* and *Mission to Moscow* for two, films designed for the box office carried no message of purpose or idealism." John Morton Blum, *V Was for Victory: Politics and American Culture during World War II* (New York: Harcourt Brace Jovanovich, 1976), pp. 25, 36. A popular account discusses OWI influence on films in a lighthearted fashion, but says that the interaction ended in mid 1943. Richard R. Lingeman, *Don't You Know There's a War On? The American Home Front, 1941–1945* (New York: Putnam, 1970), 168–210.

2. Elmer Davis to Byron Price, January 27, 1943, Box 3, Records of the Office of War Information, RG 208 (Federal Records Center, Suitland, Md.); Winkler, "Politics and Propaganda"; LaMar Seal Mackay, "Domestic Operations of the Office of War Information in World War II," doctoral dissertation, University of Wisconsin, 1966, ch. 1–2. See also *Public Opinion Quarterly* VI (Spring 1942); Harold D. Lasswell, *Propaganda Technique in the World War* (New York: Alfred A. Knopf, 1938), p. 9; and Jacques Ellul, *Propaganda: The Formation of Men's Attitudes* (New York: Vintage Books, 1965), pp. x, xiv. For Elmer Davis, see Alfred Haworth Jones, "The Making of an Interventionist on the Air: Elmer Davis and CBS News, 1939–1941," *Pacific Historical Review* XLII (February 1973), 91.

3. Although some scholars acknowledge the presence of prominent liberals in OWI, ideology has not received the emphasis that its pivotal importance in the agency merits. See Winkler, "Politics and Propaganda," pp. 13–14, 22–28, 37–41. For example, not only the questions of technique examined by Sydney Weinberg but also ideological differences fueled the "writers' quarrel" of 1943. Sydney Weinberg, "What to Tell America: The Writers Quarrel in the Office of War Information," *Journal of American History* LV (June 1968), 76, 88. For New Dealers in OWI, see Harold Gosnell to Files, September 14, 1945, in "Preparation of War Histories by Agencies: OWI, 1942–1945," item 127, series 41.3, Bureau of the Budget Records, RG 51, National Archives. See also Norman Markowitz, *The Rise and Fall of the People's Century: Henry A. Wallace and American Liberalism, 1941–1948* (New York: Free Press, 1973), ch. 2, and Blum, *V Was for Victory*, ch. 7–9. In this essay the term *ideology* is used not to imply "a rigid, doctrinaire, black-and-white understanding of the world, but, rather, . . . the system of beliefs, values, fears, prejudices, reflexes, and commitments—in sum, the social consciousness" of a group. See Eric Foner, *Free Soil, Free Labor, Free Men: The Ideology of the Republican Party Before the Civil War* (New York: Oxford University Press, 1970), 4.

4. Lowell Mellett and Nelson Poynter were not on OWI payroll but drew their salary from the Executive Office of the President. *Reduction of Nonessential Expenditures. Hearings before the Joint Committee on Reduction of Nonessential Federal Expenditures* (Washington, D.C.: 1942), pp. 1140–55, 1208–25, 1308–13; Lowell Mellett, "The Office of Government Reports," *Public Administration Review* I (Winter 1941), 126; Margaret Hicks Williams, "'The President's' Office of Government Reports," *Public Opinion Quarterly* V (Winter 1941), 548–62; Clayton R. Koppes interviews with Poynter, January 8, 1974, and Dorothy Jones, December 6, 1974; Dorothy B. Jones, "Quantitative Analysis of Motion Picture Content," *Public Opinion Quarterly* VI (Fall 1942), 411–27. See also Richard Dyer MacCann, *The People's Films: A Political History of U.S. Government Motion Pictures* (New York: Hastings House, 1973), pp. 129–35. This essay, however, considers only OWI's attempt to influence feature films produced by the movie industry.

5. Davis press conference, December 23, 1942, Box 1442, Records of the Office of War Information; *Reduction of Nonessential Expenditures*, 1213–14; *Movies at War, Reports of War Activities, Motion Picture Industry, 1942–1945*, vol. 1, no. 1, pp. 1–5.

6. James Agee, *Agee on Film: Reviews and Comments* (New York: McDowell, Oblensky, 1972), p. 329. Leo C. Rosten, *Hollywood: The Movie Colony, The Movie Makers* (New York: Harcourt, Brace and Company, 1941), pp. 30–39, 133–62, 246–47; Robert Sklar, *Movie-Made America: A Social History of American Movies* (New York: Random House, 1975), pp. 173–76, 188, 195–97; Thornton Delehanty, "Czars Fall on Hollywood," *North*

American Review 241 (Winter 1936–37), 268; Dudley Nichols, "The Writer and the Film," *Theatre Arts* XXVII (October 1943), 591–602; Rotha and Griffith, *Film Till Now,* 445–46; Ruth Inglis, *Freedom of the Movies: A Report on Self-Regulation from the Commission on Freedom of the Press* (Chicago: University of Chicago Press, 1947), p. 128; Charles Higham, *The Art of the American Film* (Garden City, N.Y.: Anchor Press/Doubleday, 1974), pp. 199–201; Donald Ogden Stewart, *By a Stroke of Luck* (New York: Paddington Press, 1975), p. 199; Andrew Bergman, *We're in the Money: Depression America and Its Films* (New York: New York University Press, 1971), p. 169; Jacobs, "World War II and the American Film," 1.

7. Jones to Poynter, "War Features Inventory as of Sept. 15, 1942," Box 1435, OWI Records; Gregory D. Black and Clayton R. Koppes, "OWI Goes to the Movies: The Bureau of Intelligence's Criticism of Hollywood, 1942–1943," *Prologue* 6 (Spring 1974), 44–59.

8. Henry A. Wallace, "The Price of Free World Victory: The Century of the Common Man," *Vital Speeches of the Day* VII (June 1, 1942), 482–85; Robert A. Divine, *Second Chance: The Triumph of Internationalism in America during World War II* (New York: Atheneum, 1967), pp. 64–66; "Government Information Manual for the Motion Picture Industry," Summer 1942, April 29, 1943, January 1944, Box 15, OWI Records.

9. "Government Information Manual for the Motion Picture Industry," Summer 1942, April 29, 1943, January 1944, Box 15, OWI Records; Eddie Mannix to Executives, Producers, Writers, and Directors at MGM, August 24, 1942, Box 1433E, OWI Records.

10. Script Review, "For Whom the Bell Tolls," October 14, 1942, Box 3530, OWI Records; Robert Warshow, *The Immediate Experience: Movies, Comics, Theatre & Other Aspects of Popular Culture* (Garden City, N.Y.: Doubeday, 1962), 33–39; Warren I. Susman, "The Thirties," Stanley Coben and Lorman Ratner, eds., *The Development of an American Culture* (Englewood Cliffs, N.J.: Prentice-Hall, 1970), pp. 200–6, 214.

11. Manuel Quezon to Lowell Mellett, August 17, 1942; Mellett to Sam Goldwyn, August 20, 1942; Goldwyn to Mellett, August 22, 1942, Box 1433B; Script Review, "Kim," August 4, 1942, Box 1438; Leo Rosten to Mellett, June 23, 1942, Box 888; Mellett to Victor Saville, September 23, 1942, Box 3527; Poynter to Mellett, August 25, 1942; Mellett to Poynter, September 1, 1942, Box 1438, OWI Records; *Harrison's Reports,* September 6, 1942.

12. Feature Review, *Little Tokio, U.S.A.,* July 9, 1942, Box 3518, OWI Records.

13. Poynter to Mellett, July 23, September 2, 1942, Box 3518; Davis to Norman Thomas, September 23, 1942, Box 3, OWI Records; Twentieth Century-Fox press release, "Synopsis of *Little Tokio, U.S.A.,*" *Little Tokio, U.S.A.,*" file (Margaret Herrick Library, Academy of Motion Picture Arts and Sciences, Beverly Hills, California); James R. Mock and Cedric Larson, *Words That Won the War: The Story of the Committee on Public Information, 1917–1919* (Princeton, N.J.: Princeton University Press, 1939), pp. 142–56.

14. Jones to Poynter, August 6, 1942, Walter White to Mellett, August 17, 1942, Mellett to Maurice Revnes, August 18, 1942, Mellett to Poynter, August 27, 1942, Box 1433E; Poynter to Mellett, August 25, 1942, Feature Review, *Tennessee Johnson,* November 30, 1942, Mellett to Louis B. Mayer, November 25, 1942, Box 3510, OWI Records.

15. Script Review, "So Proudly We Hail," November 19, 1942; Poynter to Mark Sandrich, October 28, 1942, June 22, 1943; "Re Chaplain Speech—So Proudly We Hail," November 25, 1942, Box 3511, OWI Records.

16. Script Review, "Air Force," October 27, 1942, Box 3515; Script Review, "Bombardier," October 19, 1942, Box 3522; Script Review, "Corregidor," November 21, 1942; Feature Review, *Corregidor,* March 3, 1943, Box 3515; Feature Review, *Guadalcanal Diary,* October 26, 1943; Feature Review, *Desert Victory,* April 22, 1943, Box 3518, OWI Records; Manny Farber, "Love in the Foxholes," *New Republic* 109 (September 27, 1943), 426; Agee, *Agee on Film,* pp. 52–53, 65; Sklar, *Movie-Made America,* p. 255; Jacobs, "World War II and the American Film," 13.

17. Feature Reviews, *Keeper of the Flame,* December 7, 1942, Box 1435, *Pittsburgh,* November 30, 1942; Poynter to Mellett, December 2, 1942, Box 3520, OWI Records;

"Fascist Flame," *Newsweek* XXI (March 22, 1943), 80–81; "Keeper of the Flame," *Time* XLI (January 25, 1943), 86, 88; Stewart, *By a Stroke of Luck!* pp. 261–63.

18. Jones to Poynter, November 6, 1942, Box 1433; Feature Review, *Lucky Jordan,* November 17, 1942, Box 1435; Ulric Bell to Robert Riskin, December 10, 1942, Box 3; Poynter to Mellett, October 6, 19, 29, 1942; Office of Censorship Circular, September 9, 1942, Box 1438, OWI Records. See also Michael Wood, *America in the Movies* (New York: Basic Books, 1975), pp. 37–38.

19. Davis to Mellett, September 7, 1942, Mellett to Davis, September 9, 1942, Box 890; Davis press release, September 11, 1942, Box 3510, OWI Records; William Tuttle, Jr., "Aid-to-the-Allies Short of War versus American Intervention, 1940: A Reappraisal of William Allen White's Leadership," *Journal of American History* LVI (March 1970), 840–58; Mark L. Chadwin, *The Warhawks: American Interventionists before Pearl Harbor* (New York, 1970), pp. 51–52.

20. Poynter to Mellett, October 6, 20, 1942, Box 1438; Davis to Henry L. Stimson, December 3, 1942; A. D. Surles to Davis, December 11, 1942, Box 1, OWI Board Minutes; October 31, 1942, Box 41, OWI Records; Winkler, "Politics and Propaganda," 55–62.

21. Mellett to Goldwyn, December 9, 1942, Box 1443; Bill Goetz to Mellett, December 21, 1942, Goetz to Gardner Cowles, Jr., December 22, 1942, Jean Herrick to Cowles, December 19, 1942, Box 12A, OWI Records; *Variety,* December 23, 1942.

22. Davis press conference, December 23, 1942, box 1442; OWI Board Meeting Minutes, December 22, 26, 1942, Box 41; Mellett to Goetz, December 26, 1942, Box 12A; H. M. Warner to Mellett, December 16, 1942, Box 1443, OWI Records; Mellett to Poynter, December 30, 1942, Box 16; Lowell Mellett Papers (Franklin D. Roosevelt Library, Hyde Park, New York).

23. Bell to Riskin, December 9, 1942, February 23, 1943, Box 3; Feature Reviews, *Casablanca,* October 28, 1942, *Hangmen Also Die,* February 22, 1943, Box 3523; Poynter to Dudley Nichols, October 9, 1942, Box 3515, OWI Records; Leo Braudy, *Jean Renoir: The World of His Films* (Garden City, N.Y.: Anchor Books, 1972), p. 139; André Bazin, *Jean Renoir* (New York: Simon and Schuster, 1973), pp. 264–68; Raymond Durgnat, *Jean Renoir* (Berkeley, Calif.: University of California Press, 1974), pp. 236–37; Higham, *Art of the American Film,* p. 266.

24. Script Review, "Mission to Moscow," November 30, 1942; Poynter to Bob Buckner, December 3, 1942; Feature Review, *Mission to Moscow,* April 29, 1943; Bell to Riskin, April 29, 1943, Box 3523, OWI Records; Manny Farber, "Mishmash," *New Republic* 108 (May 10, 1943), 636; Agee, *Agee on Film,* pp. 37–39; Jack Warner, *My First Hundred Years in Hollywood* (New York: Random House, 1965), p. 290. See also Melvin Small, "Buffoons and Brave Hearts: Hollywood Portrays the Russians, 1939–1944," *California Historical Quarterly* LII (Winter 1973), 330–33; Charles Higham, *Warner Brothers* (New York: Scribner, 1975), pp. 158–71.

25. Script Review, "The North Star," May 12, 1943, Box 1434, OWI Records; Lillian Hellman, *An Unfinished Woman* (Boston: Little, Brown, 1969), p. 125; Richard Moody, *Lillian Hellman: Playwright* (New York: Pegasus, A Division of Bobbs-Merrill, 1972), p. 140; Elliot Paul, "Of Film Propaganda," *Atlantic* CLXXVI (September 1945), 123; "The New Pictures," *Time* XLII (November 8, 1943), 54; *Variety,* October 28, 1942.

26. Script Reviews, "One Destiny," January 4, March 24, April 27, 1943, Box 1434; "America," November 5, 1942; Feature Review, *America,* William S. Cunningham to Revnes, February 17, 1944, Box 3525, OWI Records; Hermine Rich Isaacs, "Salute to the Living: Films in Review," *Theatre Arts* XXVIII (November 1944), 669; "An American Romance," *Time* XLIV (October 16, 1944), 94.

27. Poynter to Bell, February 13, 1943, Box 1438; Bell to Riskin, March 31, 1943, Box 3510; Bell to Riskin, April 3, 1943, Box 15, OWI Records; Bell to Poynter, May 19, 1943; Poynter to Bell, June 4, 1943; Poynter to Mellett, June 5, 26, 1943, Box 16, Mellett Papers.

28. Bell to Davis, January 9, 1943; Davis to Price, January 16, 1943; Price to Davis, January 23, 1943; Milton S. Eisenhower to Bell, December 31, 1943, Box 3; Bell to Davis, March 8, 1943, Box 3509; Bell to Phil Hamblet, February 23, 1943, Box 3518, OWI Records.

29. Bell to Louis Lober, December 15, 1943; Cunningham to Lober, June 29, 1944, Box 3509; Bell to Riskin, November 1, 1943, Box 3; Feature Review, *Buffalo Bill*, Box 3518; "Report of Activities of the Overseas Branch, Bureau of Motion Pictures, Hollywood Office, January 1, 1943–August 14, 1943," Box 65, OWI Records; *Motion Picture Herald*, August 14, 1943; Winkler, "Politics and Propaganda," pp. 84–85. Richard R. Lingeman erroneously concludes that the Hollywood liaison efforts ended with the budget cut. Lingeman, *Don't You Know There's a War On?* p. 188. Although the revised censorship code was issued about the same time as Mellett's letter to the studios, the two events appear not to be connected.

30. Bell to Watterson Rothacker, November 12, 1943; Feature Review, *Where Are Your Children*, November 8, 1943; "Cuts Required by Rothacker for 'Where Are Your Children'" [December 1, 1943], Box 3530; Feature Reviews, *The Dangerous Age*, March 30, 1944, *Youth Runs Wild*, July 25, 1944, Box 3515, OWI Records. Michael Wood suggests that this typical Hollywood treatment of social problems is representative of "middle class American liberalism." Wood, *America in the Movies*, pp. 126, 129, 125.

31. Script Review, "Wilson," September 20, 1943; Feature Review, *Wilson*, August 1, 1944, Box 3518, OWI Records; Agee, *Agee on Film*, pp. 110–13; Divine, *Second Chance*, pp. 169–72.

32. Feature Review, *Thirty Seconds over Tokyo*, September 12, 1944, Box 3517, OWI Records; Dorothy B. Jones, "The Hollywood War Film: 1942–1944," *Hollywood Quarterly* I (October 1945), 1–14.

33. Bell to Lober, December 15, 1943, Box 3530; "Report of Activities of the Overseas Branch, Bureau of Motion Pictures, Hollywood Office, January 1, 1943–August 15, 1943," "Report on Activities, 1942–1945," September 18, 1945, Box 65, OWI Records.

34. Riskin to Bell, October 22, 1943, Box 3510; Riskin to Edward Barrett, August 12, 1944, Box 19, OWI Records; Koppes interview with Jones, December 6, 1974; Robert B. Randle, "A Study of the War Time Control Imposed on the Civilian Motion Picture Industry," master's thesis, University of Southern California, Los Angeles, 1950, pp. 85–86.

35. Warshow, *Immediate Experience*, p. 38; Agee, *Agee on Film*, p. 330; Ellul, *Propaganda*, p. 256.

Thomas Doherty

Teenagers and Teenpics, 1955–1957: A Study of Exploitation Filmmaking

Exploitation filmmaking is a commercial strategy first practiced in earnest by the American motion picture industry during the latter half of the 1950s. Its distinctive product is the "teenpic," a film targeted at teenaged moviegoers to the pointed exclusion of other age groups. The purpose of this study is to trace the economic and demographic realities that encouraged—indeed, forced—the film industry to turn increasingly to teenagers for financial sustenance. *Rock Around the Clock* (1956), the first acknowledged teenpic, will serve as a kind of synecdoche for this investigation. Its history should bring into sharper focus the nature of exploitation filmmaking, one of the ways Hollywood responded to the loss of its mass audience at mid-century.

Hollywood and the Teen Marketplace

"The Big Bands are breaking up," says an impresario at the beginning of *Rock Around the Clock* (hereinafter *RATC*), "the handwriting's on the wall." The observation could have as well applied to the big Hollywood studios. By the mid-1950s the motion picture industry had lost its

From *Current Research on Film: Audiences, Economics, and Law*, vol. 2, ed. Bruce A. Austin (Norwood, N.J.: Ablex, 1986), pp. 47–61. Reprinted with permission of the author and Ablex Publishing Corporation.

preeminent place in American cultural life. Although the promise of spectacle, novelty, or controversy might occasionally lure the mass audience back to theaters, the certainty of a market and the assurance of regular production—the hallmarks of classic Hollywood—had evaporated under the heat of television, divestiture and shifting demographics.[1-4] In short, filmmaking had become a haphazard business; each picture was a hit-or-miss proposition. If theatrical movies were to have a future as an industry, they would have to find, and discover the means to cultivate, a new, reliable audience with plenty of free time and spending money. Teenagers fitted the bill.

Teenagers had always been around of course, but, prior to the 1950s, neither Hollywood nor anyone else had taken particular notice of them. By 1955, they were impossible to ignore: a statistical anomaly in population distribution had converged with unparalleled economic prosperity to produce the nation's first generation of true teenagers. They were distinct from previous generations of American young people in numbers, affluence and self-consciousness: there were more of them, they had more money, and they were more aware of their unique status. By the late 1930s, the population trough of the worst years of the Great Depression had begun to reverse itself. Throughout the war years, there began the marked increase in the birth rate that, after 1946, exploded into the famous postwar baby boom.[5-7] The wartime babies reached adolescence during the mid-1950s the majority coming of age in homes that, by the standards of their parents and the rest of the world, were luxurious. The increasing uniformity of public school education throughout the states and a national media that doted on their idiosyncracies further standardized their experience. In 1958, when Dwight Macdonald referred to "a new American caste" with "a style of life that was sui generis," he was speaking of this pre–baby boom generation.[8] They, not their celebrated younger siblings of the great baby boom of 1946–57, were the original teenagers.

Many responded to the sudden prominence of the American teenager with fear and trembling. Throughout the 1950s, cultural guardians likened this "new American caste" to savage hordes descending on a city under siege. But even as editorial writers, law enforcement officials, and parents were shoring up the barricades against them, the business community was welcoming their arrival at the gates. With good reason: there was a fortune to be made selling trinkets to the barbarians.

Newsweek labeled them "the dreamy teenage market,"[9] and *Sales Management* christened the thirteen to nineteen bracket "the seven golden years."[10] In 1959, *Life* reported what was by then old news: "The American teenagers have emerged as a big-time consumer in the U.S. economy. . . . Counting only what is spent to satisfy their special teenage demands, the youngsters and their parents will shell out about $10 billion this year, a billion more than the total sales of GM."[11] Moreover, as a study for the Bureau of Business Research later documented, those billions were all "largely discretionary,"[12] which, in entrepreneurial terms, meant that teenage pocket money was basically up for grabs.

Unlike other industries, however, Hollywood was curiously shy in its courtship of the American teenager. Partly the reason for this was that until the mid-1950s Hollywood had only the faintest idea of who its audience was. The only statistical information the industry required was the daily box office report; such data, by themselves, are not amenable to age-aggregate partitioning. As Martin Quigley, Jr., the influential editor of *Motion Picture Herald*, observed in 1957: "In the 'good old days' of dimming memory, no one in the industry—be he producer, distributor, or exhibitor—took any interest in the question *Who Goes to the Movies?* The answer was plain—Everyone. . . ."[13] Filmmakers were equally confident about predicting what kind of movies "Everyone" wanted. By and large, the forceful personalities who controlled the studio system had depended on little more than hustle and instinct to anticipate and gauge audience tastes. The oft-cited technique of Columbia's Harry Cohn, who claimed he could detect an unprofitable picture if his behind squirmed during the screening, was representative. The prospect of "the whole world wired to Harry Cohn's ass" (as screenwriter Herman J. Mankiewicz retorted) may have been daunting, but his methodology made a certain sense. Moguls like Cohn, Warner, and Mayer had a kinship with their audience that their urbane successors lacked. By the mid-1950s, though, both the audience for motion pictures and the studio executive making them had changed. As the moguls and classic producers who came to power during the go-getting 1920s were replaced by 1950s-style organization men, the distance between the middle-aged financiers who made the movies and the ever-younger audience who patronized them rendered Cohn's seat-of-the-pants methods hopelessly antiquated. At the same time, the scale of the industry—the complexities and logistics as well as the money at stake—made filmmaking a bigger gamble than ever. Yet compared to their fellows in the automobile or fashion industries, motion picture executives still made production decisions in a stunningly haphazard way.[14]

In January 1946, the Motion Picture Association of America (MPAA) first acknowledged modern business and marketing procedures by creating a special department of research. The next year, in a special issue of the *Annals of the American Academy of Political and Social Science,* MPAA department head Robert W. Chambers lamented that so many Hollywood businessmen made decisions in a statistical vacuum. Reiterating the viewpoint of MPAA President Eric Johnston, Chambers noted that "from the standpoint of statistical knowledge . . . the motion picture industry probably knows less about its audience than any other major industry in the United States."[15] He commended the industry for taking its first steps towards the emerging science of demographics and spoke of the need for continued movement in that direction.[16] Elsewhere in the same issue, communications theorist Paul F. Lazarsfeld presented a quantitative analysis of movie audiences. Lazarsfeld reported that "scrutiny of available data" showed "age [as] the most important personal factor by which the movie audience is characterized" and that "the decline of movie attendance with increasing age is very sharp."[17] His most significant finding, though, concerned movie "opinion leaders": "In an overwhelming number of cases they are young people, many of them below twenty-five years of age. This is a very remarkable result. Our general notion is that the young learn from the old. In the movie field, advice definitely flows in the opposite direction."[18] In other words, Lazarsfeld was telling the industry that, in 1947, at the height of its prestige as a business and maturity as an art form, its future was with youngsters.

This was not the conventional wisdom. Despite pleas from exhibitors, the MPAA refused to abandon its concept of moviegoing as a family outing. In 1950, Leo Handel's landmark study, *Hollywood Looks at Its Audience,* exhaustively documented the juvenilization of the movie audience.[19] Still, statistical reports notwithstanding, moviemakers remained almost willfully blind to the changing nature of their business. "You can show them (any data) you want," said one frustrated exhibitor, "that's still a long way from getting them to comply."[20] Understandably reluctant to surrender cultural dominance in the entertainment marketplace, they ignored survey after survey which uniformly reported that the nation's typical moviegoer was a teenager. "Hollywood executives hire you to help them," complained market analyst Albert E. Sindlinger. "But when you don't tell them what they want to hear, sometimes they don't trust your accuracy."[21] Walter Brooks, writing in his "Manager's Round Table" column for *Motion Picture Herald,* voiced a common industry attitude to bearers of unwelcome tidings such as Sindlinger: "You can prove anything by the statisticians. . . . The statisticians assemble all sorts of figures to prove what has happened and to predict what will happen in the future. Personally, we think the statisticians themselves should be laid end to end—to prove that what they find depends on who pays their fees."[22] Though the great audience for movies no longer existed, the industry did its best to maintain the cherished fiction of service to a grand, broad-based public.

There were two main reasons for Hollywood's astigmatism. First, the industry didn't operate like other industries in the way it went about selling its products. Moviemakers came out of a show business, carnival tradition of ballyhoo. Few had faith or expertise in modern marketing techniques which other industries had used for decades, much less in newfangled forms of consumer seduction such as motivational research and depth psychology. Second, most professionals—producers, directors, and screenwriters—had adult artistic sensibilities. Whether nurtured in the studio system or recently graduated from television or New York stages, they were serious craftsmen unwilling to let juveniles dictate the exercise of their talents. Thus, many in the film industry worked against their own economic interests by making movies for an audience that no longer attended that often: married adults with children.[23,24]

Though the concept of the movie theater as "the center of family entertainment" was encouraged at the industry's highest levels, a growing chorus of voices from the exhibition end of the business and in the trade press called for a recognition of the new demographic realities. A survey for the *Motion Picture Herald* Institute of Industry Opinion reported in 1956, "The need for pictures appealing to the 15 to 25 age group was listed as most important by all classes of exhibition and by production as well, but distribution placed it fifth. The heavy percentage of opinion for this one factor . . . is an oustanding factor of the survey."[25] Quigley used his editorial forum to inform readers that "the most important single area for the present and future well-being of the motion picture industry is the youth of the country . . . the teens up through the mid-twenties."[26] *Variety* agreed, noting at the close of 1956 that "the demand for teenage pictures . . . is coming from all quarters—from small theatres as well as large circuits, from rural towns as well as big cities. The cry to assuage [the] teenage market is so great that some observers are already expressing the fear that the only outlet for mature films will be the art house."[27]

Despite the research evidence and urging from certain quarters of the industry, many moviemakers remained recalcitrant. In 1958, producer Sam Goldwyn expressed the anachronistic sentiments of the hold-outs: "I believe in making pictures a man can take his whole family to see."[28] At that late date, of course, most men were not doing any such thing. Quigley warned that "it would be futile to adopt an ostrich-head-in-the-sand attitude and pay no heed to the fact that in relation to their numbers those in the 15 to 25 age-group are the motion pictures' best customers."[29] Even for those who acknowledged the importance of the teenage audience, the time-honored mandate of "entertainment for the entire family" died hard. For example, one exhibitor with a better grasp of statistics than adolescent behavior suggested that "what we need today at the theater is a gimmick to create an incentive to teenagers to come to their neighborhood theaters, enjoy themselves, and bring their families with them."[30]

Such naive remarks highlight the industry's twin dilemma: moviemakers had both to *recognize* that the teen audience was crucial to their economic future and to *court* it successfully. Having identified the problem, they still had to propose a solution. "We know that the juvenile audience is off even though there are more kids around than ever," said one advertising-publicity director, "What we need is a study to indicate to us which way we could get those patrons back again."[31] Appropriately, though, a statistical study by a market research firm was not the light which showed the way. Rather, it was the example of Sam Katzman, one of Hollywood's legendary fast-buck boys. The success of Katzman's teenpics led the industry into an earnest and enduring exploitation of the teenage moviegoer.

"Jungle Sam" Katzman

At the peak of his production schedule in the early 1950s, Sam Katzman churned out an average of seventeen features and three serials a year, none of which lost money or cost over $500,000. One of the industry's most active and successful independents, he specialized in the kind of disposable, low-budget fare whose profit margin was modest but certain. In 1953, for example, cued by the popularity of "sex and sandals" epics such as *Samson and Delilah* (1949), *Quo Vadis* (1950), and *The Robe* (1952) Katzman underwent a prolific Middle Eastern phase, supplying theaters with (successively) *Siren of Baghdad, Flame of Calcutta, Serpent of the Nile,* and *Prisoners of the Casbah.* His production of the lucrative Jungle Jim series featuring Johnny Weismuller earned him the moniker "Jungle Sam," but the nickname might just as well have been a tribute to his knack for survival within a treacherous industry and a volatile market. Unfettered by artistic pretensions, Katzman was the definitive exploitation filmmaker. "Lord knows, I'll never make an Academy Award movie," he said, "But then I'm just as happy to get my achievement plaque from the bank every year."[32]

Early on, Katzman saw the box office potential of tailoring a motion picture to a matching audience. Following modern business procedures, he always knew his markets, produced pictures with those markets in mind, and merchandized them accordingly. Throughout the 1940s and early 1950s, he catered alternately to preteens (what the trade press called "the cap pistol set") with matinee fare like *Adam Man vs. Superman* (1950) and *Captain Video* (1952) and to a slightly older group composed largely of adolescent boys. In 1946, a series of "quickies" (low-budget high-speed productions) Katzman made for Monogram and Columbia—*Junior Prom, Freddie Steps Out, High School Hero,* and *Betty Co-ed*—attuned him to an emerging audience for films that were neither kiddie nor Mom-and-Pop fare. After television became the nation's most popular babysitter, Katzman increasingly turned his production efforts to films with a decidedly adolescent appeal. "We got a new generation," he told *Time* in 1952. "But they got the same old glands."[33] Katzman stimulated adolescent glands with exotic locales (all filmed in California), freakish creatures (apes, dwarves, and monsters) and disheveled actresses. These items, he felt, had an intrinsic appeal for his target group, an exploitation value that could be grafted onto the flimsiest of storylines.

Given his demanding production schedule, though, not even Katzman could rely on the same half-dozen exploitative elements for every title. For new and exciting ideas he was guided by contemporary journalism: Katzman turned newspaper headlines into film titles. In this the producer was hardly breaking new ground. Since the fast-paced days of silent cinema, "as timely as today's headlines" has been a publicity hook for motion pictures. An economical (in the broadest sense of the word) source of inspiration, the press has long provided the movies with juicy subject matter and, importantly, free publicity. In 1901, Edwin S. Porter did little more than visually render newspaper accounts of contemporary events in *The Execution of Czolgosz, Terrible Teddy and the*

Grizzly King, and *The Sampson-Schley Controversy.*[34] But in Porter's day filmmakers could crank out dramatizations of current events while the story still dominated the front pages. They could take advantage of transitory public curiosity and reap maximum publicity value from the newspapers' continued coverage of the event that inspired the film in the first place. With the rise of classic Hollywood, such speed was no longer possible, nor, so long as the studios had guaranteed exhibition outlets, was it necessary. As the old system faltered and competition for a dwindling audience's attention and time intensified, filmmakers were forced to redefine their industry. Katzman's special contribution was to reintroduce something of the speed of early silent production to the motion picture industry at mid-century.

By minimizing the time lapse between the event and the film that exploited it, Katzman was virtually assured of an intrigued audience and some free publicity. The success of his quickie productions underscored a truism of exploitation filmmaking: be the first, not the best; quickness counts for more than quality. Katzman began work on an atomic thriller the day after he heard the news of the first H-bomb explosion. A few days after the outbreak of the Korean War, Columbia solicited a suitable war movie. Katzman quickly conjured up a title (*A Yank in Korea*) and delivered the completed product six weeks and two days later.[35,36]

Given this modus operandi, Katzman's decision in early 1956 to make a rock 'n' roll exploitation film was predictable. Timely, controversial, and the province of teenagers, rock 'n' roll music was obviously grist for his production mill. Less predictable were the profound, longrange effects this latest assembly-line quickie was to have on the motion picture industry. *RATC* became the first hugely successful teenpic, the picture that announced the coming ascendancy of the teenage audience. As such, its production history, exploitation campaign, and ultimate impact bear a closer look.

Rock around the Clock

Exploitation filmmakers are careful businessmen. Generally, they are too careful to attempt a radically new formula. More often than not, they capitalize on successful gambits by the major film companies. In 1955, the profit margins and controversy generated by MGM's *Blackboard*

Jungle and Warner's *Rebel without a Cause* cued Katzman and several other sharp-eyed independents to the exploitation potential of rebellious youth. Though purportedly adult films, *Jungle* and *Rebel* immediately found their own level and were enthusiastically embraced by the nation's young people. A survey for Gilbert Youth Research Organization reported *The Blackboard Jungle* as the favorite film of high school students, and *Rebel without a Cause* star James Dean their favorite actor.[37] These two films were usually acknowledged as having spawned the many of the youth movies of the later 1950s—an eclectic assortment of high- and low-budget films dealing with juvenile delinquency, drag racing, high school vice, dating rituals, horror, space aliens, and, of course, rock 'n' roll.

Over the titles to *The Blackboard Jungle*, director Richard Brooks made an audacious choice in background music: "Rock around the Clock," a minor hit by an up-and-coming band named Bill Haley and the Comets. An amalgam of country and western and rhythm and blues music, the tune marked the first appearance of rock 'n' roll in a major motion picture. Largely on the strength of its use in *The Blackboard Jungle*, "Rock around the Clock" gained new life on the *Billboard* pop music charts.[38] By the end of 1955, the song had sold some 2 million copies, providing Bill Haley with a lifetime meal ticket.[39,40]

The scale of Haley's show business success was impressive, but there was nothing, at least in the very early days, to indicate that something more than entertainment as usual was going on. After all, shrieking, swooning, and other manifestations of (often well-staged) audience hysteria had been a part of pop music trends since the 1920s: Rudy Vallee, Bing Crosby, Frank Sinatra, and, most recently, the "nabob of sob," Johnny Ray, had each in his turn inspired progressively wilder reactions from claques of devoted fans. Few imagined that "Rock around the Clock" would become, in the words of rock historian Lillian Roxon, "the Marseillaise of the teenage revolution . . . the first inkling teenagers had that they might be a force to be reckoned with, in numbers alone."[41] At the close of 1956, the song, Haley, and the attendant rock 'n' roll hoopla had all the markings of the usual, short-lived musical fad—and as a fad, it had clear exploitation possibilities for "Jungle Sam" Katzman.[42–44]

In mid-January 1956, Katzman started production on *RATC*; by month's end, shooting was complete. Columbia Pictures, his usual distributor, had placed the first rock 'n' roll musical in selected theaters by March. Directed by Fred Sears and featuring Bill Haley and the

Comets, the Platters, and disc jockey Alan Freed, the film was a variation on the venerable Big Band musicals of the 1940s, a form then undergoing something of a resurgence with *The Glenn Miller Story* (1954) and *The Benny Goodman Story* (1955). In terms of production quality and narrative complexity, *RATC* wasn't especially different from the material Katzman had been marketing for years: mildly controversial, timely, teen oriented, and cheap (under $300,000). Indeed, with the exception of the rock 'n' roll exploitation angle, *RATC* had a lot in common with an earlier Katzman production, *Teenage Crime Wave* (1955): same director, same teenage topicality, and same filmic antecedent (*The Blackboard Jungle*).

RATC was a model of exploitation filmmaking in two important ways: it was first out of the gate and it had the best title. The rock 'n' roll craze had caught Katzman's nominal competition in quickie production off guard. American International Pictures, Distributors Corporation of America, Allied Artists and Universal-International all took months to fabricate their own rock 'n' roll teenpics. Foresight was evident in the film's very title: by beating his rivals to the title registration office and filing for the immediately recognizable catchphrase "rock around the clock," Katzman secured thousands of dollars in free publicity. Articulating another commandment of exploitation filmmaking, the producer defined his narrative guidelines: "We don't get stories. We get titles and then write stories around them or to fit them."[45] Not even a businessman as prescient as he, though, could have realized how big a score he had on his hands or how powerful an influence *RATC* was to have on the motion picture industry.

Although reviewers for mainstream periodicals ignored the film's initial release, the trade press sensed its potential from the beginning. "Nothing massive or pretentious here, but it's as tasty as a charlotte russe . . ." commented *Motion Picture Herald*.[46] *Variety* enthusiastically predicted that it would "prove a handy entry for exhibitors packaging a show aimed [at] the sweater-levi crowd."[47] Handy it was. In relation to its production costs, the film's financial return was remarkable. With reported worldwide grosses of $2.4 million, or eight times the initial production costs, *RATC* was easily "one of the most spectacularly successful pictures of the year."[48] According to *Film Daily Year Book*, 479 features were released in the U.S. market in 1956, of which 272 were American-produced.[49] *Variety* lists only 109 pictures that grossed $1 million or more in their first full play off.[50] For Hollywood accountants, however, a picture's total gross receipts are less important than its profit margin, the ratio between box office take and a film's negative costs. In these terms, *RATC* was as impressive as larger-grossing, but far more expensive, productions such as *Guys and Dolls* or *The King and I*, the box office champions of 1956. In an era in which Hollywood producers were banking more and more on fewer and fewer films, *RATC* showed that with the right project, they might gain much while risking little.

Don't Knock the Rock

There was one significant marketing problem, however: the possibility that the controversy over rock 'n' roll would reach a point of diminishing returns. In late 1955 and early 1956, minor incidents of violence had erupted during live rock 'n' roll shows and in movie theaters during the "Rock around the Clock" title sequence in *The Blackboard Jungle*. Columbia's release of *RATC* exacerbated an already heated dispute over the music's presumed incitement to violence and juvenile delinquency. Though it is probably true that the average 1950s parent was more worried about fluoridation than rock 'n' roll, the national media found the rock 'n' roll phenomenon natural fodder and devoted reams of copy to its colorful stars, fans, and detractors. In retrospect, the intensity of the opposition to the suggested insidious influences of rock 'n' roll music is easy to overestimate, because historians of the early rock era delight in citing wild pronouncements by contemporary fearmongers.[51] Nonetheless, it seems appropriate to quote several statements reflecting something of the level of public discourse on the subject. The nascent racism lurking beneath much of the anti–rock 'n' roll sentiment was brought to the surface by Asa Carter, executive secretary of the North Alabama White Citizens' Council, who condemned the music as an NAACP conspiracy to infect white teenagers via the nation's jukeboxes.[52] More in line with the Freudian temper of the times was Dr. Francis Braceland, a noted psychiatrist, who called rock 'n' roll a "cannibalistic and tribalistic form of music," and explained somewhat anachronistically that "it is insecurity and rebellion that impels teenagers to affect 'ducktail' haircuts, wear zoot suits, and carry on boisterously at rock 'n' roll shows."[53] On balance, the adult attitude was perhaps more condescending than alarmist. In 1957, one critic posed what was by then a rhetorical question: "Catering to the teenager's taste has leveled our song standards to the point of vulgarity, banality, and infantilism . . . can this happen to the movies under the prospect of their getting hungry enough to start indulging the banal, untrained, irresponsible tastes of the average teenager?"[54]

RATC was launched directly into the maelstrom. Many exhibitors who played the film encountered resistance from law enforcement authorities, newspaper editorialists, and parents groups concerned that exposure to rock 'n' roll music unleashed the sleeping delinquent in otherwise well-behaved teenagers. Soon after the film's release, a front-page story in *Variety* warned: "Rock 'n' roll—the most explosive show biz phenomenon of the decade—may be getting too hot to handle. While its money-making potential has made it all but irresistible its Svengali grip on the teenagers has produced a staggering wave of juvenile violence and mayhem. Rock 'n' roll is now literally [box office] dynamite—not only a matter of profit, but a matter for the police."[55] By the standards of later decades, the juvenile mayhem (screaming, foot-stomping, and an occasional scuffle) has an almost benignly nostalgic flavor to it. After a screening of *RATC* in Minneapolis, for example, teenagers snake-danced downtown and broke store windows before "police quelled the youthful rioters."[56] According to *Billboard*, the police at one live rock 'n' roll show were reportedly so jumpy "they even frowned when the kids applauded the acts."[57]

Exhibitors were caught between their desire for teenage dollars and their dread of teenage violence. In a delicate balancing act, the publicity department at Columbia exploited the controversy ("Now's the time to book Columbia's *RATC* while it's headline news in the USA!") while trying at the same time to allay the fears and to flame the greed of theater owners. "Except for minor incidents, we've had no trouble thus far," said a Columbia spokesman. "It's doing fantastic business."[58] Reflecting the industry's two minds about the teenage audience the trade press counseled exhibitors to temper the usual ballyhoo with sound judgment. "All these rock 'n' roll stars mean something to rock 'n' roll addicts, and they are very numerous! It's the most. . . . They'll be dancing in the streets, in the lobby, and in the aisles," exalted *Motion Picture Herald*'s adviser on selling approaches, who was cautious enough to conclude his pitch with the warning: "but don't let them dance all night, the all-night dancethons can get out of control—and do you more harm than good."[59]

Exhibitor misgivings aside, the financial success of *RATC* sent an unmistakable message to the motion picture production companies: there was money to be made from teenagers by capturing the rock 'n' roll craze on film. By the end of 1956, a half-dozen rock 'n' roll pictures had completed production. The then recently organized American International Pictures showed the acumen that was soon to make it the dominant force in teenpics by leading the pack with *Shake, Rattle, and Rock* (released October 1956); Twentieth Century-Fox had Elvis Presley ready by Thanksgiving vacation in *Love Me Tender* (released November 1956), and for the Christmas holidays the company was busily promoting its second rock 'n' roll offering, *The Girl Can't Help It* (released December 1956); Distributor Corporation of America weighed in with Vanguard Production's *Rock, Rock, Rock* (released December 1956); and Universal-International submitted *Rock, Pretty Baby* (released January 1957). Even the Abbott and Costello comedy series tried to muscle in with the deceptively-titled *Dance with Me Henry* (released December 1956). Katzman, for his part, hoped lightning would strike twice with a sequel, *Don't Knock the Rock* (released January 1957).

Katzman's decision to produce *Don't Knock the Rock* is worth added note as an example of how exploitation filmmaking feeds on itself. *Don't Knock the Rock* exploits not only the rock 'n' roll controversy, but its parent film, *RATC*, as well. Having scored once, the exploitation filmmaker can usually milk further exploitation values out of the original, successful exploitation. Producer Herman Cohen did much the same thing the next year for American International Pictures, following up the hugely-successful *I Was a Teenage Werewolf* with *I Was a Teenage Frankenstein*. Discussing his exploitation methods with *Variety*, Katzman confided that he never worked too far ahead of a trend and never made more than two or three exploitation pictures on the same subject unless something unusual presented itself.[60] By Katzman's calculations, the second exploitation picture generally did about 75 percent of the business of the first and the "third begins to level off to the point it's advisable to search for something new."[61]

Calypsomania

For exploitation filmmakers, the trick is to hit the crest of the wave ride it, and jump off before wiping out. Attempts by Katzman and several other producers indicate that it is also necessary to catch the right wave. Often a good thirty years older than their target audience, moviemakers in the 1950s sometimes found it difficult to anticipate and cultivate teenage tastes. In early 1957, soon after his success with two rock 'n' roll teenpics, Katzman was reported to be biding his time "waiting for something to happen" on which "to base future productions."[62] He opted for calypso music, a new and provocative rhythm which, in late 1956 and early 1957, enjoyed a brief vogue on popular music charts.[63] The "calypso invasion" was spearheaded by Harry Belafonte's "Banana Boat Song" and the Easyriders much-recorded "Marianne." Like all musical crazes, calypso music inspired dances, fashions, and public curiosity. Having always looked upon rock 'n' roll as a temporary affliction anyway, some in the entertainment industry assumed that calypso would displace rock 'n' roll and become the next big teenage music sensation. The Rev. Norman O'Connor, described as a "recognized jazz authority," was quoted in both *Newsweek* and *Variety* predicting that rock 'n' roll was fading fast. "Rock 'n' roll is a stage in popular music similar to the Charleston, jazz, swing, and the jitterbug of the past two generations and is now on its way out," he claimed. "The present fad is now giving way to calypso music."[64,65]

Low-budget-film producers, with the precedent of *RATC* fresh in mind, stampeded to the title registration office. The titles they filed for included *Calypso Rhythm, Calypso Holiday, Calypso Nights, Bop Girl Goes Calypso, Calypso-Gripso, Calypsomania, Calypso Kid, Banana Boat Calypso,* and *Mad Craze from Trinidad.*[66] An Allied Artists entry, *Calypso Joe,* and a Sam Katzman film, *Calypso Heat Wave,* were soon neck-and-neck in a race to cash in on the presumed calypso market. In May 1957, Allied Artists won: *Calypso Joe,* promised their ads, was "ready right now for a calypso-crazy nation." *Calypso Heat Wave* followed a couple of weeks later.

But there was to be no payoff in the calypso sweepstakes and the calypso cycle was short-lived. The craze was a show business flash in the pan and an exploitation false alarm. Weighing the prospects of *Calypso Heat Wave,* a trade reviewer noted, "It's none-too-subtly aimed at the teenage market and there will have to find its greatest appeal. Against it is the fact that the calypso song craze is on the wane and some say already dead."[67] By the time *Bop Girl Goes Calypso* appeared several weeks later, it could confidently be pronounced dead on arrival, a "mild musical badly outguessed by events . . . vitiating the potential it might have had earlier as a musical programmer."[68] The remaining calypso titles went unused.

Despite the failure of the calypso cycle, the quick and substantial killings made by the first wave of rock 'n' roll pictures had effectively established the power of the teenage filmgoer. (Many of Harry Belafonte's fans were adults, and the motion picture industry had learned that record sales might not translate into ticket sales unless teenagers were buying the records.) At the close of 1956, *Variety* commented on the importance of the new audience and the kind of pictures it patronized: "The product shortage has brought about a new theory of assembling a show, a practice that has been adopted by several indie producers and distributors. This consists of packaging so-called exploitation pictures. These are low-budget films based on controversial and timely subjects that make newspaper headlines. . . . In the main these pictures appeal to 'uncontrolled' juveniles and 'undesirables.' . . . Theatermen realize that they are holding a hot potato, but out of desperation are reaching for any straw that spells [box office]. The exploitation pix and rock 'n' rollers, while not drawing the audience 'we want,' are nevertheless bringing crowds to pay-windows."[69] Indeed, *Rock, Pretty Baby, Rock, Rock, Rock,* and *Don't Knock the Rock* were each extraordinarily lucrative in relation to their production costs. The success of *Love Me Tender*, the medium-budget Elvis Presley vehicle, was even more impressive. A perfunctory western with no overt rock 'n' roll music *Love Me Tender* set box office records across the country. Its release was timed to coincide with the school system's Thanksgiving break; at one theater in San Francisco, 200 teenagers lined up for tickets five hours before classes were dismissed, at which time the deluge began.[70] Though it had been in release for less than six weeks, *Love Me Tender* was twenty-second on *Variety*'s year-end list for 1956, grossing $3.75 million.[71] The first of a decade-long series of sequels followed, with the rock 'n' roll musicals *Loving You* (released August 1957) and *Jailhouse Rock* (released November 1957). With *Love Me Tender* still going strong, Presley finished 1957 with three pictures in *Variety*'s top twenty: *Love Me Tender* (number 10, grossing a cumulative $4.5 million), *Jailhouse Rock* (number 15, grossing $4 million), and *Loving You* (number 19, grossing $3.7 million). Presley's chief rival for teenage affections, Pat Boone, achieved comparable success in his two 1957 vehicles, *Bernadine* (number 14, grossing $4 million) and *April Love* (number 18, grossing $3.7 million). Frank Tashlin's *The Girl Can't Help It* had a heftier budget and loftier ambitions than most of the field (and, of course, Jayne Mansfield's presence up-front gave it broader demographic appeal), but its formidable lineup of rock 'n' roll talent was responsible for much of the $2.8 million it accrued. At the close of 1957, *Variety*'s year-end list of box office hits for the first time included a goodly number of films whose success could be attributed *only* to teenagers.[72]

Conclusion

Teenagers had made up the most significant part of the moviegoing audience at least since World War II, but it wasn't until 1955–57 that the motion picture industry began to seriously acknowledge them. Though some segments of the business had devoted sporadic attention to the teenage audience with inexpensive serials, B westerns, or "weirdie" science fiction quickies, there was no industry-wide consensus of the importance of that market, much less an earnest assault on it, prior to *RATC*. The success of *RATC* and its progeny testified convincingly to the power—and the future ascendency—of the teenage audience. Henceforth, the industry campaign to woo this group would be concerted and conscious: it signaled new production and marketing strategies and gave prominence to a new kind of motion picture, the teenpic. Since the 1950s, this process has only accelerated, and teenpics, once the industry's embarrassing underside, have lately become its foundation. Successive generations of teenagers have demanded—and received—the kind of motion pictures that satisfy their special tastes and reflect their distinctive styles: *Easy Rider* (1969) and *Saturday Night Fever* (1977) are two obvious touchstones. More than any other group, teens dictate the terms of commercial American cinema. Exploitation filmmakers for their part now solidly in the Hollywood mainstream, have become so skilled at taking the pulse of their audience that calypsomania-like miscalculations are more and more uncommon. The awesome effectiveness of saturation advertising, simultaneous nationwide exhibition, and a bewildering array of other sophisticated marketing techniques have refined the pioneering exploitation methods of entrepreneurs like Sam Katzman to new levels of predictability and profits. The question for the 1950s exploitation filmmaker was which diet would satisfy the teenage taste; the contemporary exploitation filmmaker is more likely to ask: how can I create an appetite? The nature of that new relationship between filmmaker and audience is one focus for future research in mass communication.

NOTES

1. Biskind, Peter. *Seeing Is Believing: How Hollywood Taught Us to Stop Worrying and Love the Fifties*. (New York: Pantheon Books, 1983).

2. Dowdy, Andrew. *"Movies Are Better Than Ever": Widescreen Memories of the Fifties*. (New York: William Morrow and Company, 1973).

3. Higham, Charles. *Hollywood at Sunset*. (New York: Saturday Review Press, 1972).

4. MacCann, Richard Dyer. *Hollywood in Transition.* (Boston: Houghton Mifflin, 1962).

5. "Film 'Future': GI Baby Boom." *Variety,* March 5, 1958, 1, 27.

6. *Statistical Abstract of the United States.* (Washington, D.C.: Bureau of the Census, 1955), p. 32.

7. *Statistical Abstract of the United States.* (Washington, D.C.: Bureau of the Census, 1982–83), p. 3.

8. Macdonald, Dwight. "A Caste, A Culture, A Market—I." *The New Yorker,* November 22, 1958, 57–95.

9. "The Dreamy Teen-Age Market: 'It's Neat to Spend.'" *Newsweek,* September 16, 1957, 94.

10. Cateora, Philip R. *An Analysis of the Teenage Market.* (Austin: Bureau of Business Research, University of Texas, 1963), p. 19.

11. "A New, $10-Billion Power: The U.S. Teen-Age Consumer." *Life,* August 3 1959, 78.

12. Cateora, *Analysis,* p. 164.

13. Quigley, Martin Jr. "Who Goes to the Movies . . .and Who Doesn't." *Motion Picture Herald,* August 10, 1957, 21.

14. Austin, Bruce A. *The Film Audience: An International Bibliography of Research.* (Metuchen NJ: Scarecrow Press, 1983), pp. xx–xxv.

15. Chambers, Robert W. "Need for Statistical Research." *Annals of the American Academy of Social and Political Science* 254, November 1947, 169.

16. Ibid., pp. 170–71.

17. Lazarsfeld, Paul F. "Audience Research in the Movie Field." *Annals of the American Academy of Social and Political Science* 254, November 1947, 162–168.

18. Ibid., p. 167.

19. Handel, Leo A. *Hollywood Looks at Its Audience: A Report of Film Audience Research.* (Urbana: University of Illinois Press, 1950).

20. "More Data About Audience Tastes? Great! But How Does East Get Studios to Act on Findings?" *Variety,* March 23, 1956, 16.

21. "The Fans: They Like—and Dislike." *Newsweek,* August 4, 1958, 69.

22. Brooks, Walter. "You Can Prove Anything by the Statisticians." *Motion Picture Herald.* January 7, 1956.

23. Austin, *The Film Audience.*

24. Garrison, Lee C. Jr. *The Composition, Attendance Behavior and Needs of Motion Picture Audiences: A Review of the Literature.* (Los Angeles: Graduate School of Management, UCLA, 1971).

25. Ivers, John D. "Aim at Youth and Reduce Violence, Panelists Insist." *Motion Picture Herald,* September 8, 1956, 12.

26. Quigley, Martin Jr. "Youth Must Be Served." *Motion Picture Herald,* June 23, 1956, 7.

27. Hollinger, Hy, "'Lost Audience'; Crass vs. Class." *Variety,* December 5, 1956, 1, 86.

28. "Avoids Gats and Gams," *Variety,* June 4, 1958, 1.

29. Quigley, Martin Jr., "For the Young Audience," *Motion Picture Herald,* September 15, 1956, 7.

30. Morrison, James W. "Teenage Incentive." *Motion Picture Herald,* January 5, 1957, 7.

31. "More Data," p. 5.

32. "Meet Jungle Sam," *Life,* March 23, 1953, 82.

33. "Jungle Sam," *Time* December 1, 1952, 62.

34. Musser, Charles. *Before the Nickelodeon: The Early Cinema of Edwin S. Porter* (1983). Documentary Motion Picture.

35. "Jungle Sam," p. 62.

36. "Meet Jungle Sam," p. 82.

37. "Attendance," *Motion Picture Herald*, March 17, 1956, 9.

38. *Billboard*, May 28, 1955, 46.

39. "Haley Rocks 4th Disc Into 1,000,000 Circle," *Variety*, April 4, 1956, 1.

40. Cohn, Nik. *Rock From the Beginning*. (New York: Stein and Day, 1969), pp. 17–21.

41. Roxon, Lillian. *Rock Encyclopedia*. (New York: Grosset and Dunlap, 1969), p. 216.

42. Ehrenstein, David and Bill Reed. *Rock on Film*. (New York: Delilah Books, 1982), pp. 13–20.

43. McGee, Mark Thomas and R. J. Robertson. *The J. D. Films: Juvenile Delinquency in the Movies*. (Jefferson NC: McFarland and Company, 1982), pp. 40–41.

44. Thompson, Richard. "Sam Katzman: Jungle Sam, Or, the Return of 'Poetic Justice I'd Say.' In Todd McCarthy and Charles Flynn (Eds.), *Kings of the Bs: Working Within the Hollywood System*. (New York: E. P. Dutton and Company, 1975).

45. "Jungle Sam," p. 62.

46. "Rock Around the Clock," *Motion Picture Herald*, March 17, 1956, 818.

47. "Rock Around the Clock," *Variety*, March 21, 1956, 6.

48. "Rock 'n' Roll B. O. 'Dynamite.' *Variety*, April 11, 1956, 4.

49. Alicoate, Jack (ed.), *The 1957 Film Daily Year Book of Motion Pictures*. (New York: Wid's Film and Film Folk, 1957), p. 111.

50. "Rock 'n' Roll B. O. 'Dynamite,'" p. 1.

51. Belz, Carl. *The Story of Rock* (2d ed.). (New York: Harper and Row, 1972), pp. 56–59.

52. "Segregationist Wants Ban on 'Rock and Roll.'" *New York Times*, March 20 1956, 33.

53. "Rock-and-Roll Called 'Communicable Disease.'" *New York Times*, March 28, 1956, 33.

54. Finley, James Fenlon., "TV for Me, If Teens Rule Screens." *Catholic World* 184 (1103), February 1957, 380–381.

55. "Rock 'n' Roll B. O. 'Dynamite,'" p. 55.

56. "New 'Rock' Explosion of Hot Youth: Branch Mgr. Discounts Morals TNT," *Variety*, May 2, 1956, 1.

57. Bundy, June. "Freed Replies to R&R Press Slurs." *Billboard* April 28, 1956, 22.

58. Ronan, Thomas P. "British Rattled by Rock 'n' Roll." *New York Times*, September 12, 1956, 40.

59. "Selling Approach." *Motion Picture Herald*, June 2, 1956, 43.

60. "$5,600,000 Estimate for Katzman's 12–16 Columbia Pix Up to $6,200,000." *Variety*, March 6, 1957, 5.

61. Ibid., p. 7.

62. "$5,600,000 Estimate," p. 7.

63. Schoenfeld, Herm. "Hot Trend: Trinidado Tunes," *Variety*, December 26, 1956, 1, 42.

64. "Warning: Calypso Next New Beat: R.I.P. for R 'n' R?" *Variety*, December 12, 1956, 1, 79.

65. "The Calypso Craze," *Newsweek*, February 25, 1957, 72.

66. "Calypso Films to Flood Market?" *Variety*, March 13, 1957, 1.

67. "Calypso Heat Wave," *Variety*, June 5, 1957, 6.

68. "Bop Girl Goes Calypso," *Variety*, July 17, 1957, 6.

69. Hollinger, Hy, "Teenage Biz vs. Repair Bills," *Variety*, December 19, 1956, 20.
70. "Presley Sets House Record," *Motion Picture Herald*, December 1, 1956, 42.
71. "109 Top Money Making Films of 1956," *Variety*, January 2, 1957, 4.
72. "Top Grossers of 1957," *Variety*, January 8, 1957, 30.

Annotated Bibliography

Because the literature on how Hollywood works is vast, I used the following principles in guiding selections for this annotated bibliography: (1) I did not include items on directors or other upper-level workers unless the study specifically attempted to contextualize the individuals with the mode of production. I encourage more sensitive reading of standard descriptions of these people's work, from which we can learn much. (2) I did not include items about how the industry as an economic institution worked. That factor is a major determinant on the mode of production, however, so understanding the industry is a prerequisite for investigating the production practices. (3) I did include essays on the making of a film or on union activities if the essays included significant descriptions of the work processes. This brief bibliography indicates how many possible research avenues exist for those interested in labor history and its relation to filmmaking and film viewing.

Adamson, Joseph. "The Seventeen Preliminary Scripts of *A Day at the Races*." *Cinema Journal* 8:2 (Spring 1969), 2–9.
> Of value for its description of the unusual scripting processes for Marx brothers movies during the 1930s. Also see Groch.

Altman, Charles F. "Towards a Historiography of American Film." *Cinema Journal* 16:2 (Spring 1977), 1–25.
> A very useful historiographical article that creates thirteen types of approaches to production and distribution (technology, personality, social, studio, auteur, genre, ritual, social, etc.) and includes proposals about the causal issues implied by the approaches as well as short bibliographies for each.

Baker, Wayne E., and Robert R. Faulkner. "Role as Resource in the Hollywood Film Industry." *American Journal of Sociology* 97:2 (September 1991) 279–309.
> An excellent examination of which workers seem to have more power in "new Hollywood" and how those workers use roles and conventions for their own purposes.

317

Balio, Tino. "When Is an Independent Producer Independent? The Case of United Artists after 1948." *Velvet Light Trap* 22 (1986), 53–64.
> Includes a description of what United Artists management considered when putting together a package in the 1950s and 1960s as well as a brief synopsis of a project's typical production sequence.

Bernstein, Matthew. "Fritz Lang, Incorporated." *Velvet Light Trap* 22 (1986), 33–52.
> A study of the working relations and conflict among top management in a small, independent company operating in the late 1940s.

———. "Institutions and Individuals: *Riot in Cell Block II.*" *Velvet Light Trap* 28 (Fall 1991), 3–31.
> A detailed case study of how a producer (Walter Wanger) operated in a small company (Monogram) in the early 1950s. Also important is the essay's discussion of the influence of and deviations from formulaic material in the making of a movie.

Carringer, Robert L. *The Making of Citizen Kane.* Berkeley and Los Angeles: University of California Press, 1985.
> An exceptionally detailed study of the making of one of the most famous of all U.S. films. It provides a good idea of both the system as it was experienced and the deviations that invariably occurred, especially during the undertaking of a prestige project of the sort *Citizen Kane* was.

Deneroff, Harvey. "'We Can't Get Much Spinach'! The Organization and Implementation of the Fleischer Animation Strike." *Film History* 1:1 (1987), 1–14.
> Useful for details about how labor was structured during routine situations in animation units as well as for its information about worker resistance. Also see Langer on the Fleischer studios.

Deschner, Donald. "Anton Grot: Warners Art Director, 1927–1948." *Velvet Light Trap* 15 (Fall 1975), 18–22.
> Helpful in understanding the routine activities of an art director at a major studio.

Gomery, Douglas. *The Hollywood Studio System.* New York: St. Martin's Press, 1986.
> A valuable and short reference book that is excellent in describing the individual studios from an industrial approach. Useful for understanding the specific influences operating at various companies throughout the studio era.

———. "Orson Welles and the Hollywood Industry." *Persistence of Vision* 7 (1989), 39–43.
> A handy reevaluation of Orson Welles and Hollywood that argues Welles worked as an independent for minor studios *using them* rather than being exploited by them.

Groch, John R. "What is a Marx Brother? Critical Practice, Industrial Practice, and the Notion of the Comic Auteur." *Velvet Light Trap* 26 (1990), 28–41.

A study of how the Marx brothers movies were produced, arguing that MGM within its studio system created their so-called subversive comedy. Also see Adamson.

Grupenhoff, Richard. "The Rediscovery of Oscar Micheaux, Black Film Pioneer." *Journal of Film and Video* 40:1 (Winter 1988), 40–48.

Although more recently some scholars have questioned the view expressed here that the style existing in Micheaux's films should be explained as due to his interests in economical production, this essay does provide an important description of the work procedures of a major African-American director operating on the margins of the U.S. film industry.

Jacobs, Lea. "Industry Self-Regulation and the Problem of Textual Determination." *Velvet Light Trap* 23 (1989), 4–15.

A comparative examination of the representational constraints created when the film industry's self-regulation checks were reconstituted into the Production Code Administration in 1934.

Jeter, Ida. "The Collapse of the Federated Motion Picture Crafts: A Case Study of Class Collaboration in the Motion Picture Industry." *Journal of the University Film Association* 31:2 (Spring 1979), 37–45.

An important argument about considering the class consciousness of various members of management and labor when considering how and why organized labor was relatively unsuccessful in altering those members' working conditions or the larger structures of the mode of production during the 1930s and 1940s.

Jewell, Richard B. "Hollywood and Radio: Competition and Partnership in the 1930s." *Historical Journal of Film, Radio and Television* 4:2 (1984) 125–41.

An important study of how management used radio to promote the medium of motion pictures, its narratives, and its stars.

Jowett, Garth S. "Giving Them What they Want: Movie Audience Research before 1950." In *Current Research in Film: Audiences, Economics, and Law,* vol. I, ed. Bruce A. Austin. Norwood, N.J.: Ablex, 1985, pp. 19–35.

Audience preferences are a consideration for any production system. This essay describes the ad hoc tactics used by the film industry through about 1950 as well as sociological studies that might have influenced the views of some individuals in the industry.

Langer, Mark J. "Institutional Power and the Fleischer Studios: *The Standard Production Reference.*" *Cinema Journal* 30:2 (Winter 1991), 3–22.

An insightful essay on the operating procedures at the Fleischer studios in the 1930s and early 1940s.

———. "*Tabu:* The Making of a Film." *Cinema Journal* 24:3 (Spring 1985), 43–64.

A solid case study of how *Tabu* was created that argues a more complex image of two filmmakers working as independents in the studio era of the late 1920s. In particular, the essay criticizes representing Murnau's and Flaherty's break as "an expression of the individual artist against the hegemony of the studio system" (p. 61).

Leab, Daniel J. *"The Iron Curtain* (1948): Hollywood's First Cold War Movie." *Historical Journal of Film, Radio and Television* 8:2 (1988), 153–88.

> A fine study of the social, industrial, and political causes for choosing a film subject, pointing out well the variety of political opinions operating among filmmakers at any historical moment as well as the relations of those opinions to broader regulatory and commercial influences.

McConnell, Robert L. "The Genesis and Ideology of *Gabriel over the White House." Cinema Journal* 15:2 (Spring 1976), 7–26.

> A detailed case study of the making of the film that points out how political interests of individuals such as William Randolph Hearst could provide the financial and political support for an unusual independent film during the studio era.

Nielsen, Michael. "Toward a Workers' History of the U.S. Film Industry. In *Labor, the Working Class and the Media,* ed. Vincent Mosco and Janet Wasko. Norwood, N.J.: Ablex, 1983 pp. 47–83.

> An extremely useful synopsis of below-the-line working conditions and labor organizing through the 1970s.

Pryluck, Calvin. "The Aesthetic Relevance of the Organization of Film Production." *Cinema Journal* 15:2 (Spring 1976), 1–6.

> An important mid-1970s call for recognizing that "various aspects of institutions constrain or facilitate the production of certain kinds of films at any particular time" (p. 1).

Schatz, Thomas. *The Genius of the System: Hollywood Filmmaking in the Studio Era.* New York: Pantheon Books, 1988.

> Focusing on four companies (Universal, MGM, Warner Bros., and Selznick-as-independent), this important book argues for appreciating certain features of the studio system (from the mid 1920s through about 1960). It focuses especially on the roles of producers in their relations with directors and other members of the production team.

Staiger, Janet. "Blueprints for Feature Films: Hollywood's Continuity Scripts." In *The American Film Industry,* 2nd ed., ed. Tino Balio. Madison: University of Wisconsin Press, 1985, pp. 173–94.

> An explanation for the creation by 1915 of the continuity script and a description of its function within the work process.

———. "'Tame' Authors and the Corporate Laboratory: Stories, Writers and Scenarios in Hollywood." *Quarterly Review of Film Studies* 8:4 (Fall 1983), 33–45.

> A study of the reasons for and development of the specialization of writing skills within the Hollywood mode of production.

Vertrees, Alan David. "Reconstructing the 'Script in Sketch Form': An Analysis of the Narrative Construction and Production Design of the Fire Sequence in *Gone with the Wind." Film History* 3 (1989), 87–104.

> A meticulous and revealing case study (and reevaluation) of the contributions of production designer William Cameron Menzies on *Gone with the Wind.*

Contributors

ROBERT C. ALLEN is Smith Professor and Associate Dean of the College of Arts and Sciences at the University of North Carolina. He is author of *Horrible Prettiness: Burlesque and American Culture* and coauthor, with Douglas Gomery, of *Film History: Theory and Practice.*

GREGORY D. BLACK is Chair of Communication Studies at the University of Missouri–Kansas City and coauthor of *Hollywood Goes to War: How Politics, Profits & Propaganda Shaped World War II Movies.* His new study of censorship in the 1930s is *Hollywood Censored.*

DAVID BORDWELL is Jacques Ledoux Professor of Film Studies at the University of Wisconsin–Madison. His most recent books are *Ozu and the Poetics of Cinema,* *Making Meaning: Inference and Rhetoric in the Interpretation of Cinema,* *The Cinema of Eisenstein,* and, with Kristin Thompson, *Film History: An Introduction.*

EDWARD BUSCOMBE is Head of Publishing at the British Film Institute. He has taught at the University of Iowa, New York University, Queen's University (Kingston, Ontario), and the University of Texas at Austin. He is the editor of *The BFI Companion to the Western.* His most recent publication is a volume on *Stagecoach* in the BFI Film Classics series.

DERRAL CHEATWOOD obtained his Ph.D. in sociology from Ohio State University in 1972 and is currently Professor of Criminal Justice at the University of Baltimore. In addition to his work in criminology, Dr. Cheatwood has written on the sociology of humor, the use of media in teaching, models of accountability in modern art, and still photography and film. He recently concluded a Fulbright in Germany and is currently doing research on prison films.

THOMAS DOHERTY is Assistant Professor of American Studies at Brandeis University and author of *Teenagers and Teenpics: The Juvenilization of the American Movies in the 1950s* and *Projections of War: Hollywood, American Culture, and World War II.*

DENISE HARTSOUGH's dissertation (University of Wisconsin, 1987) examines why a corrupt studio union won a 1939 election against a dissident group. Her article on a film union's response to television appears in *Labor History*. Other work appears in *Wide Angle* and the *Historical Journal of Film, Radio and Television*. She holds a visiting faculty position at Michigan State University.

RICHARD B. JEWELL is Associate Professor and former Chair of Critical Studies at the University of Southern California School of Cinema-Television. He is the author of *The RKO Story* and numerous articles on the history of American film.

PAUL KERR is a producer/director for British TV. Since 1990, he has been series editor of BBC 2's weekly program about world cinema, entitled "Moving Pictures." Previously he was series producer on "The Media Show" for Channel Four and a senior producer on BBC 2's nightly arts strand, "The Late Show." He has written widely about film and television. Among his publications are *MTM: Quality Television* and *The Hollywood Film Industry*.

CLAYTON R. KOPPES is Professor of History at Oberlin College. He is the prize-winning author of *JPL and the American Space Program* and coauthor of *Hollywood Goes to War: How Politics, Profits & Propaganda Shaped World War II Movies*.

JAMES LASTRA is Assistant Professor of English at the University of Chicago. He is currently completing essays on surrealism and experimental cinema, as well as a book devoted to the study of representational technologies and the American cinema, focusing on the early cinema period and the coming of sound.

RICHARD MALTBY is Senior Lecturer in American Film at the University of Exeter. He is author of *Harmless Entertainment: Hollywood and the Ideology of Consensus* and, with Ian Craven, *Hollywood Cinema: An Introduction*. He is currently completing *Reforming the Movies: Politics, Censorship, and the Institutions of the American Cinema, 1908–1939*.

MARTIN F. NORDEN teaches film as Associate Professor of Communication at the University of Massachusetts at Amherst. He has published numerous articles on moving-image media and is the author of *The Cinema of Isolation: A History of Physical Disability in the Movies*.

THOMAS SCHATZ is G. B. Dealey Regents Professor of Communication in the Department of Radio-Television-Film at the University of Texas at Austin. He is the author of *Hollywood Genres*, *Old Hollywood/New Hollywood*, and *The Genius of the System*.

JEFFREY SCONCE is a Ph.D. candidate in the Department of Communication Arts at the University of Wisconsin–Madison and a coordinating editor of *Velvet Light Trap*. His dissertation is a social history examining concepts of presence and the supernatural in the reception of telecommunications technology.

JANET STAIGER is Professor of Radio, Television, and Film at the University of Texas at Austin. She is coauthor of *The Classical Hollywood Cinema: Film Style and Mode of Production to 1960* and author of *Interpreting Films: Studies in the Historical Reception of American Cinema*.

Index

Rosten, Leo C., 19, 47, 280
Rotha, Paul, 293n1
Rothacker, Watterson, 290–91

Sanders, Clinton R., 7
Sarris, Andrew, 64–65
scandals, 135
Schary, Dore, 32, 61
Schatz, Thomas, 7, 10–11
Schenck, Joseph, 228, 245n19
Schenck, Nicholas, 228, 237, 239, 247n51
Schickel, Richard, 20
Schrader, Paul, 64–65, 67
science fiction genre, 313
Scola, Kathryn, 262–64
Sconce, Jeffrey, 11
Scott, Gordon, 166–67, 177–78
Screen, 50–51, 53
Screen Actors Guild, 227
Screen Gems, 60
Sears, Fred, 306
self-regulation of subject matter, 12–13, 59, 232, 242, 251–75, 279–93, 319; *see also* censorship; production code
Selznick, David O., 11, 82, 140–61, 162n19, 320
Selznick International Pictures, 27, 242; *see also* David O. Selznick Productions
serials, 33, 61, 313
series, 35, 60–61, 179–80
Seventh Heaven, 128, 134–38
sharp-focus style, 96, 98, 117, 119; *see also* deep-focus cinematography
She Done Him Wrong, 268
Shea, T. E., 217
Sheehan, Winfield, 132, 134, 136
Sheffield, Johnny, 164–66, 176–77
Sherwood, Robert, 280, 286, 292
Since You Went Away, 161n10
Sindlinger, Albert E., 301
Sklar, Robert, 253–54
Small, Edward, 41–42
So Dark the Night, 58–59, 68–69
So Proudly We Hail, 284–85, 287

social problem pictures, 259, 297n30, 304
social theory: relation of films to industrial organization, 19–24, 36, 251, 254; relation of films to politics, 25, 36, 55, 273–74, 320; relation of films to society, 21–24, 36, 164, 273–74
Society of Sound Engineers, 218
soft style, 95–104, 112, 114
sound: types of equipment, 123n40, 132, 207; uses of, 206–7, 215, 222
sound engineers, 200–23, 235, 238
specials, 128–29
Spitz, Leo, 41, 45, 236–37, 239
Staiger, Janet, 141, 200, 204
Stagecoach, 107, 177
standardization, 47, 53, 74, 99–103, 115, 141; *see also* mode of production
standards, *see* conventions of product; conventions of production
Stanwyck, Barbara, 266, 271, 274
stars, 10–11, 34, 74–75, 134, 140, 160–61, 161n1, 255; *see also* actors
stereotypes, 163, 169, 172–73, 193–96, 265, 293
Stevens, George, 46
Stevenson, Robert, 145, 147–52, 156–57, 161n10
Stewart, Donald Ogden, 32
Story of Temple Drake, The, 270, 273
story sources, 128, 133–34, 141, 161n2
Stranger on the Third Floor, The, 102
strikes, 227–29, 231–32, 234–35, 237–38, 240, 242, 246n32, 269, 318; *see also* labor relations; resistance to mode of production
Struss, Karl, 96–97
Studio Basic Agreement (SBA), 227–28, 230, 232–34, 238–39, 246n35, 247–48n57
studio house style, 48, 53–54, 75–76, 88–89, 130, 134, 171, 176, 318
Studio Relations Committee (SRC), 251, 258–59, 266, 270–71, 278n68